Musical Lives

Selected by **Nicholas Kenyon**

OXFORD
UNIVERSITY PRESS

OXFORD
UNIVERSITY PRESS

Great Clarendon Street, Oxford OX2 6DP

Oxford University Press is a department of the University of Oxford.
It furthers the University's objective of excellence in research, scholarship,
and education by publishing worldwide in

Oxford New York

Auckland Bangkok Buenos Aires Cape Town Chennai
Dar es Salaam Delhi Hong Kong Istanbul Karachi Kolkata
Kuala Lumpur Madrid Melbourne Mexico City Mumbai Nairobi
São Paulo Shanghai Singapore Taipei Tokyo Toronto

Oxford is a registered trade mark of Oxford University Press
in the UK and in certain other countries

Published in the United States
by Oxford University Press Inc., New York

First published 2002

British Library Cataloguing in Publication Data

Data available

Library of Congress Cataloging in Publication Data

Data available

ISBN 0-19-860528-5

10 9 8 7 6 5 4 3 2 1

Typeset in DanteMT
by Alliance Interactive Technology, Pondicherry, India
Printed in Great Britain
by T. J. International, Padstow, Cornwall

Musical Lives

Preface

'The best record of a nation's past that any civilization has produced': G. M. Trevelyan's view in 1944 of the *Dictionary of National Biography* highlights the achievement of its first editor Leslie Stephen. Between 1885 and 1900 quarterly volumes rolled out from the presses in alphabetical order by subject. A national institution had come into existence, making its distinctive contribution to the national aptitude for the art of biography.

In his initial prospectus for the *DNB*, Stephen emphasized the need to express 'the greatest possible amount of information in a thoroughly business-like form'. Dates and facts, he said, 'should be given abundantly and precisely', and he had no patience with the sort of 'style' that meant 'superfluous ornament'. But he knew well enough that for 'lucid and condensed narrative', style in the best sense is essential. Nor did he content himself, in the many longer memoirs he himself contributed to the *DNB*, with mere dates and facts: a pioneer in the sociology of literature, he was not at all prone to exaggerate the individual's impact on events, and skilfully 'placed' people in context.

Stephen's powerful machine was carried on by his work-horse of a successor Sidney Lee, who edited the first of the ten supplements (usually decennial) which added people who died between 1901 and 1990. It was in these supplements that all except the first two of the memoirs published in this volume first appeared, so they were often written soon after the subject died; their authors were frequently able to cite 'personal knowledge' and 'private information'. In such cases there is always a balance to be struck between waiting for written sources to appear and drawing upon living memory while still abundant and fresh. Stephen had no doubts where he stood: he published book-length biographies of his Cambridge friend Henry Fawcett and of his brother Fitzjames within a year of their deaths, and cited Boswell's *Johnson* and Lockhart's *Scott* as proof that the earliest biographies are often the best. Furthermore, memoirs of the recently dead were included in the *DNB* right up to the last possible moment, the press often being stopped for the purpose. Roundell

Palmer, for example, died on 4 May 1895 and got into the 43rd volume published at the end of June.

So the memoirs published in this series are fully in line with what was *DNB* policy from the outset. Furthermore, all have the virtue of reflecting the attitudes to their subjects that were taken up during their lifetimes. They may not always reflect what is now the latest scholarship, but as G. M. Young insisted, 'the real, central theme of history is not what happened, but what people felt about it when it was happening'. So they will never be superseded, and many are classics of their kind—essential raw material for the most up-to-date of historians. They have been selected by acknowledged experts, some of them prominent in helping to produce the new *Oxford Dictionary of National Biography*, which will appear in 2004. All are rightly keen that this ambitious revision will not cause these gems of the *DNB* to be lost. So here they are, still sparkling for posterity.

Brian Harrison
Editor, *Oxford Dictionary of National Biography*

Musical Lives—selection from the DNB

Introduction

British music in the twentieth century saw a remarkable revival; it has been argued that not since Dunstable 600 years ago has the music of this country led the world as it has during the last hundred years.

This collection of musical lives tells one important part of that story, for biographies are a vital resource in the process of understanding why and how such a radical change was possible in the fortunes of British music. They add up to a partial view, of course, coloured by the time in which they were written, the priorities of those who commissioned the *Dictionary of National Biography*, and above all the rapidly shifting perspective of our understanding of the forces that shape musical life. But there are fascinating and entertaining portraits here, both in the evocation of vanished lives, and in the occasional waspishness of the writing (which seems to come naturally to *DNB* contributors). You can read of Dame Ethel Smyth conducting her *March of the Women* with a toothbrush from her Holloway Prison cell window, and of Sir Thomas Beecham on a summer walk down Piccadilly hailing a taxi and throwing his coat in, ordering the taxi to follow him. You will find one conductor described as 'a small, dishevelled and sometimes cantankerous man', and another whose full diary of engagements 'sometimes led to a perfunctoriness bordering upon indolence'. And you cannot but empathize with the composer who 'never made a public speech in his life, save for the three short sentences with which he opened the Faringdon cinema'.

As well as individual vignettes, there are broader themes to be explored. It was Richard Strauss who famously hailed Edward Elgar, after the first continental performance of *The Dream of Gerontius* in 1902, as 'the first English progressivist composer' (Strauss can be forgiven for not knowing much about Dunstable). Did British music go on being 'progressivist' in the twentieth century? Elgar looked backwards as well as forward in a way that can stand as a metaphor for the whole of this era. In the moving final bars of the Adagio of his First Symphony, completed in 1908, there is a piercing moment when, through the elegiac sounds of the strings, the muted sounds of horn, trombones, and harp suddenly sound the echo—or is it a pre-echo?—of distant conflicts. It is a disturbing vision, which takes the symphony far from the 'noble paean in praise of the Edwardian era' that the author of Elgar's *DNB* entry heard. How we now hear the moment probably depends, paradoxically, on the conflicts which the twentieth century experienced after Elgar wrote the piece. But that passage sums up Elgar's own emotional stance, torn between assertion and self-doubt, and that is reflected too in the division between what Nikolaus Pevsner memorably described as the 'abject inferiority complex' of British cultural life, and our immense and sometimes blinkered pride in our past.

The rules of the *DNB* dictate that all the musical figures included in this selection died during the twentieth century, up to 1990 when the old *DNB* drew its final line. As a result, many of them lived much of their lives in the nineteenth century, and I immediately bend the rules by beginning with two vital figures who died in 1900: friends, collaborators, and highly innovative figures in very different ways. Sir George Grove and Sir Arthur Sullivan (who jointly found part of Schubert's *Rosamunde* music in Leipzig and played leapfrog to celebrate) did much to create the climate for the twentieth-century revival in the twin worlds of music scholarship and creative composition; they both escaped from the often stifling tradition in which they had been brought up and opened a window on the fresh air of Europe. They set the tone for everything that follows here.

There are over 2,500 articles in the *DNB* which mention music, not only as a profession but as a hobby or interest; they all testify to the continuing importance of music in our national life. Many twentieth-century biographees profess a love of music or a more intense involvement, from the novelist Agatha Christie, who trained as a musician and might have become one had she been a more confident performer, to the philosopher R. G. Collingwood, who composed songs. Among those who are listed as musicians by the *DNB*, many more than could be included here, there are composers, conductors, and performers. Musical historians are also prominent as a category and one administrator, the omnipresent Sir Hugh Allen, is given a unique category: 'musical statesman'. (Though he was neither composer nor performer, his 'pre-eminent musico-political position' ensured that 'it could safely be said that there were few musical happenings in the country about which Allen had not been consulted', an exhausting epitaph.)

Such biographies as these create a very particular picture of our musical life, since they concentrate on professional figures rather than amateurs, on those who ran institutions rather than those who made an impact with audiences, on serious music rather than light music, on men rather than women (there are no *DNB* entries for Dora Bright, Liza Lehmann, Iris Lemare, Amy Shuard, Maud Valérie White, Grace Williams), on creators rather than executants—whom the *DNB* seems hardly to regard as prima facie musicians, though critics certainly are. In arranging this selection from the existing *DNB* biographies, I considered first the alphabetical order of previous volumes in this series, and then a thematic arrangement; but I have settled instead on a simple chronological sequence of biographies by birth date, which at least begins to tell an evolving story.

Well-loved artists who performed in the twentieth century (I could have included Sir Charles Santley or the admirable Lady Hallé, but they are essentially nineteenth-century performers) start from Dame Nellie Melba and Dame Myra Hess, and include several pianists from Solomon and Clifford Curzon to John Ogdon; among other instrumentalists the violinist Jelly d'Aranyi and her sister are in the *DNB* and have been included here, as are the oboist Leon Goossens, the horn player Dennis Brain, and the viola player Lionel Tertis. But the bassoonist Archie Camden, the cellist Beatrice Harrison, the violinist Albert Sammons, and the horn player Alan Civil, among many others, did not gain entry to the *DNB*, yet they surely affected their professions in as important ways as did composers included here. The regions suffer too: Dan Godfrey, who conducted an astonishing repertory (including the work of twenty-seven women composers) in Bournemouth in the early years of the century, is mentioned only in his father's entry.

On the whole it is the composer biographies that find the *DNB* writers at their most confident and comprehensive—though it tends to be the most innovative figures, such as Frank Bridge, who receive the least imaginative treatment; was Cornelius Cardew altogether too radical to be included? Julian Herbage nicely defends John Ireland against the charge of never having written a symphony on the grounds that 'neither did Debussy or Ravel'. Roger Nichols sums up Lennox Berkeley in words that could apply to rather too many: 'the history of 20th-century music may not have been greatly changed by his passing across it, but without him it would have been immeasurably the poorer'. Frank Howes probably thought he was flattering Ethel Smyth in her entry, but there is something acutely patronizing in his depiction of her fighting 'too many battles, some of them unnecessary and none of them conducive to the frame of mind in which music can be composed'.

Two major figures, Sir Charles Stanford and Sir Hubert Parry, tower over the start of the century and stand at the head of the line of those who taught many significant twentieth-century composers and ran our music colleges. But did they really create the English musical renaissance? It was a paradoxical combination of influences that refreshed British composition at this time: on the one hand the music of Europe, the impact of Wagner and Bayreuth, and on the other the burgeoning English folk-song revival led by Cecil Sharp in the first years of the twentieth century. This also had its links to Germany's exploration of its past: Constant Lambert was probably right when he wrote that the 'self-conscious Englishry' of the folk-song revival 'was in itself peculiarly un-English'. But it had a profound effect on our music which can be traced in many of these biographies: Vaughan Williams paying tribute to Holst (his 'music has been called cold and inhuman; it is only cold from its burning intensity'); the all-too-short life of George Butterworth; and Frank Howes writing of the emancipation of British music from continental dominance—which he credited to Vaughan Williams and Holst, but which in reality belongs to a whole group of composers as diverse as Frederick Delius and Ethel Smyth, Frank Bridge and Benjamin Britten. The often productive tug-of-war between English tradition and continental influence is a theme which surfaces in many of these biographies.

The lively lives of conductors produce some good entries. James Dalton disposes admirably of the myth of Stokowski's Slavonic origins (he was born two minutes from Oxford Circus, but his name was always Stokowski, never Stokes); Jack Brymer is warmly appreciative of Beecham including the 'many almost unrehearsed performances' he drew from orchestras over the years; Michael Kennedy is sympathetic to Barbirolli's depression. Conductors who perhaps should be in the *DNB* include those stalwarts of the Proms Basil Cameron and Clarence Raybould, as well as Stanford Robinson and Albert Coates; as with other performers the new edition of *The New Grove*, the *Oxford Dictionary of Music* by Michael Kennedy, and most recently the new *Oxford Companion to Music* by Alison Latham may be used to fill out the picture of those who did not have quite the right progressions, or connections, or clubs, to make it into the *DNB*.

It is with light music and popular music that we are on far less secure ground. Early song composers and singers, vastly popular in their day, find little place in the *DNB*. Marie Lloyd (Matilda Wood) is an early entrant, but I have not included Noel Coward, Ivor Novello, and Stanley Holloway, who are in Michael Billington's fine parallel collection of *DNB Stage and Screen Lives*. Eric Coates and Albert Ketèlbey are here, as are Semprini, Geraldo (Gerard Walcan-Bright), Joe Loss, and Victor Silvester. Jack Hylton and Mantovani are not, yet what an influence they had! And if the presence of Billy Fury and John Lennon seems bizarre in this company, that is simply because they were the representatives of a vital new generation who should be much more fully represented; they are here simply because they had the ill fortune to die first. The *DNB*'s unease about popular culture reflects a much wider later tendency, memorably summed up by the historian L. C. B. Seaman: 'the hostility to mass culture so frequently expressed from the 1920s onwards was often the result of a narrow educational system, a too early hardening of the spiritual arteries, and above all, of an ingrained distaste for the masses as such.'

There are many important stories that can be traced intermittently through the biographies: one is the revival of early music with Sir Richard Terry at Westminster Cathedral (Sylvia Townsend Warner, who assisted on *Tudor Church Music*, is included in the *DNB* collection *Literary Lives*), E. H. Fellowes and *The English Madrigal School*, Arnold Dolmetsch at Haslemere, Imogen Holst at Dartington and Aldeburgh, and the development of historical performing practice in the work of the conductors Boyd Neel and Thurston Dart—a period crowned by the brief brilliance of David Munrow. Another is the development of recording, through whom some of the great performers here made their mark on a very wide public: Richard Tauber, Isobel Baillie, Kathleen Ferrier, Peter Pears. Immigrants to this country are another rich theme, from Egon Wellesz onwards, though the *DNB* 1990 deadline excludes such major contributors to our national culture as Sir Georg Solti, Lord Menuhin, and Berthold Goldschmidt. And then there are the scholarly developments from the antiquarian Barclay Squire and the fount of all programme notes, Donald Tovey, through E. J. Dent and his involvement with the ISCM to the successive editors of *Grove's Dictionary*: Fuller Maitland, H. C. Colles, and Eric Blom. One thing academics cannot forgive is an unproductive academic, so Sir Jack Westrup receives a steely rebuke for the fact that while Professor at Oxford 'his energies were not directed more towards the writing of books' and that 'instead he indulged [*sic*] in much editing, writing articles, compiling lexicons, and lecturing abroad'. Among writers, I have chosen the great popularizers: Percy Scholes, Ernest Newman, Neville Cardus, and Walford Davies for his popular broadcasts as well as his music.

The huge growth of opera is slimly represented, and ballet would have been another collection entirely. John Christie and Karl Ebert of Glyndebourne are here; Lilian Baylis of Sadler's Wells is in *Stage and Screen Lives*. Of those who ran the Royal Opera, David Webster is recalled by his successor John Tooley, and Garrett Moore (Lord Drogheda) by Tooley's successor Jeremy Isaacs—whose wife, while at the *Financial Times*, must have been a recipient of the Droghedagrams immortalized in this entry. Publishing, a huge influence on twentieth-century music only beginning to be properly studied, creeps in with Leslie Boosey and Hubert Foss.

Introduction

How honest are these biographies? Some are certainly sanitized; there is no drink in Constant Lambert's entry, a startling omission; Malcolm Sargent's personal life goes unexplored; we learn nothing of the so-called 'lawsuit' which caused Eugene Goossens's departure from his Australian post (the discovery of a collection of pornography in his luggage); but Robert Matthew Walker is graphic on John Ogdon's illnesses. While partners are not given the stature of wives, Donald Mitchell is absolutely clear about Peter Pears in the context of Britten's life ('the two men made their life together'), we read of Rutland Boughton's non-divorce ('Boughton's complete candour overcame many objections'), though the exact status of Lady Jessie Wood in Henry Wood's life is never explained.

On the whole, performers are not criticized for their performances, though I treasure Desmond Shawe-Taylor's observation on Maggie Teyte that 'a slightly excessive use of the downward portamento occasionally introduced a sentimental touch into otherwise immaculate interpretations'. If the old *DNB* seems to have valued performance far less than it should, that is only because in traditional scholarship, performers, like women, were regarded as completely secondary. In this respect the *DNB* is both a mirror of its era and points to what can be improved in the future.

This cannot of course be a comprehensive book about twentieth-century music when so many of its greatest figures are still alive. Our final entries form a melancholy sequence of hugely creative lives cut all too short by murder (John Lennon), suicide (David Munrow), or tragic illness (Jacqueline du Pré). But I was glad, even though it was possible only because of his early death, to be able to include that unique comic genius Gerard Hoffnung. In the end, one marvels at the sheer energy and creativity of all these people. 'Recreation: none', John Betjeman recalls of the *Who's Who* entry of Lord Berners (Sir Gerald Tyrwhitt-Wilson): 'This was quite true, for there was hardly a moment of the day when he was not either composing, painting or writing.' The story of our music is unfinished and incomplete, but there will be much valuable raw material here for those who take on the absorbing and much-needed task of chronicling the full richness of British musical culture as it flourished during the now-completed twentieth century.

For help and advice I would like to thank Leanne Langley, Alison Latham, Jennifer Doctor, and Yvette Pusey.

NICHOLAS KENYON

April 2002

Contents

Contents

Contents

Contents

Contents

GROVE George

(1820–1900)

Sir

Writer on music and first director of the Royal College of Music, born on 13 Aug. 1820 at Clapham, in a house which is now occupied by the site of Wandsworth Road railway station, was the son of Thomas Grove of Charing Cross and Penn, Buckinghamshire. He went to a school on Clapham Common, kept by a Mr. Elwell, where he had as one of his schoolfellows George Granville Bradley, afterwards dean of Westminster, whose sister he subsequently married. He next entered Stockwell (afterwards Clapham) grammar school, then under Charles Pritchard, the astronomer. After finally leaving school he was articled for three years to Alexander Gordon to learn the profession of a civil engineer. At the end of his articles he went to Glasgow for two years, where, in the factory of Robert Napier (1791–1876), he gained further experience in the practical part of his profession. He was admitted a member of the Institution of Civil Engineers on 26 Feb. 1839. When his old master (Gordon) received an order to erect an iron lighthouse at Morant Point, on the eastern extremity of the island of Jamaica—the first ever put up—Grove was despatched to superintend its erection. An iron plate at the foot of the lighthouse, first permanently lighted on 1 Nov. 1842, records Grove's name as the engineer. Scarcely had he returned to London before Gordon again sent him off to Bermuda, where the government were about to build a lighthouse on Gibbs' Hill, of which a sketch appeared in the 'Illustrated London News' of 20 April 1844, and which was first lighted on 1 May 1846. Upon his return from Bermuda Grove entered the office of Mr. C. H. Wild, one of Robert Stephenson's chief assistants, who sent him to Chester to look after the erection of the 'general station' there. From Chester he was transferred to Bangor, where he served under Edwin Clark, Stephenson's resident engineer, at the Britannia bridge. An account of the first floating of the tubes is recorded in the 'Spectator' of 23 June 1849, which is interesting as being Grove's first appearance in print.

Engineering was, however, soon to be abandoned. In 1849 Grove became secretary to the Society of Arts, and shortly afterwards he accepted a similar post at the Crystal Palace, Sydenham, where the Great Exhibition building of 1851 was re-erected, and opened by Queen Victoria 10 June 1854. For a period of twenty years he rendered invaluable service to the Crystal Palace, especially in regard to the development of the music there, which subsequently attained world-wide fame under the nurturing influence and enthusiastic sway of Grove and August Manns, the musical director of the palace, conjointly. The daily and weekly orchestral performances at Sydenham prompted those admirable analytical notices of musical compositions with which the name of George Grove was so long and is so favourably associated. He had always shown a great fondness for music, but had never received any technical training in the art. Entirely self-taught, his knowledge was acquired solely by 'picking up' information. 'I wish it to be distinctly understood,' he said, 'that I have always been a mere amateur in music. I wrote about the symphonies and concertos because I wished to try to make them clear to myself and to discover the secret of the things that charmed me so; and from that sprang a wish to make other amateurs see it in the same way.' The first analytical programme compiled by Grove was that of the Crystal Palace concert on 26 Jan. 1856 to celebrate the centenary of the birth of Mozart. Week by week during the concert season for forty years Grove continued to write those analyses, which have been reprinted over and over again, not only at the Crystal Palace but in many concert programmes in London and elsewhere, including America. The most important of these interesting notices were published in a volume in 1884, and, after being amplified and carefully revised, were reissued as 'Beethoven and his Nine Symphonies' in 1896. At the palace, in co-operation with August Manns, Grove did much to make the music of Schubert—one of his special favourites—known. In the autumn of 1867 he, in company with Sir Arthur Sullivan, paid a memorable visit to Vienna, where they were successful in unearthing Schubert's 'Rosamunde' music, which had been neglected for more than forty years. A full account of this discovery is related by Grove in the Appendix to the English translation of Kreissle's 'Life of Schubert' (1869). At the end of 1873 he resigned the post of secretary to the Crystal Palace Company (though he still retained connection with the building which owed so much to him by being made a director), upon the acceptance of an offer from Messrs. Macmillan, the publishers, to an important position on their editorial staff. He edited 'Macmillan's Magazine' for some years, and wrote for Macmillan's series of 'History Primers' a primer of geography (1875), which has been translated into French and Italian.

The great work of his life—a work which will carry his name down to posterity—was the 'Dictionary of Music and Musicians.' The prospectus, dated 'March 1874,' stated that the work was not to exceed *two* volumes of some 600 pages; it ultimately attained to four volumes and an exhaustive index, totalling together 3,313 pages. The first volume appeared in 1878, and the fourth in 1889; an index volume was issued in 1890. Grove was not only the projector and editor of the 'Dictionary,' but, in addition to many other articles, he contributed three important monographs on Beethoven,

Mendelssohn, and Schubert—his favourite trio of composers—which are models of biographical literature. He made two special journeys to Germany to obtain materials for his Mendelssohn article, and more than two to Vienna for his monographs on Beethoven and Schubert.

In 1883 he took a very active part in the movement, initiated by King Edward VII when prince of Wales, for the formation of the Royal College of Music at Kensington, and was appointed the first director of that institution. For eleven years he threw all his energies into the work of organising and getting into working order that great music school. He resigned the office of director at Christmas 1894, when he was succeeded by Professor Sir C. Hubert H. Parry.

Grove's interests in life were very varied. In his earliest days he had been instilled with a knowledge of the Bible, much of which he knew by heart. Fired by a remark made by James Fergusson (1808–1886), author of 'The Handbook of Architecture,' that there was no full concordance of the proper names in the Bible, Grove set to work, and with the aid of his wife made a complete index of every occurrence of every proper name in the Old Testament, New Testament, and Apocrypha, with their equivalents in Hebrew, LXX, Greek and Vulgate Latin. This was in 1853–4. His next Bible study was a step in a similar direction. In 1854 he made the acquaintance of Arthur Penrhyn Stanley (afterwards dean of Westminster), who became his lifelong friend and who appointed Grove his literary executor. Stanley (then canon of Canterbury) was at the time engaged on the appendix to his 'Sinai and Palestine,' the first step in the topography of the Bible, with the result that it engendered a strong desire in Grove to visit the Holy Land. He paid two visits to Palestine—in 1859 and 1861—the outcome of these journeys being the formation in 1865 of the Palestine Exploration Fund, of which Grove was virtually the founder and institutor. He became hon. secretary to the fund and laboured incessantly on its behalf. A further contribution to biblical literature was the editorial assistance he rendered to (Sir) William Smith (1813–1893) in the preparation of his 'Dictionary of the Bible.' In addition to writing about a thousand pages of the book, he rewrote some of the articles but retained the initials of the original writers. He also furnished the index to Clark's 'Bible Atlas' (1868), in which the places are recorded in English and Hebrew, followed by the texts in which the names of the places occur.

The mental and physical activity of Sir George Grove was quite remarkable. He translated Guizot's 'Etudes sur les Beaux-Arts' (1853), and contributed a sketch, 'Nabloos and the Samaritans,' to Sir Francis Galton's 'South Africa' (1853). He contributed prefaces to Otto Jahn's 'Life of Mozart,' Hensel's 'Mendelssohn Family,' W. S. Rockstro's 'Life of Handel,' 'A Short History of Cheap Music, as exemplified in the Records of the

House of Novello, Ewer, & Co.,' 'The Early Letters of Schumann,' and to Mr. F. G. Edwards's 'History of Mendelssohn's Oratorio "Elijah."' He was also a frequent contributor to periodical literature.

Grove was the recipient, on 19 July 1880, of a gratifying testimonial—a thousand guineas and a gold chronometer—presented to him by the Archbishop of Canterbury on behalf of the subscribers. He was knighted on 22 May 1883, and on 26 May 1894 was made a companion of the Bath. Alfred Ernest, duke of Saxe-Coburg and Gotha, decorated him with the cross of the Order of Merit, and he received the honorary degrees of D.C.L. Durham and LL.D. Glasgow Universities. Upon his retirement from the directorship of the Royal College of Music in 1894 he still continued to take a warm and active interest in music and musicians. He was an exceedingly kind-hearted man, and took a special delight in giving a helping hand to young men. A great letter writer, his communications were characteristically reflective of his mercurial temperament, wide knowledge, boundless energy, and yet not without a touch of humour in forms of expression. For the last two years of his life he suffered from paralysis, which death relieved at his wooden house at Lower Sydenham, on 28 May 1900. His remains are interred in Ladywell cemetery, Lewisham. Grove's pupils at the Royal College of Music presented him with a bust by Mr. Alfred Gilbert, R.A.; and the teaching staff with his portrait by Mr. C. W. Furse. Other portraits of him were painted by Henry Philips, Mr. H. A. Olivier, and Mr. Felix Moscheles. A George Grove memorial scholarship has been founded at the Royal College of Music.

Grove married, in 1851, Harriet, daughter of the Rev. Charles Bradley, who survived him.

[Life and Letters by C. L. Graves, 1903; Musical Times, October 1897, containing a biographical sketch by the present writer, information for which was verbally supplied by Grove, and Musical Times, July 1900; Musical World, 24 and 31 July 1880.]

Frederick George Edwards

published 1901

SULLIVAN Arthur Seymour

(1842–1900)

Sir

Composer, younger son of Thomas Sullivan, was born at 8 Bolwell Terrace (now Street), Lambeth Walk, London, on 13 May 1842. His father, an excellent musician, played the violin in the orchestra of the Surrey Theatre, and afterwards became bandmaster at the Royal Military College, Sandhurst (1845–56); subsequently—until his death, 22 Sept. 1866, at the age of sixty-one—he held a professorship at the Royal Military School of Music, Kneller Hall, from its institution in 1857. Thomas Sullivan's elder son, Frederick (1837–1877), distinguished himself as an actor. The mother of the two boys, Mary Clementina, daughter of James Coghlan, came of an old Italian family named Righi.

Arthur Sullivan was cradled in music. At Sandhurst he obtained a practical knowledge of all the instruments in his father's band—'not a mere passing acquaintance, but a lifelong and intimate friendship.' He was sent to a boarding-school kept by W. G. Plees, at 20 Albert Terrace, Paddington. On 12 April 1854, aged nearly twelve, Sullivan was admitted one of the children of the Chapel Royal, St. James's, and two days later he was entrusted with the singing of a solo at one of the services. 'His voice was very sweet,' records Thomas Helmore, the master of the children, 'and his style of singing far more sympathetic than that of most boys.' The children were boarded at 6 Cheyne Walk, Chelsea, with Helmore, who not only laid the foundations of Sullivan's musical education on a solid basis, but remained his attached friend till death. During his choristership Sullivan composed in 1855 a setting of 'Sing unto the Lord and praise His name.' This 'full anthem' was sung in the Chapel Royal when the dean (Bishop Blomfield of London), to show his appreciation of the youthful effort, rewarded the boy composer with half a sovereign. His first published composition, a sacred song, 'O Israel,' was issued by Novello & Co. in November of the same year (1855).

In June 1856 Sullivan was the youngest of seventeen candidates who entered for the recently founded Mendelssohn scholarship to perpetuate the memory of Mendelssohn in England. The result was a tie between Sullivan and Joseph Barnby, the youngest and oldest competitors. In a final trial, however, Sullivan became the victor. He entered, under the terms of the scholarship, the Royal Academy of Music as a student, though he did not leave the choir of the Chapel Royal until 22 June 1857. His teachers at the Royal Academy were Sterndale Bennett and

Arthur O'Leary for pianoforte, and John Goss for composition. During his student period at Tenterden Street a setting by him of 'It was a Lover and his Lass,' for duet and chorus, was performed at the academy concert of 14 July 1857, and an overture on 13 July 1858. The latter work was praised by the 'Musical World' of 17 July 1858 (the leading musical journal of the day) for its cleverness, 'and an independent way of thinking, which, in one so young as the Mendelssohn scholar, looks well.' Outside his academy studies he took an active part in composing music for, and, clad in the academy uniform, in conducting the orchestra of, the Pimlico Dramatic Society, an amateur organisation which had the advantage of his brother Fred's assistance in the capacity of stage manager and director-in-chief.

In the autumn of 1858 Sullivan was sent by the Mendelssohn scholarship committee to the Conservatorium, Leipzig. He studied there under Moritz Hauptmann (counterpoint), Julius Rietz (composition), Ignatz Moscheles and Louis Plaidy (pianoforte), and Ferdinand David (orchestral playing and conducting). At Leipzig his publicly performed compositions included a string quartet; an overture, 'The Feast of Roses,' suggested by Thomas Moore's 'Lalla Rookh' (26 May 1860); and the music to Shakespeare's 'Tempest'—the last-named being his *exit opus* from the Conservatorium.

Sullivan returned to England in April 1861, when he immediately had to set about earning his own living. He took a course of lessons on the organ from George Cooper in order to qualify himself for an organist appointment. In the summer of 1861 he became organist and choirmaster of St. Michael's church, Chester Square, the adult members of his choir being composed of policemen! The turning-point of his life as a composer was reached by the performance of his wonderfully beautiful 'Tempest' music, played under the conductorship of Mr. August Manns at the Crystal Palace Saturday concert of 5 April 1862. Among the audience on that occasion was Charles Dickens, who said to the composer: 'I don't profess to be a musical critic, but I do know that I have listened to a very remarkable work.' The professional critics fully endorsed the opinion of the great novelist, and Sullivan at the age of twenty-one suddenly found himself famous. The 'Tempest' music, which was repeated at the concert on the following Saturday, must be placed among his best work. In melodic charm, dainty orchestration, and poetic fancy, Sullivan never surpassed this spontaneous composition of his youth. The arrival of the princess of Wales (Queen Alexandra) in London in March 1863 prompted a song, 'Bride from the North,' and a processional march. Sullivan's success as a song composer may be said to date from his five Shakespearean songs, produced at this time, of which 'Orpheus with his lute' stands out pre-eminently as a composition of sterling merit. The post of organist at the Royal Italian Opera, Covent Garden Theatre, which he held for a time under Costa's conductorship, resulted in the composition of the ballet of 'L'Ile enchantée,' produced at Covent Garden on 16 May 1864. In the same year he made his first appearance as a composer at one of the great musical festivals by the production of his cantata 'Kenilworth' (libretto by H. F. Chorley) at Birmingham, 8 Sept. 1864. 'Kenilworth' contains a duet, 'How sweet the moonlight sleeps,' which is 'far too good to be forgotten.' He lost much time over an opera (libretto also by Chorley) entitled 'The Sapphire Necklace,' of which only the overture came to maturity, and which has been frequently performed in the concert-room. From 1865 to 1869 Sullivan held his first appointment as a *chef d'orchestre* in the conductorship of the Civil Service Musical Society.

The year 1866 was an important one in his career. He was offered by Sterndale Bennett, the principal, a professorship of composition at the Royal Academy of Music. He also became professor of 'pianoforte and ballad singing' at the Crystal Palace School of Art. His only symphony (in E) was produced at the Crystal Palace on 10 March 1866. On 11 July he gave a concert at St. James's Hall, made additionally notable by the co-operation of Jenny Lind and the veteran Ignatz Moscheles. The sudden death of his father, on 22 Sept. 1866, furnished the promptings for the composition of his 'In Memoriam' overture, written for the Norwich musical festival, and first performed there 30 Oct. 1866. A concerto for violoncello and orchestra was performed (the solo part played by Signor Piatti) at the Crystal Palace concert of 24 Nov.

The chief event of this eventful year (1866) was the beginning of Sullivan's comic opera career. His first venture in this extraordinarily successful field of artistic creativeness was 'Cox and Box: a new Triumviretta,' an adaptation by Sir F. C. Burnand of the well-known farce by Maddison Morton, 'Box and Cox,' made still more comic by Burnand's interpellations, and set by Sullivan 'with a brightness and a drollery which at once placed him in the highest rank as a comic composer.' This amusing piece was privately performed at the residences of Burnand and Mr. Arthur J. Lewis (the latter on 27 April 1867), and in public at the Adelphi Theatre on 11 May 1867, at a benefit performance organised by the staff of 'Punch' for their late colleague, C. H. Bennett. 'Contrabandista' (libretto also by Burnand) followed in December. Then came a pause till the production of 'Thespis, or the Gods grown old; an operatic extravaganza,' libretto by Sir W. S. Gilbert (Gaiety Theatre, 26 Dec. 1871). This work was important in that it furnished the first fruits of that remarkable Gilbert and Sullivan collaboration which for nearly thirty years was extraordinarily prolific in results, and in fact inaugurated a new era in comic opera in this country. Its landmarks, so to speak, may be indicated by 'Trial by Jury' (1875), 'H.M.S. Pinafore' (1878), and 'The Mikado' (1885), the most popular of the series. In 'Trial by Jury' the composer's brother Frederick distinguished himself in the part of the Judge, and this comicality, by introducing the late Richard D'Oyly Carte as manager, initiated what may be called the Savoy Triumvirate—Gilbert, Sullivan, Carte. On 10 Oct. 1881 the Savoy Theatre, built by D'Oyly Carte specially for the Gilbert and Sullivan operas, was opened. A complete list of these works, with places and dates of their production, will be found at the end of this article.

To return to the more serious side of Sullivan's career, an overture, 'Marmion,' was commissioned by the Philharmonic Society and first performed at their concert of 3 June 1867. In the same month he became the first organist and choirmaster of St. Peter's church, Cranley Gardens, Kensington (consecrated 29 June 1867). This post he held for a short time concurrently with that of St. Michael's, Chester Square; but early in 1872 he entirely relinquished his ecclesiastical offices. These appointments, however, were largely the means of bringing into existence his anthems, hymn tunes, and other sacred music. In October 1867 he visited Vienna in company with his friend Sir George Grove, an expedition made memorable by the discovery of some valuable manuscripts of Schubert (Hellborn, *Life of Franz Schubert*, English transl., with appendix by George Grove, ii. 297).

As Sullivan had now fully established his reputation as a composer, it is not surprising that commissions began to reach him. For the Worcester musical festival of 1869 he composed his first oratorio, 'The Prodigal Son,' Sims Reeves taking the principal part on its production on 8 Sept. The Birmingham festival of the following year brought forth his 'Overture di Ballo' (performed 31 Aug. 1870), 'which, while couched throughout in dance-rhythms, is constructed in perfectly classical forms.' In the spring of this year he delivered at the South Kensington Museum a course of lectures (illustrated by part singing) on the 'Theory and Practice of Music,' in connection with a scheme entitled 'Instruction in Science and Art for Women.' For the opening of the International Exhibition on 1 May 1871, he composed the cantata 'On Shore and Sea' (words by Tom Taylor), and exactly a year later his festival 'Te Deum,' to celebrate the recovery of King Edward VII, then prince of Wales, from his serious illness, was performed at the Crystal Palace by two thousand executants in the presence of thirty thousand people. In November of the same year he became the first conductor of the Royal Amateur Orchestral Society. His second oratorio, 'The Light of the World,' was composed for the Birmingham festival of 1873, and first performed 27 Aug. In the following year he edited the musical section of 'Church Hymns, with Tunes,' published by the Society for the Promotion of Christian Knowledge. At Manchester, on 26 Feb. 1874, after a performance of 'The Light of the World' he was presented with an old English silver goblet and a purse containing 200*l.* In July 1874 he was appointed conductor of the Royal Aquarium orchestra: this post he held till May 1876. His other conducting engagements, in addition to those already mentioned, were: Messrs. Gatti's promenade concerts at Covent Garden Theatre during the seasons of 1878 and 1879; the Glasgow Choral Union orchestral concerts for two seasons, 1875–7; the Leeds musical festival (triennial) from 1880 to 1898; and the Philharmonic Society (London) from 1885 to 1887.

Sullivan was appointed the first principal of the National Training School of Music (South Kensington) in 1876, which office he held till 1881, when he was succeeded by Dr. (afterwards Sir John) Stainer. On 1 June 1876, in company with his old master, John Goss, he received the degree of Doctor in Music (*honoris causa*) at the university of Cambridge. A similar distinction was bestowed upon him at Oxford three years later, the occasion being the first time that honorary degrees in music were conferred by the university. In 1878 he acted as British Commissioner for Music at the International Exhibition at Paris, when he was decorated with the Order of the Légion d'honneur of France. A visit to America in November 1879, in company with Sir W. S. Gilbert and D'Oyly Carte, was in the nature of a triumphal reception.

To inaugurate his conductorship of the Leeds festival—in succession to Michael Costa—he composed his sacred music drama 'The Martyr of Antioch' (the words selected from Dean Milman's poem), performed 15 Oct. 1880. At the festival of 1886 (16 Oct.) his setting of Longfellow's 'Golden Legend' was first produced with a success that has ever since been accorded to this his finest as well as his most popular choral work. The Leeds festival of 1886 was made additionally memorable by a very remarkable performance under Sullivan of Bach's Mass in B minor. Apart from the succession of his comic operas, the outstanding event in the latter years of Sullivan's life was his serious (or 'grand') opera 'Ivanhoe,' produced at the Royal English Opera House (now the Palace Theatre), Shaftesbury Avenue, 31 Jan. 1891.

Delicate as a child, Sullivan suffered much ill-health during the greater part of his life. He died, somewhat suddenly, at his residence, 1 Queen's Mansions, Victoria Street, Westminster, on 22 Nov. 1900. His funeral partook of the nature of a public ceremony, and, after a service in the Chapel Royal, St. James's, where he had so often sung as a boy, his remains were interred in the crypt of St. Paul's Cathedral. Shortly before his death he returned to his early love, church music, by composing, at the request of the authorities of St. Paul's Cathedral, a 'Te Deum' for chorus and orchestra to celebrate the cessation of hostilities in South Africa when that happy consummation should take place (Sir George Martin's letter to the *Times*, 29 Nov. 1900).

Sullivan, who was unmarried, received the following distinctions: fellow of the Royal Academy of Music (his *alma mater*); Mus. Doc. Cantabr. (1876) and Mus. Doc. Oxon. (1879), both *honoris causa*; Order of the Légion d'honneur of France, 1878; Order of the Medjidieh from the sultan of Turkey, 1888; Order of Saxe-Coburg and Gotha; the Royal Victorian Order. He was knighted on 22 May 1883.

A portrait of Sullivan by Sir J. E. Millais, painted in 1888, is destined for the National Portrait Gallery. A mural tablet was placed above his grave in the crypt of St. Paul's Cathedral. A memorial tablet was fixed to the house where he was born on 20 July 1901, and a public monument was erected in the Embankment Gardens, London.

As a composer Sullivan was typically British (see his letter, signed 'A British Musician,' to the *Times*, 20 July 1897, on the subject of neglect of native music by British military bands). Melody, that rare gift, he possessed in a degree that may be classed as genius. The influence of his early training in the choir of the Chapel Royal is traceable in all his vocal music, solo and concerted, which is always grateful to sing and interesting to the singer. He was a master of orchestration, his treatment of the wood-wind being in many instances worthy of Schubert. Here again the seed sown in the band-room at Sandhurst bore rich fruit. Moreover, not a little of the humour of the comic operas is due to his masterfulness in extracting fun from his lifelong friends, the instruments. His creative achievements may be summarised in the words of his friend and early encourager, Sir George Grove: 'Form and symmetry he seems to possess by instinct; rhythm and melody clothe everything he touches; the music shows not only sympathetic genius, but sense, judgment, proportion, and a complete absence of pedantry and pretension; while the orchestration is distinguished by a happy and original beauty hardly surpassed by the great masters' (Grove, *Dict. of Music and Musicians*, iii. 763 *a*).

The following is an attempt at a complete list of Sullivan's compositions:

Oratorios and Cantatas.—'Kenilworth' (H. F. Chorley), Birmingham festival, 8 Sept. 1864; 'The Prodigal Son,' Worcester festival, 8 Sept. 1869; 'On Shore and Sea' (Tom Taylor), composed for the opening of the Royal Albert Hall, Kensington, 1 May 1871; Festival 'Te Deum,' Crystal Palace, 1 May 1872, to commemorate the recovery of King Edward VII, then prince of Wales; 'The Light of the World,' oratorio, Birmingham festival, 27 Aug. 1873; 'The Martyr of Antioch' (Dean Milman), Leeds festival, 15 Oct. 1880;

'The Golden Legend' (Longfellow, adapted by Joseph Bennett), Leeds, 16 Oct. 1886; Exhibition ode (Tennyson), opening of the Colonial exhibition, Royal Albert Hall, 4 May 1886; Imperial Institute ode (Lewis Morris), composed for the laying of the foundation-stone by Queen Victoria, 4 July 1887; Imperial March, opening of the Imperial Institute by Queen Victoria, 10 May 1893.

Operas and Plays.—'Cox and Box' (F. C. Burnand), Adelphi Theatre, first public performance 11 May 1867; 'The Contrabandista' (F. C. Burnand), St. George's Hall, 18 Dec. 1867; 'Thespis, or the Gods grown old,' Gaiety Theatre, 26 Dec. 1871; 'Trial by Jury,' new Royalty Theatre, 25 March 1875; 'The Zoo: an original musical folly' (B. C. Stephenson, who wrote the libretto under the pseudonym W. M. Bolton Rowe), St. James's Theatre, 5 June 1875; 'The Sorcerer,' Opera Comique, 17 Nov. 1877; 'H.M.S. Pinafore,' the same, 25 May 1878; 'Pirates of Penzance,' 3 April 1880; 'Patience,' the same, 23 April 1881. The following were produced at the Savoy Theatre: 'Iolanthe,' 25 Nov. 1882; 'Princess Ida,' 5 Jan. 1884; 'The Mikado,' 14 March 1885; 'Ruddigore,' 22 Jan. 1887; 'The Yeomen of the Guard,' 3 Oct. 1888; 'The Gondoliers,' 7 Dec. 1889; 'Haddon Hall' (Sydney Grundy), 24 Sept. 1892; 'Utopia (Limited),' 7 Oct. 1893; 'The Chieftain,' enlarged version of 'Contrabandista' (F. C. Burnand), 12 Dec. 1894; 'The Grand Duke,' 7 March 1896; 'The Beauty Stone' (A. W. Pinero and Comyns Carr), 28 May 1898; 'The Rose of Persia,' 29 Nov. 1899; 'The Emerald Isle' (Basil Hood), an unfinished opera, but completed by Edward German, and produced at the Savoy Theatre, 27 April 1901 (unless otherwise stated, all the foregoing are settings of librettos by W. S. Gilbert); grand opera, 'Ivanhoe' (Julian Sturgis), produced at the Royal English Opera House, 31 Jan. 1891.

Incidental Music to Plays.—'The Tempest' (op. 1), Crystal Palace, 5 April 1862; 'Merchant of Venice,' Prince's Theatre, Manchester, 19 Sept. 1871; 'Merry Wives of Windsor,' Gaiety Theatre, 19 Dec. 1874; 'Henry VIII,' Theatre Royal, Manchester, 29 Aug. 1877; 'Macbeth,' Lyceum Theatre, 29 Dec. 1888; 'The Foresters,' by Tennyson, Daly's Theatre, New York, 25 March 1892; 'King Arthur,' Lyceum Theatre, 12 Jan. 1895.

Orchestral Compositions.—Procession March, composed in celebration of the marriage of King Edward VII, then prince of Wales, and performed at the Crystal Palace on 14 March 1863; Symphony in E, Crystal Palace, 10 March 1866. Overtures: 'In Memoriam' (of his father), Norwich festival, 30 Oct. 1886; 'Marmion,' Philharmonic Society, 3 June 1867; 'Di Ballo,' Birmingham festival, 31 Aug. 1870; Concertino for violoncello and orchestra, Crystal Palace (Piatti soloist), 24 Nov. 1866. Ballets: 'L'Ile Enchantée,' Covent Garden Theatre, 16 May 1864; 'Victoria and Merrie England' (ballet), Alhambra, 25 May 1897.

Pianoforte Compositions.—Reverie in A, Melody in D (originally published as 'Thoughts'), 1862; 'Day Dreams,' six pieces, 1867; and 'Twilight,' 1868.

Violoncello Compositions.—Concerto in D (composed expressly for Signor Piatti), 1866; and Duo concertante for pianoforte and violoncello, 1868.

Songs and Duets.—Nearly one hundred. Of these 'The Lost Chord' (a setting of Adelaide Procter's words) has attained extraordinary popularity. The cycle of (eleven out of twelve) songs entitled 'The Window, or the Loves of the Wrens,' lyrics by Tennyson, published in 1871, take high rank in the realm of the art-song.

Part-songs (secular).—Ten. The settings of Sir Walter Scott's lines, 'O hush thee, my babie' (for mixed voices), first performed by Barnby's choir, St. James's Hall, 23 May 1867, and 'The long day closes' (for male voices), words by H. F. Chorley, are the best known.

Sacred Music.—Thirteen anthems; Morning Service in D; part-songs, arrangements of tunes, &c. (a complete list of these appeared in the *Musical Times*, January 1901, p. 24); Hymn tunes, about fifty, of which 'St. Gertrude,' a setting of the Rev. S. Baring-Gould's words, 'Onward, Christian soldiers,' was composed for the 'Hymnary,' 1872, but the tune first appeared in the 'Musical Times,' December 1871. A practically complete collection of his hymn tunes is published by Messrs. Novello, the well-known music publishers of London.

Sullivan edited 'Church Hymns with Tunes' (1874), and Messrs. Boosey's edition of operas, and he wrote additional accompaniments to Handel's 'Jephtha' for the performance of that work at the Oratorio concerts, St. James's Hall, 5 Feb. 1869.

[Grove's Dict. of Music and Musicians, iii. 761, iv. 797; Lawrence's Sir Arthur Sullivan, Life-story, Letters, and Reminiscences, 1899; Willeby's Masters of English Music, 1893; James D. Brown and S. S. Stratton's British Musical Biography, 1897; Fredk. R. Spark and Joseph Bennett's History of the Leeds Musical Festival, 1892; Musical Times, December 1900 p. 785, January 1901 p. 21, February 1901 p. 99, March 1901 p. 167, April 1901 p. 241; Brit. Mus. Cat.]

Frederick George Edwards

published 1901

PARRY Sir Charles Hubert Hastings

(1848–1918)

Baronet

Composer, musical historian, and director of the Royal College of Music, was born at Bournemouth 27 February 1848. He was the second son and youngest child by his first wife of Thomas Gambier Parry, of Highnam Court, Gloucestershire. Gambier Parry was a lover of the arts, a collector of Italian pictures, and himself a painter of more than ordinary amateur ability. He was a keen supporter of the 'high-church' movement. Though the religious forms of Hubert's youth were completely outgrown later, and the growth involved some violent reaction from them, the life at Highnam laid a stable foundation for his habit of associating seriousness with art and beauty with seriousness.

Hubert Parry's predilection towards music appeared early. Childish compositions, beginning with single and double chants, appear in notebooks which have been preserved from the age of nine. A list of his compositions when he was sixteen contains every form of Anglican church music, with piano and organ pieces, fugues, canons, madrigals, and songs interspersed. He was then at Eton, and the diaries which contain this list give a vivid picture of the zest with which he entered into every phase of public school life. That the keeper of 'School Field' should take a leading part as pianist and singer in the concerts of the Eton Musical Society was sufficiently unusual. He further surprised every one by passing the examination for the degree of bachelor of music at Oxford during his last 'half' at Eton. The method is typical. Education was for him the accumulation and sorting of diverse experiences. He had no exclusions. He would learn how things were done from the men who knew, whether the thing were the structure of a fugue or the rigging of a yacht. When he knew, he would use the knowledge in his own way. In music, Handel and Mendelssohn, imbibed at a succession of Gloucester festivals, were his first heroes. At Oxford, where he matriculated as a commoner of Exeter College in 1867, concerted chamber music became an absorbing interest, and he was instrumental in founding the University Musical Club. He spent his first long vacation at Stuttgart, studying orchestration and kindred matters with Henry Hugo Pierson, learning German, attending the opera, and also taking lessons in viola-playing.

In 1873 Parry settled permanently in London, having married in the previous year Lady Elizabeth Maude Herbert, second daughter of Sidney, first Lord Herbert of Lea. He was at this time a member of Lloyds, and though his diaries and correspondence show that he was fully determined to make music the central interest of his life, the idea of the musical profession as a career was naturally not then entertained. In one sense it may be said that he never was a professional musician, since he was never under the necessity of earning a living by music. Yet his desire to do something of worth imposed on him a stern discipline of study. At first his ambition was towards piano-playing, and during a winter which he spent at Cannes for his wife's health, he gave several concerts with the violinist, Guerini. In London he sought out as his piano teacher Edward Dannreuther, who soon became his closest friend and counsellor. Every new composition was submitted to Dannreuther's judgement for many years after the days of pupillage were passed, and the words 'Dann approves' occur constantly in the record of his undertakings. It was through Dannreuther that Parry went to the first Bayreuth festival (1876) and came under the spell of *Der Ring des Nibelungen*. When Wagner visited London in the following year, Parry formed an acquaintance with him through Dannreuther, and revelled in every opportunity of steeping himself in Wagner's music.

The Wagnerian gospel found the most immediate response in Parry's soul. He was going through a necessary period of revolt against many of the narrow traditions of his upbringing, social, artistic, and religious. In composition he concentrated chiefly on instrumental music. He wrote for the violin and piano a fine Partita in D minor and a Duo for two pianos in E minor, long a favourite work (published by Breitkopf and Haertel). A whole series of concerted chamber works for piano and strings came out at the private concerts which Dannreuther gave regularly at his house in Orme Square, and a Nonet for wind, 'written as an experiment', as also the now well-known Fantasia and Fugue for organ (Novello, 1913) belong to these years. A concert of Parry's chamber music given at the house of Mr. A. J. Balfour in Carlton House Terrace in 1879 has been generally referred to as a landmark in his career. In none of these compositions does the influence of Wagner seem peculiarly strong, but they certainly showed an independence of thought which was disquieting to some of Parry's friends. His father shook his head sadly over the heterodoxy of 'poor dear Hubert'. A letter to one of the nearest of these friends shows Parry's own standpoint. He says, 'I like my compositions as little as possible. I feel that they are far from what they ought to be; but I take a good deal of pains and do not write ill-considered reflections of Wagner, and though I feel the impress of his warmth and genius strongly I am not tempted to tread in the same path in the matter of construction, because what is applicable to the province of dramatic music is entirely alien to instrumental music. I have my own views on the latter subject. . . .'

Towards the end of 1875 Sir George Grove had invited Parry to collaborate with him as assistant editor of the monumental *Dictionary of Music and Musicians*, and the research which Parry's own articles entailed, together with the varied duties of editorship, stimulated that wide historical outlook seen later in his literary works, particularly *The Art of Music* (1893), *The Oxford History of Music*, vol. iii (1902), and *Style in Musical Art* (1911).

The customary division of a composer's work into periods is always dangerous; in the case of so continuous and consistent an artist as Parry it is doubly so, yet it is necessary if such a summary of his activities as this is to be anything more than a catalogue. What may be called the formative period came definitely to an end with the production in 1880 at the Crystal Palace of a piano concerto written for Dannreuther's performance. The same year 'Scenes from Shelley's Prometheus Unbound' for solo voices, chorus, and orchestra was given at the Gloucester festival and was the first fruit of the type of work with which Parry was to make an indelible impression on the taste of his generation.

The spirit of splendid rebellion in the poem was Parry's inspiration; he brought to its expression all that growth towards freedom which he had acquired in years of probation. Naturally the technical influence of Wagner, the Wagner of *The Ring*, is evident; the subject encouraged it, for here he was nearer to 'the province of dramatic music' than he had been before. There is also more warmth of colouring and scenic suggestion in the orchestral music than in any of Parry's later work. But the quality of the melody, the sensitiveness to the English language, and the subtle beauties of the writing for the choir, are unmistakable. Here was a new voice in music; it happened to be an English voice.

In spite of the mixed reception of 'Prometheus', the way was now open for wider activities in composition. Two symphonies followed quickly on one another, that in G and the one known as the 'Cambridge', not only because it was written for the Cambridge Musical Society but because it had as background a 'programme' of undergraduate life. The Cambridge Society had rescued 'Prometheus' from its fate in an admirable performance, and in the years in which the Society was guided by (Sir) Charles Stanford many of Parry's works were given there as they appeared. A setting of Shirley's ode, 'The Glories of our Blood and State', appeared in the same year as the Cambridge symphony, and showed that Parry's mind was already turning to what became ultimately the dominating issue of his life—reflective choral music.

The music to 'The Birds' of Aristophanes (Cambridge, 1884) led to his one experiment in opera, 'Guinevere', a romantic opera in three acts, which he composed with enthusiasm in 1886, though with many misgivings about the libretto. A single attempt to get it performed led to nothing; Parry laid aside the score and with it all aspirations towards opera, the conditions of which became increasingly distasteful to him in later years. Yet his music to the comedies of Aristophanes at various times, 'The Frogs' (Oxford, 1891), 'The Clouds' (1905), and 'The Acharnians' (1914) shows that he retained a sympathy with and a certain instinct for the theatre, though he regarded these things rather as an academic 'rag' than as the serious business of his art.

The period was completed with the noble setting for double choir and orchestra of Milton's ode 'At a solemn Music' ('Blest Pair of Sirens'). It has since become the most famous of all his works. Parry, together with many of his Eton and Oxford friends, had delighted in singing the choruses of the Mass in B minor, for the first English performance of which the Bach Choir had been originally formed. He wrote 'Blest Pair' for these friends at the suggestion of Grove, and its instant success amongst them, when the Bach Choir sang it in 1887, made amends for all the carping disparagement with which professional critics had pursued his earlier works.

His first oratorio 'Judith', given at Birmingham in the following year, marks a fresh stage in Parry's career. 'Judith', like 'Blest Pair', was a popular success, and from this time onward till he succeeded Sir George Grove as director of the Royal College of Music (1895) Parry was pouring out large works with almost unparalleled activity and conducting performances of them all over the country. They covered a wide range of expression. Two further symphonies, the 'English' in C and one in E minor, were produced in London in 1889; the same year came his first work for a Leeds festival, Pope's 'Ode on Saint Cecilia's Day'; 'L'Allegro ed Il Penseroso' (Norwich, 1890) again showed his understanding of the measured stateliness of Milton's verse, and from that he turned first to the majesty of the Latin psalm 'De Profundis', written for triple choir (Hereford, 1891), then to the melody of Tennyson in the choric song from 'The Lotus Eaters' (Cambridge, 1892). Yet this is pre-eminently the period of oratorios, three in number, 'Judith', 'Job' (Gloucester, 1892), and 'King Saul' (Birmingham, 1894).

'Judith' has been called a reactionary work, and with a certain justice. It is distinctly disconcerting, notwithstanding the intrinsic beauty of many of the numbers, to find Parry in the very zenith of his powers reverting to the stereotyped form of the Old Testament oratorio, with all its paraphernalia of massive choruses and arias. But Parry's attitude to the form was not one of complaisant acceptance. His preface makes it clear that his main interest lay in 'popular movements and passions and such results of them as occur a hundred times in history, of which the Israelitish story is one vivid type out of many'. In these works the musical experiences of his youth are sifted. He goes back in order to go forward, reviews the whole position of oratorio, and passes beyond both the conventional religious standpoint and the dramatic attractions of narrative. In the best moments of the two Birmingham works he reaches the epic expression of human feeling. 'Job' goes farther. Every convention of oratorio, even the choral *finale*, is discarded, in order that the one purpose, the growth of the soul through pain, may be traced out in the cry of lamentation, in the answer of the Lord 'out of the whirlwind', and in the peaceful peroration for orchestra alone. In the last two scenes of 'Job' we have the clue to that long chain of works which was eventually to sum up Parry's thought on the puzzle of life.

Meantime, however, there were busy years in which Parry's responsibilities as director of the Royal College of Music (he had held a professorship there since its inception in 1883), as choragus and subsequently as professor of music at Oxford, and his literary work, all made disastrous inroads on his time for composition. Most of the larger productions of the 'nineties show signs of that hasty workmanship which has seriously damaged Parry's reputation with a generation much concerned about technique, points of effect, and especially orchestration. Even the Symphonic Variations, probably his most successful composition for orchestra alone, has suffered from his carelessness in marking *nuances*, and certain festival works have sunk into oblivion after one imperfect performance largely on that account. The wonder is that the stream of composition went on comparatively unchecked, and that in the smaller works, from the songs collected in the various series of 'English Lyrics' to the 'Ode to Music' written for the opening of the new concert hall at the Royal College of Music, there is so much of the same lofty melody and sure handling of the voices which are the lovable qualities of Parry's art.

In the year after the South African War, the Royal Choral Society produced at the Albert Hall 'War and Peace', a symphonic ode for solo voices, chorus, and orchestra. Parry wrote the words himself (as he had often done—partially at any rate—in the case of previous works) and threw into rough and vigorous verse, suitable to his music, his thoughts on the conflicting passions of war and peace. Musically he rose to his full stature in the treatment of this theme, and it proved to be the precursor of a series of works, which in differing forms address themselves to one or other aspect of the same problem. Several cantatas, produced at a succession of Three Choirs festivals, beginning with 'Voces Clamantium' (Hereford, 1903), use the imagery and poetry of the Biblical writers to illustrate his message. Their very titles proclaim it: 'The Love that casteth out Fear', 'The Soul's Ransom', and 'Beyond these Voices there is Peace'. Each has compellingly fine musical moments, but each left him feeling that the message 'Look where thy Hope lies' was incomplete.

In 'A Vision of Life' (Cardiff, 1907) he again wrote his own poem, and wrestled with the same theme, surveying as in a dream the greatness and pitifulness of human struggle throughout salient epochs in the world's history. Even his last orchestral symphony (1912) shares in the thought, for the first three of its four linked movements bear the titles 'Work', 'Love', and 'Play', and the whole is summed up in a mood of optimism by a *finale* labelled 'Now'. Nor was this all, for in his last years he was much occupied with a book, *Instinct and Character* (unpublished, though typed copies have been deposited, and may be seen, in the British Museum, Bodleian, and Royal College of Music libraries), which endeavoured to examine the grounds of human action, reaction, and progress and to show where his hope lay for the future of mankind.

All this shows the impossibility of estimating Parry solely as the musical artist, even though it is through his music that he has done most towards 'winning the way'. The joyous freshness of the 'Ode on the Nativity', his last work for a Three Choirs festival (Hereford, 1912), shows that his purely musical inspiration still ran clear, and the boyish sense of fun was ready to break out again in such things as 'The Pied Piper' and the music to 'The Acharnians'. Nor must it be forgotten that during these years he so steeped himself in the mind of J. S. Bach, that he was able to produce the most intimately sympathetic study of 'a great personality' in music which the literature of this country possesses.

Parry's vivid interest in many things outside music, his love of the open air and the sea (he was a member of the Royal Yacht Squadron, and sailing his own yacht was easily first among his favourite recreations), his sympathy with young people, his constant desire to explore new ways of thought, even those ways in modern music which were most antipathetic to him—all contributed to keep his nature sane and sweet. He could be intolerant, hasty, and even forbidding. He never 'suffered fools gladly', but only fools failed to get at the essential simplicity and truth of the man. It was primarily his example and presence as head of the musical profession which compelled that enlarged outlook on the part of musicians themselves and that favourable change in their position amongst their fellows which in the last generation has brought new life to the art in England. He made music a man's concern.

The 'Songs of Farewell', six motets for unaccompanied voices, together with some solo songs and organ preludes, are the product of Parry's last years. The European War had shattered everything most dear to him, and he did not see the end of it. Its shadow is cast on his music, yet in these motets he holds to the convictions he had so hardly won, and in 'Never weather-beaten Sail', 'There is an old Belief', and 'Lord, let Me know mine End', there is a serenity and confidence which places them among the really great achievements of music.

He died at Rustington 7 October 1918, and was buried in the crypt of St. Paul's Cathedral.

Parry was knighted in 1898, and was made a baronet on the occasion of King Edward's coronation in 1902. His wife and two daughters survived him, but he left no male heir. The estate of Highnam Court, which he inherited from his father, passed to his half-brother. A tablet to his memory, bearing an inscription by the poet laureate (Mr. Robert Bridges), has been placed by public subscription in Gloucester Cathedral.

[Unpublished Diaries and Letters; personal knowledge. A fairly complete list of Parry's compositions to date of publication, 1907, is included in the second edition of Grove's *Dictionary of Music and Musicians*, edited by J. A. Fuller-Maitland. For further biographical details, see C. L. Graves, *Hubert Parry: His Life and Works*, 2 vols., 1926, published since this article was written.]

HENRY COPE COLLES

published 1927

STANFORD Charles Villiers

(1852–1924)

Sir

Composer, conductor, and teacher of music, was born in Dublin 30 September 1852, the only child of John Stanford, of Dublin, examiner in the court of Chancery and clerk of the crown, co. Meath, by his wife, Mary, daughter of William Henn, of Dublin, master in Chancery. He was educated at Henry Tilney Bassett's school in Dublin. His early Dublin life was spent in a favourable intellectual atmosphere. His father was an enthusiastic amateur vocalist and violoncellist. His music teachers, Arthur O'Leary (under whom he studied in London), Michael Quarry, and Sir Robert Prescott Stewart, were all of them able musicians and all of them Irishmen. Quarry, in particular, exercised a great influence upon Stanford by instilling into him a love for the music of Bach, Schumann, and Brahms, little of which had, in those days, penetrated to Ireland. These early influences never lost their spell and can be traced in Stanford's works up to the last.

Stanford

Stanford did not definitely decide to adopt music as a profession until 1870, when he was eighteen years of age. His father, in accepting the situation, insisted upon a general university education first and a specifically musical study abroad afterwards. This plan was carried out, but not without some difficulty. Stanford went up to Queens' College, Cambridge, as choral scholar in 1870, but he achieved such distinction in the musical life of Cambridge as an undergraduate that in 1873 he was appointed organist of Trinity College, and his university activities prevented any prolonged musical study abroad. Nevertheless, from 1874—the year in which he took his degree with a third class in the classical tripos—to 1876 he was given leave of absence for considerable periods in order to visit Germany for musical instruction. He studied first with Carl H. C. Reinecke in Leipzig and afterwards with Friedrich Kiel in Berlin. Stanford's reputation as a composer soon extended beyond Cambridge. As early as 1876 he attracted attention in London by his music to Tennyson's *Queen Mary*, written, at the poet's suggestion, for the Lyceum production, and by a symphony which gained a prize in a competition organized by the Alexandra Palace authorities. In 1877 his name figured in the Gloucester Festival programme with an overture. In 1882 a second symphony appeared, and his orchestral serenade was produced at the Birmingham Festival. His music to the *Eumenides* of Aeschylus (1885) took Cambridge by storm, and had much to do with consolidating his position as a musician of distinction.

It is surprising that with his manifold and varied activities, which increased when he settled in London in 1892, Stanford's output as a composer was so continuous. Whatever else claimed his attention—and he touched nothing timidly or half-heartedly—the time reserved for creative work was seldom allowed to be disturbed. He was a rapid worker. He scarcely ever made a sketch. Even complicated works were written straight into score, in ink, without previous preparation. Stanford was certainly the most versatile British composer of the latter half of the nineteenth century. There was no department of music in which he did not seek to challenge comparison with the foremost composers of his age, and there were few departments in which he failed to achieve some measure of distinction.

Stanford's efforts in the cause of English opera deserve special mention. If he gained only temporary successes with his stage works his fate in this respect must in part be attributed to the difficult conditions which beset operatic production in England. His first opera, *The Veiled Prophet of Khorassan* (1881), enjoyed only two performances, one in Hanover, and one in London. *Savonarola* (1884), *The Canterbury Pilgrims* (1884), *Much Ado about Nothing* (1901), and *The Critic* (1915), in which Sheridan's 'tragedy rehearsed' became an 'opera rehearsed', fared little better. His last opera, *The Travelling Companion*, published by the Carnegie Trust in 1919, has not up to the present time (1934) received an adequate professional presentation. The nearest approach to a popular success which Stanford secured on the stage was with his *Shamus O'Brien*, a romantic light opera, which had a run of several weeks at the old Opera Comique Theatre, London, in 1896.

Stanford's large-scale choral works, although many of them are forgotten, were highly esteemed in their day, and certainly left their influence upon the work of later writers. 'The Three Holy Children' (1885) and 'Eden' (1891) have not been heard in recent years, but his 'Requiem' (1897) and especially his 'Stabat Mater' (1907) created a more lasting impression, and may be regarded as representing his finest work for chorus and orchestra. On a smaller scale, in the form of secular ballads, his 'The Revenge' (1886), 'Phaudrig Crohoore' (1896), and 'The Last Post' (1900) remain conspicuous examples of the best type of British choral writing, and have won both professional and popular acceptance.

For orchestra alone Stanford completed seven symphonies, the best-known of which are No. 3, 'The Irish' (1887), and No. 5, 'L'Allegro ed il Penseroso', inspired by Milton's poems (1895). His six 'Irish Rhapsodies' are, however, more representative of his genius, and their national character, combined with the imperishable poetic beauty of the native melodies from which the main themes are derived, give them a place of special significance in modern music. No. 1 (1902) is the most obstinately popular, but No. 2 (1903) is a finer work, and No. 4, 'The Fisherman of Lough Neagh' (1913), is probably the most satisfying example of Stanford's orchestral writing which exists.

Stanford was also a prolific writer of chamber music—skilfully wrought, but mostly of a severely classical type which seldom reflected his personality attractively. There are eight string quartets; two string quintets; a pianoforte quintet and quartet; several trios and duet sonatas for various combinations, &c. None of these are publicly performed with any regularity, although many of them are in the repertories of amateur players.

Stanford's church music, on the other hand, has established itself firmly in the services of all English cathedrals and important churches. His settings of the canticles are healthy, vigorous, and far superior in quality to those of most of his contemporaries. No religious music is better loved in Great Britain than 'Stanford in B flat' (1879), whilst his four later services, and several anthems, have almost equal claims upon the affection of church musicians. Medievalists have taken exception to some of his methods, and complained that this music is not always devout in style, but Stanford took a liberal view of the Church's needs for various occasions.

Stanford

The mastery of design and fluency which distinguish Stanford's services and anthems are features also in his secular part-songs, notably the 'Elizabethan Pastorals', of which there are three sets; in the infinitely charming vocal pieces for children; in the much-esteemed compositions for organ, as well as in his smaller instrumental solos, too numerous to mention in detail. Fleeting trifles many of them are, but sometimes they reveal his individuality with greater clearness than more elaborate works.

It is, however, as a writer of solo songs that Stanford's reputation appears to be most securely established. Through the art of his friend, Plunket Greene, he won especial fame for his settings for baritone voice with choral and orchestral accompaniment. Early and brilliant examples are the 'Three Cavalier Songs', settings of Browning's poems, with male chorus (1882), but his 'Songs of the Sea' (1905) and 'Songs of the Fleet' (1910) are his finest essays in a form which he made peculiarly his own. They strike a note of romantic patriotism at once stirring and dignified. In writing for solo voice with pianoforte he excelled in settings of modern Irish poems, several collections of which won wide acceptance. The high-water mark in this type of song is reached with 'An Irish Idyll' (1901), but the succeeding collections, 'Cushendall' (1910), 'A Fire of Turf' (1913), and 'Songs from Leinster' (1914), all maintain an excellent standard and contain many of his happiest thoughts.

As a conductor Stanford gained extensive experience with the Cambridge University Musical Society (1872–1893), but he will chiefly be remembered as director of the Bach Choir, London (1885–1902), and of the Leeds Festival, where he succeeded Sir Arthur Sullivan and officiated from 1901 to 1910. He also had chief charge of the Royal College of Music orchestra during the period of his professorship at that institution. It has been well said by one of his pupils, George Dyson, that 'Stanford was never a virtuoso conductor. Virtuosity of every kind was alien to his temperament. Contrasted with the more exuberant, his methods appeared to be sound rather than inspired. But he could handle large masses with a command and a dignity which revealed the nobility of masterpieces.'

Stanford was appointed professor of composition and orchestral playing at the Royal College of Music on its opening in 1883, and professor of music at Cambridge in 1887, holding both appointments until the year of his death. He earned the reputation of being the most successful composition teacher of his time in England. Many of his pupils were destined to become distinguished musicians. Amongst these were Walford Davies, Coleridge Taylor, Vaughan Williams, Gustav Holst, John Ireland, Frank Bridge, Rutland Boughton, Eugène Goossens, Arthur Bliss, and Herbert

Howells. This list alone will serve as testimony to the soundness of his training and the catholicity of his sympathies. In 1911 he published his treatise on *Musical Composition*, a little volume which was the fruit of long experience and presented an admirable epitome of his methods, set forth without didactic heaviness or pedantry.

Stanford's other contributions to literature are not numerous, and may be regarded mainly as diversions in the course of a busy life. His chapters in *A History of Music* (1916), written in collaboration with Cecil Forsyth, are terse in style and exhibit sound critical judgements. Mention should also be made of his *Studies and Memories* (1908) and *Interludes* (1922).

Stanford was the recipient of many academic distinctions, including the honorary degrees of Mus.D. of Oxford (1883) and Cambridge (1888), D.C.L. of Durham (1894), and LL.D. of Leeds (1904). He was knighted in 1902.

Stanford married in 1878 Jane Anna Maria, daughter of Henry Champion Wetton, of Joldwynds, Shere, near Guildford. They had one son and one daughter. Stanford died in London 29 March 1924 and his ashes are buried in Westminster Abbey.

Stanford's personality was very striking. He was tall in stature, and his countenance, somewhat grim in repose, assumed, in conversation, immense earnestness and animation. He was easily led by his fiery temperament into indiscretions of utterance. He delighted to triumph over enemies, but seldom bore malice. He could stab with sarcasm and heal the wound with affectionate good-humour. None could question his intense loyalty to his art, to his friends, to those who served him, and to those whom he delighted to honour.

An excellent portrait of Stanford, painted by Sir William Orpen, hangs in the hall of Trinity College, Cambridge. A cartoon of him by 'Spy' appeared in *Vanity Fair* 2 February 1905.

[Sir George Grove, *Dictionary of Music and Musicians*, 3rd ed., 1928; Sir C. V. Stanford, *Pages from an Unwritten Diary*, 1914; *Proceedings* of the Musical Association, 1926–1927; private information; personal knowledge.]

T. F. DUNHILL

published 1937

SQUIRE William Barclay

(1855–1927)

Musical antiquary, was born in London 16 October 1855. He was the only son of William Squire, of Feltham Hill, Middlesex, merchant of the City of London, by his wife, Elizabeth Ogden. He was educated privately, at Frankfurt-am-Main, and at Pembroke College, Cambridge, where he graduated B.A. in 1879, having obtained a third class in the historical tripos. He practised as a solicitor in London from 1883 to 1885, and in the latter year was appointed an assistant in the department of printed books in the British Museum, and in 1912 was made an assistant keeper, with special charge of the printed music. Although Squire retired from this office under the age limit in 1920, he was in 1924 appointed honorary curator of the King's music library which is permanently on loan to the Museum, and this bore valuable fruit in the publication of a catalogue of this collection. Part I, dealing with the Handel MSS., appeared in 1927; Part III, the printed music and musical literature, in 1929. The second portion had not been begun by Squire when he died, and is the work of Miss Hilda Andrews.

From 1890 to 1904 Squire acted as music critic for the *Saturday Review*, *Westminster Gazette*, *Globe*, and *Pilot* in succession. He wrote the libretto of (Sir) C. V. Stanford's opera, *The Veiled Prophet of Khorassan* (1881) and of (Sir) F. Bridge's cantata, 'Callirrhoe' (1888). Squire contributed many articles to all three editions of Grove's *Dictionary of Music*, and in the third edition, which is illustrated, his special interest in portraits of musicians proved of great service. He was also a contributor to the *Encyclopædia Britannica* and to other publications. He compiled catalogues of old printed music in the British Museum (2 vols., 1912), of the music in the chapter library of Westminster Abbey (*Monatshefte* for 1903), and of the printed music in the Royal College of Music (1909), of which he had been librarian since 1885. He also collaborated with Helen, Countess of Radnor in the *Catalogue of the Pictures in the Collection of the Earl of Radnor* (1909).

Squire did much valuable editorial work on English madrigals and old keyboard music, the most important of which, the *Fitzwilliam Virginal Book*, was done in co-operation with his brother-in-law, J. A. Fuller-Maitland, and was published in 1894–1899. He edited a reprint of the words of Robert Jones's *Muses' Gardin for Delights* (1901), and for the Purcell Society, of which he was honorary secretary, he edited Purcell's harpsichord music (4 vols., 1918).

During the European War, Squire worked for the Intelligence Department of the Admiralty (1916–1918), and from 1918 to 1920 he served in the historical section of the Foreign Office. His report on the *Tribes of Tunisia* (1916) was officially adopted by the French government. He died, unmarried, in London 13 January 1927.

Squire became a fellow of the Society of Antiquaries in 1888 and of the Royal Geographical Society in 1894. He was elected an honorary fellow of Pembroke College, Cambridge, in 1925. In 1918 he became a knight of grace of the order of St. John of Jerusalem, and in 1926 received the C.V.O.

As an historian and archaeologist Squire's habitual care and accuracy made him regarded as a sound authority, and his readiness to place his great knowledge, not only of music, but of matters artistic and genealogical, at the disposal of all genuine applicants for information, will not be readily forgotten by students in the British Museum Library and elsewhere.

[Private information; personal knowledge.]

H. THOMPSON

published 1937

MAITLAND John Alexander Fuller- (1856–1936)

Musical critic and connoisseur, was born in London 7 April 1856, the only child of John Fuller-Maitland, by his wife, Marianne, only child of George Noble, of Duffryn, Glamorganshire. He was grandson of Ebenezer Fuller-Maitland, a prominent member of the Clapham Sect. In 1862 his father built the house in Phillimore Gardens, Kensington, which Fuller-Maitland inherited, and which was for fifty years his home and a very famous centre for musical gatherings.

Owing to delicate health, Fuller-Maitland was educated privately, except for three terms at Westminster, but in 1875 he entered Trinity College, Cambridge: this proved to be the turning-point in his career, for he then came under the influence of (Sir) C. V. Stanford and W. Barclay Squire and entered upon what he called five or six years of 'musical amateurity'. He was invited about 1881 by (Sir) George Grove to contribute to his *Dictionary of Music and Musicians*, and in 1882 Grove introduced him to John (later Viscount) Morley, editor of the *Pall Mall Gazette*, of which Fuller-

Maitland then became the musical critic; but W. T. Stead succeeded Morley as editor in 1883, and in 1884 Fuller-Maitland was dismissed. The same year, however, he became the musical critic of the *Guardian* and in 1889 he succeeded Francis Hueffer as musical critic of *The Times*. This post he held until 1911 when he retired to Borwick Hall, near Carnforth. He married in 1885 Charlotte Elizabeth (died 1931), eldest daughter of William Squire, of Feltham Hill, Middlesex, and sister of Barclay Squire; there were no children of the marriage. He died at Borwick Hall 30 March 1936.

For many years Fuller-Maitland was a prominent figure in English musical life. Criticism was his chief activity; and the influence which he wielded was wide and wholesome. He was not endowed with originality of insight, nor with special gifts of style; but he had high ideals, extensive knowledge, and untiring enthusiasm. His tastes were in the main conservative; but he took a keen interest in many different kinds of music. He was an early researcher into folksong and medieval choralism, and (in collaboration with Squire) produced the authoritative edition of the *Fitzwilliam Virginal Book* (1894–1899); he was a Purcell scholar, and contributed vol. iv (*The Age of Bach and Handel*, 1902) to the *Oxford History of Music*. Among those who were, roughly speaking, his contemporaries, Brahms, Joachim, Parry, and Stanford were nearest to his heart; and he wrote books on all four. He also edited, with many personal contributions, the second edition of *Grove's Dictionary* (1904–1910). Perhaps the most significant book of his large output is *A Door-keeper of Music* (1929), an autobiography from childhood to retirement: attractively full of good sense and pleasant humour, it portrays in vivid fashion many varied scenes of the social and artistic life of Victorian and Edwardian England.

Fuller-Maitland received the honorary degree of D.Litt. from Durham University and was an associate of the Royal Academy of Fine Arts, Brussels.

[*The Times*, 31 March 1936; *Cambridge Review*, 30 October 1936; J. A. Fuller-Maitland, *A Door-keeper of Music*, 1929 (portrait); *Grove's Dictionary of Music and Musicians*, 4th ed., vol. ii, edited by H. C. Colles; personal knowledge.]

BRUCE L. RICHMOND
ERNEST WALKER

published 1949

ELGAR Sir Edward William

(1857–1934)

Baronet

Composer, born at Broadheath, near Worcester, 2 June 1857, the fifth child and eldest surviving son of William Henry Elgar, by Ann, daughter of Joseph Greening, of Weston, Herefordshire. The father came from Dover to Worcester in 1841, and was organist of St. George's Roman Catholic church there. He also established a music shop in the city.

Edward Elgar was brought up in a family where there was much talk of music and in a district where there was regular music-making. He often sat with his father in the organ-loft at St. George's and after a time played the organ there, eventually succeeding his father as organist (1885–1889). He went to a local teacher for violin lessons and realized one of his earliest ambitions when, as a violinist, he joined the orchestra of the Worcester Glee Club, and, like his father, played in the orchestra at the meetings of the Three Choirs. Soon after his coming of age, Elgar was conducting some of the local concerts, with members of his family in the orchestra. Works by Mozart, Rossini, and others were played, but first of all had to be arranged by the young conductor for the slender orchestra of the club. By trial and experience he began to learn how to transfer a part written for one instrument to another, and how to treat the orchestral garment at his disposal so that it did not seem too threadbare.

Elgar's education insisted chiefly upon self-reliance. He had been to a kindergarten and later to a boys' school, Littleton House, near Worcester, where during a scripture lesson he formed the first dim resolve to compose one day a work on the subject of Christ's Apostles. He left school at the age of fifteen and for a short time served as an apprentice in a solicitor's office. Then he had the idea of becoming a solo violinist and began to give lessons with the intention of saving enough money to have violin lessons himself in London from a good teacher. Everything had to be worked out carefully in terms of money, and at length in 1877, 'living on two bags of nuts a day', as he himself used to describe the venture, he embarked on a series of violin lessons from Adolf Pollitzer. As a result he found himself gradually coming to the decision that he would devote his life and thought, not to the violin, but to the composition of music.

But the knowledge which Elgar had gained was casual. He began to perceive that, if he would realize his dreams, it was not enough to continue arranging music for the Glee Club and the Worcestershire County Asylum band. He studied Mozart and, by stern application, taught himself the externals of symphonic form. He went to Leipzig for two weeks in 1882 and heard all the music available there. Not long afterwards, in 1883, an orchestral composition of his called 'Intermezzo: Serenade Mauresque' was performed at a Birmingham concert.

A visit by Dvořák to England must be regarded as one of the early influences in Elgar's life, not in the matter of style but as an incident which stirred the young composer's enthusiasm. Another influence can be dated from 1886 when Miss Caroline Alice Roberts came to him as a pupil. She was the only daughter of Sir Henry Gee Roberts, and they were married in 1889. The Elgars settled in London, but in 1891 they moved to Malvern and thence (1904) to Hereford, where they remained until 1911. In 1912 they made their headquarters at Severn House, Hampstead, where they remained until Lady Elgar's death eight years later.

It was about the time of his marriage that Elgar, encouraged by his wife, decided to give most of his time to composition. Without a doubt, his wife's belief in his genius was a prime factor in his development at this period. The development was not spectacular but very sure. He began to think in terms of the larger forms of composition. For the Worcester festival of 1890 he was ready with the 'Froissart' overture. Three years later (1893) he had finished a work which he described as 'a symphony for chorus and orchestra' called 'The Black Knight', and in another three years (1896) he had completed his first oratorio, 'The Light of Life', and his choral work, 'Scenes from the Saga of King Olaf'. It was in this last work that Elgar became fully confident of his powers, and in 1899 he produced a work, 'Variations on an original theme for orchestra', generally known by the title 'Enigma variations', which left no more doubt in the public estimation of his genius. This fine work, which has become one of the best known of all Elgar's orchestral compositions, was first played under Hans Richter in 1899. When Sir Arthur Sullivan died in 1900 it became apparent to many that Elgar, although a composer of another build, was his true successor as first musician of the land. It was in that year that his masterpiece appeared, the oratorio 'The Dream of Gerontius', a setting of part of Newman's poem. This was first performed on 3 October at the Birmingham festival under Richter. The performance itself was disappointingly below standard, but after the work had been given in Germany with a German translation of the text (at Düsseldorf in 1901 and again in 1902) with Julius Büths as conductor, it was accepted at its proper worth in the composer's own country. It was 'Gerontius' which moved Richard Strauss to drink to the success of 'the first English progressive musician, Meister Elgar'. Meanwhile the university of Cambridge had anticipated this toast by conferring upon Elgar in 1900 the honorary degree of doctor of music.

This was the beginning of Elgar's most sustained period of creative energy and it lasted until 1920, which was the year of his wife's death. From time to time he turned aside to the smaller forms and produced songs, incidental music for plays, and music for occasions (the 'Coronation Ode', 1902, and the 'Coronation March', 1911), but for the most part during these years he was at work upon some full scale orchestral or choral work. The unfolding of his genius showed him to be essentially a symphonic writer. This was already to be discerned in the oratorios 'The Apostles' (1903) and 'The Kingdom' (1906), which were the first two works of an uncompleted trilogy, and again in a number of orchestral works such as the first four 'Pomp and Circumstance' marches (1901–1907, the first of which contains the popular tune later known as 'Land of Hope and Glory'), the overtures 'Cockaigne' (1901) and 'In the South (Alassio)' (1904), and the superb 'Introduction and Allegro' for strings (1905). But the full flower of his imagination was not shown until the two symphonies and the violin concerto were completed and performed. These achievements, together with the symphonic study 'Falstaff' (1913), with their richness, expansiveness, and majesty, can be truly appraised only against the background of the Edwardian age, although the violin concerto is more contemplative than the others. This concerto was dedicated to Fritz Kreisler who was soloist in the first performance in 1910. The first symphony (Symphony in A flat, 1908) may be thought of as a noble pæan in praise of the Edwardian era, the second symphony (Symphony in E flat, 1911) as an epic, and the violoncello concerto (1919) as an elegy on the same theme. This last-named work and three examples of chamber music plainly reveal the disillusioning influence of the war years of 1914 to 1918, especially the concerto, with its spare orchestration and plangent cadences.

When in 1924 Elgar was made master of the king's musick, it was evident that there were some in authority who heard in his music a voice of exceptional eloquence. But there were others, steadily increasing in numbers, who knew that Elgar was far greater than a mere laureate, and that, like Sibelius, he was a composer whose music, although imbued with national feeling, spoke with universal appeal. English people had been slow to appreciate his work until the 'Enigma variations' was heard, but thereafter approval and understanding increased with almost every composition. He received numerous honours: he was appointed a member of the Order of Merit in 1911 (being the first musician to receive the order), was knighted in 1904, created a baronet in 1931, and appointed K.C.V.O. in 1928 and G.C.V.O. in 1933. Besides his Cambridge doctorate already mentioned, he received honorary doctorates of music from the universities of Durham, Oxford, Yale, and London, and honorary degrees from several others, and among foreign honours are to be reckoned those of corresponding member of the Institut de France and honorary member of the Regia Accademia di Santa Cecilia.

After Lady Elgar's death, Elgar produced no major work. Some very personal orchestrations of Bach and Handel, some music for the Wembley British Empire Exhibition (1924), some incidental music for a play, No. 5 of the 'Pomp and Circumstance' marches, planned as a set of six (1930), and the 'Nursery Suite' (1931, dedicated to the Duchess of York and the Princesses Elizabeth and Margaret) were almost the only evidence which the public had to indicate that the composer had not completely given up writing music. A few friends knew that he had sketched some music for an opera which was to be based on Ben Jonson's play *The Devil is an Ass*, and on the occasion of his seventy-fifth birthday (1932) it was announced that the British Broadcasting Corporation had commissioned him to write his third symphony. Elgar made some sketches for this work, but before he could come to grips with the great undertaking, a fatal illness overtook him, and he died at Worcester 23 February 1934. He was buried in his wife's grave in the churchyard of St. Wulstan, Little Malvern. He was survived by his only child, a daughter.

Among symphonic composers of all nations, Elgar's name shines because of his orchestral writing, and in this respect he did much to raise the standard of orchestral playing in England. By the members of English orchestras he was greatly beloved, and in turn memories of early days, when he was a humble bandsman, made him deeply appreciative of their work, and led him to take great pains in helping them to understand the intricacies of his scores. His reward has been that the best of the English orchestras have the secret of bowing his melody and of breathing his rich harmony, and have mastered the idiom of his phrase and the curve of his eloquence.

In the history of music Elgar will be remembered as the man who so far lifted the status of English music that the once fashionable description of England as 'the land without music' became an absurdity. 'Falstaff', one of the finest of all works written for a modern orchestra, is called a symphonic study and the symphonic aspect cannot be too much emphasized. The music's behaviour, that is, is guided by an inner logic of its own rather than by a series of scenes and events, although it is still true that the agreement between that inner logic and the 'programme' is a remarkable feature of the music. When Elgar's finely imaginative achievement in 'Falstaff' is contemplated and some of the excellent music which he wrote in an earlier work, the cantata 'Caractacus' (1898), is then recalled, it is impossible not to be set wondering what heights the composer would have reached in the Ben Jonson opera which he was sketching. But, although destiny's plan included no opera by Elgar, the splendid attainments of succeeding English composers, especially in symphonic writing, have been so much the more notably excellent for the vantage-ground gained by Elgar in his oratorios, symphonies, concertos, the 'Enigma variations', the 'Introduction and Allegro' and in 'Falstaff'.

A portrait of Elgar by Talbot Hughes no longer exists, but a drawing by (Sir) William Rothenstein (1910) in the Royal Library at Windsor Castle is reproduced in *Music and Letters*, January 1920. A bronze cast of a bust by Percival Hedley (1927), is in the National Portrait Gallery.

[Basil Maine, *Elgar. His Life and Work*, 2 vols., 1933; R. J. Buckley, *Sir Edward Elgar*, 1904; Ernest Newman, *Elgar*, 1906; W. H. Reed, *Elgar*, 1939; *Grove's Dictionary of Music and Musicians*, 4th ed., vol. ii, edited by H. C. Colles; Louise B. M. Dyer, *Music by British Composers. A Series of Complete Catalogues, No. 2. Sir Edward Elgar*, 1931; personal knowledge.]

BASIL MAINE

published 1949

DOLMETSCH (Eugene) Arnold

(1858–1940)

Musician and musical craftsman, was born at Le Mans, France, 24 February 1858. He came of a family of musicians. His grandfather, of Bohemian origin, settled in Zürich in 1808. There his father, Rudolf Arnold Dolmetsch, was born and became a pianoforte maker but was himself a musician who played Bach's fugues on the clavichord. His mother was Marie Zelie Guillouard. Arnold was the eldest son. He was thus early apprenticed to the craft of instrument making and the art of playing. After his father's death he went to the Brussels Conservatoire for a general musical education and studied the violin with Henri Vieuxtemps. In 1883 he entered the newly founded Royal College of Music in London and was encouraged by its director, Sir George Grove, not only in his professional career as music master at Dulwich College but in his investigations into the early English instrumental music which he found in the British Museum in 1889.

Thereafter the study of old music, the way to play it, the instruments on which to play it, how to play them, and, when the stock of old specimens ran out, the making of new lutes, virginals, clavichords, harpsichords, recorders, and ultimately of viols and violins, became Dolmetsch's lifework. His chief contributions to the English musical renaissance, which throughout his lifetime was growing from roots pushed into native soil by the revivals of folk-music and Tudor music, was the rediscovery of a school of English composers for consorts of viols, of whom the chief were John Jenkins (1592–1678) and William Lawes, and the re-establishment of the recorder (first made by him in 1921) as an instrument of popular music. In 1915 he published *The Interpretation of the Music of the Seventeenth and Eighteenth Centuries*. He soon after settled at Haslemere, Surrey, and established workshops there. In 1925 he founded an annual summer festival of chamber music at which old music unearthed from many a library was performed on the instruments for which it had been composed and in the right style. These performances by his family and pupils were not always highly polished in execution, but Dolmetsch was unabashed. He formulated his principles in these words: 'This music is of absolute and not antiquarian importance; it must be played as the composer intended and on the instruments for which it was written with their correct technique; and through it personal music-making can be restored to the home, from which two centuries of professionalism have divorced it.' His sons and daughters, who were all four turned by him into versatile executants, certainly formed a domestic consort. His restoration of the recorder opened a new line of amateur effort. His improved harpsichords encouraged the use of that instrument for the *basso continuo* of eighteenth-century operas and oratorios. His work for viols and lute was of the greatest antiquarian, although of less general musical, interest. In the words of Sir Henry Hadow his lifework as a whole certainly 'opened the door to a forgotten treasure-house of beauty'.

In 1928, in honour of Dolmetsch's seventieth birthday, the Dolmetsch Foundation was incorporated for the 'encouragement of the revival of early instrumental music'. In 1937 he was granted a civil list pension; in 1938 he was created a chevalier of the Legion of Honour; and in 1939 he received the honorary degree of doctor of music from Durham University. He was naturalized in 1931. He died at Haslemere 28 February 1940.

Dolmetsch was twice married: first, in 1877 to Marie Morel, of Namur; secondly, in 1903 to Mabel, daughter of John Brookes Johnston, of Denmark Hill. By his first wife he had a daughter, Hélène (1880–1924), who was a fine player of the viola da gamba. By his second wife he had two sons, the elder of whom was killed in the war of 1939–1945, and two daughters.

There are portraits of Dolmetsch by Sir Max Beerbohm, Sir William Rothenstein, and Nevill Lytton at Haslemere, and by Edmond Xavier Kapp at Bedales Junior School.

[Arnold Dolmetsch, *Dolmetsch and his Instruments* (privately printed at Haslemere), 1929; Robert Donington, *The Work and Ideas of Arnold Dolmetsch*, Dolmetsch Foundation, 1932; *Musical Quarterly*, April 1933; *Grove's Dictionary of Music and Musicians*, 4th ed., vol. ii, edited by H. C. Colles.]

FRANK HOWES

published 1949

SMYTH Ethel Mary

(1858–1944)

Dame

Composer, author, and feminist, was the daughter of Lieutenant-Colonel (later Major-General) John Hall Smyth, C.B., an artillery officer stationed at Woolwich, who had fought in the Indian Mutiny and was living at Sidcup, where Ethel Mary, the fourth of a family of six girls and two boys, was born 23 April 1858. Her mother was the daughter of a Norfolk Stracey who had married a Mr. Charles Struth and subsequently in Paris a Mr. Reece, from whom she was eventually separated. Emma, daughter of the first marriage, who became Mrs. Smyth, was thus subject to French education and to French ways, the effects of which she never quite lost even in the conventional atmosphere of an English officer's home. Her own background in the deliberate obscurity of her mother's life in Paris gave her some sympathy with her own rebellious daughter (whom she called 'the stormy petrel') when paternal opposition to a musical career for Ethel was at its height.

In the course of Ethel's education at home and at a boarding-school at Putney, musical talent showed itself early, although not with extraordinary precocity. It was taken in hand at a critical moment by the composer of the tune for the hymn 'Jerusalem the Golden', Alexander Ewing, then a captain in the Army Service Corps and a neighbour of the Smyths who had moved to Frimley. His wife (Juliana Horatia Ewing) gave Ethel, then a girl of seventeen, some help in the writing of English, and prophetically declared that she would turn her into a writer some day. The battle for a musical career, which had begun at the age of twelve, was not decided until 1877 when after furious opposition from her father she got her way and went off to Leipzig to study at the Conservatorium. At Leipzig she obtained admission to the circle dominated by Brahms, studying with Heinrich von Herzogenberg, and forming a friendship with his wife Elisabeth which is the main theme of the autobiographical *Impressions that*

Remained. Her first works, the product of her studies and couched as was natural enough in the idiom of German romanticism of the early 'eighties, were a Quintet for strings and a Sonata for violin and piano, which were obviously promising. She continued to compose assiduously, at first in the forms of chamber music, but in 1890 a Serenade in D in four movements for orchestra gained a performance at the Crystal Palace concerts and later in the same year an overture, 'Antony and Cleopatra', was performed there and in 1892 repeated by (Sir) George Henschel at one of his London concerts.

To the next year belongs the Mass in D, her most impressive work outside the category of opera. It is an oratorio setting in the style of the Viennese Masses which culminated in Beethoven's Mass in D, and although not a challenge to Beethoven on his own ground it is an assertion of the composer's ability to handle with confidence the largest forms on the highest themes. The work, although in the appropriate style, is not derivative, and when it was revived in 1924, thirty-one years after its original performance at the Royal Albert Hall under Sir Joseph Barnby, the freshness of the invention and the mastery of its construction and its orchestration were noted as signs of its vitality. Sir Donald Tovey honoured it with one of his analytical notes, in the course of which he says that 'no choral work within modern times is more independent of all classical or modern antecedents except those of artistic common-sense'. Her other important oratorio 'The Prison', composed at the end of her long career—it was first performed in 1931 when she was seventy-three—was not successful, although it was based on a philosophical text by Henry B. Brewster, brother-in-law of Elisabeth von Herzogenberg, who figures largely in the composer's memoirs and certainly influenced her thought. Its intellectual sincerity is not matched by a similar imaginative intensity and its scrappiness suggests that the dissipation of her great energies and enthusiasms, however much they enriched her life, was not favourable to artistic creation.

For Ethel Smyth was an inveterate crusader. Her first battle was for her own career as a musician. Having got her training she fought for recognition not merely as a woman composer but as a composer without prefix or suffix. She actually secured performances of her operas in German theatres: *Fantasio* was produced at Weimar in 1898 and at Carlsruhe in 1901; the one-act *Der Wald* in Berlin and at Covent Garden in 1902, in New York in 1903, and at Strasbourg in 1904; *Der Strandrecht*, which became *The Wreckers*, at Leipzig and Prague in 1906. The first performance in England and in English was given at His Majesty's Theatre in 1909 under (Sir) Thomas Beecham and it had revivals at Covent Garden (1931) and Sadler's Wells (1939). *The Boatswain's Mate* (after the story by W. W. Jacobs) would have been first given at Frankfurt but for the war and actually had its première in London in 1916. Her other operas were in one act: one, described as a dance dream, *Fête Galante*, produced at the Birmingham Repertory Theatre in 1923; the other, a farcical comedy, *Entente Cordiale*, produced at Bristol in 1926. This is a very considerable achievement in the notoriously hazardous and incalculable field of opera. *The Boatswain's Mate*, although suffering from a mixture of styles—it begins as a ballad opera with spoken dialogue and ends with continuous music—could safely take its place in a repertory of English comic opera along with the Savoy operas if ever the equivalent of an Opéra Comique were established in London. *The Wreckers*, of which the libretto was written by Henry B. Brewster, remains her greatest artistic achievement and her greatest success.

In the volume of her autobiography entitled *As Time Went On* . . . the conjunction of those two disparate ideas, achievement and success, forms the theme of some discussion on why she failed to obtain practical recognition in her own country by the performance of her works. (Incidentally there was not in her output a great deal of orchestral music, such as might have found its way into the programmes of the promenade concerts—the Concerto for violin and horn (1927) is her only large-scale symphonic work.) She did, however, win the recognition of an honorary doctorate of music from Durham in 1910, from Manchester University in 1930, and was the first woman recipient of the honorary degree at Oxford in 1926. She also received the honorary degree of LL.D. from St. Andrews in 1928. In 1922 she was appointed D.B.E.

Ethel Smyth was the first woman to compose music in the largest forms of opera, oratorio, and concerto, and to convince the sceptical world of music in England and in Germany that musical talent in a woman was not confined to salon music, such as Madame Chaminade wrote gracefully, but could take its place beside that of the most serious-minded men. In battling for musical emancipation she was caught up into the larger movement for women's suffrage and found herself in 1912 marching through the streets with the militant suffragettes to her own 'March of the Women', composed for the movement, and subsequently conducting its strains with a toothbrush from the window of a cell in Holloway prison. The daughter of a soldier she was a fighter, and like many bonny fighters she fought too many battles, some of them unnecessary and none of them conducive to the frame of mind in which music can be composed.

About the reception of her literary work she could have no complaints. After the *Impressions that Remained* (2 vols., 1919) she maintained a succession of racily written sequels—*Streaks of Life* (1921), *A Final Burning of*

Boats (1928), *Beecham and Pharaoh* (1935), *As Time Went On* ... (1936), and *What Happened Next* (1940). In them the reader gets a true impression of the vigour and vitality of one who was full of high spirits, serious purpose, and English eccentricity. She had a charming singing voice with which she entertained the private circle of her friends, and a striking appearance, in tweeds and three-cornered hat, when she sometimes mounted the platform to conduct her own works in public. As an emancipated woman, an author, and a composer, she was a prominent figure who long outlived her Victorian origin and retained into extreme old age the vital qualities which made her all those things at once. She died, unmarried, at Woking 9 May 1944. A bust by Gilbert Bayes is at the Sadler's Wells Theatre. A portrait in oils, showing her in the robes of a D.Mus. of Oxford, was painted in 1936 by Neville (later the Earl of) Lytton and is now at the Royal College of Music.

[Her own writings; private information; personal knowledge.]

FRANK HOWES

published 1959

SHARP Cecil James

(1859–1924)

Musician, author, and collector and arranger of English folk-songs and dances, was born in London 22 November 1859, the eldest son of John James Sharp, slate-merchant, by his wife, Jane Bloyd. He was educated at Uppingham School and at Clare College, Cambridge. He had inherited a love of music from his father, and in his early days had studied music, practically and theoretically. While at Cambridge he entered fully into the musical activities of the university. After taking his degree (a third class in the mathematical tripos), Sharp went in 1882 to Adelaide, where he held the legal post of associate to the chief justice of South Australia. He was also during this period assistant organist of the cathedral and conductor of the Philharmonic Society. From 1889 to 1891 he was co-director of the Adelaide College of Music. While in Australia he composed two light operas and some smaller pieces. Early in 1892 he returned to England. In 1893 he married Constance Dorothea (died 1928), daughter of Priestley Birch, of Woolston, near Kingsbridge, Devon, and had one son and three daughters. He became conductor of the Finsbury Choral Association (1893–1897), music master at Ludgrove School (1893–1910), and principal of the Hampstead Conservatoire of Music (1896–1905). From 1910 to 1912 he held no official position. From 1912 to 1924 he was director of the English Folk-Dance Society. From 1919 to 1923 he held the post of occasional inspector to the Board of Education with special reference to the teaching of folk-dance. In 1923 he received the honorary degree of Mus.M. of Cambridge University. He died at Hampstead 23 June 1924, after a short illness.

Such are the external facts of Sharp's career, but interest centres in the last twenty-five years of his life and in the gradual growth under his influence of the knowledge of the English traditional arts of music and dancing. In 1902 his experience as singing-teacher at Ludgrove School led him to prepare and publish *A Book of British Song*. This contains both traditional melodies (gleaned from William Chappell's *Popular Music of the Olden Time*, 1838, and other printed sources) and 'composed' music of a simple kind. It was probably his work on this book which led Sharp to realize the essential importance of traditional art, and in 1903 he decided to find out for himself how far traditional music survived in England and what was its quality. His first experiment was made in September 1903 at Hambridge, in Somerset, where, with the help of the vicar, the Rev. C. L. Marson, he made an exhaustive search of the neighbourhood with surprising results. A selection from the songs which he discovered, called *Folk-Songs from Somerset*, was published in 1904 and aroused great interest. That such beautiful and vital melodies should have been sung for generations in 'unmusical' England was indeed a remarkable discovery.

Opinion had, however, been ripening. (Sir) Hubert Parry had in 1893 published his *Art of Music*, in which he applied the theory of evolution to music and showed the line of succession from the simplest of folk-tunes to the most elaborate symphony. Already, also, a certain number of traditional melodies had been collected. In 1898 the Folk-Song Society had been founded, and in 1904 Sharp was elected on to its committee. Nevertheless, his ideas were not cordially welcomed by the leading members of the society, whose ideal was that of quiet research, while Sharp was above all a teacher and a propagandist. He used scholarship and research as a means to an end; for he believed in folk-song, not as a relic of the past, but as a thing of living beauty. These simple and lovely melodies have awakened in thousands of people a musical consciousness hitherto dormant. In 1906, after the Board of Education had published a list of recommended songs for children in which no distinction was made between songs which were traditional and those which were merely popular, Sharp vainly urged the Folk-Song Society to make a protest.

Meanwhile Sharp persistently pressed the claims of folk-song by lectures, articles, and letters to the newspapers, thereby arousing some bitter opposition. In 1907 he tabulated his experiences in his book *English Folk-Song: some Conclusions*. The theories set out therein are not new, nor do they pretend to be so. They are the logical conclusions of the evolutionary theory of music and that of the communal authorship of folk-song already vaguely formulated by others. It should be noted that Sharp claimed communal authorship, but not communal origin, for the folk-song. He held, together with Jacob Grimm and others, that folk-music, developing as it does by purely oral tradition without being stereotyped by print or writing, tends to evolve as it passes through the minds of generations of singers; that therefore no individual singer can at any given moment be said to be the author of the song, but that it truly represents the communal mind of those to whom it belongs. Moreover, he held that the law of the survival of the fittest applies here, and that the process is one not of disintegration but of evolution.

All this time Sharp was collecting more songs and publishing the cream of them in further volumes of *Folk-Songs from Somerset* (five series, 1904, 1905, 1906, 1908, and 1909). His example fired others, and it soon appeared that there was hardly a village in England where this native art did not survive.

Sharp's final adventure in search of songs was his visits to the Southern Appalachian Mountains in North Carolina, Tennessee, Kentucky, and Virginia in 1916 to 1918. In these remote parts of the United States there lives a people descended from early English colonists segregated by natural surroundings from the rest of the world. They have preserved the customs, speech, and above all the songs, which they brought with them from England in the early eighteenth century. When Sharp heard of this community he characteristically determined to get at the facts of the alleged survivals, and he paid several visits (lasting forty-six weeks in all) to the Appalachian Mountains, although he was in indifferent health and had to make his investigations in circumstances of the most primitive discomfort.

Sharp noted down altogether nearly five thousand tunes and variants, about one-third being collected in the Appalachian Mountains. Of these he published some five hundred for use with pianoforte accompaniment, and a further thousand are printed in the *Journal of the Folk-Song Society* and other scientific publications. The rest remain in his manuscript books which he left to Clare College, Cambridge. These figures conclusively dispel the idea that Sharp imagined that all folk-songs were of equal value.

The other main subject of Sharp's activities was the folk-dance, in which he was practically first in the field. This was a much more difficult problem than the folk-song, for it takes only one man to sing a song while it takes six to dance a morris, and by the time Sharp began to collect there were few complete morris 'sides' left. Most of the dances had, therefore, to be reconstructed from the explanations and partial demonstrations of old and infirm men. Further, there is no recognized notation of the dance as there is of the song; so the only thing to do was to invent a notation for the purpose. Sharp's first dance researches, dating from 1905 (he had previously, in 1899, noted the tunes of several morris-dances from Headington, Oxfordshire), were in the Midlands, the home of the morris-dance. In 1910 he turned his attention to the corresponding ceremonial dance of northern England, the sword-dance. Less artistically important, but, as it proved, socially more far-reaching, was the country dance. This is not a ceremonial dance for experts, but a form of social enjoyment; moreover it is danced by both sexes, whereas the morris and sword dances are traditionally danced by men only. Sharp collected some examples of the country dance from living tradition, but most of those which he published were transcribed by him from the seventeen editions of John Playford's *Dancing Master* (1650–1728). Here his unfailing instinct enabled him to select those dances which reflect the spirit of tradition, even though some of them have no doubt been consciously worked on by individuals.

Sharp was, of course, not content merely to collect; he also wanted to teach, and between 1907 and 1914 he published over three hundred dances with their tunes. He recognized, however, that these things cannot be learned from books only. In 1905 he had come into contact with Mary Neal and her Espérance club for working-girls in Cumberland Market, London; and it was here that practical folk-dance teaching was first undertaken. For a time Sharp and Miss Neal worked together; but the object of the Espérance club was social regeneration rather than artistic excellence. Miss Neal held that Sharp's interpretation of the dances was formal and pedantic and robbed them of the joyousness which it was the object of her club to encourage: Sharp considered that the joy of doing a good thing well was the ultimate object to be secured. So the two parted company, and Sharp found new allies in the Chelsea College of Physical Training, where he established a school of folk-dance in 1909.

In 1911 Sharp founded the English Folk-Dance Society, the object of which was to 'preserve and promote the practice of English folk-dances in their true traditional forms'. From this time forward his life became that of an inspiring teacher and an efficient and autocratic organizer, and with the exception of a few flying visits to discover new folk-songs and dances and the expeditions to America already recorded, the rest of his life was devoted to the society which he founded. The English Folk-Dance Society prospered far beyond his expectations, and since his death it has gone on growing. In 1931 the membership was 1,689, besides fifty-two local branches (including two in the United States) with a membership of over twenty-two thousand, and early in 1932 an amalgamation with the Folk-Song Society was effected.

On Sharp's death a fund was opened to build a house where his memory could be kept alive by preserving, practising, and teaching folk-songs and dances. In June 1930 Cecil Sharp House in Regent's Park Road, London, was opened, and on its foundation-stone are inscribed the words: 'This building is erected in memory of Cecil Sharp who restored to the English people the songs and dances of their country.'

Sharp won the admiration of all who came into contact with him, even those whom his uncompromising methods of controversy had antagonized before they got to know him. His absorption in his mission did not prevent him from taking an intelligent interest in all that was going on in the world, about which he always had something pregnant to say. In politics he inclined to the Fabian socialist view. His favourite composers were Beethoven, Wagner, and Handel. He suffered all his life from ill-health, but this only added to the energy with which he worked for the causes that he loved.

A portrait by Sir William Rothenstein hangs in the library at Cecil Sharp House.

[*The Times*, 27 June 1924; *Journal* of the Folk-Song Society, December 1924; *English Folk-Dance Society News*, November 1924; A. H. Fox Strangways, *Cecil Sharp*, 1933; private information; personal knowledge.]

R. Vaughan Williams

published 1937

STRANGWAYS Arthur Henry Fox

(1859–1948)

Schoolmaster, music critic, and founder-editor of *Music and Letters*, was born 14 September 1859 at Norwich, the eldest son of Captain (later Colonel) Walter Aston Fox Strangways of the Royal Artillery, and his wife, Harriet Elizabeth, second daughter of John Edward Buller, of Enfield. In the paternal line he was descended from Sir Stephen Fox.

Fox Strangways was educated at Wellington College and Balliol College, Oxford, where he was placed in the third class in *literae humaniores* in 1882. For the next two years he studied music, especially the piano, at the Hochschule in Berlin, but he did not at once enter the musical profession.

He was a schoolmaster first at Dulwich College (1884–6), then at Wellington (1887–1910). In 1893 he also became organist but relinquished this on becoming a tutor in 1901. On his retirement from Wellington he visited India, where his field-work and researches resulted in *The Music of Hindostan* (1914) which still holds its place as an authoritative work. On his return in 1911 he wrote occasional criticisms of concerts for *The Times* and shortly afterwards joined the staff, writing regularly in the absence on war service of his senior colleague, but by far his junior in years, H. C. Colles. In 1925 he joined the staff of the *Observer* as music critic, where he remained until the outbreak of war in 1939. A selection from his weekly articles edited by (Sir) Steuart Wilson was published in 1936 under the title *Music Observed*. He was a considerable contributor to the third edition of *Grove's Dictionary of Music and Musicians* (1927) which Colles edited. In 1933 he wrote in collaboration with Miss Maud Karpeles the life of his friend and colleague, founder of the English Folk-Dance Society, Cecil Sharp.

His main contribution to musical journalism was the establishment of *Music and Letters*, a quarterly review appearing first in January 1920, of which he was sole proprietor as well as editor. The avowed objects were expressed in a manner wholly characteristic of the editor who wrote that music was 'a subject of rational enquiry like any other' and that it was not needful to be 'so busy with ideas as to be careless of words'. In this spirit he continued the journal until the end of 1936, when it was rescued from disappearance by the transfer of its responsibilities to Mr. Richard Capell. In the earlier years of the journal Fox Strangways had interested himself in printing translations into English of German *lieder*, most of which were his own versions. In 1924 a volume called *Schubert's Songs Translated* and in 1928 a similar volume of Schumann, and later a small album of Brahms, were issued, all in conjunction with (Sir) Steuart Wilson. After his retirement to Devon in 1939 in his eightieth year, Fox Strangways completed single-handed the translation of all the songs of Brahms, Hugo Wolf, and Richard Strauss, and most of the songs of Liszt. These versions in typescript were deposited in the music library of the British Broadcasting Corporation in 1947. As well as this not inconsiderable task he planned and partly completed an anthology of English verse never set to music, but of suitable quality, as a useful time-saver for students without literary experience. He died, unmarried, 2 May 1948 at Dinton, near Salisbury, the birthplace of Henry Lawes.

Fox Strangways brought into the field of musical journalism an intellect trained to exactitude of observation and of subsequent expression. His twenty-five years of schoolmastering had not narrowed his interests; he had contrived to combine with his duties the pleasure of riding to hounds. Although he lacked sympathy with all forms of fiction, he had a strong vein of poetry and romanticism in his nature and a deep appreciation of the profounder emotions which music could arouse. This was well expressed in the final sentences of his article on Indian music in *Grove's Dictionary*: this music, he wrote, 'reveals man in the presence of God. We do not and we shall not make much out of it without patience and practice, but it is worth both. We say no less, but we can say no more, of our own.'

Two pencil drawings of Fox Strangways were made by Sir William Rothenstein.

[*Grove's Dictionary of Music and Musicians*; *Music and Letters*, July 1948; private information; personal knowledge.]

Steuart Wilson

published 1959

MELBA Nellie

(1861–1931)

Dame

Prima donna, whose married name was Helen Porter Armstrong, was born 19 May 1861 at Doonside, Richmond, a suburb of Melbourne, Australia, the elder daughter and third child of David Mitchell, by his wife, Isabella Ann Dorn. Both parents were natives of Forfarshire; the mother was of Spanish descent. David Mitchell, a man of strong character, had arrived in Australia with one sovereign in his pocket and became a pioneer in a number of enterprises, in all of which he succeeded, and his children therefore grew up in good circumstances. Music was one of the interests and accomplishments of the household. Nellie Mitchell, encouraged to sing from her earliest childhood, sang at six years of age at a school concert organized by her aunts in the Richmond town hall, gaining an enthusiastic encore. Later she was sent to the Presbyterian Ladies' College in East Melbourne, where the professor of singing was Madame Christian, who, a former colleague of Sir Charles Santley, had settled in Australia and later became a nun. Madame Christian was a pupil of the famous singing teacher Manuel Garcia, and from her Nellie Mitchell first learnt the principles of vocalism of the great school which Madame Mathilde Marchesi, also the pupil of Garcia, and at one time deputy for him, later unfolded fully to her, and to which, as she always insisted, she owed the development and preservation of her voice. Before leaving Australia she had some lessons from an old Italian opera singer, Signor Cecchi, but in her autobiography, *Melodies and Memories* (1925), she does not refer to them with satisfaction.

David Mitchell was averse to his daughter embarking on the career of a professional singer, but after her marriage in December 1882 (dissolved in 1900) to a young Irishman, Charles Nesbitt Frederick Armstrong, youngest son of Sir Andrew Armstrong, first baronet, of Gallen Priory, King's County, manager of a sugar plantation in Port Mackay, she lived a desolate and lonely life in the heart of the bush in a small house with a galvanized iron roof. At length her father paid her passage to England, and after giving a farewell concert Nellie Armstrong in the spring of 1886 sailed for England with her only child, a son. Her reception in London was by no means encouraging. She sang to Sir Arthur Sullivan, who said that after a year's further study he might be able to offer her a small part in *The Mikado*. Wilhelm Ganz, however, accompanist and friend of Patti, arranged opportunities for her to sing at Prince's Hall, Piccadilly, and at the Freemasons' Hall in the City, but the audiences were small, and the experience, in spite of some congratulations, Mrs. Armstrong found disheartening. She therefore, having been given in Australia a letter of introduction to Madame Mathilde Marchesi, decided to go to Paris and present it. The famous teacher, testing her voice thoroughly, recognized its possibilities, and also found a character full of determination to pursue the hard path of a serious student of singing. So sure was Marchesi of the success in store for Nellie Armstrong that in the middle of the first interview she went out of the room to inform her husband that she had 'found a star'.

After a year's lessons, the famous *entrepreneur* Maurice Strakosch, hearing her in Madame Marchesi's studio, offered 'Melba'—as she called herself at her first appearance in Paris—a ten years' contract, which was duly signed. Immediately afterwards came a better offer from the management of the Théâtre de la Monnaie in Brussels. This Marchesi advised Melba to accept, assuring her that Strakosch, an old friend, would not make any difficulty. He did, however; but an *impasse* was dramatically solved by his sudden death, and Melba's appearance on 13 October 1887 as Gilda in Verdi's *Rigoletto* was an extraordinary triumph, the entire Brussels press proclaiming the advent of an artiste of the first rank.

Soon after this, (Sir) Augustus Harris engaged the successful débutante for his first season of Italian opera at Covent Garden, and Melba made her début there as Lucia in Donizetti's *Lucia di Lammermoor* on 24 May 1888. At the conclusion of the opera it was clear that she had captured the public, and she had instantly won the suffrages of society, making more friends among the wealthy patrons of the Royal Italian Opera than any prima donna of the period. There was some reserve, however, on the part of the press from the point of view of complete operatic artistry, but the extraordinary beauty of the strikingly fresh voice, perfectly even through its compass of two and a half octaves (B flat to F sharp), used with an art that seemed nature in perfection, was freely recognized.

On 8 May 1889 Melba made her first appearance at the Paris Opéra as Ophélie in Ambroise Thomas's *Hamlet* and studied the parts of Marguerite in *Faust* and Juliette with Gounod himself. Sarah Bernhardt also went to infinite pains in assisting Melba to realize, in a way suited to her individuality, the dramatic possibilities of the characters which she had to assume on the operatic stage, but she never became a really good actress. Yet the critics, on her first appearance, hailed her as such and did not appreciate her voice.

Less than a month later Melba returned to Covent Garden, largely through the influence of Lady de Grey (later Marchioness of Ripon), who overcame some hesitation on the prima donna's part, and she appeared (15 June) in the first performance ever given in England of Gounod's *Roméo et Juliette* in French, with Jean de Reszke as Romeo and Edouard de Reszke as the Friar. A marked advance in Melba's acting and singing had taken place: the association of Melba with the brothers De Reszke was an operatic landmark, and thenceforth she took part regularly in every Covent Garden season.

Melba's position was now assured, and her public life was passed in singing at various capitals of the world, although it was not until 1893 that she first visited the United States, where she sang at the World's Fair in Chicago. Her visit to St. Petersburg in 1891 was noted for two things; the Tsar's command to lay aside the tradition that only Russian should be sung at the Imperial Opera House, so that Melba and her colleagues could sing *Roméo et Juliette* in French, and the invitation given to her to sing in private to Anton Rubinstein, who was already in failing health. Again when in the following year she sang at the Scala at Milan at the beginning of a brilliant tour in Italy, Verdi went to hear her, and, inviting her to his house, went with her through the Desdemona music in *Otello* and praised her rendering. In 1893, in fulfilment of a promise made to the composer, she introduced the part of Nedda in *Pagliacci* to the British public at Covent Garden. For her, Saint-Saëns composed the title-role of *Hélène* which she studied while travelling in the train during a tour of Canada and the United States in 1903, and in which she sang at Monte Carlo in 1904. The last opera which she added to her list of twenty-five was *La Bohème*, and she sang in it first at Philadelphia in 1898, having studied it with the composer in

Italy earlier in the year. So much did the part appeal to her, that she exerted her personal influence and got *La Bohème* accepted at Covent Garden, and 'Melba nights' there became for a generation of opera lovers her appearance in that role.

It is not surprising that when she revisited her native land in 1902, after an absence of sixteen years, 'Australia's queen of song' was greeted with a rare enthusiasm. She never forgot Australia, visiting it not infrequently, and after her retirement in 1926 she settled there finally at Coombe Cottage near Coldstream in Victoria. In 1918 she was appointed D.B.E. and was thenceforth known as Dame Nellie Melba: in 1927 she received the G.B.E. Another order which she received was that of Science, Art, and Music, which was pinned on her breast in 1904 by Queen Alexandra after a state concert at Buckingham Palace in honour of the Archduke Francis Ferdinand.

Melba's kindness of heart was wide and her charitable acts many. When in 1906 Oscar Hammerstein's enterprise in grand opera at the Manhattan Opera House seemed doomed to disaster, and she was advised by friends in New York not to fulfil her engagement, she came to the rescue, although the circumstances called for considerable courage; but her success was greater than ever before, and the audiences were extraordinary. She raised over £100,000 for the Red Cross during the war of 1914–1918. Towards young singers she constantly showed interest, inculcating the method she used, which she held could alone bring out the full beauty of the human voice, and preserve it. She showed her *camaraderie* by appearing in 1922–1923 in London with the British National Opera Company, an organization which was making a praiseworthy effort to further the cause of opera in English.

Melba's voice was not of an instantly arresting strength, but it had that power of expansion in a large building which is a characteristic of beautiful singing. It was this 'Stradivari' quality which won the admiration of the violinists Joachim and Sarasate. The technique was invariably impeccable: scale passages were like strings of pearls, and Melba's shake was perfect in its distinctness, evenness, and limpidity. Melba was favoured in appearance by nature and she preserved her physical advantages by careful living. When she retired, her intonation was still perfect, her technique unimpaired, and her voice still wonderfully fresh and 'girl-like'. She died at Sydney 23 February 1931.

A bust of Melba was made by (Sir) Bertram Mackennal in September 1899. Melba presented it to the National Gallery, Melbourne, and it was unveiled by Lord Brassey, then governor of Victoria.

[Nellie Melba, *Melodies and Memories*, 1925; Agnes G. Murphy, *Melba. A Biography*, 1909; Herman Klein, *Great Women Singers of My Time*, 1931; *Grove's*

Dictionary of Music and Musicians, 4th ed., vol. iii, edited by H. C. Colles; Arthur Mason in *Musical Opinion*, 1 April 1931; personal knowledge.]

J. Mewburn Levien

published 1949

DELIUS Frederick (1862–1934)

Musician, was born at Bradford 29 January 1862, the second son in a family of four sons and ten daughters of Julius Delius, a well-to-do wool merchant, of Bradford, by his wife, Elise Pauline, daughter of Christian Kroenig, of Bielefeld, Westphalia. Both his parents were German-born but his father, who was also from Bielefeld, had become a naturalized Englishman in 1850. There was much music-making, both amateur and professional, in the home. The young Frederick soon began to prefer Chopin and Grieg to Mozart and Beethoven, a trend of taste which remained undeviating to the end.

After receiving some education at Bradford Grammar School and the International College at Isleworth (1876–1879) Delius, who wished to make music his career, was ordered into the family business and there was actually a brief period of unavailing endeavour in the woollen industry until the domestic crisis so familiar in the lives of artists came to a head. In this case the unusual compromise, reached after some heat, was that Frederick Delius, aged twenty-two, should go out and plant oranges in Florida. There the solitude of the grove, the resplendent tropical scenery, and the strange music of the negroes combined to set the youth's imagination ablaze. He must get a pianoforte. While negotiating for this in Jacksonville he fell in with a convalescent Brooklyn organist, T. F. Ward, who returned to the grove with Delius and the pianoforte to become his informal teacher. This six-months' course proved of greater value than all the formal instruction which Delius was subsequently to undergo. In 1885 he left the grove and set up as a teacher of pianoforte and violin first at Jacksonville and later at Danville, Virginia.

Meanwhile Delius's parents had altogether lost touch with their errant and now independent offspring. But they eventually succeeded in causing a message to reach him in which they offered terms of well-nigh unconditional surrender. At all events in August 1886 Delius became installed as a student at the Leipzig Conservatorium. Now at last he could hear orchestras and operas to his heart's content and live for nothing but music. There was also the formal instruction at the conservatorium, but no trace of this can be found in his subsequent output except in certain of the weaker passages. The great event of this sojourn was the meeting with Grieg, who was probably the second person—Ward being the first—to perceive the genius in the younger man. In the spring of 1888 an orchestra was hired with the contents of a barrel of beer to play a suite by Delius called 'Florida'. The conductor was Hans Sitt, one of Delius's masters; the audience, Grieg, Christian Sinding, and the composer. The new work received an enthusiastic ovation. Delius, after about eighteen months in Leipzig, accompanied Grieg to London where he was giving some concerts. Now there was arranged a special dinner party at which Grieg finally persuaded Julius Delius of his son's quality. This auspicious occasion marks the end of parental opposition to Frederick's musical career. When Grieg died in 1907 Delius 'felt that he had lost his best friend'.

Delius then (1888) became a whole-time composer. He never did anything else. He moved to France where he lived for the rest of his life. He worked mostly in Paris for eight years, consorting with literary folk, painters, and sculptors—notably Gaugin and Strindberg—rather than with French musicians with whom he had but little in common; to this day his music is unknown in France. In 1897 two friends of his, girl students of painting, invited him for the week-end to a house which they had taken for the summer at Grez-sur-Loing, near Fontainebleau. He accepted and stayed on until death. So did one of the young ladies, Jelka Helen (von) Rosen, whom shortly afterwards he married. Born of a German diplomatic family, she had linguistic talent and a rare literary and artistic perception. Wonderful though she was as a wife, particularly during her husband's last stricken years, she was more than that. She helped in the selection and arrangement of the words for most of the choral output of his best years, a literary task which, unaided, the composer was not at all well qualified to perform. Notable too were her wit and charm, which even life with Delius failed to impair.

From then until 1921 all the great works were composed in the quiet home at Grez with the garden running down to the river. Here the couple mostly remained except when the war came too dangerously near for comfort. Then having buried the wine, they sought the temporary shelter of these shores. Otherwise there would merely be trips to Germany and England in order to hear Delius's works performed, and to the Norwegian mountains for the summer holidays. He had learnt to love these in youth during one of his wool-trade visits to Sweden.

It is a tale of toil, frustration, gradual recognition, and ultimate triumph. Before the end of the century faint signs of recognition were stirring. Hans

Haym and Alfred Hertz, of Elberfeld, and Julius Buths, of Düsseldorf, began to show interest. In 1899 Delius gave a choral-orchestral concert in the St. James's Hall, London. Hertz came over to conduct the programme which included the tone poem 'Over the Hills and Far Away' (which had already been given at Elberfeld under Haym), the music which now forms the close of 'A Mass of Life', and excerpts from the opera *Koanga*, the negro opera inspired by his sojourn in Florida. Press and public gave this concert a fairly good though puzzled reception; yet the general impression remains that a considerable curiosity to hear more of this unknown composer was aroused.

Nevertheless, it was left to Germany to carry on the good work with performances of 'Appalachia' (choral–orchestral variations on an old slave song, also inspired by Florida) at Düsseldorf (1905), 'Sea-Drift' (cantata with words taken from a poem by Walt Whitman) at Essen (1906), and the opera *A Village Romeo and Juliet* at Berlin (1907). Delius's renown was established in Germany by virtue of these three works alone, and his subsequent compositions were repeatedly played with abundant success up and down the country ('Brigg Fair' for instance was in 1910 alone played by thirty-six different orchestras) until the outbreak of war in 1914.

But about 1910 a young conductor called Thomas Beecham had already appeared to put English lovers of music in general and of Delius in particular under an unlimited debt. He was the first to discover the key to this composer's *tempi* and to his peculiar mode of utterance. Fortunately he has directed the recording of most of Delius's large works for the concert hall. These are the authoritative renderings ecstatically approved throughout by the composer, so that there can never be any excuse for future arbitrary individual 'readings', for the tradition is now established once and for all. But the list is still (1945) incomplete.

Soon after 1924 Delius lost his sight and the use of his limbs. It seemed that his muse must be stilled for ever. Meanwhile there was a steady increase in performances of Delius, although Sir Thomas Beecham was at that time in temporary self-imposed retirement. In 1920 there occurred at the Queen's Hall the first performance of 'The Song of the High Hills' under Albert Coates, and later (1925) the first post-war performance of 'A Mass of Life' under Paul Klenau, both at concerts of the Royal Philharmonic Society. Sir Henry Wood also was including certain smaller works in his promenade and Saturday symphony concerts at the Queen's Hall, while (Sir) Hamilton Harty in the north was doing good work. But with Sir Thomas Beecham's return in 1926 the composer rapidly became—what his most fervent admirers had never envisaged—a genuine popular success. That he had at last won the ear of the musical multitude was proved by the six-day Delius festival held at the Queen's Hall in the autumn of 1929 under Beecham and in the presence of the composer in his bathchair. With the disappointing exception of 'The Song of the High Hills' the cream of his orchestral output with and without *soli* and chorus was included. In the same year the King appointed Delius a C.H. In 1932 he received the freedom of the city of Bradford and in 1933 an honorary degree from Leeds University. In 1929 the university of Oxford invited him to come and receive the honorary degree of D.Mus., but at the last moment he was unable to visit Oxford.

In 1928 Mr. Eric Fenby, a young Yorkshire musician, offered his services as amanuensis and they were gratefully accepted. The task consisted largely in constructing finished articles from previously existing sketches, but there was also actual invention of new material. The process of dictation evolved by this unique partnership is fascinatingly described in Mr. Fenby's book *Delius as I knew him* (1936). The most outstanding work realized by this collaboration is 'Songs of Farewell' for double chorus and orchestra given at a Courtauld–Sargent concert in 1932.

Delius died at Grez-sur-Loing 10 June 1934. After temporary burial in Grez churchyard, his body was next year removed to Limpsfield in Surrey. At the service on that occasion Sir Thomas Beecham read the funeral oration and conducted a detachment of picked orchestral players in certain Delius pieces fitting for the occasion. Delius's widow was placed beside her husband a few days later. There were no children of the marriage.

'But it's not music' expostulated Delius one day, humming a misquotation from Beethoven. His bitterly caustic tongue, at strange variance with his music, in a harsh almost rasping accent, half Bradford, half foreign, would thus give pungent expression to his distaste for the classics. Another violent antipathy was towards the verbal discussion of composition technique. A notable English pundit was one day holding forth upon this subject in a musical company until Delius, bearing it no longer, interpolated the observation 'Well, at any rate music is a thing to be listened to, not talked about.' Both these traits explain to some extent his curious isolation in musical realms, for apart from a superficial affinity with Grieg's his music derives from nothing and leads nowhere. Professional critics have decried his lack of 'form' and amateur listeners have complained of monotony of texture. Both strictures are half just. He disdained the use of mechanical expedient to secure semblance of 'form', so that the innocent listener, deprived of such adventitious aids to sustained attention, cannot always follow the composer's thought and tends to become drowsy with the sheer sensuous beauty of sound from moment to moment. So with his operas, which are not 'dramatic' according to any hitherto known conventions. Yet the carefully wrought and beautiful performances under Beecham at the Royal College of Music of *A Village Romeo and Juliet* (1934) convinced the audiences of the work's innate though highly individual dramatic purpose. Intensely susceptible to the beauties of nature and to the emotions, joys, and sorrows of life, Delius made these the inspiration of all his most lovely works, the titles of which usually indicate the character of each one.

There are three portraits of Delius by James Gunn: a painting which represents him listening to his 'Mass of Life' (1929) is in the possession of the City Art Gallery, Bradford; a sketch in oils (1932) and another portrait (also 1932) are in private possession.

[Philip Heseltine, *Frederick Delius*, 1923; Clare Delius, *Frederick Delius. Memories of my Brother*, 1935; Eric Fenby, *Delius as I knew him*, 1936; R. H. Hull, *Delius*, 1928; Arthur Hutchings, *Delius*, 1948; *Grove's Dictionary of Music and Musicians*, 4th ed., vol. ii, edited by H. C. Colles; personal knowledge.]

PATRICK HADLEY

published 1949

GERMAN Edward

(1862–1936)

Sir

Composer, whose original name was Edward German Jones, was born at Whitchurch, Shropshire, 17 February 1862, the elder son and second child of John David Jones, by his wife, Betsy Cox. His father held the post of organist at the Congregational chapel, and in his early years the son frequently deputized for the father. Edward was educated at Bridge House School, Chester, and on leaving there in 1878 began to study for an engineering career. Teaching himself the violin, he soon led the orchestra of the Whitchurch choral society and his ability impressed the conductor, Professor Walter Hay, of Shrewsbury. Supported by Hay, he persuaded his parents to have him trained for the musical profession, and after studying under Hay's direction, he entered the Royal Academy of Music in September 1880. About this time he adopted his two christian names and gave up the surname of Jones. In 1885 he won the Charles Lucas medal for composition, and became a sub-professor of the violin. An operetta, *The Two Poets*, was produced at the St. George's Hall in December 1886, and was taken on tour with moderate success. Later he changed its name to *The Rival Poets*, and under this title it achieved much popularity. In 1887 his first symphony was performed at a Royal Academy concert in the St. James's Hall.

German succeeded W. G. McNaught as professor of the violin at Wimbledon School, and through the help of Alberto Randegger began conducting in the autumn of 1888 at the Globe Theatre for the production of *Richard the Third* in 1889. His incidental music to this was very favourably received, and shortly after he met (Sir) Henry Irving, who commissioned him to write the music for the production of *Henry the Eighth* at the Lyceum Theatre in 1892: the three dances have become famous. There followed a succession of compositions incidental to theatre productions, mostly Shakespearian: they include the overture and incidental music to *English Nell*, by Edward Rose and Anthony Hope (Prince of Wales's Theatre, 1900). *The Emerald Isle*, left unfinished by the death of Sir Arthur Sullivan, was completed by German, and produced at the Savoy Theatre in 1901. *Merrie England* (1902) and *A Princess of Kensington* (1903) followed, and later (1907), *Tom Jones*. In 1904 appeared his 'Welsh Rhapsody'. In 1907 he toured the United States of America, conducting and directing productions. Collaborating with Sir W. S. Gilbert, he produced *Fallen Fairies* in 1909, and two years later he was commissioned to write the coronation march and hymn for King George V and Queen Mary. Thereafter little of note took place until 1919, when he wrote 'Theme and Six Diversions' for the Royal Philharmonic Society. From 1922 to 1928, German was busily engaged in conducting and examining, and during those years his compositions were constantly being performed. In 1928 he was knighted. From that time on he lived in comparative retirement (receiving, however, the gold medal of the Royal Philharmonic Society in 1934) and died in London 11 November 1936. He was unmarried.

Highly popular with his fellow musicians, German's work and personality were much admired by such men as Sullivan, Elgar, Parry, Stanford, and Mackenzie. Revolutionary changes in musical thought were taking place during his lifetime. Although striving to keep an open mind on the new tendencies, German admitted that they contained a great deal which he did not and could not understand. During his trip to America he was interviewed by the press on the question and is reported to have said: 'Young England is full of splendid promise, but there is danger ahead in sacrificing the beauties of art to mere sensation.' Of his own work it has been said that he takes a high place among 'those few specially gifted composers who were able to combine artistic achievement with strong popular appeal'.

[*The Times*, 12 November 1936; *Musical Times*, December 1936; W. H. Scott, *Edward German*, 1932; *Grove's Dictionary of Music and Musicians*, 4th ed., vol. ii, edited by H. C. Colles; private information.]

Edric Cundell

published 1949

GREENE Harry Plunket (1865–1936)

Singer, was born at Old Connaught House, co. Wicklow, 24 June 1865, the son of Richard Jonas Greene, barrister, of Dublin, by his wife, Louisa Lilias, fourth daughter of John Plunket, third Lord Plunket, and granddaughter of William Conyngham Plunket, first Lord Plunket, lord chancellor of Ireland. He was educated at Clifton College, and afterwards studied singing at Stuttgart and Florence and in London. He was professor of singing at the Royal Academy of Music (1911–1919) and at the Royal College of Music (1912–1919). He married in 1899 Gwendolen Maud, younger daughter of Sir C. H. H. Parry, and had two sons and a daughter. He died in London 19 August 1936.

Greene's contribution to music in this country was due in equal proportions to his timely arrival as an adept interpreter for Sir C. V. Stanford, Parry, Sir Arthur Somervell, and that generation of English composers, and to his native charm of character and vivid poetic imagination. He made his first appearance in England as a bass-baritone in 1888, and soon established his reputation as a singer, first by his 'joint partnership', from 1893 onwards, in recitals with the pianist Leonard Borwick in the classical repertory of German *Lieder* and Brahms songs, and secondly as a specialized interpreter of the regular series of cantatas and oratorios which Parry wrote for the Three Choirs festivals, especially 'Job' at Gloucester in 1892.

Music in that generation was only just becoming a profession for men of education and social position. Sir F. A. G. Ouseley had set a precedent despite discouragement from the dean of Christ Church, Oxford, who would not permit a baronet and a gentleman commoner to read for a degree in music. Parry further enlarged the bounds, but in the executive ranks of the profession, particularly among singers, Greene was an arrival from a new and welcome sphere, to be joined later by such men as Gervase Elwes and James Campbell McInnes. Each of these brought special gifts into the common purpose of establishing the rising generation of British musicians. Greene was the first in the field, and was in particular the 'creator' of the Stanford Irish song-cycles in which his native charm of manner was irresistible (before political differences had clouded the outlook) and he was a partner on equal terms in the Charles Stanford-Henry Newbolt combination of patriotic and sea songs which were of a far higher degree of merit than anything that had previously been set down.

The effect of Greene on his generation was remarkable: it was due to his charm and humour combined with his magnificent presence, his perfect diction in speech and song, now beguiling and now commanding, and, above all, to his fresh-air outlook which banished the hackneyed insincerities of the shop-ballad and raised the standard of public taste. In this campaign he was particularly influential as an adjudicator in the competition festival movement, both in this country and in Canada.

Greene was a writer of considerable distinction not only on music (*Interpretation in Song*, 1912) but on his favourite recreation of fishing (*Where the Bright Waters Meet*, 1924). He also wrote *Charles Villiers Stanford* (1935).

A portrait of Greene by James Gunn was commissioned by many of his friends on his seventieth birthday and is at present in the keeping of his family.

[*The Times*, 20 August 1936; *Grove's Dictionary of Music and Musicians*, 4th ed., vol. ii, edited by H. C. Colles; H. P. Greene, *From Blue Danube to Shannon*, 1934; personal knowledge.]

STEUART WILSON

published 1949

TERRY Richard Runciman

(1865–1938)

Sir

Musician and musical antiquary, was born at Ellington, Northumberland, 3 January 1865, the elder son of Thomas Terry, schoolmaster, of Newcastle-upon-Tyne, by his wife, Mary Ballard, daughter of Walter Runciman, of Dunbar, and sister of Walter, later first Lord Runciman, of Shoreston. His career as a professional musician opened in 1887 when he abandoned a choral scholarship at King's College, Cambridge, after two years only at that university, and one year previously at Oxford. Leaving Cambridge he went as music master to Elstow School, near Bedford, and three years later as organist to St. John's Cathedral, Antigua. He came home from the West Indies in 1893 at a time of spiritual crisis; his decision then to join the Roman Catholic Church reset the course of his life, and the career that gave him international fame had its inception in 1896 when he was appointed to direct the music at the Benedictine school of Downside. Here his supreme talent for choir training enabled him to present the liturgical music by sixteenth-century Catholic composers that he thenceforth made his lifelong study, bringing to light through unremitting researches the hitherto unknown masters of the Tudor polyphonic school which culminated in William Byrd.

In 1901, at the instigation of Cardinal Vaughan, Terry came to London to direct the new choir of Westminster Cathedral, and during his twenty-three years there he initiated the Tudor music revival by presenting to the public through living performance almost the entire corpus, then only existent in obsolete manuscript notation, of early English works for the Roman rite. The perfection of his choir and the musical importance of his services at Westminster made the cathedral a focus of attention, and his work there in Tudor polyphony was a powerful motive force to the young composers of his day, a fact publicly recognized in the honorary degree of doctor of music conferred upon him by Durham University in 1911 and in the knighthood of 1922. Terry's research in early manuscripts left its mark primarily upon performance, and his vitality of mind and heart, allied to an unerring musical taste and scholarship, made him a potent influence, although his legacy to the world in print is by comparison exiguous.

As a Roman Catholic Terry contributed materially to the improvement of church music by his published works on hymnology, carols, and plainsong, but it is as the father of the Tudor music revival that he has a permanent place in history. His public success in other musical spheres was considerable, as journalist, lecturer, examiner, and shanty-collector, which last owed much to his seafaring Runciman inheritance.

Terry married in 1909 Mary Lee (died 1932), daughter of Jasper Stephenson, of Aydon-Castle, Northumberland, and had a son and a daughter. He died in London 18 April 1938.

A portrait of Terry in doctor's robes, by Philip Hagreen, is in private hands.

[Hilda Andrews, *Westminster Retrospect. A Memoir of Sir Richard Terry*, 1947; *Grove's Dictionary of Music and Musicians*, 4th ed., vol. v, edited by H. C. Colles; personal knowledge.]

HILDA ANDREWS

published 1949

ELWES Gervase Henry [Cary-]

(1866–1921)

Singer, born 15 November 1866 at Billing, Northamptonshire, was the elder son of Valentine Dudley Henry Cary-Elwes, of Billing Hall and Brigg Manor, Lincolnshire, by his second wife, Alice, daughter of the Hon. and Rev. Henry Ward, and niece of the third Viscount Bangor, of Castle Ward, North Ireland. He was educated at the Oratory School, Edgbaston, under Cardinal Newman, and at Woburn School under Lord Petre; and subsequently, from 1885 to 1888, at Christ Church, Oxford. Deciding to enter the diplomatic service, he went in 1889 to Munich for a year: there he studied German and French and also the violin. Returning to London he engaged in further study for his career, and in 1891, on the advice of Sir Nicholas O'Conor, took a post as honorary attaché to the British embassy at Vienna, where he spent a year; he also widened his musical knowledge by composition lessons, and became personally acquainted with Brahms. He then moved to Brussels, where he spent three years, incidentally studying singing with Demest. This was his last diplomatic appointment. Owing to his father's failing health, he resigned his profession in 1895 and returned to England, settling down on his father's Lincolnshire property and working at forestry. Five years afterwards he was advised by Sir Alfred Scott-Gatty to adopt singing as a career; and he studied in London with Henry Russell and for two winters with Bouhy in Paris, completing his technique under his chief master, Victor Beigel. He sang in public for the first time in Paris in December 1902, and in London in the spring of 1903. He owed to Miss May Wakefield (the organizer of the Westmorland festivals) and to Professor Johann Kruse some of his earliest important engagements. Subsequently he sang several times in Belgium and Holland, and also, in 1907, toured Germany with Miss Fanny Davies. He went three times to America, and on his third visit was killed (12 January 1921) by an accident at Boston (Backbay) station, either overbalancing himself or being struck by a moving train.

Elwes married in 1889 Lady Winefride Mary Elizabeth Feilding, fourth daughter of the eighth Earl of Denbigh, and had six sons and two daughters. In 1909 he succeeded, on his father's death, to the family property: at the same time he discontinued the use of the name Cary which he had previously borne.

Some few months after his death, a 'Gervase Elwes memorial fund' was instituted by his friends and admirers, the income being utilized for the assistance of young musicians of talent and for the furtherance of various musical causes in which he had taken personal interest. On 14 December 1922 a portrait-bust of Elwes, the work of Malvina Hoffman and the gift of herself and other American admirers, was unveiled at Queen's Hall, the scene of most of Elwes's important London concerts.

For many years Elwes held a position of special prominence in the English musical world. A man of a personality both lofty and winning, he was in touch with an unusually large circle: a singer of great accomplishment and high artistic conscience, he always refused to compromise with unworthy music. His tenor voice was not in itself exceptional in power or sensuous charm, but it was more than adequate for all purposes of artistry; and his singing was marked by rare intellectual insight and, so to speak, spiritual dignity and feeling. He was especially at home with Bach and Brahms and in the title-rôle of Elgar's *The Dream of Gerontius* (a work with which he had the most intimate sympathy): but he was by no means a narrow specialist and was always active in the encouragement of young composers.

[Private information; personal knowledge.]

Ernest Walker

published 1927

BANTOCK Granville Ransome

(1868–1946)

Sir

Composer, was born in London 7 August 1868, the eldest son of George Granville Bantock, a gynaecologist and surgeon of sufficient eminence to challenge Lister's new ideas of antisepsis. Dr. Bantock was born in the north of Scotland, where his father was factor to the Duke of Sutherland, from whom the name Granville is derived. He married Sophia Elizabeth Ransome, who came of a family of East Anglian Quakers.

Bantock was educated at a private school and the Royal Academy of Music, to which, however, he only proceeded after an attempt at a scientific training at the City and Guilds Institute, undertaken at the instance of his father who cherished the ideas first of the Indian Civil Service and then of chemical engineering as a career for his musical son. In September 1889 young Bantock had his way and began the study of composition at the Academy under Frederick Corder. Here he remained for four years, turning his hand to the practice of clarinet, violin, and piano, as well as other instruments in varying measures of assiduity. The experience served him well since his chief distinction as a composer lies in his instrumentation at a time when, with the exception of Sir Edward Elgar, his elders and contemporaries among English musicians did not emulate the romantic, virtuoso orchestration of the post-Wagnerians on the continent. He won the Macfarren scholarship at the end of his first term with some wholly untutored music which included Satan's monologues from *Paradise Lost*. The choice was characteristic, for he regarded himself as a rebel against all the established orders and to the end of his life went his own way. The long list of compositions comprising under 146 headings (many of them containing several titles) show more pagan than Christian themes, as many oriental as western titles, exotic sources of inspiration in profusion, and sympathy with the early Socialists. However, his time at the Academy passed smoothly and prolifically and at the end of it he obtained work as conductor of George Edwardes's touring musical comedies, which took him round the world.

Contact with the theatre might, in a country with better operatic conditions than those prevailing in Britain at the end of the nineteenth century, have led to a more profitable employment of Bantock's talents, for seen in retrospect they are rich in descriptive ability and defective in the self-subsistent musical interest required for non-dramatic forms of music. But it was not to be: in 1897 he was appointed director of music at New Brighton in Lancashire. Here he fought battles for the improvement of public taste and for contemporary composers. Sibelius was one of his novelties and in return for his introduction to the English public Sibelius dedicated his third symphony to Bantock. But Bantock was all too successful in outgrowing the conditions of the job and it came to an end in 1900 after giving a fillip to English music.

Not long before he left the north in 1900 to take up the post of principal of the music school attached to the Midland Institute at Birmingham, Bantock married (in 1898) Helen Francesca Maude, daughter of Hermann von Schweitzer, a research chemist; there were three sons and one daughter of the marriage. Other issues of it were the 'Helena Variations' for orchestra and many poems from his wife's pen which became song-texts. In 1901 he was made fellow of the Royal Academy of Music.

Bantock's versatility, product of his wide-ranging curiosity and impressionability, and the facility of his technique prejudiced the development of a personal style: the more he wrote the less did he consolidate a recognizable individuality. In his large output of music in every form the orchestral works, the overture 'The Pierrot of the Minute', the tone-poem

'Fifine at the Fair', and the 'Hebridean' Symphony, show his instrumental mastery; the choral cantata with orchestra and soloists 'Omar Khayyám' is probably his greatest achievement, since it concentrates in one work his partiality for oriental subjects, his powers of musical illustration, and a capacity less frequently manifested for large-scale organization. Another *tour de force* is 'Atalanta in Calydon', a choral symphony for unaccompanied voices in twenty parts which are treated in a semi-orchestral manner. His interest in virtuoso choralism had been aroused by the competition festival movement and he wrote a huge quantity of part-songs for all sorts of vocal combinations with and without accompaniment. His only opera was *The Seal-Woman*, described as a Celtic folk-opera based on Hebridean tunes, but he wrote much incidental music for plays as diverse as *The Bacchae, Macbeth*, and Arnold Bennett's *Judith*. Programme music and grandiose orchestration in the manner of Richard Strauss appeared in the first decade of the twentieth century to be the line of advance for English music, but the war of 1914–18 deflected it into less cosmopolitan channels, so that Bantock's music seemed even before his death, and still more subsequently, to be not only outmoded but too rootless to leave a permanent mark on the art. But it represented a phase in the revival and he served his generation well. He remained in Birmingham until 1934, when he retired from the professorship at the university in which, in 1908, he had succeeded Elgar, for whom the chair was created. He was knighted in 1930. The rebel thus became an academic and the recipient of official honours. After his retirement he went to London and interested himself in the work of the Trinity College of Music, undertaking on its behalf another tour round the world. He died in London 16 October 1946.

Burly and bearded, Bantock was a good mixer among men of many sorts and had wide sympathies, as his choice of literary texts, his travels, and his democratic leanings in their different ways amply testify. There is a portrait (1920) by J. B. Munns at the Barber Institute, university of Birmingham.

[H. Orsmond Anderton, *Granville Bantock*, 1915.]

Frank Howes

published 1959

NEWMAN Ernest

(1868–1959)

Musical critic, whose real name was William Roberts, was born 30 November 1868 in Everton, Lancashire, the only child of Seth Roberts, a tailor, and his second wife, Harriet Spark, whose first married name was Jones. Both parents also had families by their first spouses. William Roberts was educated at Liverpool College and University College, Liverpool. He was intended for the Indian Civil Service, but illness prevented him from taking the examination and he became a clerk in the Bank of Liverpool (1889–1903), meantime contributing to a number of progressive journals articles not only on music but on literature, religion, and philosophical subjects. He published his first book, *Gluck and the Opera*, in 1895, as Ernest Newman. The pseudonym was intended to signify his outlook, but it corresponded to some psychological need, since he thereafter adopted it in private as well as public life, although he never legally ratified the change. In 1897 he published *Pseudo-Philosophy at the End of the Nineteenth Century*, a criticism from the point of view of aggressive rationalism of writings by Benjamin Kidd, Henry Drummond, and A. J. Balfour, under the name Hugh Mortimer Cecil, but he did not use this name again.

In a series of articles contributed to *Cassell's Weekly* from March 1923 Newman described how he contrived to find time for an immense amount of reading and for self-education in music during his time at the bank. He had only one half-hour lesson in harmony, which was enough to convince him that he could do better for and by himself than by formal instruction, but he worked at composition for five years and at playing the piano, and made himself an expert score-reader.

His first musical journalism was written for (Sir) Granville Bantock in his *New Quarterly Musical Review*. He also owed to Bantock commissions to write programme-notes for his concerts at New Brighton, and later (1903) when Bantock was principal of the Birmingham and Midland Institute school of music, an invitation to join the staff. In 1905 Newman published his *Musical Studies* and left Birmingham to become music critic of the *Manchester Guardian*, in which his trenchant pen and independence of view sometimes upset the Hallé committee and Hans Richter but established his critical reputation. So much so that in 1906 the *Birmingham Daily Post* recalled him to Birmingham where he remained until 1919.

During these years Newman wrote studies of Wagner (1899 and 1904), Strauss (1908), Elgar (1906), and Hugo Wolf (1907). This last book remained for thirty years the best monograph on its subject and was translated into German. In 1914 came *Wagner as Man and Artist* which showed Newman's analytical powers, his independence—it was critical of *Mein Leben* and consequently not well received at Bayreuth—his appreciation of the Wagnerian music-drama, and his extreme care over documentation and detail. It led him on to his *magnum opus, The Life of Richard Wagner* in four volumes published in 1933, 1937, 1945, and 1947, which itself gave rise as a by-product to a study of *The Man Liszt* (1934). Newman had no illusions about Wagner's moral character and no doubts about his unique genius. Such was the clarity of his mind in the small things as well as the great that the biography, which involved a stupefying mass of material, is likely to remain definitive, unless Bayreuth improbably yields up further material of some wholly unexpected importance.

When he went to London in 1919 Newman began to write regularly for the *Observer*, but in the following year he joined the *Sunday Times* and thereafter, until 1958, he was its music critic, writing a weekly article and noticing the more important events in London music. His critical aim was objectivity—not for him the adventures of the soul among masterpieces—although he professed no interest in anything but the best, at any rate not until the second-rate had acquired historical interest. Although he could not turn criticism into a science, as he would have liked to do, he set out his critical creed in *A Musical Critic's Holiday* (1925), and in *The Unconscious Beethoven* (1927) a method of what soon came to be known as style criticism. A collection of his articles was published in 1919 entitled *A Musical Motley*; and from the *Sunday Times* two other selections were culled by Felix Aprahamian in 1956 and 1958. These served to show Newman's great range, which was sometimes overlooked because of his undoubted predilection for the nineteenth century and for opera, on which he published *Opera Nights* (1943), *Wagner Nights* (1949), and *More Opera Nights* (1954). He had translated most of Wagner's opera texts by 1912 and he was also responsible for translations of Weingartner's *On Conducting* (1906) and Schweitzer's *J. S. Bach* (1911).

Newman rigidly refused all honours until in extreme old age he no longer had the energy to decline them: Finland conferred on him the Order of the White Rose in 1956; Germany the Grosse Dienstkreuz in 1958; and the university of Exeter the D.Litt. in 1959. In 1955 he was presented with a *Festschrift*, a collection of essays by colleagues and admirers, *Fanfare for Ernest Newman*, edited by Herbert van Thal who later (1962) edited a further selection of Newman's essays and papers in *Testament of Music*.

In conversation Newman was as witty and kindly as he was witty and formidable in writing. In both and behind his amused smile was to be detected an underlying pessimism. In extreme age Beethoven's late quartets became his bible, for though he affected boredom with listening to music and was a rationalist by creed his values were determined by the big things in music. In appearance he was slight in build and after an illness in early middle life totally bald.

Newman was twice married: first, in 1894, to Kate Eleanor (died 1918), daughter of Henry Woollett, an artist descended from the engraver William Woollett; secondly, in 1919, to Vera, daughter of Arthur Hands, a Birmingham jeweller. There were no children of either marriage. He died at Tadworth, Surrey, 7 July 1959.

[Vera Newman, *Ernest Newman*, 1963; private information; personal knowledge.]

FRANK HOWES

published 1971

DAVIES (Henry) Walford

(1869–1941)

Sir

Musician, was born at Oswestry 6 September 1869, the seventh child and fourth surviving son of John Whitridge Davies, who founded and conducted a choral society there, and was choirmaster of the Congregational church. His wife, Susan, was the daughter of Thomas Gregory, jeweller, of Oswestry. In 1882 Walford Davies was admitted a chorister at St. George's chapel, Windsor, by the organist, Sir George Elvey. When his voice broke, he became organist of the royal chapel of All Saints, Windsor Great Park, pupil assistant to (Sir) Walter Parratt (Elvey's successor), and secretary to Dean (afterwards Archbishop) Randall Davidson. In 1890 he was awarded an open scholarship for composition at the Royal College of Music, (Sir) Hubert Parry becoming his teacher for that subject. During this period he was organist of St. George's church, Campden Hill, for three months, and St. Anne's church, Soho, for one year, resigning the latter appointment owing to illness. In the following year he became organist of Christ Church, Hampstead, and in 1895 was appointed teacher of counterpoint at the Royal College of Music, a post which he held until 1903, returning again as superintendent of the choir training class from 1910 to 1916. He proceeded Mus.D. (Cambridge) in 1898.

In the same year Davies succeeded E. J. Hopkins as organist of the Temple Church. For the next twenty-one years the music of this church was his chief concern and its services, already famous for their music, attracted a large congregation. His principal innovation was the monthly 'cantata service', which included Bach's cantatas, the Passion music, and the Christmas Oratorio at their appropriate seasons. He conducted the London Bach Choir from 1902 to 1907, and the London Church Choirs' Association annual festivals in St. Paul's Cathedral from 1901 to 1913. In 1915 he organized concerts for troops, and compiled and edited the *Fellowship Song Book*. Three years later he became musical director to the Royal Air Force with the rank of major and in 1919 he was appointed O.B.E.

In the same year he accepted the professorship of music at University College, Aberystwyth, and with it the post of director of music and chairman of the National Council of Music for the university of Wales. Here he laboured unceasingly for the musical enlightenment of the principality, and in 1922, on Lloyd George's retirement from office, he was knighted. He finally ended his connexion with the Temple in 1923. In 1924 he gave the Cramb lectures at Glasgow, broadcast for the first time from Savoy Hill, and was appointed Gresham professor of music in the university of London. He resigned his professorship at Aberystwyth in 1926, but retained his chairmanship of the National Council of Music until his death. He was organist and director of the choir of St. George's chapel, Windsor, from 1927 to 1932, and in the latter year was appointed C.V.O. On the death of Sir Edward Elgar in 1934, he was appointed master of the King's musick. In the following year he organized the remarkable jubilee concert in the Royal Albert Hall, which brought singers from all over the United Kingdom to sing British music in the presence of King George V and Queen Mary. He took a prominent part in arranging the music for the coronation of King George VI, and was promoted K.C.V.O. in 1937. At the outbreak of hostilities in 1939 he removed to Bristol with the British Broadcasting Corporation to which he had been a musical adviser since 1926. He was a member of C.E.M.A. which later became the Arts Council. He died at Wrington, near Bristol, 11 March 1941, and was buried in the graveyard of Bristol Cathedral. His elder brother, Edward Harold Davies, who had for many years been professor of music in the university of Adelaide and director of music at the Elder Conservatorium, died in 1947.

Davies's creative work had made its mark while he was still a student at the Royal College of Music. From 1902 to 1912 he contributed important works for solo voices, chorus, and orchestra for several of the principal festivals, including a cantata (Leeds, 1904) founded upon the old morality play *Everyman*, which remains his most important and best-known work on a large scale, and the 'Song of St. Francis' (Birmingham, 1912). Of his smaller works, the songs and the 'Six Pastorals' for vocal quartet, strings, and piano (1897) have a delicacy and charm all their own. His love of children is well illustrated in the 'Four Songs of Innocence' (1900), in the 'Nursery Rhymes' for vocal quartet (1905 and 1909), the 'Sacred Lullabies' (1909), and the 'Peter Pan' Suite for string quartet (1909). The well-known and popular 'Solemn Melody' for organ and strings, originally written for the Milton tercentenary celebrations, was produced at a Promenade concert in 1908.

As organist, choirmaster, and composer Davies's influence on the church music of his generation was conspicuous. Of his many compositions, the anthems 'God created man' (1899), the 'Walk to Emmaus' (1899), and the well-known introit 'God be in my head' (1908) all display his individual style. He was one of the first members of the Church Music Society, for which he lectured, wrote pamphlets, and edited works.

A remarkable power of getting into touch with every kind of audience made Davies one of the most effective judges at competition festivals. This gift was developed further through the advent of broadcasting, an art in which he proved himself a master. His courses of lectures to schools, and to adult listeners, became widely popular by reason of his exceptional power of thinking aloud, and thinking with his listeners, who thus felt drawn into his confidence.

Davies married in 1924 Constance Margaret, daughter of William Evans, canon of St. David's, and rector of Narberth. Honorary degrees were conferred upon him by the universities of Leeds (LL.D., 1904), Glasgow (LL.D., 1926), Dublin (Mus.D., 1930), and Oxford (D.Mus., 1935). He also held the honorary diplomas of F.R.C.O. (1904), F.R.A.M. (1923), and F.R.C.M. (1926).

A charcoal drawing by Evan Walters is in the National Museum of Wales.

[*The Times*, 12 March 1941; H. C. Colles, *Walford Davies*, 1942; *Grove's Dictionary of Music and Musicians*; personal knowledge.]

Henry G. Ley

published 1959

WOOD Henry Joseph

(1869–1944)

Sir

Musical conductor, was born in London 3 March 1869, the only child of Henry Joseph Wood, an optician and model engineer who was a keen amateur 'cellist and for twenty-five years tenor soloist at St. Sepulchre's church, Holborn. His mother Martha, daughter of Evan Morris, a Welsh farmer, possessed a natural soprano voice, and it was she who awakened her son's interest in music and provided him with his early tuition. Otherwise the child was self-taught, and it is remarkable evidence of his gifts that at the age of ten he often acted as deputy organist at St. Mary Aldermanbury. It was as an organist that he first came before the public, the recitals of 'Master Henry J. Wood' being a feature of the Fisheries and Inventions exhibitions of 1883 and 1885. From 1878 until he was fifteen Wood was educated at a school in Argyll Street, where he carried off all the prizes for painting, drawing, and music. At this time painting was nearly as strong an interest as music and for some years he continued to study in his spare time at the Slade School of Fine Art and the St. John's Wood School of Art. In 1911 he gave an exhibition of fifty sketches in oil at the Piccadilly Arcade Gallery in aid of the Queen's Hall Orchestra Endowment Fund.

After a short period of private tuition from Ebenezer Prout and his son Louis, Wood studied for two years at the Royal Academy of Music, where his professors were W. C. Macfarren for piano, Charles Steggall for organ, Ebenezer Prout for composition, and Manuel Garcia for singing. The association with Garcia determined his ambition to become a singing teacher, and he gained valuable experience by accompanying at the lessons given by Garcia and other eminent professors of the time. After leaving the Academy and during the period in which he was attempting to secure a foothold in the musical profession, Wood published a number of songs and wrote several works on a more ambitious scale, but soon realized that his vocation did not lie in composition. His ability as an accompanist and his knowledge of singing led him inevitably to the musical stage and to conducting.

His first professional experience as a conductor was gained with the Arthur Rousbey Opera Company in 1889, and in the following year he was engaged by R. D'Oyly Carte to superintend the rehearsals of *Ivanhoe* for Sir Arthur Sullivan. This led to his appointment as assistant conductor at the Savoy Theatre, and further operatic experience included a season with the

Carl Rosa Opera Company in 1891, with Leslie Crotty's Georgina Burns Light Opera Company in 1892, and Signor Lago's Italian opera season later in the same year when Tchaikovsky's opera *Eugene Onegin* was produced for the first time in England on 17 October at the Olympic Theatre, London. In between these conducting engagements he continued his work both as an accompanist and teacher of singing, in partnership with Gustav Garcia in his operatic school in Berners Street.

In 1894 Wood paid a visit to the Wagner Festival at Bayreuth, and there became acquainted with Felix Mottl. This meeting resulted in his being engaged as musical adviser to Schulz-Curtius for the Wagner concerts given at the newly built Queen's Hall. The manager of the hall, Robert Newman, had decided to run a series of promenade concerts, and saw in the twenty-five-year-old conductor the ideal musical director for the series. The financial backing for the concerts was assisted by a music lover and throat specialist, George Clark Cathcart, who provided £2,000, on condition that the existing high pitch, ruinous to singers' voices, should be abandoned and the lower French pitch introduced. So came into being, in August 1895, the most remarkable and influential series of concerts in the history of British music. Newman was to be associated with them for over thirty years, Wood for fifty. Although tribute must surely be paid to the manager, the series will always be associated, and rightly so, with the name of its founder-conductor.

The direction of a nightly series of promenade concerts, taking place over a period of anything from eight to ten weeks, both established Wood's reputation and encouraged Newman to embark on an ambitious and comprehensive scheme for his new hall. In 1896 a short series of symphony concerts was inaugurated, and in the following year the schedule at Queen's Hall included promenade concerts, symphony concerts, Sunday orchestral concerts, and concerts by the Queen's Hall Choral Society. As a recognition of these achievements, Queen Victoria commanded a performance of the Queen's Hall Orchestra under Wood at Windsor Castle 24 November 1898. In 1899 came the first London Musical Festival, shared by Lamoureux with his Paris Orchestra and Wood with his Queen's Hall Orchestra, the two joining forces for the final concert.

Despite this heavy schedule of London concerts, Wood found time in the following years to train and conduct an increasing number of choral societies and orchestras in the provinces. In 1898 he accepted the post of director of the Nottingham Sacred Harmonic Society and later founded the Nottingham City Orchestra. In 1900 he was appointed conductor of the Wolverhampton Festival Choral Society, in 1902 of the Sheffield, in 1904 of the Westmorland, and in 1908 of the Norwich, festivals. Such activities could only have been undertaken by a man of phenomenal energy who possessed also the most detailed technical knowledge of his work, a man who prepared everything minutely in advance, not only for himself, but for all those with whom he was associated. A mere clockwork precision, however, was far from his ideal. Wood was one of the earliest British conductors to insist on the importance of interpretation, and his scores were invariably marked with a wealth of expressive detail. It was characteristic that when he was about to conduct Bach's B minor Mass at the Sheffield Festival of 1911, he sent each member of the choir 168 pages of notes on details of interpretation.

In 1898 Wood married his first wife, Olga, daughter of Princess Sofie Ouroussoff, of Podolia, Russia. She had been his singing pupil, and to her he owed a broadening and refining of his musical outlook and an increased interest and enthusiasm for Russian music. This artistically fruitful marriage was unhappily short. His wife died in 1909. Meanwhile a critical situation had arisen at Queen's Hall owing to the bankruptcy of Robert Newman in 1901. After some negotiation a syndicate was formed by (Sir) Edgar Speyer and activities were again carried on under Newman's management. This successful régime was responsible for such important musical events as the visits of Strauss, Debussy, Sibelius, and Grieg to conduct their own compositions at Queen's Hall. During this period also, Wood received international recognition, being invited in 1904 to conduct the New York Philharmonic-Symphony Orchestra, an invitation never previously extended to a British-born conductor.

Wood was knighted in 1911 and in the same year married Muriel Ellen, daughter of Major Ferdinand William Greatrex of the 1st (Royal) Dragoons, by whom he had two daughters. His provincial activities at this time had reached a peak, and included the Sheffield, Norwich, Birmingham, Wolverhampton, and Westmorland festivals, the Cardiff orchestral concerts, the Gentlemen's concerts and later Brand Lane's concerts at Manchester, the Liverpool Philharmonic, and concerts at Leicester and Hull. Meanwhile his Queen's Hall concerts continued to reflect the most important trends in contemporary music. As a single instance, Schönberg's revolutionary 'Five Orchestral Pieces' were played at a promenade concert in 1912, the year of their first world performance.

In the war years of 1914–18 Wood and Newman carried on at Queen's Hall, and when in 1915 public opinion forced Speyer to leave the country, the Queen's Hall orchestral concerts were taken over by the publishing firm of Chappell, the lessees of the hall, and the orchestra was renamed the New Queen's Hall Orchestra. Three years after the end of hostilities Wood was chosen, together with Arthur Nikisch and Gabriel Pierné, to conduct at the international festival at Zürich, and in the same year he was awarded the gold medal of the Royal Philharmonic Society. In 1926 he conducted the Handel Festival at the Crystal Palace. Two years earlier he had enlarged his important work as a teacher by taking over the orchestral classes at the Royal Academy of Music, and interesting himself in the conducting students there. It was characteristic of Wood that the dates of these classes were always the first to be entered into his bulky engagement diary, and nothing was allowed to disturb them. The debt of orchestral players to Wood is indeed immense, and all who came into contact with him admit how much he taught them. Their sobriquet 'Old Timber' was not merely a play on words, but a symbol of solid admiration and heartfelt respect.

Academic recognition of his services to the cause of music was given by Manchester University in 1924 by the conferring of an honorary D.Mus. Oxford followed suit in 1926, Cambridge in 1935, and London in 1939, and Birmingham awarded him the honorary degree of M.Mus. in 1927. In 1924 he was elected a fellow of the Royal College of Music and in 1928 he became an honorary freeman of the Worshipful Company of Musicians. He was appointed an officer of the Legion of Honour (1926) and received the Order of the Crown of Belgium (1920). Tempting offers were made from America and in 1926 Wood conducted at the Hollywood Bowl, choosing his programmes from the music of living British composers. Realizing the importance of the work still to be done in England, he had declined in 1918 the offer of an appointment for six months in every year with the Boston Symphony Orchestra.

In 1926 the death of Robert Newman severed an association which had lasted for over thirty years, and in the same year Chappells announced that they were unable to continue financing the promenade concerts. Negotiations between Wood and the British Broadcasting Corporation resulted in the Corporation's sponsoring the 1927 season, and the historic series of concerts became not only financially secure but were also broadcast for the first time. Programmes were freed from previous commercial considerations, and with the formation of the B.B.C. Symphony Orchestra in 1930 rehearsals became increasingly satisfactory. At a press interview Wood declared that he was on the threshold of realizing his lifelong ambition 'of truly democratizing the message of music and making its beneficial effect universal'.

On 5 October 1938, the occasion of his jubilee as a conductor, a concert was held at the Royal Albert Hall, the proceeds of which, together with a Jubilee Fund, were devoted to the endowment of nine beds for orchestral musicians in London hospitals. A fund was also founded within the British Musicians' Pension Society for the benefit of orchestral players' dependants. At the same time Wood presented to the Royal Academy of Music his library of 2,800 orchestral scores and 1,920 sets of parts, and also established a Henry Wood Fund to assist necessitous students.

Wood now awaited the consummation of his life-work, the jubilee of the promenade concerts, but on the outbreak of hostilities in 1939 the season was abruptly cut short, and early in 1940 the fate of the series appeared to be in the balance. Eventually a season was sponsored by the Royal Philharmonic Society, Wood conducting the London Symphony Orchestra, until continuous air raids brought the season to a close in September. The Queen's Hall was destroyed by enemy action 10 May 1941, but the promenade concerts that year were given without interruption at the Royal Albert Hall, and in the following year the B.B.C. was once more able to undertake their management.

In 1944 Wood was appointed C.H. and shortly before his jubilee promenade season he formally handed over the trusteeship of the concerts to the B.B.C., it being mutually agreed between Wood and the Corporation that these should in future be known as 'The Henry Wood Promenade Concerts' in order that their aims and ideals should be perpetuated. Wood was able to achieve his ambition of conducting on the opening night of his fiftieth promenade season, but his health had for some time been failing and he died 19 August 1944 in hospital at Hitchin. His ashes were laid to rest in St. Sepulchre's church, Holborn, where a St. Cecilia window was dedicated to his memory in 1946.

Of Wood, Sir Hugh Allen wrote: 'No one has had greater influence on the music of his time and generation, nor given himself so unsparingly to its service.' By his thoroughness, integrity, enthusiasm, and human understanding Wood did more than any other man to spread the love of orchestral music and raise its level of performance. He was the first British conductor to found a stable and permanent orchestra and to train it fully at rehearsal. As early as 1904 he had refused to allow the system by which deputies could be provided, and in 1913 he was the first conductor to introduce women into a British orchestra. His meticulous insistence on tuning, his innovation of sectional rehearsals for each department of the orchestra, and his careful marking of orchestral parts so as to secure unanimity of bowing, phrasing, and dynamics provided a basis for the present high standard of British orchestral playing. As a teacher of orchestras, choirs, and singers he influenced and developed almost every sphere of British music, while his constant encouragement of British composers was one of the greatest contributory factors in this country's musical renaissance. His selfless devotion to music was equalled only by the thoroughness which he brought to every aspect of his art.

A portrait of Wood by Frank O. Salisbury is in the National Portrait Gallery, which also possesses a pencil drawing by Madame H. E. Wiener. A portrait by Flora Lion, is in the Savage Club, which has also in its keeping a portrait by Meredith Frampton. In a memorial room at the Royal Academy of Music is a bust by Donald Gilbert, together with eight oil-paintings by Wood and other mementoes of him. These are the gift of Lady (Jessie) Wood, and it is a condition of the gift that the bust will occupy every year its dominant position on the platform at the Henry Wood Promenade Concerts.

Wood's publications include *The Gentle Art of Singing* (4 vols., 1927–8, and abridged in 1 vol., 1930) and *About Conducting* (1945).

[Sir Henry Wood, *My Life of Music*, 1938; Rosa Newmarch, *Henry J. Wood*, 1904, and *A Quarter of a Century of Promenade Concerts*, 1920; Bernard Shore, *The Orchestra Speaks*, 1938; Symposium, *Sir Henry Wood: Fifty Years of Proms*, 1944; Robert Elkin, *Queen's Hall*, 1944; Thomas Russell, *The Proms*, 1949; Jessie Wood, *The Last Years of Henry J. Wood*, 1954; *Musical Times*, September 1944; *Grove's Dictionary of Music and Musicians; The Times*, 21 August 1944; personal knowledge.]

JULIAN HERBAGE

published 1959

ALLEN Hugh Percy

(1869–1946)

Sir

Musician and musical statesman, was born at Reading 23 December 1869, the youngest of the seven children of John Herbert Allen, who was in business with Huntley & Palmers of Reading. His mother, Rebecca, was the daughter of Samuel Bevan Stevens, a member of the firm of Huntley, Bourne & Stevens which made the tins for Huntley & Palmers' biscuits.

There is not much evidence that the home was one in which music was seriously cultivated, nor do we hear of any particular success achieved by the boy at Kendrick School, Reading, but the arrival of Dr. Frederick John Read as organist of Christ Church, Reading, when Allen was eight, was a milestone in his life. Determined to have lessons from Read, Allen obtained local organistships—Coley (1880), Tilehurst (1884), Eversley (1886), and in 1887 he combined the latter post with some teaching at Wellington College. In that year he went as assistant to Read who had been appointed organist of Chichester Cathedral. This settled Allen's life-work. Chichester gave him experience in cathedral services, the training of a choir, and the responsibilities of a cathedral organist. As yet, however, he had no paper qualifications. He therefore took his B.Mus. examinations at Oxford in 1892, and in the same year was appointed organ scholar of Christ's College, Cambridge. Here appeared the first signs of his power to influence others musically. Contemporaries speak of his ability to make people do more than they thought possible. The college music society, the college orchestra (a new venture, and a real *ad*venture in 1892), the university musical club, performances of Greek plays—all these gained by his infectious enthusiasm and his drive. He graduated in arts in 1895 and in 1896 took his D.Mus. examinations at Oxford, although he was prevented by regulations from taking the degree until 1898.

In 1897 Allen was appointed organist of St. Asaph Cathedral, and in the one year that he spent there vastly improved the standard of singing and radically altered the repertoire. The next year he went to Ely Cathedral. Here he was not slow to forge musical links with Cambridge. Performances of the St. Matthew Passion, Brahms's Requiem and 'Schicksalslied' must have astonished this quiet cathedral town, and the importation of singers and orchestral players from Cambridge must have created abnormal activity on an otherwise sleepy railway line.

In 1901 the organistship of New College, Oxford, was vacant. Four distinguished musicians were shown the short list of four names, and their opinions were invited. All of them warned the college not to appoint Allen. If ever serious advice was wisely rejected, it was then, for Allen gave New College unstinted and selfless devotion for eighteen years. As at St. Asaph and Ely, the choir at New College was soon required to sing much difficult music, and the weekly service lists show both progressiveness and catholicity. In 1908 the college showed its appreciation of Allen's work by offering him a fellowship, at that time a most unusual recognition of a mere musician. The crowds at the Christmas carol services were testimony to the regard felt for organist and choir, not only by the university but also by the city. There was, however, a wider sphere awaiting Allen in the amalgamation of two choral societies (of different traditions and understandable rivalry) into the Oxford Bach Choir. Allen then formed an orchestra to accompany the choir in the fine works which he taught them, and music was soon raised to a position in Oxford which it had never before occupied and became an integral part of the life of university and city.

It was not surprising that Allen should be approached by musical authorities outside Oxford. He became director of the Petersfield Festival (1906), conductor of the London Bach Choir (1907–20), director of music at

University College, Reading (1908–18), director of music at Cheltenham Ladies' College (1910–18). In 1913, and again in 1922, 1925, and 1928 he was one of the conductors at the Leeds Festival. The stories of his forgetfulness of rehearsals and his refusal to answer letters and telegrams are legion, but all these places bear the marks of Allen's influence.

In 1918 Sir Walter Parratt resigned the professorship of music at Oxford, and there was no doubt about his successor. Oxford was glad to have at last a resident professor. But when Sir Hubert Parry died later in the year Allen was appointed director of the Royal College of Music, and Oxford thought it would lose him. As usual with Allen, nothing of the sort occurred. He retained his professorship, kept his rooms at New College, and for another seven years conducted the Oxford Bach Choir. His activity was ceaseless and it is said that he once went from Oxford to London and back three times in a day.

Allen's arrival at the Royal College of Music coincided with post-war expansion. The number of students rose from 200 to 600 and many of the director's plans for extension of work, which were made quickly and, as it seemed, temporarily, eventually became permanent. For nineteen years he directed the affairs of the College, but in 1937 he felt he ought to retire. Retirement with Allen was a synonym for change of occupation; to the end of his life he retained his Oxford professorship and made Oxford his headquarters, keeping a watchful eye on musical activities, advising, encouraging young people, working (which meant in his case fighting) for the creation of a music faculty, which the university granted in 1944. New premises and the setting up of a Music School occupied him continuously from this time until his death.

Allen's position in the musical world was very distinguished, but most unusual. This was not curious, for most things about him were unusual. From the time of his first appointment his aim was to spread the love of music, and to teach people, both individually and in large numbers, how to make music. In Oxford he galvanized generations of undergraduates of both sexes into musical action, and showed them, with a technique of his own, how to get hold of music and how to get inside it. He was criticized for being content with less than perfect performances, but his critics, while having a modicum of truth on their side, failed to perceive his aim. In Allen's mind rehearsals were more important than performances. At rehearsals he could talk and teach, at performances he could only glower and frown when he was not satisfied. Nevertheless, members of his choir and orchestra have spoken of many occasions when they sang and played far better than they knew how—all because of Allen's inspiring command. Thousands of young people came under his influence in the provinces, and when he went to London thousands more were added. Many of these went out into the world carrying with them the infection of his enthusiasm which they transmitted to others. In this way, Allen probably did more good musically than anyone else of his generation.

Partly because of his twofold offices in London and Oxford, but chiefly because of the man himself, Allen gradually became a focal point for musical employers and potential employees. His advice and help were sought by many musical organizations. The Incorporated Society of Musicians owes its reconstitution and its revivification chiefly to him; Kneller Hall sought his help; he was a member of the council of the corporation of the Royal Albert Hall; the Royal Philharmonic Society needed, and got, his advice; the British Broadcasting Corporation made him chairman of its music advisory committee in 1936. There was a time, just before he retired from the Royal College of Music, when it could be safely said that there were few musical happenings in the country about which Allen had not been consulted.

This pre-eminent musico-political position has tended to obscure the eminence of Allen as a musician. Those who knew him well will remember his executant ability. They will remember, perhaps enviously, his uncanny power of sight-reading, whether of an orchestral score or an eight-part vocal score with clefs now obsolete. His knowledge of actual music was vast. Bach and Brahms were his special favourites, but Beethoven's Mass in D he sometimes felt was the greatest of all. He was an authority on the composers of the earlier German school, especially Heinrich Schütz, but could talk knowledgeably about Schönberg. A lesson with him in score-reading was memorable.

Musical historians of the future will have no easy task in assessing his place. He did not compose; he was not well known as a player: few realized how much actual music he knew, but there will be few accounts of musical events of his time which do not mention him. His work was with human beings. He was a human dynamo; but to state that, and that only, will give but little impression of him either as man or musician.

One might have thought that Allen's only interest was music, but there was a love of the sea in his bones, which cemented his friendship with Parry. Astronomy intrigued him, and he knew more about it than most amateurs. His mind travelled to vast spaces—the sea, light years, the stars.

It was natural that honours should come to Allen, although he set but little store by them. He was knighted in 1920, appointed C.V.O. in 1926, promoted K.C.V.O. in 1928 and G.C.V.O. in 1935. Besides his Oxford doctorate he was an honorary Mus.D. of Cambridge (1925), D.Litt. of Reading (1938), Litt.D. of Sheffield (1926), and D.Phil. of Berlin. He was also an honorary fellow of Christ's College, Cambridge (1926); and in 1937 he was master of the Worshipful Company of Musicians.

In 1902 Allen married Edith Winifred, daughter of Oliver Hall, of Dedham, Essex; they had one son and one daughter. On 17 February 1946 Allen was knocked down by a motor-cyclist in Oxford and the severe injuries which he received caused his death three days later on the 20th. A sudden death, with a touch of violence about it, seemed characteristic of the man.

A portrait of Allen by L. Campbell Taylor is at the Royal College of Music and a pencil drawing by J. S. Sargent is at New College, Oxford.

[Cyril Bailey, *Hugh Percy Allen*, 1948; personal knowledge.]

W. K. STANTON

published 1959

ATKINS Ivor Algernon

(1869–1953)

Sir

Organist and choirmaster, the fifth child and third son of Frederick Pyke Atkins, professor of music and for many years organist of St. John's, Cardiff, by his wife, Harriet Maria Rogers, was born 29 November 1869 at Llandaff.

He was educated privately before passing into the hands of Charles Lee Williams at Llandaff Cathedral. In 1885 he became pupil-assistant to George Robertson Sinclair and served in that capacity at the cathedrals of Truro and (from 1890) at Hereford. In 1892 he matriculated, through the Queen's College, Oxford, as a non-resident musical scholar, and was admitted to the degree of bachelor of music. Thus qualified, he was appointed, in 1893, organist of Ludlow parish church. There he enlarged his experience, and in 1897 he was appointed organist at Worcester Cathedral, a post carrying with it the duty of conducting the triennial festival of the Three Choirs.

At first conditions at Worcester were not easy. His taste was offended by the facile music which bulked large in the repertory. And it was not until the Edwardian decade was drawing to its close that Atkins's views prevailed. Then, in his zeal for reform, he discarded much Victorian music and by 1930 had revived the works of his Tudor predecessors, Thomas Tomkins and Nathaniel Patrick. He also showed proofs of his scholarship by reviving the use of portions of the thirteenth-century *Worcester*

Antiphonar and producing for the Worcestershire Historical Society an account of the early organists of Worcester Cathedral (1918); by a preface to *Worcester Mediaeval Harmony* (1928), and (with Neil R. Ker) the *Catalogus Librorum Manuscriptorum Bibliothecae Wigorniensis 1622–23* (1944). Atkins was cathedral librarian for twenty years (1933–53) and was elected F.S.A. in 1921.

He was an excellent organist but his daily work did not involve the regular exercise of a conductor's skill. During his first festival in 1899 his conducting was criticized adversely; notwithstanding, from 1902 onwards his great powers of organization and all-round musicianship carried him through. His greatest service to the festival, enlarging the repertory, was the fruit of broad musical sympathies. In 1902, while the repercussions of the secession of John Henry Newman were still felt, his courageous introduction of *The Dream of Gerontius* was the beginning of the close association of (Sir) Edward Elgar with the Three Choirs. In the same year he gave a first festival commission to (Sir) Walford Davies, thus inaugurating the enterprising policy with regard to new works which distinguished all his programmes.

Atkins's love of Bach was supreme. He produced a valuable edition of the *Orgelbüchlein* (1916) and, with Elgar, prepared an edition of the *St. Matthew Passion* (1911), and established that work as a regular feature of the festival. He also edited the *St. John Passion* (1929), Brahms's *Requiem* (1947), and the *Worcester Psalter* (1948). Although not ambitious as a composer, he produced a cantata, 'Hymn of Faith' (1905), and several anthems, services, and songs.

In 1914 the declaration of war led to a break in the sequence of the festivals which lasted for six years. Many influential persons felt that it would be impossible to revive them. But in 1920 Atkins undertook the immense task. The revived festival at Worcester was almost entirely his own creation and its success brought the honour of knighthood in the following year.

Thereafter, until he conducted his last festival at Worcester in 1948, his life was uneventful and his employment never varied. At Easter 1950 he retired.

Atkins became an honorary R.A.M. in 1910; doctor of music in 1920; a fellow of St. Michael's College, Tenbury Wells, in 1921. He was president of the Royal College of Organists in 1934–6.

In 1899 Atkins married Katharine May Dorothea, daughter of the Rev. Edward Butler, of Llangoed Castle, and had one son. Atkins died at Worcester 26 November 1953. Lady Atkins, who was prominent in the life of the city and the first woman to become high sheriff of Worcester, died in 1954.

[Watkins Shaw, *The Three Choirs Festival*, 1954; *Grove's Dictionary of Music and Musicians*; *Berrow's Worcester Journal*, *passim*; personal knowledge.]

A. T. Shaw

published 1971

WOOD Matilda Alice Victoria

(1870–1922)

Music-hall comedian, professionally known as Marie Lloyd, was born at 36 Plumber Street, Hoxton, 12 February 1870, the eldest of the eleven children of John Wood, artificial flower-maker, by his wife, Matilda Mary Caroline Archer. In childhood she formed a troupe of little girls, the Fairy Bell Minstrels, who sang and acted in schoolrooms and mission halls. At the age of fourteen she appeared on the stage of the Grecian music-hall, which was attached to the Eagle public-house in the City Road; her salary was fifteen shillings a week and her stage name Bella Delmare, which she soon changed to Marie Lloyd. Before she was sixteen she was performing in the West end of London, and in 1886 she was earning £100 a week.

In 1891, 1892, and 1893 Marie Lloyd was engaged by Sir Augustus Henry Glossop Harris for his pantomimes at Drury Lane Theatre; she also appeared in a few other pantomimes in suburban and provincial theatres. But her real bent was for the music-halls, which during her career were developing into imposing theatres of variety. Her songs were all written and composed for her by others; but she moulded them as she pleased by means of look, gesture, and tone of voice, making most of them openly and joyfully improper; yet, attractive as she was with her golden hair and blue eyes, she kept her performance free from any personal display or invitation, and appealed to the women as much as to the men. Her power lay in her cheery vitality, her thorough knowledge of vulgar English—and especially Cockney—manners and humour, and her highly cultivated skill in swift and significant expression, which won praise from judges so good as Ellen Terry and Sarah Bernhardt. Tours in Australia, South Africa, and the United States of America showed that her very English humour could be enjoyed outside England.

Marie Lloyd's work fell into three periods. In the first she was girlish, almost childish, as when she made her first great hit with the song 'The boy I love sits up in the gallery'. Next came a long series of songs which she sang as a grown woman dressed in, and beyond, the height of fashion, such as 'Oh, Mr. Porter', 'Everything in the garden's lovely', and 'When you wink the other eye'. Last came certain studies of shabby and broken-down women, in which she mingled sadness and humour, and showed considerable skill in the impersonation of character.

Over the music-hall public Marie Lloyd held undisputed dominion. Some of the affection for her was due to her notorious generosity. She lavished both money and care on the poor and the unhappy; and in 1907 in a music-hall strike on behalf of the minor performers, she came out on strike with the rest and took her turn as picket. Overwork and domestic trouble hastened her end. She was taken ill on the stage of the Alhambra (the audience loudly applauding what they took for a very realistic piece of acting) and died at her home at Golders Green 7 October 1922, aged fifty-two.

Marie Lloyd married three times: first, in 1887 Percy Charles Courtenay, general dealer, by whom she had her only child, a daughter; secondly, in 1906 Alexander (Alec) Hurley, comedian; and thirdly, in 1914 Bernard Dillon, jockey.

[*The Times*, 3 and 6 October 1913, 23 February 1914, 16 July 1920, and 9 October 1922; Naomi Jacob, *Our Marie*, 1936.]

H. H. Child

published 1937

WALKER Ernest

(1870–1949)

Musician, was born in Bombay 15 July 1870, the son of Edward Walker, partner in a firm of East India merchants, by his wife, Caroline Cooper. His parents brought him to England in 1871 and later settled at Anerley, near the Crystal Palace, where he frequented the concerts, then under the direction of (Sir) August Manns. Educated at private schools, at the age of seventeen he was admitted to Balliol College, Oxford, where the master, Benjamin Jowett, took a special interest in him. He was placed in the second class of the honours list in classical moderations (1889) and *literae humaniores* (1891). Philosophy was his chief interest in his work for the schools and he was deeply influenced by R. L. Nettleship. He became intimate with the college organist, John Farmer, and helped him in the

Balliol Sunday evening concerts. He proceeded to take the degrees of B.Mus. (1893) and D.Mus. (1898), and was assistant organist at Balliol from 1891 until on Farmer's death in 1901 he succeeded him as organist and director of music, greatly raising the standard of the concerts. In 1913 he resigned the organistship, thinking participation in chapel services inconsistent with his views on religion, but held the directorship until 1925, when he retired in order to devote himself to composition. He was elected an honorary fellow of the college in 1926.

Walker took a large part in all the musical activities of the university, and was for many years a teacher and examiner. He did much to improve the standard of the musical degrees and, with Sir Hugh Allen, to raise the status of music in the university; in 1944 it was constituted an independent faculty.

He was a fine pianist with a catholic taste, and as an accompanist had an almost unique reputation. His compositions were scholarly, restrained, and sensitive; they fall naturally into two groups. The earlier consisted mostly of vocal music and followed the German diatonic tradition; the best known are the 'Five songs for four voices from "England's Helicon"' (1900). About 1914 diatonics gave place to harmonics and his style became more terse and enigmatic. The bulk of the music was now instrumental. Typical of this period is the 'cello and piano Sonata (composed in 1914); the passion of the first movement is unique in Walker's work.

Walker was much in request for reviews and critical articles and analytical notes to concert programmes. But his reputation as a writer rests mainly on *A History of Music in England* (1907), which has remained a classic. He also wrote *Beethoven* in the 'Music of the Masters' series (1905), and in 1946 collected some of his articles under the title *Free Thought and the Musician*; the essay which gives the title discusses the effect of rationalist views on the professional musician's life. In all his writings his scrupulous accuracy and sincerity are conspicuous.

Naturally a retiring, even shy, man, Walker was gentle and quiet in his ways, but always strong in his protest against anything false or shoddy. He was unmarried, but made many friends, especially among his pupils and fellow musicians. Early in life he tended to high church Anglicanism, but that gave way to agnosticism and ultimately to atheistic rationalism. Yet there was always something of the mystic in him, which found expression both in his music and in his lasting love of nature. He continued to live in Oxford after his retirement and died there 21 February 1949.

A drawing of Walker by Francis Dodd (1934) is at Balliol College, and another by Sir Muirhead Bone (1946) is in the possession of the Misses Deneke.

[Margaret Deneke, *Ernest Walker*, 1951, with a chapter on Walker's compositions by Ivor Keys; personal knowledge.]

Cyril Bailey

published 1959

FELLOWES Edmund Horace (1870–1951)

Clergyman and musical scholar, was born in Paddington, London, 11 November 1870, the second son and fifth child of Horace Decimus Fellowes, of the family of Fellowes of Shotesham Park, Norfolk, assistant director of the Royal Army clothing depot, and his wife, Louisa Emily, daughter of Captain Edmund Packe, Royal Horse Guards, of Prestwold Hall, Leicestershire.

Fellowes showed musical gifts at an early age and in 1878 he received an offer from Joachim to be his pupil on the violin. Instead, he proceeded in due course to Winchester and Oriel College, Oxford, taking a fourth class in theology (1892) and becoming B.Mus. and M.A. in 1896. He was ordained deacon (1894) and priest (1895) and after a short curacy in Wandsworth became precentor of Bristol Cathedral in 1897. In 1900 he was appointed minor canon of St. George's chapel, Windsor Castle, where he remained until his death and where his rendering of the priest's part in the services was of exceptional dignity and beauty. From 1924 until 1927 he was in charge of the choir between the death of Sir Walter Parratt and the appointment of Sir Walford Davies. In this capacity he toured Canada with the lay clerks in company with (Sir) Sydney Nicholson and boys from Westminster Abbey. As a minor canon of Windsor he was appointed M.V.O. in 1931; later he contributed five volumes to a series of historical monographs relating to the chapel.

While a young clergyman Fellowes acquired considerable knowledge of heraldry. But in 1911 his attention was drawn to the work of the English madrigal composers, and this proved decisive. Thenceforward he applied himself to studying and editing English music of the period *c.* 1545–1645 on which he became the leading authority. Single-handed he edited 36 volumes of madrigals, 32 volumes of lute songs, and 20 volumes of Byrd's music; he was also the most pertinacious of the editors of *Tudor Church Music*. This work was supported by important biographical and critical writings, notably *The English Madrigal Composers* (1921) and *William Byrd* (1936), breaking much new ground. Meanwhile, as honorary librarian of St. Michael's College, Tenbury Wells, Worcestershire (1918–48), he arranged and catalogued the extensive musical library left by Sir Frederick Ouseley.

By his investigation of original sources, Fellowes shed fresh light on the idiom of this music and mapped out a considerable area, making it common property. For, scholar though he was, he was a performing musician even more, and his aim was to be not only accurate and informative but comprehensive and practical. His editions were intended to get the music performed, not to rest on a scholar's desk; but they were not to be mere selections. This conception was then a novelty; it has been amply justified by the natural familiarity of later generations with the field he tilled almost as a pioneer. When estimating his technical achievement as editor, as distinct from his range, discoveries, and fruitful practical impact, it must be remembered that in Fellowes's day there was no organized training for musical research in England. He had to find his own way, and thereby contributed largely to the standards by which he will be judged. On his critical writings, whose contributions to knowledge are plain for all to see, it is a just comment that he viewed his subject in too insular a light.

Parallel to his researches ran his lifelong efforts to improve church (and particularly cathedral) music. He was president of the Church Music Society (1946–51) in succession to Archbishop Lang. When president of the Musical Association (1942–7) he was instrumental in securing for that body the appellation 'Royal'.

Disappointed by failure to attain a canonry (though he was offered a non-stipendiary Wiccamical prebend of Chichester which he was precluded from accepting), Fellowes did not lack honours of another sort. He received the honorary doctorate in music from Dublin (1917), Oxford (1939), and Cambridge (1950), and was made an honorary fellow of Oriel in 1937. In 1944 he was appointed C.H.

All his life he was an accomplished player of chamber music, and, in his earlier days, of tennis also. His interest in cricket led him to write a *History of Winchester Cricket* (1930). Rightly jealous for the things he had struggled for, Fellowes perhaps seemed forbidding to those who took things for granted; but he was the most loyal of men, kind to many a younger scholar. The essentials of his work and personality were thoroughness and tenacity.

In 1899 he married Lilian Louisa, youngest daughter of Admiral Sir Richard Vesey Hamilton, by whom he had three sons and one daughter. He died at Windsor 21 December 1951.

[E. H. Fellowes, *Memoirs of an Amateur Musician*, 1946; *The Times*, 22 December 1951; *Musical Times*, February 1952; personal knowledge.]

WATKINS SHAW

published 1971

BUTT Clara Ellen

(1872–1936)

Dame

Singer, whose married name was Clara Ellen Kennerley Rumford, was born at Southwick, near Brighton, 1 February 1872, the eldest daughter and eldest surviving child of Henry Butt, a captain in the Mercantile Marine, by his wife, Clara Hook, great-granddaughter of Theodore Hook. Both her parents sang, and Clara, beginning with piano lessons, was encouraged by them also to take advantage of some minor opportunities to cultivate her voice, which was soon discovered to be of remarkable richness and great compass. Miss Cook, the headmistress of the South Bristol High School at which Clara was educated (her parents having settled in Bristol in 1880), accidentally hearing some of Clara's already splendid low notes, got Daniel Rootham, a fine bass singer, conductor of the Bristol Festival Choir, to hear her, and he began her training, although she was still in her early 'teens. Soon she was singing in the Bristol Festival Choir and hearing famous soloists. In January 1890, when sixteen years old, she won a valuable scholarship, which was also open to instrumentalists, at the Royal College of Music, but she had to wait until she had attained the regulation age of seventeen before she could take up residence and begin her studies, which were directed by John Henry Blower. The college authorities extended her scholarship for a fourth year and then sent her for a three months' course to Duvernoy in Paris, Queen Victoria defraying the cost. Later in her career Clara Butt studied with Bouhy in Paris, and with Etelka Gerster in Berlin, and in Italy. She made her début at the Royal Albert Hall in the comparatively small contralto part of Ursula in Sir Arthur Sullivan's cantata *The Golden Legend* on 7 December 1892, and three days later sang the name part in Gluck's *Orfeo* at a performance given by pupils of the Royal College of Music at the Lyceum Theatre.

On both occasions Clara Butt's success was complete, her magnificent voice and splendid appearance (she was six feet two inches in height) launching her on a career of almost unexampled popularity. Confining herself to the concert platform (with the exception of some appearances as Orfeo at Covent Garden under Sir Thomas Beecham in 1920), she sang at all the principal festivals in England and at concerts (many of them her own, with her husband, Robert Kennerley Rumford, baritone, whom she married in 1900) at home, all over the British Empire, and in America, with striking success. Sir Edward Elgar composed 'Sea Pictures', his cycle of five songs for contralto solo with orchestral accompaniment, for Clara Butt, and she produced them at the Norwich festival in 1899. Elgar also wrote the music of the Angel in *The Dream of Gerontius* with Clara Butt in mind; and it was a suggestion from her that brought from the future master of the king's musick the patriotic song 'Land of Hope and Glory'. What has become a classic of its kind, the setting of 'Abide with Me', was composed by Samuel Liddle, her fellow student at the Royal College of Music, for Clara Butt, who sang it with an appeal of great poignancy. Her singing was remarkable for its broad effect rather than for its artistic finesse, and there could not be a greater contrast in style than between her and Patti when they appeared on the same concert platform. Her activity and generosity in organizing and singing at concerts during the war of 1914–1918 for charities—the Red Cross, Three Arts Club women's unemployment fund, etc.—knew no bounds: a week of Elgar's music at the Queen's Hall was notable as an artistic as well as a charitable achievement; and for these services she was appointed D.B.E. in 1920. She died at North Stoke, Oxfordshire, as the result of an accident in 1931, after a long and painful illness, 23 January 1936. Both her sons predeceased her, but she was survived by her husband and her daughter.

[Winifred Ponder, *Clara Butt. Her Life-Story*, 1928; *Grove's Dictionary of Music and Musicians*, 4th ed., vol. i, edited by H. C. Colles; H. Saxe Wyndham and Geoffrey L'Epine, *Who's Who in Music*, 1913; *Musical Times*, March 1936; personal knowledge.]

J. Mewburn Levien

published 1949

VAUGHAN WILLIAMS Ralph

(1872–1958)

Composer, was born 12 October 1872 at Down Ampney, Gloucestershire, into a family of mixed Welsh and English descent whose members went chiefly into the law or the Church. Sir Edward Vaughan Williams was his grandfather, Sir Roland Vaughan Williams his uncle. He was the younger son of the vicar, the Rev. Arthur Vaughan Williams, and his wife, Margaret, daughter of the third Josiah Wedgwood, grandson of the potter, who had married his cousin, Caroline Darwin, niece of Charles Darwin. His parents' two families had come to live at Leith Hill in Surrey in the middle of the nineteenth century and Ralph Vaughan Williams was to continue his association with the Leith Hill musical festival until the middle of the twentieth. He was brought up at Leith Hill Place because his father died when he was only two. There was music in both families but the child was no precocious genius. He wrote a little piece four bars long for piano when he was six, and by the time he was eleven he was playing the violin quite well, but, when he was an undergraduate at Cambridge his Darwin cousins thought he was wasting his time trying to be a composer, and he was thirty by the time he had found his real idiom. However, he relates in a musical autobiography contributed to *Ralph Vaughan Williams* (1950) by Hubert Foss that while he was still at Charterhouse he organized a concert at which one of his own works was played. Before he went up to Trinity College, Cambridge, in 1892 he spent two years at the Royal College of Music studying composition with (Sir) Hubert Parry and (Sir) Charles Stanford and he was able to take his Mus. Bac. in 1894 while still reading history in which he obtained a second in 1895. He then put in another year at the Royal College but he still had not found himself and went off to Berlin to work with Max Bruch. Years later he was still dissatisfied with his technique and in 1907–8 worked for some months at refining it with Ravel in Paris. But he had taken his Cambridge doctorate in 1901. Thereafter he was known to the world, since he declined a knighthood, as Dr. Vaughan Williams and later to younger generations as 'Uncle Ralph'.

Vaughan Williams was by creed and practice a nationalist, like those Slavonic, Latin, and Scandinavian musicians who in the nineteenth century turned against the long hegemony of German and Italian music to native sources of inspiration in order to secure emancipation for themselves and the ultimate enrichment of European music. Chief of these sources for Vaughan Williams was English folksong, but other influences were hymnody, including plainsong, to which he was led by his editorship of *The English Hymnal* (1906), Purcell, of whose works he edited a volume of the Welcome Odes for the Purcell Society (1904–6), and the Elizabethan madrigals to which he was devoted all his life both publicly and domestically. In him English music secured independence of the continental dominance which had been exerted by the powerful figures of Handel and Mendelssohn for a century and a half. He was assisted in this movement by his friend Gustav Holst, but he did not in the end establish a school, for the emancipation when it came was complete, and nationalism had spent most of its force in the early twentieth century.

Vaughan Williams had the integrity and independence of his middle-class origins, the lively conscience and streak of puritanism of his formal education, and an impressive physical presence. He belonged to that small class of Englishmen who are by temperament and upbringing radical traditionalists or conservative liberals; he could even be described as an agnostic Christian, in that while cherishing the main traditions of English life, its folksong, its hymnody, its ecclesiastical occasions, its liberal politics, its roots, he was forward-looking, outspoken, and quick to protest at official obscurantism, timidity, or intolerance, as when he publicly deprecated the banning of Communist musicians from access to the radio during the war of 1939–45. In the war of 1914–18 he enlisted as a private in the Royal Army Medical Corps and went to France and then to Salonica, but in 1917 he was transferred to the Royal Garrison Artillery and given a commission. He was sent again to France in March 1918 at the time of the great retreat. During his time in the army he had organized such music as was possible in recreation huts and after the armistice was made director of music, First Army, B.E.F., France, until he was demobilized.

His earliest music, apart from student and prentice work, consisted of songs, of which 'Linden Lea' (1902), the first published work, became and remained a classic. Another early song, 'Silent Noon' (1903), which was, however, one of a sequence of six settings of sonnets by Dante Gabriel Rossetti, also achieved a wide and lasting currency. In retrospect Rossetti seems less suited to his robust imagination than R. L. Stevenson (*Songs of Travel*, 1904) or Walt Whitman (*Towards the Unknown Region*, 1907) who provided texts for more characteristic music. By the time the latter had been given at the Leeds Festival of 1907 and had proclaimed that a new voice was to be heard in English music, a crisis in style had been resolved by Vaughan Williams's discovery of English folksong. He had been attracted in youth by Christmas carols and such few folksongs as came his way—'Dives and Lazarus' was a favourite which years later was to give him the 'Five Variants of "Dives and Lazarus" ' for harp and string orchestra

(1939)—but in December 1903 he collected 'Bushes and Briars' in Essex, the first of several hundreds of authentic folksongs taken down from the lips of traditional country singers in the course of the next few years. The modal character of these tunes unlocked for him the idiom which had been struggling to erupt and the first-fruits of the emancipation were three orchestral 'Norfolk Rhapsodies' (1906–7) and the *Fantasia on Christmas Carols* (1912). The rhapsody and the fantasia were the forms found by all nationalist composers to be more suited to thematic material derived from national tunes than conventional sonata form, which is recalcitrant to extended melody. He continued to compose songs on and off throughout his life but in diminishing numbers after about 1930, although his last completed work was a set of 'Four Last Songs' (1958).

Vaughan Williams would not have been the traditionalist he was had he failed to contribute to the long tradition of English choral music. After the success of his Whitman cantata at Leeds in 1907 it was natural for him to provide something more substantial for the premier choral festival: the *Sea Symphony*, with words again by Whitman, for the festival of 1910. More than Beethoven's Ninth is this a true choral symphony since all its four movements are vocal and at the same time are cast in one or other of the symphonic forms. As Vaughan Williams's mind gradually turned towards the symphony, which was eventually to form the central corpus of his output, this large-scale cantata took its place as the first in the canon of his nine symphonies. There is only one oratorio actually so called among his choral works with biblical words, *Sancta Civitas* (1926), of which the words are derived from the Apocalypse and prefaced by a quotation from Plato. *Hodie* nearly thirty years on (1954), however, is, in fact if not in official nomenclature, a Christmas oratorio. Of the other choral works some are occasional pieces, *Benedicite* (1929), *Dona nobis pacem* (1936), *Flourish for a Coronation* (1937), *A Song of Thanksgiving* (1944), and only *Five Tudor Portraits* (1935) is of the dimensions of a secular oratorio, although *An Oxford Elegy* and *Fantasia on the 'Old 104th'* (both 1949) employ a chorus, the one with an obbligato for a speaker, the other with an obbligato for pianoforte.

His first purely instrumental symphony was the *London*, completed before the war but revised before publication in 1920. Two other of his nine symphonies bear titles, No. 3, the *Pastoral* (1922), and No. 7, *Sinfonia Antartica* (1952), which was an overflow from the music he had composed for a film, *Scott of the Antarctic*. Nos. 4 (1935) and 6 (1948) are so angry and disturbing that they have also suggested a submerged programme, which the composer himself firmly deprecated. No. 5 (1943) had an avowed connection with *The Pilgrim's Progress*, on a setting of which the composer was contemporaneously working. Nos. 8 (1956) and 9 (1958) show a preoccupation with formal experiment and tone colour. No. 9 was performed only four months before his death and while it showed no lack of vigour it did sound a note of something like resignation not previously heard in his music. The range of experience covered is wide, although the subjective emotions explored by the German symphonists are not prominent.

Vaughan Williams also composed a good deal of dramatic music, which includes incidental music to pageants, masques, Shakespeare, Greek plays (of which the overture and suite for *The Wasps* of Aristophanes, 1909, is the chief and has an independent existence), film scores, ballets, and operas. These last are heterogeneous, ranging from the quasi-ballad opera to the text of Harold Child, *Hugh the Drover* (1924), to the full-length comedy *Sir John in Love* (1929); from the farcical extravaganza *The Poisoned Kiss* (1936) to the word-for-word setting of the tragic *Riders to the Sea* (1937) and the 'morality' *The Pilgrim's Progress* (1951). In none of these is the dramatic touch as certain as in the symphonies and choral works and they are not wholly proof against theatrical mischance, yet the work which is not only utterly characteristic but reveals supreme mastery is a stage work, the ballet *Job* (1931).

Many of his most characteristic works are not classifiable in the normal categories. Such are the *Serenade to Music* (1938) dedicated to Sir Henry Wood, *Flos Campi* (1925) which is a suite scored for solo viola, small orchestra, and small chorus, and his most important chamber work is a song sequence 'On Wenlock Edge' (1909) with accompaniment for string quartet and piano. There is an element of cussedness in his attitude to the concerto: he wrote four so called, besides two 'Romances' and a suite, for instrumental solo with orchestra. Those for violin are not virtuoso works; that for piano the composer rearranged for two keyboards to make it more effective; on the other hand it was a particular performer's virtuosity which evoked the concerto-type works for viola, oboe, harmonica, and tuba.

There is no side of music which Vaughan Williams did not touch and enrich, although some of his compositions were primarily of occasional and local significance, and for piano and organ he wrote little. His settings and arrangements of folksongs, however, are a valuable parergon. He conducted the Bach Choir from 1921 to 1928 and taught composition at the Royal College of Music for twenty years. His literary output consisted mostly of pamphlets and lectures, which were reprinted in book form, the chief being *National Music* (1934) in which his aesthetic creed was formulated. He did his share of committee work, notably in connection with the English Folk Dance and Song Society, of which he became president in 1946. The honours which came to him, an honorary doctorate of music from Oxford (1919), an honorary fellowship of Trinity College, Cambridge (1935), and the Order of Merit (1935), were no doubt for his eminence as a composer, but they were also a recognition of the manifold services he rendered to English music. It was not until he was an old man that it was realized that there was no formal portrait of him. The Royal College of Music therefore commissioned one from Sir Gerald Kelly which hangs in the college. The Manchester City Art Gallery has a bronze by Epstein and the National Portrait Gallery drawings by Juliet Pannett and Joyce Finzi and a bronze by David McFall.

In 1897 Vaughan Williams married Adeline (died 1951), daughter of Herbert William Fisher and sister of H. A. L. and Sir W. W. Fisher. In 1953 he married Ursula, daughter of Major-General Sir Robert Lock and widow of Lieutenant-Colonel J. M. J. Forrester Wood. He died in London 26 August 1958 and was buried in Westminster Abbey.

[Ursula Vaughan Williams, *R.V.W.: A Biography of Ralph Vaughan Williams*, 1964; Michael Kennedy, *The Works of Ralph Vaughan Williams*, 1964; personal knowledge.]

FRANK HOWES

published 1971

RONALD Landon

(1873–1938)

Sir

Musician, was born in London 7 June 1873, the younger son of Henry Russell, well known in contemporary circles as a writer of ballads. From early boyhood Ronald, who was educated at St. Marylebone Grammar School and Margate High School (afterwards Margate College), was clearly marked out for a musical career; his mother directed his first lessons, which were followed by private instruction from Franklin Taylor (piano) and Henry Holmes (violin). At the age of fourteen he entered the Royal College of Music, and studied composition with (Sir) Charles Hubert Parry, for whom he retained the utmost veneration.

At the age of seventeen Ronald was chosen to play piano solo in André Alphonse Toussaint Wormser's wordless play *L'Enfant Prodigue* at the Prince of Wales's Theatre (31 March 1891) and on tour. Appointed subsequently as coach and *répétiteur* at Covent Garden Theatre, he met Madame Melba, and became her accompanist for a number of years, besides conducting the orchestra for her American tour in 1895. There followed a spell of some discouragement, during which Ronald conducted a succession of theatre bands and many of the smaller orchestras in the provinces. An engagement to direct a series of concerts in Birmingham led to his meeting Max Mossel, an association that proved to be of immense mutual value. Mossel persuaded him to conduct abroad, and this venture became the turning-point in his career. He toured the capitals of Europe in 1908–1909, meeting with success wherever he went, the critics comparing his work favourably with that of the great German conductors. Ronald has been acclaimed a fine exponent of the music of Sir Edward Elgar, and it was on this tour that he introduced the A flat symphony to Rome (1909). News of these concerts having reached London, he was invited to conduct the Royal Philharmonic Orchestra in place of Hans Richter who was ill. From that time his reputation was established. In 1909 he was appointed permanent conductor of the Royal Albert Hall Orchestra (founded in 1905 as the New Symphony Orchestra), and there followed 'Harrison' concerts in the North, symphony concerts at the Queen's Hall (March 1909 until 1914), and Sunday afternoon concerts at the Royal Albert Hall (begun in October 1909).

In 1910 Ronald was appointed principal of the Guildhall School of Music, a post which he retained almost up to the time of his death. There he established the curriculum system, and brought the standard of teaching into line with that of the leading schools. He also formed a professors' club in order to bring a more corporate spirit into the building. The combination of this work with such musical commitments as conducting, journalism, and gramophone recording told on his health, and the Albert Hall concerts came to an end after the season of 1918–1919. The conductorship of the Scottish Orchestra was offered to him, and the committee of the Guildhall School of Music granted him leave of absence to undertake it. Ill health constantly handicapped his career, however, and although he conducted at the Albert Hall and the Palladium down to 1927, he had to give up much of his orchestral work from that time onwards.

Ronald's compositions, generally, were of the ballad type, and many of his songs achieved much popularity; but it was by conducting and as principal of the Guildhall School that he made his greatest contribution to music.

Ronald took no academic degrees, but the diplomas of F.R.A.M. (1921), F.G.S.M. (1922), and F.R.C.M. (1924) were conferred upon him, and in 1922 he was knighted in recognition of his services to music. He died in London after a long illness 14 August 1938. He was twice married: first, in 1897 to Mimi (died 1932), daughter of Josef Ettlinger, wholesale cloth merchant, and had a son; secondly, in 1932 to Mary (Mollie), daughter of Richard Dobson Callison.

A portrait of Ronald by John Collier was presented to the Guildhall School of Music by members of the Corporation of the City of London.

[*Musical Times*, September 1938; Sir L. Ronald, *Variations on the Personal Theme*, 1922, and *Myself and Others*, 1931; *Grove's Dictionary of Music and Musicians*, 4th ed., vol. iv, edited by H. C. Colles.]

EDRIC CUNDELL

published 1949

HOLST Gustav Theodore

(1874–1934)

Composer, whose original name was Gustavus Theodore von Holst, was born at Cheltenham 21 September 1874, the elder son of Adolph von Holst, a music teacher in Cheltenham, by his first wife, Clara, daughter of Samuel Lediard, solicitor, of Cirencester. The von Holsts were of Swedish origin though long settled in England. The painter Theodor von Holst was Gustav's great-uncle.

At an early age Holst began to learn the violin and the pianoforte. His favourite composer in these days was Grieg. Soon after entering Cheltenham Grammar School he read Berlioz's *Orchestration* and with no further instruction started to set Macaulay's 'Horatius' to music for chorus and orchestra. However, his father discouraged composition and wished him to be a virtuoso pianist, but neuritis prevented this and at the age of seventeen he was allowed to study counterpoint with G. F. Sims of Oxford.

In 1892 Holst obtained his first professional engagement as organist of Wyck Rissington, Gloucestershire. At the same time he conducted a choral society at the neighbouring Bourton-on-the-Water. Next year saw the first public performance of his work in Cheltenham, the music for an operetta, *Lansdowne Castle*. As a result of this success his father sent him to the Royal College of Music where he studied composition with (Sir) C. V. Stanford. At this time he got to know the later works of Wagner and heard Bach's B minor Mass; thenceforth Bach and Wagner became his passion until in later years the influence of English folk-song and of the Tudor composers tended to weaken the Wagnerian supremacy although Bach was never dethroned.

Meanwhile Holst had made himself proficient on the trombone and was able to eke out his modest allowance by playing on seaside piers and in a 'Viennese' dance band. The trombone took him right into the heart of the orchestra, an experience which was the foundation of his great command of instrumentation.

In 1895 the Royal College awarded Holst a scholarship. This meant free tuition but only £30 a year for 'maintenance' and his life at this time, partly on principle, but chiefly from necessity, was almost unbelievably frugal. Owing to this his neuritis became so bad that he could not hold an ordinary pen and his eyesight suffered severely. These two weaknesses persisted throughout his life. Out of his poverty, however, there grew indirectly his love of the English country. He could not afford train journeys and used to walk to his various destinations. His habit of long walks never left him. They were his relaxation after a spell of hard work and a prelude to new periods of inspiration.

In 1898 Holst became first trombone and *répétiteur* to the Carl Rosa Opera Company and shortly after joined the Scottish Orchestra as second trombone. Thus ended his *status pupillaris*. His student compositions had grown in competence but, although his intimate friends saw something beneath the surface, his work did not, in itself, show great originality or force. Strangely enough the germ of the future Holst seems to be found in his early children's operettas; otherwise he was content, unconsciously perhaps, to lay the foundations of that incomparable sureness of touch and clarity of texture which mark his mature writing.

It was now that Holst discovered the feeling of unity with his fellow men which made him afterwards a great teacher. A sense of comradeship rather than political conviction led him, while still a student, to join the Kelmscott House Socialist Club in Hammersmith. Here he met Isobel, daughter of an artist Augustus Ralph Harrison, and he married her in 1901. They had one daughter, Imogen, who followed her father's footsteps as composer and teacher.

Mysticism had always attracted Holst, and he had read Walt Whitman and Ibsen. In 1899 with no other training than a little 'grammar school' Latin he learnt enough Sanskrit to make translations of the Vedic hymns for musical setting. On these followed the *opera di camera*, 'Savitri' (1908), also on a Sanskrit subject: this was first performed at the London School of Opera under Mr. Hermann Grunebaum in 1916. These works, although mature, were but a foreshadowing of something greater—'The Hymn of Jesus'—written in 1917 and first performed at the Queen's Hall in 1920.

In 1903, although still comparatively unknown, Holst decided to give up the trombone and devote himself to writing music. He soon found that man cannot live by composition alone and he became music teacher at the James Allen Girls' School, Dulwich, and at the Passmore Edwards (later the Mary Ward) Settlement, where he gave the first English performances of several Bach cantatas. In 1905 he was appointed director of music at St. Paul's Girls' School, Hammersmith. Here he did away with the childish sentimentality which schoolgirls were supposed to appreciate and substituted Bach and Vittoria; a splendid background for immature minds. In 1913 a sound-proof music room was built at the school where he could work undisturbed. The first work written in these rooms was the 'St. Paul's' suite for strings (1913) dedicated to the school orchestra.

St. Paul's was a clean slate, but at Morley College for Working Men and Women in South London, where Holst became musical director in 1907, a bad tradition had to be broken down. The results were at first discouraging, but soon a new spirit appeared and the music of Morley College, together with its off-shoot the 'Whitsuntide festival' held at Thaxted, Essex, and elsewhere, became a force to be reckoned with. The 'Holst' room stands as a memorial to his work there which was carried on in the same spirit by his successors.

The year 1914 marked the inception of Holst's most famous work, 'The Planets', a suite for orchestra, each movement being suggested by the astrological attribute of a planet. This was completed in 1917. A private performance was given in 1918 under (Sir) Adrian Boult as a parting present to the composer on his departure to the Near East. The war had brought Holst great misery; he tried in vain to enlist and he began to think that he was useless; then the Young Men's Christian Association invited him to organize music for the troops in Salonika. In view of this official appointment he decided to discard the prefix 'von' from his name. He returned after a successful year abroad to find, rather to his dismay, that he was becoming a popular composer. The American orchestras were fighting for the first public performance of 'The Planets' which was produced at the Queen's Hall in 1919 and followed there by 'The Hymn of Jesus' in 1920.

Holst went back to his sound-proof room and in 1919 composed the 'Ode to Death' (a setting of a poem by Whitman), considered by many to be his most beautiful choral work. He also finished in 1922 his opera *The Perfect Fool*. This was played to a crowded house at Covent Garden in 1923. The audience was puzzled and did not understand his peculiar sense of humour, so well appreciated by his friends. However, the splendid ballet music has remained in the repertoire.

From 1919 to 1924 Holst was professor of composition at the Royal College of Music and he held a similar post at University College, Reading, from 1919 to 1923. An accident while conducting at Reading caused concussion. Disregarding this he went to America in 1923 in order to conduct at the musical festival at the university of Michigan at Ann Arbor, but on his return his old enemy, insomnia, became alarming and he was ordered complete rest. This enabled him soon to restart composing, first an opera, *At the Boar's Head*, founded on the Falstaff scenes of *Henry the Fourth*, and set almost entirely to English dance tunes (produced by the British National Opera Company at Manchester in 1925), and second and more important, the 'Keats' choral symphony, written for the Leeds festival of 1925. Its strength and power were obvious but it had no popular success and an entirely inadequate performance in London did not help it. Holst's dread of popularity seemed to drive him back upon himself. A certain aloofness appeared in his music; for instance, in 'Egdon Heath' (1927, first performed in 1928), written as a homage to Thomas Hardy. Even those who understood him best found it difficult to assimilate at first, although they are gradually coming round to the composer's own opinion, that this was his best work. However, some gracious smaller compositions belong to this period, notably the seven part-songs for women's voices (1925–1926), settings of poems by his friend Robert Bridges.

Holst's position as a composer is testified to by the Holst festival held in his native town of Cheltenham in 1927 and by the award of the gold medal of the Royal Philharmonic Society in 1930. He was also invited to lecture at Harvard University and to conduct his own compositions in Boston. This (his third) visit to the United States of America (1932) was interrupted by illness, but he recovered quickly and he returned to England apparently well though without some of his old energy. At this time he wrote the six choral canons which are a puzzle to many although some have succeeded in plucking out the heart of their mystery.

In these later years Holst's constant companion was his daughter, and whenever they could meet, he and his lifelong friend, Dr. Ralph Vaughan Williams, would spend whole days discussing their compositions. Holst declared that his music was influenced by that of his friend: the converse is certainly true.

Holst again fell ill in 1932, although he was able in 1933 to write the 'Lyric Movement' for Mr. Lionel Tertis, the violist. He died in London of heart failure following an operation 25 May 1934. His ashes were buried in Chichester Cathedral, close to the memorial to Thomas Weelkes whose music he greatly loved.

Holst's music has been called cold and inhuman: it is only cold from its burning intensity. It is true that he sometimes seemed to be living in a world removed from human beings, but he never lost touch with his fellow men.

A portrait of Holst, by Bernard Munns, is in Cheltenham Public Library, and a drawing, by Sir William Rothenstein (1920), is at Morley College.

[Imogen Holst, *Gustav Holst*, 1938 (chronological lists of compositions, and portraits); *Grove's Dictionary of Music and Musicians*, 4th ed., vol. ii, edited by H. C. Colles; *Music and Letters*, July and October 1920; *Musical Times*, July 1934; personal knowledge.]

R. VAUGHAN WILLIAMS

published 1949

BAIRSTOW Edward Cuthbert

(1874–1946)

Sir

Musician, was born at Huddersfield 22 August 1874, the eldest child and only son of James Oates Bairstow, wholesale clothier, and his wife, Elizabeth Adeline Watson. His father had a tenor voice and was a member of the Huddersfield Choral Society. Bairstow was educated at the High School, Nottingham, where his grandparents lived, until in 1889 his father retired and the family removed to London where he attended the Grocers' Company School at Hackney Downs, and later had coaching from a private tutor. In Huddersfield he was taught the organ by Henry Parratt (brother of Sir Walter Parratt), and in Nottingham by Arthur Page. Soon after arrival in London he had lessons from John Farmer, then organist of Balliol College, Oxford, and later (1892–9) he was a pupil of Sir Frederick Bridge, organist of Westminster Abbey. During this time he became organist of All Saints' church, Norfolk Square, Paddington. In 1894 he obtained the degree of B.Mus. at Durham University, proceeding D.Mus. in 1900. In 1899 on Bridge's recommendation he was appointed organist of Wigan parish church and conducted the choral society there and also at Blackburn. In 1906 he was appointed to the more important post at Leeds parish church. In addition to his church duties he had a busy life teaching, lecturing, performing, composing, and travelling each week to Preston and Blackburn to conduct the choral societies. At the Leeds triennial Festival in 1907 he was official organist under the conductorship of Sir Charles Stanford.

Another chapter of his life began in 1913 when he became organist and master of the choir at York Minster where he remained until his death. The increased duties of his cathedral work made it impossible for him to continue conducting the choral societies in Lancashire but, now that his reputation as a choral trainer was established, he accepted the invitation to conduct the York Musical Society, the Bradford Festival Chorus, and the Leeds Philharmonic Society. At York Minster Bairstow's devoted work with the choir and music generally became well known and widely appreciated and perhaps reached the highest level of excellence during the 1300th celebrations in 1927.

Meanwhile he had become known as a judge at musical competition festivals in this country, and in 1928 he also judged in Canada. His natural ability, teaching experience, and fearless judgements had a stimulating effect on the movement. He was much in demand, although he realized that he was not 'popular'; consequently he often remarked 'I have judged at every competition festival in the country—*once*.'

On the death of Joseph Cox Bridge in 1929 Bairstow accepted the chair of music at Durham University, his alma mater. The professorship at that time was non-resident and he was able to continue his work at York Minster. At Durham he set himself to raise the standard of the degree in music. In 1932 he was knighted, and he received the honorary degree of Litt.D. (1936) from Leeds and D.Mus. (1945) from Oxford. For various periods he held office as president of musical bodies such as the Incorporated Society of Musicians and the Royal College of Organists; of the latter he was for many years an examiner and member of the council.

Probably Bairstow's chief influence was through his many pupils. He was a born teacher. His success was due to his uncanny insight into the problems of teaching, to his sympathy, patience, perseverance, enthusiasm to stimulate the imagination of the pupil, appreciation of honest work done, and above all to his great love of music. His courage, forthright speech, and transparent sincerity made him greatly beloved by many, even though it was sometimes misunderstood by and embarrassing to a few.

He published two textbooks on music, and one on singing written in collaboration with his friend H. Plunket Greene. His published compositions include church and organ music, songs, part-songs, and chamber music. For the coronation of King George VI in 1937 he wrote the introit.

In 1902 he married Edith Harriet, daughter of John Thomas Hobson, a government inspector of alkali works. They had a happy married life, and their home at York became well known for its generous hospitality and good friendship, which was shared by many, especially fellow artists. They had two sons and a daughter. Bairstow died at York 1 May 1946.

Coleridge-Taylor

[*Musical Times*, August 1944; an unfinished autobiography in manuscript; private information; personal knowledge.]

ERNEST BULLOCK

published 1959

COLERIDGE-TAYLOR Samuel (1875–1912)

Musical composer, was born in London at 15 Theobalds Road, Holborn, 15 August 1875. His father, Dr. Paul Taylor, was a native of Sierra Leone. He was brought up by his mother, Alice, *née* Hare, at Croydon, where he lived practically all his life and where he died. His mother was poor, and Coleridge-Taylor's education began at an elementary school where his musical ability was sufficiently evident for the schoolmaster to get him admitted into the choir of St. George's Presbyterian church, Croydon. Education might have gone no farther but for the interest of Colonel Herbert Walters, who discovered the boy's talent, removed him into the choir of St. Mary's church, Addiscombe, and in 1891 sent him as a student of the violin to the Royal College of Music. Here he came under the notice of (Sir) Charles Villiers Stanford, who advised him to take to composition as his principal study. In 1893 he won a scholarship at the College. He held it for four years, and during that time gained general recognition as one of the most talented of young composers. Over twenty of his works were first heard at College concerts, including a string quartet in D minor, a clarinet quintet (which so greatly impressed Joseph Joachim that he led a performance of it in Berlin in 1897), a nonet for piano, wind, and strings, and three movements of a symphony in A minor. As a composition pupil of Stanford, Coleridge-Taylor was firmly grounded in the classics, but even in these student days his highest admiration was given to the music of Dvořák, whom he loved to extol above Brahms. Spontaneity of melody, piquancy of rhythm, and glowing colour meant more to him than the subtle intellectualities of the great Germans.

Coleridge-Taylor had surrendered his scholarship when, on 11 November 1898, the concert was given, at the College, which produced his 'Hiawatha's Wedding Feast' and made him famous. Sir Hubert Parry wrote (*Musical Times*, October 1912): 'It had got abroad in some unaccountable and mysterious manner that something of unusual interest was going to happen, and when the time came for the concert the "tin tabernacle" (i.e. the temporary concert hall of the Royal College of Music) was besieged by eager crowds, a large proportion of whom were shut out, but accommodation was found for Sir Arthur Sullivan and other musicians of eminence. Expectation was not disappointed, and "Hiawatha" started on a career which, when confirmed by the production of "The Death of Minnehaha" at the North Staffordshire festival in the following year (1899) and of a final section by the Royal Choral Society in 1900, established it as one of the most universally beloved works of modern English music.'

The production of the whole work by the Royal Choral Society at the Albert Hall on 22 March 1900 set the seal on Coleridge-Taylor's unique achievement, and he was asked to compose for one festival after another. But he could never find another book with just that simplicity of narrative, that naïve human interest combined with exotic imagery, which made Longfellow his ideal partner in song. 'The Blind Girl of Castel Cuillé' (Leeds 1901), 'Meg Blane' (Sheffield 1902), and an oratorio 'The Atonement' (Hereford 1903) were all failures in comparison with 'Hiawatha'. The only later choral work which came near to that ideal fitness between words and music was 'A Tale of Old Japan' (London 1911). Here a poem by Alfred Noyes provided the composer with a story and an 'atmosphere', the two things which he needed from words. The stage offered a similar impetus to his genius, and the incidental music which he wrote to a series of plays by Stephen Phillips, produced at His Majesty's Theatre—*Herod* 1900, *Ulysses* 1902, *Nero* 1906, *Faust* 1908—was successful because of his power of giving vivid musical characterization to externals. The personal factor, too, was easily recognizable in his purely instrumental music from the early ballade in A minor to the 'Othello' suite, the 'Hiawatha' ballet music (distinct from the cantata), and the violin concerto which were among his latest works. The 'catchy' rhythmic phrase and its repetition in varied tones, the capacity for indulging unrestrainedly in the simple human emotions of joy and sorrow without reflection and without cant, are the qualities which come from his negro ancestry.

In appearance and manners Coleridge-Taylor was very much of his father's race. There was a sweetness and modesty of nature which was instantly lovable. Success made him happy but he was easily cast down. He had little power of self-criticism, but sometimes he would accept the criticism of others too readily. In his student days on one occasion when his work had been sharply criticized by his teacher, the manuscript was found by a fellow-student thrown aside in the waiting-room of the College as not worth carrying home. It was only after his best work had been done that he conceived a desire to study African negro music and to become its apostle by composing works on native folk themes. His later publications show that he did this to a considerable extent, but it is noteworthy that after having planned the violin concerto which he wrote for the Norfolk (Connecticut) festival on these lines, he redrafted it in a more original style. His visits to America no doubt did something to awaken his racial sentiment, though he was received there, especially by his host, Mr. Carl Stoeckel, in the most warm and generous spirit. He was also stimulated in this direction by the example of Dvořák's group of works 'From the New World', but he lacked the stamina to become the leader of a movement. His compositions amount to 82 opus numbers, with many to which no number is assigned, and amongst them there is much that is ephemeral. But 'Hiawatha' holds its own, and twenty-five years after its production it was given in the form of a pageant opera in the arena of the Albert Hall (19 May 1924 and again in 1925), the composer's son, Hiawatha Coleridge-Taylor, taking part as conductor of the ballet.

Coleridge-Taylor married in 1899 Jessie, daughter of Major Walter Walmisley, a member of the same family as the composer and organist, Thomas Forbes Walmisley, and the musician, Thomas Attwood Walmisley. There were two children of the marriage, the son Hiawatha, and a daughter. Coleridge-Taylor died 1 September 1912.

[W. C. Berwick Sayers, *Samuel Coleridge-Taylor, Musician; his Life and Letters*, 1915; *Musical Times*, March 1909 and October 1912; Manuscript catalogue of compositions, by J. H. Smithers Jackson (Croydon Public Libraries); published compositions; private information; personal knowledge.]

Henry Cope Colles

published 1927

TOVEY Donald Francis

(1875–1940)

Sir

Musician, was born at Eton 17 July 1875, the youngest son of Duncan Crookes Tovey, at that time an assistant master at Eton, later rector of Worplesdon, Surrey, by his wife, Mary Fison, who came from Norfolk. Both parents were unmusical, but had remarkable literary gifts. Donald's prodigious musical aptitude was apparent at a very early age; when eight years old he is said to have embarked on composition on an extended plan. It was the acuteness of his 'ear' in childhood, and the correlation of pitch heard and pitch sung, that attracted the notice of Miss Sophie Weisse, later headmistress of a girls' school at Englefield Green. To her Tovey owed his entire upbringing and education until he was nineteen, for he never went to an ordinary boys' school; moreover it was Miss Weisse who launched him on the open seas of public music-making. These early years were more than usually important in the making of the musician, for Tovey had shown, even in childhood, his remarkable power of absorbing music, both from score and from performance, with great rapidity and an almost mathematical accuracy. It was wise policy that sent the boy to (Sir) Walter Parratt, then organist at St. George's Chapel, Windsor, for counterpoint lessons; later to James Higgs, for whom Tovey never lost his admiration; and later still at the age of thirteen to (Sir) Charles Hubert Parry, to whom he always referred as 'my master'. A visit at the age of eight or nine to Berlin, where he heard the great violinist Joseph Joachim play the Beethoven violin concerto, and also spoke with him, was an important event. Another early influence dating from boyhood which Tovey publicly acknowledged was that of the great scholar of the keyboard A. J. Hipkins. In this formative period his mind was mainly occupied by music, without, however, neglect of other spheres of knowledge; for Tovey had a strong philosophical power of thought, and more than a leaning towards astronomy and the higher mathematics, retaining to his death a fine general learning which he was able to use as a background for even his most specialist writings. That he studied the piano with Ludwig Deppe appears to be untrue, but he was brought up on his methods and supported them.

In 1894 Tovey went to Balliol College, Oxford, as the first holder of the Lewis Nettleship memorial scholarship in music, and in that same year he appeared in public at Windsor as a pianist with Joachim. At Oxford Tovey entered what was for him a new, comparatively unsheltered world. Although by nature and training shy, his abounding natural humour and an ingrained kindliness found him a place even among the athletes. He read voluminously, scores especially, and never forgot what he read. At Balliol he came into close touch with Dr. Ernest Walker, who even at that time was astonished by the accuracy and readiness of his memory in the wide range of classical music. In 1898 he graduated B.A. with classical honours; in 1921 he was awarded a doctorate of music by decree of convocation and he was elected an honorary fellow of Balliol in 1934.

No familiar musical pattern in the England of his time seemed to fit this immensely learned, deeply thinking, energetic, if absent-minded young musician. The problem of opening Tovey's career was solved by Miss Weisse who arranged for him a series of classical chamber concerts in November 1900 at the St. James's Hall, London, at which he gave not only some quite unusual chamber works of the classical school, but also played a trio and quintet of his own, with many piano solos, and wrote a series of programme notes, many of which have been reprinted. This series and another in London in 1901 were followed by recitals in Berlin and Vienna, at which Tovey played with Joachim. The year 1903 witnessed an orchestral concert, under (Sir) Henry Wood, at which he played his pianoforte concerto; this work was repeated by Hans Richter in 1906 and Tovey also played it at Aachen in 1913. All through this second period Tovey, the pianist, was playing classical chamber music with Lady Hallé, Robert Hausmann, and others. The Chelsea Concerts Society was formed in 1906 and lasted until 1912, to be succeeded by the Classical Concert Society, which was revived after the war of 1914–1918. In the middle of all this concert work came a request from the *Encyclopædia Britannica* to write the articles on music for the eleventh edition, published by the Cambridge University Press. It was a turning-point in Tovey's life, and that was a seed time for his later activities. His friendship with Mr. R. C. Trevelyan from 1905 had also brought to the surface his lifelong interest in the problems of opera, and in correspondence with the poet he was discussing 'The Bride of Dionysus' from which emerged the opera produced in Edinburgh in 1929.

In 1914 Tovey successfully applied for the Reid professorship of music in the university of Edinburgh, in succession to Frederick Niecks. He was appalled by the conflict between Germany and England, bitterly regretting the break in the exchange of musical culture between the two countries. A new venture, started in 1917, had important effects—his founding of the Reid Orchestra in Edinburgh, with students and professionals playing the great masterpieces. Tovey conducted, played, and wrote numerous occasional commentaries for programmes—now famous in their reprinted form of *Essays in Musical Analysis* (6 vols., 1935–1939). The selection was widely representative of every phase of classical music, and also of the newer developments of Elgar, Dr. Ralph Vaughan Williams, Dr. W. T. Walton, and Mr. Paul Hindemith. He originated an entirely new system of university training in music, worked enthusiastically at his lectures and his orchestra, kept up his active piano-playing, and in short blossomed out into one of the greatest personalities in the musical world of his day. He visited California in 1924–5–6, New York and Boston in 1926 and 1928, Barcelona in 1928 and 1934. He conducted a voluminous if sporadic correspondence. He lectured at Glasgow, Liverpool, Oxford, and elsewhere; broadcast several series of talks; edited (1931) Bach's 'Kunst der Fuge', finishing the last incomplete fugue and writing a rich commentary on the whole; continually absorbing music by some process of study unknown to ordinary musicians. He finished the opera, and he wrote in 1933 a 'cello concerto for Señor Pablo Casals (performed in 1934 and 1937). All this, added to his constant university work, brought on illnesses and an increasing rheumatic disability of the hands, which crippled him in his last years. He died in Edinburgh 10 July 1940. A previous union was declared null; he married in 1925 Clara Georgina, youngest daughter of Richard Wallace, merchant, of Edinburgh: there was no issue of the marriage. He was knighted in 1935.

As a pianist Tovey was without question in the first rank among players of his day, though he never embarked upon a virtuoso's career. He played chamber music with the most eminent artists only (Joachim and his quartet, Lady Hallé, Hausmann, Casals, Madame Suggia, the sisters d'Aranyi), and covered a wide area in his performances. Interested in the problems of piano-playing (one of the first indeed to play the double-keyboard-action piano of Emanuel Moor) he seemed to unfold and expound each work—its history, shape, and meaning—as he played. His philosophy of art held that each work can have perfection, and, if a great work, is perfect. As a composer he wrote, consciously, in the idiom of the German classics and has been, perhaps, unduly neglected. Yet good judges have accounted his opera to be a masterpiece of dramatic declamation and of instrumentation, and the 'cello concerto, long though it is, has magnificence.

Although five years after his death he is known chiefly as a musical historian and commentator, the writing of prose was always a secondary interest in Tovey's mind. He planned books, but never made a whole one himself. He had dreams of a complete treatise of musical instruction in four volumes, but wrote none of it. He wrote prose to assist the occasion of music, to expound music, or to clarify it, and he was surprised, and not entirely pleased, at his universal acceptance as a writer. Actually he wrote for the moment, and his writings should be classed as 'occasional', although, collected, they make a large corpus of musical learning. Apart from his profound knowledge, his sense of exploration, his deep beliefs, and examples, always apt, illustrating what he knew were more than theories, Tovey's writings are characterized, like his talk, by a brilliant and allusive humour, by reference to authors before unthought of as contributing to the practice of his art (e.g. Lewis Carroll), by the creed already mentioned that a work can, and ought to, be perfect, and by that rare continuity of thought which comes from an ever-ready mind.

Those who were not able to be his pupils at Edinburgh University may get some sense of Tovey as a teacher by reading his books assiduously and with proper humour. His work at Edinburgh was conspicuous in the history of musical instruction in Great Britain, for it was alike theoretical (in the learned meaning) and practical (in the musical). His conducting of the Reid Orchestra, not always with very good forces to command, was vivid and intensely musical.

Joachim accounted Tovey the most learned man in music that had ever lived: on the ground that he knew it all, and that nowadays there is more to know. He was capable at any moment of playing any printed classical work on the piano, whether it were written for five or ten or a hundred instruments, and whether he could ever have heard it or not. But he was far removed from the antiquary, nor did he care greatly for musicians' lives.

Tovey was a tall, large man, in youth slender and ascetic-looking, but becoming in appearance more robust as he grew older. His eyes would wander at times, as if he were thinking of something else than the subject under discussion (for Tovey discussed interminably). Yet this was not inattention: he was seeking for the modern instance, in literature or elsewhere. When he digressed from his arguments (as he did at enormous length) it was found that the deviations were perfectly apposite and illuminating. His reading, outside music, consisted of detective stories, humorous works of all grades, especially verse (he set Lear and Hilaire Belloc brilliantly to music), the *Encyclopædia Britannica*, and any book containing information about the arts. His upbringing led him towards Beethoven as the principal star in his galaxy; but in the end he came to love Haydn most of all, and he was very sympathetic towards the less formally rhythmic music of Palestrina and of the English Tudor masters.

A portrait of Tovey by Otto Schlapp hangs in the music classroom of Edinburgh University. Two portraits by P. A. de László and other pictures hang in the Donald Tovey Memorial Rooms in Buccleuch Place, Edinburgh, dedicated by Dr. Sophie Weisse to his memory, with an endowment in the keeping of the university. His library is also there, in classrooms used by the faculty of music.

[Preface by E. Walker to Sir D. F. Tovey, *A Musician Talks* (edited by H. J. Foss), 2 vols., 1941; *Music Review*, February 1942; private information; personal knowledge.]

HUBERT J. FOSS

published 1949

KETÈLBEY Albert William

(1875–1959)

Composer, was born 9 August 1875 in Aston Manor, Birmingham, the son of George Henry Ketèlbey, engraver, and his wife, Sarah Ann Aston. As a young boy he showed a remarkable talent for music and proficiency on the piano. At the age of eleven he composed a piano sonata which he performed publicly at the Worcester town hall and which earned in later years the praise of Sir Edward Elgar. Realizing the boy's promise his parents allowed him, after preliminary study in Birmingham, to compete for a scholarship at Trinity College, London. He came out many marks above the other entrants and at the age of thirteen was installed at the college as Queen Victoria scholar for composition. At the age of sixteen he was appointed organist of St. John's church, Wimbledon, and while there continued his composition studies.

After four years of organist's work, carried on mostly while still a student, Ketèlbey went on tour as conductor of a light opera company and at the age of twenty-two he was appointed musical director of the Vaudeville Theatre in the Strand. Although Ketèlbey's most notable work was in the sphere of light music, he also composed some serious music, including a quintet for wood-wind and piano, which won the Sir Michael Costa prize; a string quartet; an overture for full orchestra; a suite for orchestra; and a Concertstück for solo piano and orchestra; all of which had London performances.

But it was with the publication of pieces like 'Phantom Melody' (which won a prize offered by Van Biene), 'In a Monastery Garden', 'In a Persian Market', 'Sanctuary of the Heart', that Ketèlbey came into his own during the twenties as foremost British light composer of his day. To his music he brought the capacity to invent popular melodies with a character of their own. He was well equipped to write for the orchestra (he could play the cello, clarinet, oboe, and horn) and his orchestrations are colourful and well balanced. In Ketèlbey's day light music tended to be picturesque and romantic and it was performed principally in the palm courts of luxury hotels, in cafés and liners, and in the silent cinema. Most of his pieces have a programme-synopsis.

He was particularly successful as a composer of 'atmospheric' music specially written to accompany silent films, a highly profitable source of income in the days when every cinema of pretension employed a 'live' orchestra. His pieces appeared in the 'Loose Leaf Film Play Music Series' and included such titles as 'Dramatic Agitato', 'Amaryllis' (is suitable for use in dainty, fickle scenes), 'Mystery' (greatly in favour for uncanny and weird picturizations), 'Agitato Furioso' (famous for its excellence in playing to riots, storms, wars, etc.).

Other works by Ketèlbey were the concert pieces: 'Suite Romantique', 'Cockney Suite', and 'Chal Romano' overture; a comic opera, *The Wonder Worker*; and in lighter vein 'Gallantry', 'Wedgwood Blue', 'In the Moonlight', and 'Souvenir de Tendresse'.

His highly successful compositions enabled Ketèlbey, one of whose pseudonyms was Anton Vodorinski, to spend most of his later years in retirement in the Isle of Wight. He died at Cowes 26 November 1959.

After the death of his first wife, Charlotte Curzon, Ketèlbey married, in 1948, Mabel Maud, widow of L. S. Pritchett. He had no children.

[Private information; personal knowledge.]

MARK H. LUBBOCK

published 1971

DENT Edward Joseph

(1876–1957)

Musical scholar, was born at Ribston Hall, Yorkshire, 16 July 1876, the fourth and youngest son of John Dent Dent, barrister and for many years a member of Parliament, and his wife, Mary Hebden, daughter of John Woodall, of Scarborough. A scholar of Eton and King's College, Cambridge, Dent obtained a third class in part i of the classical tripos in 1898. He had studied music at Eton under C. H. Lloyd, and at Cambridge, where he was a pupil of Charles Wood and (Sir) Charles Stanford, he obtained his Mus.B. in 1899. In 1902–8 he was a fellow of King's College and lectured on the history of music, also teaching harmony, counterpoint, and composition. In 1926 he was appointed to the professorship of music in the university, a post which he held until 1941. During this period he reorganized the teaching of music on a broader basis, as not only the prerogative of organists and organ scholars but of those who were interested in all branches of music. His interests were numerous: at first he made a number of researches into seventeenth- and eighteenth-century Italian opera, a subject considerably neglected at that time, and published articles on it in the *Encyclopædia Britannica*, the second edition of *Grove's Dictionary of Music and Musicians*, and the *Riemann-Festschrift* of 1909. He also published a book on Alessandro Scarlatti in 1905 and another on

Mozart's operas in 1913 (2nd, revised, edition 1947). He made new translations of Mozart's *Figaro, Don Giovanni,* and *The Magic Flute* and supervised a celebrated student production of the last-named at Cambridge in 1911. His later translations included several of Verdi's operas, Berlioz's *Les Troyens*, Beethoven's *Fidelio*, and other works. He also edited and produced many works of Purcell at Cambridge, the Old Vic, the Glastonbury Festival, and elsewhere, and made a new edition of his *Dido and Aeneas* for Hamburg in 1924 which was also produced at Münster in 1926 and Stuttgart in 1927.

In 1919 Dent became the music critic of the *Athenaeum* and he was also active in the formation of the British Music Society. But he remained essentially international in outlook and it was due to him that the International Festival of Contemporary Chamber Music, held in 1922 at Salzburg, developed into the International Society for Contemporary Music, a body which has branches in many countries and gives annual festivals of modern music. He became its first president, a post he held until 1938 and again in 1945–7. He also served on the board of directors of Sadler's Wells Theatre, of which he became a governor. When the Covent Garden Opera Trust was set up in 1946 he became one of the directors and showed a very active interest in the presentation of opera of all kinds in English.

Dent wrote articles on modern English music for Adler's *Handbuch der Musik-geschichte* and on 'Social Aspects of Music in the Middle Ages' for the 1929 edition of the *Oxford History of Music*. Later he served on the editorial board of the *New Oxford History of Music*. He was an honorary doctor of music of Oxford (1932), Harvard (1936), and Cambridge (1947). He was also, in 1953, one of the first two musicians to be elected F.B.A. His other books included *Foundations of English Opera* (1928) and a masterly biography of Ferruccio Busoni (1933), a composer whom he knew well as a personal friend. His writings included many articles, forewords to books, and programme notes.

Dent composed a small number of original works, of which the most important are a set of polyphonic motets. He also made an arrangement of the *Beggar's Opera* which is much more faithful to the original than the well-known version by Frederic Austin—in fact Dent removed the preludes and codas to the songs which Austin had added unnecessarily. He also made a practical version of one of the earliest oratorios, the sacred drama *La Rappresentazione di Anima e di Corpo* of Cavalieri, *c.* 1550–1602. The first performance of this work was given in 1600 in Rome; the next recorded stage performance took place in 1949, given by the Girton Musical Society of Cambridge from Dent's edition. In 1950 Dent became the first president of the newly formed Liszt Society.

Dent was a man of immense knowledge and wide interests, but his personality was not in the least academic in the conventional sense. He inspired his pupils and widened their range of vision, and he also possessed a mordant (but never cruel) sense of humour which enabled him to puncture many inflated reputations. As president of the International Society for Contemporary Music his good sense enabled him to prevent the society being split apart by warring factions. (His account of the early days of the society, 'Looking Backward', published in *Music Today*, 1949, is a comic masterpiece.) His scholarship was always a living activity; he was always interested in promoting live performances of the music he was interested in, not merely writing articles about it in learned journals. He revived a great deal of early music at a time when the vogue for it was not nearly as marked as it later became, because he felt that this music was worth performing in the modern age for its own sake, not merely as a matter of academic interest. At the same time he kept a keen interest in modern developments, and if he did not always relish the more extreme experiments of the *avant-garde*, he was always willing to let young musicians have their say and to judge them by results. Thus he became a universally loved and respected figure, because it was felt that his judgements were entirely objective and based on knowledge and experience: even his best friends could be the target of his witty but sarcastic tongue if he felt that their work was below what they should have been able to achieve. He left his mark behind in many fields of music, not only in Cambridge, but in the whole international scene.

Dent, who was unmarried, died in London 22 August 1957. A portrait by Lawrence Gowing is at King's College, Cambridge, and the Fitzwilliam Museum has drawings by Sydney Waterlow and Edmond Kapp.

[*Grove's Dictionary of Music and Musicians*; personal knowledge.]

HUMPHREY SEARLE

published 1971

TERTIS Lionel

(1876–1975)

Viola player, was born in West Hartlepool 29 December 1876, the elder son and eldest of three children of Polish immigrants Alexander Tertis, a Jewish minister, and his wife, Phoebe Hermann. Three months later the family moved to Spitalfields where he went to the board school. His first instrument was the piano and he gave a concert when he was six. At thirteen he left home to earn a living as a pianist, and saved enough to enter Trinity College of Music in 1892, where he had violin lessons under B. M. Carrodus, continuing the piano under R. W. Lewis for three intermittent terms.

In 1895, after six months at Leipzig Conservatorium, he entered the Royal Academy of Music and studied the violin under Hans Wessely, changing to the viola in 1897. He had to teach himself, fell in love with the instrument, and dedicated his life to raising the neglected viola to full recognition as a solo instrument. Two of his friends were so inspired by his playing that they composed works for him; E. York Bowen wrote a concerto and two sonatas, and Benjamin Dale a suite.

In 1897 Tertis joined the Queen's Hall Orchestra under (Sir) Henry Wood, who promoted him to principal viola. He returned to the RAM as a sub-professor in 1899 and was appointed full professor of the viola in 1901. He left the orchestra in 1904 to concentrate on solo work, and by 1908 had made such a reputation that the Royal Philharmonic Society engaged him to play Bowen's Concerto, and in 1911 the orchestrated version of Dale's Suite under Artur Nikisch; it was in 1911 too that he gave his first performance of Bach's Chaconne, and his monumental interpretation became unsurpassed by any violinist.

In World War I he became involved with many distinguished Belgian refugee musicians, including the violinist Eugène Ysayë, who invited him to play Mozart's *Sinfonia Concertante* with him under Henry Wood. He played informal chamber music at Muriel Draper's house in Chelsea with many great artists, including Pau Casals, Alfred Cortot, Jacques Thibaud, Artur Rubinstein, and Harold Bauer. He later toured America with the Bauer Piano Quartet and played the first performance of Ernest Bloch's Suite in Washington.

Meanwhile the era of 'recording' had opened, and, accepted as the greatest exponent of the viola, he made countless recordings between 1920 and 1933, from which a selection was reissued by EMI on long-playing records in 1966 and 1974, and others by the Pearl Company in 1981. One of the highest moments in his career was in 1924 at the Albert Hall, when he performed Mozart's *Sinfonia Concertante* with Fritz Kreisler, whom he admired beyond any other violinist. He had triumphed in his task, the viola had come into its own, and none had helped him more than the composers. After Bowen and Dale came Sir Arnold Bax, Ralph Vaughan Williams, Gustav Holst, Sir Arthur Bliss, and Sir William Walton. John Ireland, Sir Edward Elgar, and Frederick Delius all sanctioned his arrangements of their works. He returned to the RAM from 1924 to 1929 to teach the viola and direct the chamber music. During this time he trained the Griller Quartet.

In 1937 fibrositis compelled him to give up playing in public, and he then directed his unabated energies (with the co-operation of the outstanding lutenist, Arthur Richardson) to the creation of the ideal viola. The first was completed in 1938, and Richardson made over a hundred himself. By 1965 there were over 600 Tertis models in existence, and in 1973 makers were producing them in seventeen countries.

In 1940 Tertis returned to the concert platform, giving charity concerts and demonstration recitals on the TM viola. He published numerous arrangements for the viola and also wrote an autobiography, *Cinderella No More* (1953), which he revised and enlarged as *My Viola and I* (1974). In 1956 he went to America to demonstrate the new viola, and two years later to South Africa. He finally retired in 1964. He succeeded in his mission because of his amazing virtuosity on the large viola, hitherto unused, and for the magnetism that seemed to flow out of that immensely strong figure, rooted to the platform like an oak tree. One became inevitably drawn into the very heart of the music he was performing.

Tertis was appointed CBE in 1950. He was also FRAM and an honorary fellow of Trinity College, London (1966). He won the Kreisler award of merit (1950), the gold medal of the Royal Philharmonic Society (1964) and of the Worshipful Company of Musicians, and the Eugène Ysayë medal and diploma of honour of the Ysayë Foundation, Brussels (1968).

In 1913 Tertis married Ada Bell (died 1951), daughter of the Revd Hugh Gawthrop. In 1959 he married the cellist Lillian Florence Margaret Warmington, daughter of Harold Henry Warmington, solicitor. He died in his Wimbledon home 22 February 1975.

[Lionel Tertis, *My Viola and I*, 1974 (autobiography); *Times Educational Supplement*, 14 December 1974; personal knowledge.]

BERNARD SHORE

published 1986

GARDINER Henry Balfour

(1877–1950)

Composer, was born in London 7 November 1877, the son of Henry John Gardiner, merchant, and his wife, Clara Elizabeth Honey. Gardiner showed from the first a notable talent for music, which was encouraged by his family as part of a normal education at Charterhouse and New College, Oxford, where he obtained a second class in honour moderations (1898) and a fourth in *literae humaniores* (1900). His musical training in the more advanced stages was completed by two periods of study at Frankfurt under Ivan Knorr, at that time a busy and successful teacher. There Gardiner was the centre of a group of young musicians who afterwards did much for English music, among them Mr. Cyril Scott, Mr. Percy Grainger, Roger Quilter, and Norman O'Neill. Although he was never in a full sense one of the 'Frankfurt Group', Frederick Delius was much associated in later years with these artists. From his studies with Knorr, Gardiner returned, as Grainger has said, 'a magnificent pianist, a resourceful conductor ... a thoroughly practical music-maker, and ... one of the most inspired composers of his generation.'

From 1900 onwards Gardiner produced a steady output of music, including a Symphony (1908), an Overture, and many smaller pieces. Important among these early works are a Quartet and a Quintet for strings, and a ballad for chorus and orchestra called 'News from Whydah' (1912) which secured wide popularity. Other works for chorus and orchestra are the specially beautiful 'April' (1912) and 'Philomena' (1923). A projected opera on the subject of Thomas Hardy's story 'The Three Strangers' was never completed, despite the fact that a great deal of work was done upon it. An extract from the music, however, entitled 'Shepherd Fennel's Dance', became very popular and has proved to be Gardiner's most frequently played, although by no means his most characteristic, composition. Some of his most personal music is to be found among his songs and the shorter pieces for pianoforte.

Gardiner's music is firm in design, masterly in effectiveness, warm in colour, and impassioned in feeling. He had learnt in Frankfurt how to use the full resources of the post-Wagnerian orchestra, and if he was to some extent, like Grainger and Delius, influenced by Grieg, he was also much affected by the English folk-songs, of which in the early days of the revival he was an active collector.

At the outbreak of war in 1914 Gardiner's career was at its height, and he returned from the army five years later in the full intention of resuming it. He found, however, that in the intervening years the musical climate had changed. The warm romanticism of pre-war days had given way to the more austere and intellectual atmosphere that is found in the later works of Gustav Holst and in the period of Ralph Vaughan Williams's Mass in G minor. This mood was foreign to Gardiner's temperament: and the realization of this, coupled with his naturally self-critical character, led him to renounce music with almost dramatic suddenness. He devoted himself exclusively to the country pursuits in which he was always interested and had the means to enjoy, and after 1924 he wrote no more music.

Gardiner influenced the music of his generation by his ready appreciation of other men's work as well as by the quality of his own. His enterprising spirit and his wealth enabled him to initiate and support some influential musical activities, including many large-scale London orchestral concerts at which important works by his contemporaries were produced. The full story of his beneficent activities cannot be told, but these were great, and many distinguished artists, including Holst and Delius, were helped by them. This generosity, like Gardiner's energy of action and utterance, was the expression of a rich and abundant nature. In everything Gardiner was a character. His judgements and reactions were decided, individual, and totally uninfluenced by the opinions of the majority or by academic considerations. He was loved by many friends. He died, unmarried, at Salisbury 28 June 1950.

[Private information; personal knowledge.]

THOMAS ARMSTRONG

published 1959

SCHOLES Percy Alfred

(1877–1958)

Musical writer and encyclopedist, was born at Headingley, Leeds, 24 July 1877, the third child of Thomas Scholes, commercial agent, and his wife, Katharine Elizabeth Pugh. Ill health limited his attendance at school (he was a lifelong sufferer from severe bronchitis), but he gave much time to miscellaneous reading and the assiduous study of the elements of music. After a couple of years earning 10*s.* a week as assistant librarian of the Yorkshire College (later the university of Leeds), he taught music at Kent College, Canterbury (1901), and Kingswood College, Grahamstown, South Africa (1904). On his return to England at the age of twenty-eight his career began to take a more definite direction. He became an extension lecturer to the university of Manchester on what was coming to be known as 'musical appreciation', and continued in this way very successfully for the next six years. Meanwhile he took his A.R.C.M. diploma and (after a false start at Durham) entered St. Edmund Hall, Oxford, gaining his B.Mus. in 1908.

In 1907, following a series of lectures for the Co-operative Holidays Association, he formed the Home Music Study Union, whose organ, *The Music Student* (in later years *The Music Teacher*), he edited from its foundation in 1908 until 1921. He married in 1908 and in 1912 made the decisive step of moving to London, his only guaranteed income being £40 a year as assistant to J. S. Shedlock, music critic of the *Queen*. With the support of such men as H. C. Colles and (Sir) Percy Buck, he was soon making his mark as a journalist and as an extension lecturer for the universities of Oxford, Cambridge, and London. From 1913 to 1920 he was music critic of the *Evening Standard*.

When war broke out in 1914 he was on a lecture tour of colleges in the United States and Canada. On his return he headed, until 1919, the 'music for the troops' section of the Y.M.C.A. in France, further developing his twin gifts of detailed organization and the ability to hold the attention of the unpractised listener. From this work came his very successful *Listener's Guide to Music* (1919).

Early in 1920 he became music critic of the *Observer*, following the abrupt departure of Ernest Newman who had accepted a substantial offer from the rival *Sunday Times*. For the next five years Scholes filled the position with notable success. His style, always fluent and readable, gained distinction. He continued to regard his role as primarily that of an educator, and was undoubtedly among the first to see the educational potentialities of broadcasting, the gramophone, and the player-piano. He gave a weekly radio talk commenting on the previous week's broadcasts: from 1926 to 1928 he was musical editor of the *Radio Times*. He was usually at work on several books at once. His home was a busy office with as many as six or more typists and co-workers, including his devoted wife.

A contract to provide pianola roll annotations for the Aeolian Company provided him with the means to detach himself from journalism. In 1928 he moved to Switzerland, and thenceforward lived in the neighbourhood of Montreux. The following year he organized an 'Anglo-American Music Educators' Conference' at Lausanne, which was repeated in 1931. He made four further lecture tours of the United States. He was now able to give time to more solid scholarship and his thesis on 'The Puritans and Music' gained him in 1934 his D.ès L. from Lausanne University.

For some time Scholes had planned a more comprehensive work, tentatively called 'Everyone's Musical Encyclopedia', for the great new body of listeners brought into being by radio and the gramophone. The book finally appeared as the *Oxford Companion to Music* in the autumn of 1938. Scholes's varied experience as teacher, lecturer, journalist, critic, and scholar was at last drawn together in one accomplishment—'the most extraordinary range of musical knowledge, ingeniously "self-indexed", ever written and assembled between two covers by one man' (*Grove*).

In 1940 he made his way to England just before the fall of France; his wartime homes were first at Aberystwyth, then at Oxford, where he was elected to the board of the faculty of music. He completed a monumental biography of Dr. Charles Burney (2 vols., 1948, James Tait Black memorial prize), a model of humane scholarship, and continued his lexicographical labours with his *Concise Oxford Dictionary of Music* (1952) and *Oxford Junior Companion to Music* (1954). After the war he returned to Switzerland, and built a house at Clarens. In 1950 the devaluation of the pound drove him back to Oxford, where he spent the next six years losing inch by inch his battle against the complications in his lifelong bronchitis brought on by advancing age and an inimical climate. Every winter he returned to Switzerland; and there, at Vevey, he died, 31 July 1958. He was survived by his wife, Dora Wingate, daughter of Richard Lean, civil engineer. There were no children.

Scholes was of middle height, and although not robust, an active walker. He worked long hours with great concentration, with methodical interruptions for exercise. His conscience was strongly protestant, totally divorced from any conventional religious expression. He was warmly humanitarian; a long-standing and articulate vegetarian and opponent of blood sports. There were those for whom his clarity of thought, total absence of humbug and affectation, and ironic humour made him seem something of a philistine. He was charitable in good causes, warm and generous in personal dealings, at the same time disinclined to give ground in business matters. Traces of his native Yorkshire speech remained with him to the end. In a letter to his publisher he once wrote, 'the epitaph I should desire for myself, were it not already applied to another and a greater man, would be "The common people heard him gladly".'

Scholes valued his well-earned academic distinctions which in addition to those already mentioned included: from Oxford the honorary degree of D.Mus. (1943), M.A. (by decree, 1944), and D.Litt. (1950), and from Leeds an honorary Litt.D. (1953). He was an honorary fellow and trustee of St. Edmund Hall, Oxford; an officer of the Star of Romania (1930), F.S.A. (1938), and O.B.E. (1957). His remarkable library, one of the largest of its kind in private hands, was acquired by the National Library of Canada, Ottawa.

[Private information; personal knowledge.]

John Owen Ward

published 1971

BOUGHTON Rutland

(1878–1960)

Composer, was born in Aylesbury 23 January 1878, the eldest child of William Rutland Boughton, grocer, and his wife, Grace Martha Bishop. He was educated at the Aylesbury Endowed School, and throughout his childhood his mother encouraged his obvious devotion to music. Before his fourteenth year he conceived a cycle of music dramas on the life of Jesus, to be enacted by soloists with the choir of the local Sacred Harmonic Society grouped round three sides of a raised platform. This conception of choral drama was his unique contribution to English music. He had never been in a theatre, but he had seen at the seaside a concert party on a raised platform, had been given Shakespeare's plays as a school prize, and had heard oratorio. It also enabled him to write music on Sunday without offending the family conscience. In the same year, 1892, he was apprenticed to the concert agency of Cecil Barth. His employer was lenient to his shortcomings and generous with material and artistic help.

In 1898 he was accepted by (Sir) Charles Stanford at the Royal College of Music. His formal education had been scanty, but his musical experience, obtained in complete isolation, was already greater than that of his fellow students, and perhaps of his teachers. This self-education did not, unfortunately, at any time include self-criticism.

In 1901 he left the College as the fund raised for his studies was exhausted. He failed as a music journalist, and, nearing starvation, accompanied singing lessons for David Ffrangcon Davies and filled in wind parts on the harmonium in the pit of the Haymarket Theatre.

Nevertheless, in 1903 he married Florence Hobley. In 1905 (Sir) Granville Bantock offered him a post in the Midland Institute in Birmingham, where he was greatly influenced by the activities of Bishop Gore and Father Adderley.

In 1907 Boughton met Reginald Buckley, poet and journalist, who had vague ideas, born of Wagnerian influences, of a music drama of the Arthurian legend. Boughton had also visualized such a scheme in his childhood's *Jesus* drama. Together in 1911 they produced a booklet *Music-Drama of the Future*. Boughton's essay, though naïve and high-flown in language, urged his point that 'the Wagnerian drama lacks just that channel of musical expression which is absolutely necessary to the English people', namely choral singing.

At that moment, Boughton's personal life became complicated. His marriage was ended in 1910 by a deed of separation—divorce was beyond his means—and he joined his life with that of Christina Walshe, an art student in Birmingham, who was a member of Boughton's Literary and Musical Fellowship. Christina's home background had been as strict as Boughton's own, but their ideas of 'social freedom' were alike. Local scandals and reproaches were inevitable and they left Birmingham, but Boughton's complete candour overcame many objections. He had the capacity for demanding and retaining the support of many distinguished friends, among them G. B. Shaw.

In the spring of 1913 Buckley and Boughton settled on Glastonbury as the Bayreuth of their new Arthurian enterprise. The first performance of the first Glastonbury Festival was held on 5 August 1914, the war taking precedence by twenty-four hours. The annual festival was suspended after 1916 when Boughton was called up, to become ultimately band-master in the Royal Flying Corps of which (Sir) Walford Davies had been appointed director of music. The festivals were resumed in 1919.

In 1921 (Sir) Barry Jackson put on Boughton's *The Immortal Hour*, an opera based on the Celtic drama by Fiona Macleod, and first performed at Glastonbury in 1914, at his repertory theatre in Birmingham. Encouraged by its success, he offered a London production, to which Boughton agreed unwillingly, as he thought the sophistication of a normal theatre would destroy its magic. In fact, it ran from October 1922 for 216 performances and was revived in 1923, 1926, and 1932, making a total of some 500 performances in London alone. This work and *Bethlehem* (1915), based on the Coventry mystery, represent the only marketable successes of Boughton's music.

Two other works achieved a temporary success: a translation of *Alkestis* by Gilbert Murray in 1922 and *Queen of Cornwall* (1924) by Thomas Hardy, both produced at Glastonbury. These two works may be said to reflect Boughton's domestic problems which in 1923 culminated in the rupture of his union with Christina and an alliance with Kathleen Davis, a senior pupil at his new school at Glastonbury.

In 1926 Glastonbury was finally abandoned, both as a festival and as a home, and the family settled at Kilcote, near Gloucester, Boughton working a small-holding with some success and deeply absorbed in composition. He was granted a Civil List pension in 1938 under the newly established rules enabling 'men of genuine distinction to continue their work without the haunting fear of immediate penury'.

Boughton's political and personal creed governed his life and influenced his music, which tempts the reader to marvel at its naïvety, from which, however, it derives its peculiar strength. He wrote in all forms, but more than half his output remained in manuscript, deposited in the British Museum. His literary remains, other than the libretti of the music dramas, are contained in two propaganda pamphlets of 1911 and two full-scale books on music: *Bach* (1907, revised ed. 1930) and *The Reality of Music* (1934). The journalistic articles have not been collected.

Boughton died in London 25 January 1960. His portrait (1911) by Christina Walshe became the possession of his son-in-law Christopher Ede, husband of Joy Boughton (died 1963), oboist, who alone of his children (three sons and five daughters) made a name for herself in music.

[Michael Hurd, *Immortal Hour*, 1962; personal knowledge.]

STEUART WILSON

published 1971

BRIDGE Frank

(1879–1941)

Musician, was born at Brighton 26 February 1879, the son of William Henry Bridge, of Brighton, and his wife, Elizabeth Warbrick. The father was a musician, a conductor under whom Frank Bridge played, usually violin, but sometimes other instruments, and even, when required, conducting. This early experience was of inestimable value to the young musician, giving him intimate knowledge of the range and colour of the orchestra, and generally laying the foundation of that skill and knowledge which he came to display. He went to the Royal College of Music as a violin student, and in 1899 won a scholarship for composition, studying under (Sir) Charles Stanford. He transferred from violin to viola without having any tuition on the latter instrument, of which he became a superb player.

So exceptional were his qualities that when Wirth, the viola of the Joachim Quartet, was prevented by illness from coming to England, Bridge was chosen to take his place (1906), and earned from Joachim and his colleagues the most enthusiastic appreciation.

In his earliest days Bridge earned his living by playing in theatre and other orchestras—he was also a member of the Royal Philharmonic Orchestra; in fact he was an expert and versatile musician who rose from quite a humble beginning. A colleague who shared his desk in a performance of the *Messiah* said it had been a revelation to hear what Bridge found in the viola part. He played in the Grimson (second violin), the Motto (viola), and the English (viola) string quartets; but when this last quartet disbanded in 1927, he practically ceased playing and concentrated on composing and conducting.

As a composer Bridge ranged over a wide field; he produced educational solos for piano, for violin, and three sets of miniature trios for young players for piano, violin, and 'cello. He won various important prizes, of which his full-sized string Quartet in E minor won a *mention d'honneur* at an international competition held at Bologna in 1906. His 'Phantasie' string Quartet in F minor won a prize in the first competition organized by Walter Willson Cobbett (1905); the 'Phantasie' Trio in C minor was awarded the first prize in the second competition (1908), the purpose of these competitions being to produce works in which the instruments should have equally interesting parts. Cobbett also commissioned him to write the very beautiful 'Phantasie' Quartet for piano and strings in F sharp minor (1910), and in 1915 his prize for a string quartet in which both violins should have equal interest was awarded to Bridge's second string Quartet, in G minor. Other compositions included a Quintet for piano and strings (1905) and a Sextet for strings (1912). Bridge's chamber music was perhaps the most important of his creative work, and is of real value. He also wrote a Sonata for piano (1921–4), one for piano and 'cello (1913–17), and another for piano and violin (1932). For orchestra his works included a symphonic poem 'Isabella' (1907), a suite 'The Sea' (1910–11, published under the auspices of the Carnegie Trust), a rhapsody 'Enter Spring' (1927), and a 'Lament' for strings (1915) written in memory of a young friend drowned at sea; 'Phantasm' for piano and orchestra (1931), also 'Oration' (1930) for 'cello and orchestra. Besides these he composed solos for organ, piano, violin, viola, 'cello, a number of songs, and a divertimento (1938) for wind instruments.

He had great gifts as a conductor and took the New Symphony Orchestra, shortly after its foundation, in repertory rehearsals; he was in charge of a season at the Savoy Theatre (1910–11) in which Marie Brema produced Gluck's *Orfeo*, and was included in the 1913 autumn season at Covent Garden. He was frequently called on in an emergency to conduct various concerts, including some of the Royal Philharmonic Society, and it is interesting to note that a number of those who played under him said that he was one of the few who really interpreted the works, for so many beat time, but so few interpret.

His one permanent position as a conductor was with the Audrey Chapman Orchestra, formed chiefly of amateurs, with professional strengthening for the concerts. The standard of playing in this orchestra under Bridge's training reached a very high level of musicianship and sensitiveness. Although he possessed these gifts as a conductor, he never attained the position which was his due, owing possibly to his very direct and penetrating criticism of those whom he conducted.

Bridge made four visits to the United States; he conducted several times in Boston, Detroit, Cleveland, and New York, having many works performed in these cities as well as in California. Mrs. Elizabeth Sprague Coolidge commissioned from Bridge the piano Trio No. 2 (1929), and also the string Quartets No. 3 (1926) and No. 4 (1937), both of which were played by the Brosa, Pro Arte, and many other organizations. In composition he had a fine technique and a masterly command of form.

In 1908 Bridge married Ethel Elmore Sinclair, a fellow student from Australia who had won the Clarke scholarship at Melbourne which brought her to the Royal College of Music, London, in 1898. Bridge died at Friston-Field, near Eastbourne, 10 January 1941. There were no children of the marriage.

[Private information; personal knowledge.]

Ivor James

published 1959

HARTY (Herbert) Hamilton

(1879–1941)

Sir

Musician, was born at Hillsborough, county Down, 4 December 1879, the third son of William Michael Harty, organist of Hillsborough church, by his wife, Annie Elizabeth, daughter of Joseph Hamilton Richards, soldier, of Bray, county Dublin. It was from the father that the more famous son had his earliest instruction in piano, viola, and theory. At the age of eight he could deputize for his father at the organ, and by the time he was twelve he had an organist's post of his own at Magheragall, county Antrim. Thence he went in succession to Belfast and Dublin to fill organ appointments. He was helped in his studies by Michael Esposito, the Neapolitan musician who for forty years was prominent in the musical life of Dublin. Harty made his mark in Dublin as an exceptionally sensitive accompanist, and on going to London in 1900 he quickly established himself as one of the best of the day. His association with singers in this capacity led naturally to the composition of songs and to the writing of piano accompaniments for Irish folk-songs. In 1901 he won a prize at the Feis Ceoil (Dublin) for a piano Trio, and a Lewis Hill prize in 1904 for a piano Quintet; but the orchestra, which was to dominate the last thirty years of his life, began to attract him. He wrote a successful 'Comedy' Overture in 1907 and the 'Ode to a Nightingale' for soprano solo with orchestra which was produced at the Cardiff Festival of that year, with his wife as soloist. He began about this time to appear as a conductor with the London Symphony and other orchestras.

Musicians who combine in themselves great abilities in three cognate but nevertheless competing activities of piano-playing, conducting, and composing—von Bülow, Busoni, and Rachmaninov were eminent continental instances—inevitably gravitate towards one at the expense of the other two. Harty never looked like becoming a great composer, even of the stature of Busoni or Rachmaninov, and his name is kept alive in concert programmes more by the brilliantly apt arrangements for full modern orchestra which he made of Handel's 'Water Music', of the same composer's 'Music for the Royal Fireworks', and of some pieces by John Field which he made into a suite in 1939. The feeling for orchestral colour and effect, which makes these transcriptions into an expression of Harty's musical personality without trespass upon the original composers', he had learned as an interpreter of Berlioz. As a conductor his personal predilections were for the romantics, although his taste was securely grounded in the classics, and he had no sympathy with the more eccentric brands of modernism of his day. Yet he had an open mind to what he regarded as legitimate developments: he performed Sibelius's symphonies, and gave the first performances of Constant Lambert's 'The Rio Grande' (in which he played the piano part, 1929), and of (Sir) William Walton's Symphony (1935).

As a composer, Harty wrote wholly within the romantic tradition and by historical accident he came just at the moment when the vein was showing signs of exhaustion. The change in the mental climate between the years before and after the war of 1914–18 made music composed in the decade before the war, to which belong Harty's tone-poem 'With the Wild Geese' (1910) and his cantata 'The Mystic Trumpeter' (1913), seem outmoded. In the last resort they were derivative from an expiring German romanticism, however much other elements, such as Harty's own Irish characteristics, succeeded in giving them a temporary independence. The violin Concerto which he wrote in 1909 made a great impression at the time, whereas the 'Irish' Symphony of 1924, which contains much fine music derived from Irish folk-song, was seen from the very fact of its romantic euphony to be speaking a dead language. Its scherzo, which reconciled the conflict of symphonic form with folk-music more satisfactorily than the other movements written more or less round a programme, may well survive as an independent piece. His songs, which evoke Celtic atmosphere with their close-knit union of the vocal and piano writing, keep a place in the long and honourable tradition of English song.

Thus, in an age of increasing specialization, Harty still followed the older continental tradition of versatility. Beginning his career as an organist, he subsequently won distinction in three other fields, piano accompanying, composition, and orchestral conducting. His thirteen years (1920–33) as conductor of the Hallé Orchestra brought him widespread fame far beyond Manchester, taking him as a conductor of international repute several times to the United States, and in 1934 to Australia. His manner with an orchestra was quiet, and his unquestioned authority was derived in part from his sterling musicianship and in part from the warmth and lively humour of his personality.

Harty was knighted in 1925; he received the honorary degree of D.Mus. from Trinity College, Dublin, in the same year, from Manchester in 1926 and from the De Paul University, Chicago, in 1936, and of LL.D. in 1933 from the Queen's University, Belfast, where the Hamilton Harty chair of music was founded in 1951. He was elected a fellow of the Royal College of Music in 1924, and received the gold medal of the Royal Philharmonic Society in 1934, after he had relinquished the conductorship of the Hallé Orchestra, which he had restored to its former distinction.

Harty married in 1904 Agnes Helen, daughter of Albert Chapman Nicholls, managing director of Cavendish House, Cheltenham. She was a well-known singer under her maiden name and was appointed C.B.E. in 1923. Harty's last years were chequered by ill health, but he still took conducting engagements. He died at Hove 19 February 1941. There were no children. A sketch drawing by William Weatherby is in the Manchester City Art Gallery; Harty was also painted by Harold Speed.

[*The Times* and *Manchester Guardian*, 21 February 1941; *Musical Times*, March 1941; P. A. Scholes, *Oxford Companion to Music*; *Grove's Dictionary of Music and Musicians*; private information; personal knowledge.]

FRANK HOWES

published 1959

COLLES Henry Cope

(1879–1943)

Musical historian and critic, was born at Bridgnorth, Shropshire, 20 April 1879, the third child and elder son of Abraham Colles, M.D., F.R.C.S. (and great-grandson of Abraham Colles), by his wife, Emily Agnes Georgiana, daughter of Major Alexander R. Dallas, and granddaughter of A. R. C. Dallas. He was educated privately and at the Royal College of Music (1895–9), where his interest in musical history was early aroused by Sir Hubert Parry. In 1899 he became organ scholar at Worcester College, Oxford, where he attracted the attention of (Sir) Henry Hadow, then dean of the college, whose lectures doubtless helped in shaping Colles's future career.

At Oxford he obtained the degree of B.A. in 1903 and the additional degree of B.Mus. in 1904, and in 1932 the university conferred upon him the honorary degree of D.Mus.; he was elected honorary fellow of Worcester in 1936. After leaving Oxford he studied at the Temple Church (1903–5) with (Sir) Walford Davies, a lifelong friend whose biography he wrote in 1942.

In 1905, at the instigation of Hadow, Colles began his career as a writer, contributing a weekly article on music to the *Academy* at the request of H. H. Child. He also began work at *The Times* in 1905 and became an assistant to J. A. Fuller-Maitland, whom he succeeded as musical editor in 1911, and he retained this post until his death. On his appointment as editor he at once inaugurated and maintained the weekly articles on musical affairs, for the most part written by himself, which attracted wide attention both in England and abroad and by their scholarship and research soon acquired considerable importance.

During the war of 1914–18 Colles served in Macedonia as a captain in the Royal Artillery, receiving the Greek Cross in 1918. On his return he was invited, in 1919, by (Sir) Hugh Allen to join the staff of the Royal College of Music as lecturer in musical history, analysis, and appreciation. In 1923 he accepted an invitation from the *New York Times* to act as 'guest music critic', remaining in America for some months. In 1927 he was Cramb lecturer at Glasgow University, taking for his subject the interdependence of the English language and the English musical genius—especially as exemplified in Purcell. The substance of these lectures was reproduced in his *Voice and Verse* (1928). He lectured also at Liverpool University, the Royal Institution, and elsewhere.

In 1927 appeared the third and revised edition of *Grove's Dictionary of Music and Musicians*, the editorship of which had been entrusted to him some years before. It was a task for which his ripe scholarship eminently qualified him. He was also responsible for a further revision and a supplementary volume in 1940.

In private life Colles was a staunch friend and a man of deep loyalties, none perhaps being more marked than that to the English Church. To her he gave steadfast service in many ways. As a writer he constantly stressed the value and importance of her great musical traditions, and the need of their continued maintenance; as a practical musician he gave strong support to the School of English Church Music founded by his friend Sir Sydney Nicholson, the Church Music Society, and St. Michael's College, Tenbury Wells. His wide knowledge on musical matters was also placed at the service of the British Council.

Colles's attitude to contemporary music may have been regarded as conservative, yet in the main he was not unsympathetic and, at any rate, he had unusual sanity of judgement. His daily criticisms were helpful and constructive, yet where condemnation was called for he was fearless.

Colles's published works show ease, clearness, and accuracy. They include *Brahms* (1908); *The Growth of Music* (1912–16), a much-used textbook of musical history; *Oxford History of Music*, volume vii *Symphony and Drama, 1850–1900* (1934), a critical and well-proportioned survey of an interesting period in music; a collection of Colles's shorter writings was edited by his wife, with a short memoir, and published as *Essays and Lectures* in 1945.

In 1906 Colles married Hester Janet (died 1952), daughter of Thomas Matheson, a member of Lloyd's. Colles died in London 4 March 1943. A chalk drawing by Mrs. Campbell Dodgson was in the possession of his widow.

[*The Times*, 6 March 1943; *Times Literary Supplement*, 13 March 1943; *Music Review*, vol. iv, 1943; H. J. Colles, 'H. C. C.—a Memoir' in *Essays and Lectures*, 1945; personal knowledge.]

IVOR ATKINS

published 1959

BEECHAM Sir Thomas

(1879–1961)

Second baronet

Conductor, was born 29 April 1879 at St. Helens, Lancashire, the elder son and second child of (Sir) Joseph Beecham, chemist, of St. Helens and later Huyton, and Josephine Burnett. His family background was that of the very prosperous business started by his grandfather, Thomas Beecham, a famous name in the world of digestive pills, which were sold at first personally by their inventor, and later marketed and advertised in vast quantities. There was good personal rapport between Beecham and his grandfather, better than that between him and his father.

At an early age Beecham showed two personal gifts—a good memory for words, and a passion for music. He was taught the piano from the age of six. He was also interested in sport, and in spite of his short stature, played football and cricket for Rossall School, Lancashire, which he attended from 1892 to 1897 and where he was a house-captain. He later went for eighteen months to Wadham College, Oxford (1897/8), where he practised the piano, played football, and indulged in bouts of foreign travel to hear his favourite operas. It soon became obvious that music was to be his chosen life's work. He was given, at twenty, and obviously by family influence, the opportunity to conduct his first professional orchestra—the Hallé, upon a visit to St. Helens, who were faced with an empty podium because Dr Hans Richter, who had been asked to conduct, had other engagements. Previously Beecham had learnt something about conducting with his own St. Helens Orchestral Society—which he had founded two years previously—and seemed to find no difficulty in leading the Hallé orchestra through an almost unrehearsed performance, a capacity he was to demonstrate superbly with a succession of orchestras over the next sixty years.

Having left Oxford without taking a degree, Beecham went to live in London in 1900, where he studied musical composition with Charles Wood, Frederic Austin, and other teachers. In 1902, aged twenty-two, Beecham joined, as one of its conductors, a small London touring opera company directed by Kelson Trueman, and soon had committed its repertory to memory. In 1903 he married Utica ('Utie') Celestia, daughter of Charles Stuart Welles, of New York, an American diplomat, at a time of serious discord in his own family. There were two sons of his marriage. It was a short-lived union of which he rarely spoke in later years, although the separation which soon followed seemed sad rather than bitter. They were divorced in 1943 and Utica, Lady Beecham, died in 1977.

An injury to his wrist in 1904 destroyed Beecham's ambition to be a concert pianist. Most of that year he spent travelling on the Continent with his wife, attending performances and collecting musical scores. In December 1905 he gave his first public orchestral concert in London, with players of the Queen's Hall orchestra. Press notices were poor, and Beecham himself far from satisfied. In 1906, helped by the clarinettist Charles Draper, he founded the New Symphony Orchestra, which expanded to sixty-five players in 1907, all of whom were carefully selected. This time Beecham's arresting style triumphed, and it was obvious that Britain had an important young conductor. It was at this stage that he met Frederick Delius, whose music was to be such an important part of

Beecham's work. In 1908 he presented several works by his new friend, with whom he went to Norway on holiday. In 1910, backed by his father, whose friendship he had now regained, Beecham mounted the first of his many Covent Garden opera seasons, a mammoth affair with thirty-four works represented, many of them very grand in scale and quite unknown in Britain. There were works by Richard Strauss (*Elektra* and *Feuersnot*); Wagner (*Tristan and Isolde*); Debussy (*L'Enfant Prodigue*); four of the less familiar Mozart operas; and many works by lesser composers. This did not prevent—indeed it inevitably produced—very heavy financial losses; but it could well be taken as a pattern for many of Beecham's finest achievements in the years which followed. In 1911 he presented Diaghilev's Russian Ballet with Nijinsky and in 1913 he introduced Chaliapin in a season of Russian opera, as well as giving the first London performance of Richard Strauss's *Der Rosenkavalier*. The tragic international events which followed in 1914 cut short Beecham's operatic activities, but he remained indefatigable in his fight to keep music going, and sustained both the Hallé Society and the London Symphony Orchestra with financial and artistic help. His greatest achievement at this time was the touring of his opera company, working in theatres large and small up and down the country, performing more than thirty different operas, including such works as *The Boatswain's Mate* by (Dame) Ethel Smyth and Isidore de Lara's *Nail*, all at prices so low as to put them within reach of everyone. In 1916 Beecham succeeded to his father's baronetcy, having been knighted earlier in the same year. A final financially disastrous Covent Garden season in 1920 left him fighting to stave off bankruptcy, and until 1923 he was almost absent from the musical scene. From then until 1929 his life seems to have been a gradual climb back to the pinnacle he had achieved so early. In that year he presented the first Delius Festival in London, which was attended by the now blind and paralysed composer, who for the first time began to receive the public appreciation he deserved.

In 1932, after heated negotiations, lasting some years, with the BBC and the London Symphony Orchestra for the foundation of a full-time permanent symphony orchestra in London, Beecham founded, with the assistance of Courtaulds, the excellent London Philharmonic Orchestra, which still exists (1979). With them he was to present many excellent concert and opera seasons until 1939, when war once again changed the London scene. In 1934 Delius died and the Delius Trust, planned by Beecham, took over the task of presenting his music on records and in concert-halls. In 1936 Beecham took his orchestra to Nazi Germany, and had the audacity to include in his party his secretary Berta Geissmar, the expatriate German who travelled safely and openly with him. Two occasions are remembered from this tour—the evening when Beecham refused to precede Adolf Hitler into the concert-hall, thus avoiding having to salute the arrival of the Führer, and the concert at Ludwigshaven, in the concert-hall of BASF, manufacturers of recording equipment, which marked the first recording ever made on tape of any orchestra. From 1939 to 1944 Beecham travelled constantly abroad, in the USA and Australia, and his reputation as a wit and a raconteur grew as rapidly as his stature as a conductor.

Upon his return to London in 1944, and after trials and arguments with both the London Philharmonic Orchestra and what was soon to be the Philharmonia under Walter Legge's direction, in 1946 he formed the Royal Philharmonic Orchestra, which was to be his last orchestra and the one with which he was to be longest in association. In 1946 he gave an important series of concerts in the second Delius Festival; and in 1947, in the presence of the eighty-three-year-old composer, a Richard Strauss Festival.

In 1950 he presented his orchestra in a lengthy tour of North America—an enterprise which somehow supported itself without government help and with Beecham's own generous donation of his services to balance a precarious budget. In the years which followed, Beecham busied himself with almost every possible aspect of orchestral and operatic activity at the very highest level. His recordings were among the finest produced anywhere. He conducted extensively in Britain, America, and Paris. He was made a Companion of Honour in 1957, an event which was clouded for him by the death of his second wife, Betty, daughter of Daniel Morgan Humby, a surgeon, of London. She was a pianist who was formerly the wife of the Revd H. C. Thomas, of London, and they had been married in 1943, after Beecham terminated his long association with Lady Cunard. Beecham's publications included an early autobiography, *A Mingled Chime* (1944), which described his life only until 1924, and should have been augmented by a later volume; and a biography of Frederick Delius (1958). In 1956 he gave the Romanes lecture at Oxford.

In 1959 he married his personal secretary, Shirley Hudson, who was with him in the United States in 1960, when illness forced him to return to London, where he died 8 March 1961. He was succeeded in the baronetcy by his elder son, Adrian Welles Beecham, born in 1904.

Beecham was often a harsh taskmaster and could sometimes be inconsiderate to those working for him. Punctuality was not among his most noticeable virtues. Nevertheless, such peccadilloes were easily overlooked in view of his effervescent enthusiasm which communicated itself to musicians and public alike. Orchestral players will long remember him as not only a great conductor, but a witty and stimulating person who could inspire them to produce their best and showed obvious pleasure in what he heard. He was a man of wide reading, which informed and enlivened his conversation, and he was renowned for his wit. Sometimes his interpretations of the music he conducted were controversial—for example, it was felt that he failed to bring out the heroic nature in some passages by Beethoven. But he succeeded in giving a freshness of outlook to performances and often astonished the public by his vitality, his flamboyance of manner, and his deep musical understanding. His own favourite composer was Mozart.

In appearance Beecham, although invariably an impressive figure, changed considerably over the years. In youth he was, judging from the many photographs and cartoons of the time, slim, elegant, dark-haired, and something of a dandy. The famous story of his summer evening walk along Piccadilly when he is said to have hailed a cab, thrown in his redundant overcoat, and said 'Follow me' as he continued his stroll is probably exaggerated, but contains a germ of the truth about the 'Beech' of the time. By his fifties he had already become a more sturdy character, but by no means rotund; now white-haired and with his famous 'goatee' beard jutting formidably (especially if he were arguing or directing a more dramatic musical work), he took on a more pinkish hue and a somewhat more benign aspect in moments of repose. With the passing years the figure became stouter, but Beecham was never anything like a fat man, and to the very end he presented an impressive pair of shoulders to orchestras the world over. Sitting down at this time he seemed gigantic; it was when he stood that he was revealed as a very short man—his legs were surprisingly short, belying every other physical aspect of this remarkable man. One feature remained constant through the years—the large and lustrous eyes, at once the agents of fear and confidence in the hearts of the players who faced him, and possibly the most important tool in his conducting equipment.

Apart from photographs and cartoons, portraits of Beecham seem to be few and rarely successful. Simon Elwes painted a portrait in 1951, but it is generally regarded as not a good likeness. In the Royal Festival Hall there is an excellent if somewhat skeletal bust in bronze which catches the mercurial conductor very much in action with a typical sideways cut-off which was extremely characteristic of his technique. There is a portrait of Beecham in oils by Gordon Thomas Stuart (1953) and a drawing by Guy Passet (1950), both in the possession of Alan Denson. One of six bronze bust casts by David Wynne (1957) is at the National Portrait Gallery, and others are at the Festival Hall, Bristol, and Aberdeen. Several caricatures were drawn by Edmund Dulac. There is also a portrait by Dorothy E. F. Cowen (1952). Sketches made at the Queen's Hall, London, during the Delius Festival of 1929, by Ernest Procter, are in the National Portrait

Gallery, and the Royal Philharmonic Orchestra has a sculpture by Muriel Liddle (1979).

[Charles Reid, *Thomas Beecham*, 1961; Neville Cardus, *Sir Thomas Beecham*, 1961; Humphrey Proctor-Gregg, *Beecham Remembered*, 1976; Ethel Smyth, *Beecham and Pharaoh*, 1935; Sir Thomas Beecham, *A Mingled Chime, Leaves from an Autobiography*, 1944; Harold Atkins and Archie Newman, *Beecham Stories: Anecdotes, Sayings and Impressions*, 1978; Alan Jefferson, *Sir Thomas Beecham: A Centenary Tribute*, 1979; personal knowledge.]

JACK BRYMER

published 1981

IRELAND John Nicholson (1879–1962)

Composer, organist, and pianist, youngest child of Alexander and Annie Ireland, was born at Inglewood, Dunham Massey in the sub-district of Altrincham, Cheshire, 13 August 1879. Both parents were well known in literary circles, his father being editor and part-owner of the *Manchester Examiner* and his mother the biographer of Jane Welsh Carlyle. Owing to his mother's delicate health he was sent as a boarder to a dame-school in Bowdon and later to Leeds Grammar School. At fourteen he entered the Royal College of Music, London, studying piano with Frederic Cliffe and organ with Sir Walter Parratt. A year later both his parents died, but he was able to continue his musical studies through a small allowance. At sixteen he was the youngest student to be awarded a fellowship of the Royal College of Organists, and a year later he was appointed assistant organist and choirmaster of Holy Trinity church, Sloane Street. In 1897 he received a composition scholarship and studied with (Sir) Charles Stanford until 1901. In 1908 he was made a Mus.B. of Durham University which in 1932 conferred on him an honorary doctorate.

In 1904 Ireland was appointed organist and choirmaster of St. Luke's, Chelsea, a post he held for twenty-two years, during which time he composed the greater part of his church music. In 1909 his Phantasy Trio in A minor won the second prize in W. W. Cobbett's chamber music competition and the following year his Violin Sonata in D minor was given first prize out of 134 works submitted from all over the world. It was, however, with his second Violin Sonata (1917) that he achieved full recognition, and he 'awoke one morning to find himself famous'. Meanwhile he had become acquainted with the writings of Arthur Machen, whose work was characterized by mystery, romanticism, and the macabre. Ireland had always been attracted by the prehistoric atmosphere and relics of the remoter parts of the Sussex Downs and the Channel Islands, and the influence of Machen can be heard in the individual musical style of the piano suite *Decorations* (1913) and the orchestral *The Forgotten Rite* (1913).

In 1923 Ireland was appointed professor of composition by the Royal College of Music and examiner for the Associated Board of the Royal Schools of Music, and in the following year the academic distinctions FRCM and honorary RAM were given him. The next fifteen years were his most prolific as a composer. During this period he wrote his Cello Sonata and Piano Sonatina, performed at festivals of the International Society for Contemporary Music in 1924 and 1929, Piano Concerto in E flat (1930), *Legend*, for piano and orchestra (1933), *A London Overture* (1936), and the choral work *These Things Shall Be*, commissioned by the BBC for the coronation of King George VI in 1937, together with the greater part of his large and important contribution to song and piano music.

Retiring from his professorial duties at the Royal College in 1939—his composition pupils included E. J. Moeran, Alan Bush, Humphrey Searle, Benjamin Britten, and Geoffrey Bush—he planned to spend the rest of his life in Guernsey, but the German occupation of the Channel Islands in 1940 forced him to return to England. However, his stay in Guernsey had given him the inspiration for one of his finest piano works, the Island Sequence, *Sarnia* (1941). During the war years he lived outside London and, still active as a composer, wrote the Epic March (1942) and after the war the Overture *Satyricon* (1946) and music for the film *The Overlanders* (1947). In his final decade he left the studio in Gunter Grove, Chelsea, which had been his home for almost the whole of his creative life, and retired to Rock Mill, a converted windmill looking out over the South Downs and Chanctonbury Ring. His failing eyesight did not permit much creative work, but his friend Mrs Norah Kirby was at hand to relieve him of business worries and cope with the many friends and young music students who were eager to visit him. Shortly after his eightieth birthday a John Ireland Society was formed which has done much to propagate his music both in public concerts and on gramophone records, and which has sponsored the publication of some of his early chamber music.

Ireland described himself as 'England's slowest and most laborious composer' and certainly his output of major works was comparatively small. He never wrote a symphony, but neither did Debussy or Ravel, two elder contemporaries whose music he greatly admired, and who influenced his individual pianistic style. Even in his songs and piano music he wrote with great deliberation and self-criticism, and never let a work be published until he was satisfied with it in every detail. As a song-writer the literary background he inherited from his parents found full and prolific expression in his setting of English poets from Shakespeare and Blake to Masefield, Housman, Thomas Hardy, and many other poets of the present century. Many years ago the music critic Edwin Evans summed up the quality inherent in his music as 'a scrupulous artistic sincerity'.

Friendship was an essential ingredient of his life, and he valued the company of his intimate friends, whom he preferred to meet individually. In 1927 he married Dorothy Phillips, a piano student at the Royal College of Music, but the marriage was never consummated and was soon annulled.

Ireland died 12 June 1962 at Rock Mill and was buried at Shipley, Sussex, the headstone on his grave being of prehistoric sarsen stone. There is a memorial window to him in the musicians' chapel of the Church of the Holy Sepulchre, Holborn, and a plaque at his birthplace. A portrait by Arnold Mason is privately owned; the National Portrait Gallery has one by G. Roddon. A portrait bust by Konstam is privately owned.

[John Longmire, *John Ireland: Portrait of a Friend*, 1969; Appreciation and Biographical Sketch in *Catalogue of Works* compiled by Norah Kirby, 1968; *Cobbett's Cyclopedic Survey of Chamber Music*, 2nd edn., 1963; private information; personal knowledge.]

JULIAN HERBAGE

published 1981

MAYER Robert

(1879–1985)

Sir

Businessman, patron of music, and philanthropist, was born 5 June 1879 at Mannheim, Germany, the third of the four sons (there were no daughters) of Emil Mayer, hop merchant and later brewer, of Mannheim, and his wife Lucie Lehmaier, of Frankfurt. He was educated at Mannheim Gymnasium and Conservatoire. He displayed musical gifts from his earliest years, and was encouraged by an encounter with Johannes Brahms. Increasing distaste for Prussian militarism led Mayer's father to send him in 1896 to settle in Britain, where his first job was with a firm of stockbrokers. On leaving that he went into the non-ferrous metal business, in which he remained until 1929. He became a naturalized British citizen in 1902, and from 1917 to 1919 served in the British army.

In 1919 he married Dorothy Moulton, the daughter of George Piper, OBE, civil servant at the War Office, of London. They had a daughter and two sons, the elder of whom died in 1983. Dorothy was a soprano singer of considerable distinction who was notable for introducing to the public the work of young composers (particularly English ones) while they were still unknown. She encouraged Mayer to support music and in particular to promote the musical development of children. Following the example of Walter Damrosch's special concerts for children in America, they instituted the Robert Mayer Concerts for Children, the first of which was given in the Central Hall, London, on 29 March 1923. Mayer chose his conductors well: the first season was conducted by (Sir) Adrian Boult; and most of the seasons thereafter until 1939, when the concerts had to be suspended, were directed by (Sir) H. Malcolm W. Sargent. The combination of Sargent's musicianship and skill with the young audience, Dorothy's enthusiasm, and Robert's generosity and determination ensured that the Robert Mayer concerts became and remained an important institution in the musical life of London. They spread to a large number of provincial centres in the 1930s and made a significant contribution to the renaissance of music in England, as well as later in Ireland where Mayer supported his wife's foundation for the promotion of music.

In 1929 Mayer retired from a formal business career, his means being by now sufficient to fund his work for music. He was co-founder with Sir Thomas Beecham of the London Philharmonic Orchestra in 1932. In 1939 he was knighted for his services to music.

The concerts for schoolchildren started again after the war, which Mayer spent in the United States, and in 1954 Mayer established Youth and Music, an organization modelled on the continental Jeunesses Musicales and catering for young people from fifteen to twenty-five. Its main activity was to take blocks of seats at concerts and opera performances and make them available at affordable prices to groups formed in places of education and work. Thus many who had been introduced to orchestral music by the children's concerts were enabled to develop their appreciation of music in the years after they had left school.

In addition to these activities Mayer supported talented musicians in various ways: he would, for example, assist groups of players or singers to undertake concert tours abroad, or help promising students to continue a course of training when other support was not available.

In later years Mayer's philanthropy was not confined to musical causes. There were three threads that ran through it—music, young people, and the improvements of relations with citizens of other countries—and they were related in his mind: he saw music as a civilizing force in society and in international relations. He became interested in the problems of juvenile delinquency, and in 1945 published a book *Young People in Trouble*. He supported the Elizabeth Fry Fund, the International Student Service, the Children's Theatre, the Transatlantic Foundation, the Anglo-Israel Foundation, and many other such causes. In his nineties he was a strong supporter of the movement for British membership of the European community.

His wife died in 1974, when he was ninety-five. It seemed at first as if all the light had gone out of his life. But his irrepressible energy and vitality triumphed over age and bereavement, and within a few months his small, brisk, neat—almost dapper—figure was to be seen in London concert halls and opera houses as often as ever, and his imagination was once again at work on plans for expanding the scope of Youth and Music. His hundredth birthday was celebrated by the publication of an autobiography confidently entitled *My First Hundred Years* (1979) and by a gala concert at the Royal Festival Hall in the presence of the Queen, who afterwards bestowed upon him the insignia KCVO.

Mayer was appointed CH in 1973. He was an honorary fellow or member of the Royal Academy of Music, the Royal College of Music, the Guildhall School of Music, and Trinity College London; and was given honorary doctorates at Leeds (1967), the City University, London (1968), and Cleveland, Ohio (1970). He was awarded the Albert medal of the Royal Society of Arts in 1979. The international dimension of his activities was recognized by the award of the grand cross in the Order of Merit in the Federal Republic of Germany (1967) and membership of the Ordre de la Couronne in Belgium (1969).

In 1980 he married Mrs Jacqueline Noble (née Norman), who cared for him with devotion through his last years of increasing frailty and withdrawal from public activity, until he died in London 9 January 1985 at the age of 105.

[*The Times*, 15 January 1985; private information; personal knowledge.]

Robert Armstrong

published 1990

CHRISTIE John

(1882–1962)

Founder of Glyndebourne Opera, was born 14 December 1882, at Eggesford, Devon, the only child of Augustus Langham Christie, a country squire, and his wife, (Alicia) Rosamond Wallop, third daughter of the fifth Earl of Portsmouth. His family had acquired large estates over the past hundred years since their ancestor came from Switzerland to settle in England, and now owned the manor house at Glyndebourne and some ten thousand acres, as well as an extensive property in north Devon. Unfortunately Augustus Christie suffered from a nervous instability verging upon insanity, and the early life of the son was spent away from his father. His childhood was unhappy, which had the effect of making him fiercely independent and often rebellious; so that at the age of six, being strong and well able to look after himself, he was sent away to school, where he quickly earned a reputation for indiscipline. In 1896 he went to Eton, like his father and grandfather, where, despite his small stature, he made his mark by unconventional behaviour and by the capricious use of his intelligence according to whether he liked or disliked his masters. From there he was sent in 1900 to the Royal Military Academy, Woolwich, but he injured his foot in a riding accident, and, much to his satisfaction he abandoned a military career and in 1902 passed into Trinity College, Cambridge. Here he spent three years reading natural sciences, which he liked, and developed a keen interest in music and the motor car. After getting a second class degree (1905) he became a master at Eton in 1906 and spent sixteen years there (apart from two years on war service), which proved, as he often said, to be the happiest of his life. At that time Eton masters were allowed very considerable freedom, and he was conspicuous among a somewhat eccentric community for a novel approach to his duties and methods. But he enjoyed teaching and had the gift of inspiring loyalty among his pupils and made many friends among his colleagues. The years 1914–16 saw him in France, where, as a captain in the King's Royal Rifle Corps he showed absolute fearlessness in action, which won him the Military Cross and the admiration of his men. But trench warfare proved too severe a strain on his injured foot and he returned to Eton, staying there another six years, until he decided to give up teaching in order to pay more attention to the development of his inherited assets. In 1913 his father had let him have virtual control of Glyndebourne, which he made his own home and used for entertaining his friends. In 1920, when he gained legal ownership of the estate, he at once set about improving the amenities of the house. He had already built on a large room which was to become the centre of his musical activities. Here he had installed a cathedral organ, buying up an organ company for the purpose, and developed the estate workyard, which later grew into a most successful commercial enterprise. He also acquired a controlling interest in various other businesses; for he felt strongly that a landlord should do something constructive with his money and property, and he had no use for the idle and parasitic rich. As yet he confined his musical interests to performances in the Organ Room, but in 1930 he became engaged to (Grace) Audrey Laura St. John-Mildmay (died 1953), a gifted soprano with the Carl Rosa Opera Company, daughter of the Revd Aubrey Neville St. John-Mildmay (later tenth baronet), and they were married the next year. Almost at once he made plans to give complete operas at Glyndebourne, but his wife saw that this would not be practicable unless it were done 'properly' (as she put it). Therefore her husband, who trusted her professional judgement implicitly, decided to build a theatre on to the back of his country house. So Glyndebourne Opera was founded.

When this announcement was made, the music world was incredulous, the press derisive, and even his closest friends thought that such a wild scheme could not possibly succeed. But he went ahead, and by summer 1934 the opera house had been built with a large and excellently equipped stage but a relatively small auditorium holding about three hundred people. A first-rate team was assembled under the leadership of the conductor Fritz Busch and the producer Carl Ebert, with John Christie himself and his wife at hand to keep things under control. Recent visits to Salzburg and elsewhere had made them both ardent Mozartians, and the first season opened with *Le nozze di Figaro*. It was immediately pronounced a triumphant success both by the musical intelligentsia and by the lay public, and an equally good reception was given to *Cosi fan tutte* which followed. During the next four years the repertoire was extended to the other three best-known Mozart operas and to Verdi's *Macbeth* and Donizetti's *Don Pasquale*. In five productions of three of these operas Audrey Mildmay sang with great charm and distinction, while in the same period managing to have a daughter and a son and to act as an exemplary hostess to her many guests. She was indeed a person of rare quality. The first three seasons had cost John Christie about £100,000 of which £21,000 had been lost on the running costs of the Opera, but in 1937 he was able to make a small profit and thus to prove that such a thing could be done. Then war started, and Glyndebourne became a home for London children. Audrey Christie, much against her will, took her own children to Canada, where she eked out a precarious existence by giving concerts, but was able to return home in 1944. At once Christie set about considering means of reviving the Opera, but financial problems were acute, since he did not feel it reasonable to spend more of his private fortune for the benefit of the public. A few concerts with Sir Thomas Beecham and opera performances (the world premières of Benjamin Britten's *The Rape of Lucretia* and *Albert Herring*, and Gluck's *Orpheus* with Kathleen Ferrier) were given in 1946–7, while Glyndebourne was engaged in creating the Edinburgh Festival, where it performed opera exclusively from 1947 to 1949. But it was not until 1950 that support from the John Lewis Partnership enabled Glyndebourne to put on its own festival again. Then in 1952 the Hungarian textile manufacturer, Nicholas Sekers (later knighted for his services to music) organized the supporters of Glyndebourne into a group known as 'The Glyndebourne Festival Society' (the first scheme of its kind in Britain), and this substantially assisted the opera to remain solvent. Shortly afterwards the decision was taken to place it under a charitable Trust, the first to be registered for the benefit of the performing arts, and now the normal procedure in this field. But before this could come into effect Glyndebourne suffered a tragic blow with the death in 1953 of Audrey Mildmay at the age of fifty-two. Fortunately she had lived to see the Opera on its way to permanent existence, and her principles and ideals are alive to this day. The year after, John Christie became a Companion of Honour as a reward for his work and the Trust was set up. Thenceforth he played a less active part, and his son George took over most of the executive control. Christie lived another seven years, mentally as alert as ever but physically much handicapped by failing eyesight. In the last months of his life he became almost completely blind in his one remaining eye (he had lost the use of the other some fifty years before and had eventually had it removed), but even now, bearded and confined to a wheelchair, he was still the same genial host and stimulating company that he had always been. At last in 1962 he was no longer well enough to attend the opening night of the season, and on 4 July he died at Glyndebourne, aged seventy-nine.

In any estimate of the character and achievement of this remarkable man, perhaps the most obvious conclusion would be that he had to an extraordinary degree the ability to reconcile the ideal with the practical. Most people who knew him well would agree that among his many qualities the most vital were a highly original and creative mind, dynamic and inexhaustible energy, and unfailing and unbounded optimism. He was fifty when he established a new and challenging objective in his life, and from that moment he pursued this purpose with a ruthless and unflagging singleness of aim. Many thought of him as impossibly eccentric, but a closer acquaintance with the man himself showed that most of his decisions were amply justified in the event, even if he sometimes gave curious reasons for making them. Cast in a mould somewhat larger than life, it was not surprising that he should advise others to 'think big' (to use his own phrase) and to ignore and despise littleness of mind and action. Above all he believed that life was not worth living without what he called 'amusement'. By this he did not mean that a man should show a shallow or frivolous attitude to his problems, but rather that he must be capable of sifting out whatever grains of humour might be found in the chaff of experience. All through his life John Christie applied this philosophy in handling difficult situations and people, and he had the rare gift of settling disputes by making them appear ridiculous. He did not suffer fools gladly, and he had no time for those who bored him or did not try to see his point of view; nor was he particularly ready to see their own. Nevertheless he did what no man has ever done before in producing opera at his own country house and persuading people to come from all over the world to hear it. As he often said, the object of Glyndebourne was not just to put on good performances of opera but to aim at perfection, and, in the opinion of many, he came nearer to realizing this ideal than anyone else in the history of opera.

There is a portrait of Christie by Kenneth Green (1937) which hangs in the dining room at Glyndebourne, and a bronze bust by Oscar Nemon (1960) in the garden surrounding the opera house.

[Wilfrid Blunt, *John Christie of Glyndebourne*, 1968; Spike Hughes, *Glyndebourne*, 1965; Glyndebourne Festival programmes; private information; personal knowledge.]

NIGEL WYKES

published 1981

STOKOWSKI Leopold Anthony

(1882–1977)

Orchestral conductor, was born 18 April 1882, in London, the eldest child (a sister was born in 1884 and a brother in 1890) of Kopernik Joseph Boleslaw Stokowski, cabinet maker, of London, and his wife, Annie Marion Moore, of Irish parentage. He was a student at the Royal College of Music, London, first from January 1896 to December 1899, specializing in piano- and organ-playing for which his teacher was (Sir) H. Walford Davies, and also studying composition with (Sir) C. V. Stanford; he later re-entered the college in November 1903, finishing in July 1904. He also made several visits to France and Germany. He became Bachelor of Music of Oxford University in 1903, taking his degree through Queen's College, a procedure followed by many RCM students at about this time; the manuscript of his exercise for the degree, 'The Redeemer', for mezzo-soprano soloist, chorus, and string orchestra, is preserved in the Bodleian Library. He became an American citizen in 1915.

Stokowski's professional career began with various posts as organist and choirmaster. From 1900 to 1901 he was at St. Mary's, Charing Cross Road, and was appointed to St. James's, Piccadilly, in March 1902. In 1905, after an approach by the rector of St. Bartholomew's, New York, he accepted the organist's appointment at this wealthy and fashionable church, holding the post for three years. Here he was introduced to Olga Samaroff (born Lucie Hickenlooper, from San Antonio, Texas), a concert pianist who had studied in Paris and Berlin, and it was she who engineered his first appointment as a conductor, of the Cincinnati Symphony Orchestra, which he held from 1909 to 1912. Immediately on resigning from the Cincinnati conductorship, Stokowski was appointed conductor of the Philadelphia Orchestra, to begin at the start of the 1913–14 season. In fact he took over at once, from the autumn of 1912, remaining with the orchestra until 1936. From then on, Stokowski seldom had a regular orchestra for more than a short time, but embraced more varied musical activity. From 1937 he conducted music for Hollywood films (among them *One Hundred Men and a Girl*, 1937, and Walt Disney's *Fantasia*, 1940), appearing in some of them himself. In 1940 he formed the All-American Youth Orchestra (later the All-American Orchestra, 1941) and was co-conductor, with Toscanini, of the NBC Orchestra from 1941 to 1944. He was with the New York City Symphony Orchestra (1944–5), and was musical director of the Hollywood Bowl (1945–6), the New York Philharmonic (1947–50), the Houston Symphony Orchestra (1955–60), and the American Symphony Orchestra (1962–72).

Stokowski was possibly the greatest celebrity among twentieth-century conductors, a magician of the orchestra although a controversial interpreter. His first appointment, in Cincinnati, was achieved despite an almost complete lack of previous conducting experience, but he immediately showed such ability as an orchestral trainer combined with a showman's flair that the standard of the orchestra rose dramatically in a very short time. A comparable transformation occurred in Philadelphia and by 1916, with the performances of Mahler's *Symphony of a Thousand* in Philadelphia and New York, both orchestra and conductor were considered unequalled in the USA. Stokowski was indebted to Edward Bok, publisher and member of the Philadelphia Orchestra board, for the provision of adequate rehearsal facilities and assistance in the endowment of the orchestra. In 1924 Mrs Mary Curtis Bok formed the Curtis Institute in Philadelphia for the training of musicians; Stokowski became the teaching conductor for the first three years, continuing his direct association with the school until 1930. Many of the Philadelphia Orchestra members were active as teachers in the school, which in turn provided a very high proportion of recruits for the orchestra. Stokowski throughout his life showed great enthusiasm for performing new works, and is said to have given about two thousand first performances, most of the works being by American composers. His policies frequently brought him into conflict with the orchestra board and with concert managers, his last years in Philadelphia being particularly acrimonious in this respect.

Noteworthy among his American premières were: several works of Schönberg, including *Pelléas et Mélisande* and *Five Pieces for Orchestra*, during the 1920s; Stravinsky's *Les Noces* (at the Metropolitan Opera, 1929); Stravinsky's *Le Sacre du Printemps* (the first American production of the ballet, also at the Metropolitan Opera, 1929–30 season); Mussorgsky's *Boris Godunov*, in the original version (1929–30 season); Berg's *Wozzeck* (March 1931), which is said to have involved eighty-eight preliminary rehearsals and sixty on-stage rehearsals, all directed by Stokowski; and Charles Ives's Symphony no. 4 (a first performance in the American Symphony Orchestra's 1965–6 season). Several works by Rachmaninov were first performed during the Philadelphia years, among them the Symphony no. 3 and, with the composer as soloist, Piano Concerto no. 4 and *Rhapsody on a Theme of Paganini*.

Although Stokowski made some notable contributions to opera and ballet performances, his unyielding and overbearing nature made collaboration with choreographers and producers practically impossible, and he remained primarily a concert conductor, albeit a highly spectacular one. He was tall, striking looking, in his later years sporting a mane of white hair and, for most of his career, dispensed with a baton, carving out elegant designs of the greatest clarity with his arms and hands. He was keenly interested in recording and left a large legacy of records made over a period of more than fifty years; several of these date from the 1970s when he was living in England and recorded with a specially chosen orchestra in London. His preferred composers are, not surprisingly, late Romantic and Slavonic, while classical composers such as Haydn and Mozart appear scarcely at all, and Bach exclusively in his symphonic transcriptions. The unconventional orchestral layouts which he devised were aimed at achieving the most effective balance in particular acoustical conditions; the tendency was to place the strings on the left and wind instruments on the right, with sometimes a surrounding arc of double basses at the rear.

He was tireless in striving to enable living composers to have their works performed, as he was to encourage young people to play in orchestras and to listen to concerts. The founding of the Curtis Institute enabled him to fill many of the places in the Philadelphia Orchestra with American-born and -trained musicians, in contrast to the state prevailing previously, where a high proportion of players in American orchestras came from Europe. His view was basically one of not discriminating against the American, and he extended it over the contentious areas of sex and race, refusing to countenance discrimination against women and negroes, if they were the best candidates for the positions to be filled. He did not conduct in England between 1912 and 1951, but thereafter was a regular summer visitor, and in 1972 at the age of ninety performed the same programme (with the London Symphony Orchestra) which he had given sixty years earlier.

Stokowski was married three times: first, to Olga Samaroff, on 24 April 1911; there was one daughter, born in 1921. The marriage was dissolved in 1923 and he married, secondly, in 1926, Evangeline Brewster Johnson, daughter of the chemist who established the pharmaceutical company. There were two daughters of this marriage, which was dissolved in 1937. Thirdly, he married Gloria Vanderbilt di Cicco, in April 1945. There were two sons of this marriage, which was dissolved in 1955. Stokowski died 13 September 1977 at his home in Nether Wallop, Hampshire, England.

He was elected FRCM and an honorary fellow of Queen's College, Oxford (1951), and was awarded a D.Mus. by the University of Pennsylvania and LL D by the University of California.

[H. C. Shonberg, *The Great Conductors*, 1967; H. Kupferberg, *Those Fabulous Philadelphians*, 1969; D. Wooldridge, *Conductor's World*, 1970; E. Johnson (ed.), *Stokowski: Essays in Analysis of his Art*, 1973; A. Chasins, *Leopold Stokowski: a Profile*, 1979; H. Stoddard, *Symphony Conductors of the USA*, 1957; *New Grove Dictionary of Music and Musicians* (article on Stokowski), 1980; personal knowledge.]

JAMES DALTON

published 1986

TYRWHITT-WILSON Sir Gerald Hugh

(1883–1950)

Fifth baronet, and fourteenth Baron Berners

Musician, artist, and author, was born at Apley Park, Bridgnorth, 18 September 1883, the only child of Lieutenant (later Commodore) Hugh Tyrwhitt (third son of Baroness Berners, who had married Sir Henry Thomas Tyrwhitt) and his wife, Julia Mary, daughter of William Orme Foster, M.P., of Apley Park. Berners's two volumes of autobiography, *First Childhood* (1934) and *A Distant Prospect* (1945), give an account of his life until he left Eton. From these two books which are written in a delightful and deceptively simple style, we may gather that he did not take willingly to the sporting country life for which his parents and grandmother intended him, but he retained a knowledge of animal life, particularly birds and plants. Eventually he entered the diplomatic service as an honorary attaché in the embassies at Constantinople (1909–11) and Rome (1911–19). In 1918 he inherited from his uncle the barony of Berners, and the Tyrwhitt baronetcy, in the next year taking the additional name of Wilson. He sold much of the Berners property and bought Faringdon House in Berkshire where he lived for the remainder of his life, entertaining his many friends and occasionally visiting London and Rome where he owned a house overlooking the Forum.

Berners's chief delight in life was music, and the second volume of his autobiography movingly describes how at Eton his appreciation developed and his mind opened to pleasure in the arts generally. The book is probably the best of his prose works. He did not live to finish the third volume which has not been published. He wrote in addition five humorous light novels, satirizing various aspects of English social life: *The Camel* (1936), *Far from the Madding War, Count Omega, Percy Wallingford and Mr. Pidger*, and *The Romance of a Nose* (all published in 1941). He also wrote a prose lampoon *The Girls of Radcliff Hall* (1937) published in Faringdon.

In the world of music Berners will be remembered chiefly for his contributions to ballet music between 1926 and 1946 but earlier works by which he first became well known as a composer should not be forgotten. Berners received much of his musical education abroad and studied for a short time with Stravinsky and Casella. Among his earliest published works are 'Trois petites marches funèbres' of 1914 ('Pour un homme d'état', 'Pour un canari', 'Pour une tante à héritage') which at once demonstrated his skill in portraying humour and satire. These pieces were followed by others including 'Fragments psychologiques' and 'Valses bourgeoises'. Berners's sense of parody inspired several songs set to German, English, and French words, and his parodies of national styles are also seen in two orchestral works 'Three Pieces for Orchestra' of 1916 ('Chinoiserie', 'Valse sentimentale', and 'Kasatchok') and 'Fantaisie Espagnole' of 1918. Later Berners turned to opera and set to music Mérimée's one-act comedy *Le Carrosse du Saint-Sacrament* which was produced in Paris in 1924 in a triple bill which included works by Stravinsky and Sauguet.

In 1926 appeared 'The Triumph of Neptune', the first of the series of ballets for which Berners supplied the music. This score was written for the Diaghilev ballet. Another, 'Luna Park', was included in (Sir) C. B. Cochran's 1930 revue. These were followed by three scores composed for the Sadler's Wells Ballet Company. The first, 'A Wedding Bouquet', for which Berners also designed the costumes and which employs a chorus with words by Gertrude Stein, was produced at Sadler's Wells Theatre in 1937. The second, 'Cupid and Psyche', followed in 1939, while 'Les Sirènes' was produced at Covent Garden in 1946. Although Berners achieved early in his career a reputation as a specialist in musical humour and parody, these are not by any means the principal characteristics of all his compositions. Everywhere considerable technical skill and originality are evident, and it is a regret that his music is so rarely heard today.

Berners was also a talented landscape painter in oil and held exhibitions at the Lefevre Galleries, London, in 1931 and 1936. He painted mostly in the manner of early Corot, of whose early paintings he had a fine collection. Another manner he employed for slightly satiric paintings was that of the Douanier Rousseau. He also collected works by Derain, Sisley, Matisse, Dufy, and Constable.

In *Who's Who* Berners recorded '*recreation*: none'. This was quite true, for there was hardly a moment of the day when he was not either composing, painting, or writing. He was extremely self-critical and destroyed much that he did. Personally he was shy and quiet, but he had a remarkable gift for making friends and a loyalty to them which no reverses in their fortunes would shake. He was a man of few words and nearly all of those were extremely amusing. His wit was barbed and mischievous, but never harmful. He delighted in making jokes, whether practical or verbal, which exposed pretentiousness or hypocrisy. He was no respecter of persons nor the upholder of any political creed. He never made a public speech in his life, except for the three short sentences with which he opened the Faringdon cinema. He died unmarried at Faringdon House, 19 April 1950, when the barony passed to his cousin, Vera Ruby, wife of

Harold Williams. The baronetcy became extinct. A caricature by Sir Max Beerbohm and a portrait by Gregorio Prieto are at Faringdon House.

[*Miniature Essays: Lord Berners*, published by J. & W. Chester, Ltd., 1922; *Catalogue of Paintings by Lord Berners*, with a foreword by Clive Bell, 1931; *Catalogue of Three Exhibitions*, Alex. Reid and Lefevre, Ltd., 1936; private information; personal knowledge.]

J. Betjeman

published 1959

BAX Arnold Edward Trevor

(1883–1953)

Sir

Composer, eldest son of Alfred Ridley Bax and his wife, Charlotte Ellen Lea, was born in Streatham 8 November 1883. His father, a man of independent means, was a fellow of the Society of Antiquaries and a regular subscriber to the Saturday concerts of Sir August Manns at the Crystal Palace. Clifford Bax, the author and playwright, was a younger brother. According to Bax's autobiographical *Farewell, my Youth* (1943) he could not remember the time when he was not able to read music at the piano 'with the same unthinking ease with which a man reads a book'. His early education was private, and in 1898 he became a student of the Hampstead Conservatoire, then in the charge of Cecil Sharp. Even in youth, however, Bax was not interested in English folksong, and two years later he entered the Royal Academy of Music, studying composition with Frederick Corder and pianoforte with Tobias Matthay. He won the Battison Haynes prize for composition in 1902, and in the following year, which saw his first public appearance in St. James's Hall as a composer, he was awarded the Macfarren scholarship for composition, which he held until he left the Academy in 1905. He distinguished himself also by winning the Charles Lucas medal for composition and the Walter Macfarren prize for piano playing. In addition to these achievements he was considered unique in his ability to read complex modern scores at the piano. Later he was to be elected an associate (1910) and a fellow (1921) of the Academy.

A formative influence during his early years was his private study of scores by Wagner, Strauss, and Debussy, whose music was then largely frowned on in academic circles. On leaving the Academy he twice visited

Dresden, where he heard the original production of Strauss's *Salome*. But already another influence had entered his life. In 1902 he had come across 'The Wanderings of Oisin' by W. B. Yeats and in his own words, 'in a moment the Celt within me stood revealed'. For a time, indeed, he adopted a dual personality, and published three books of tales as 'Dermot O'Byrne'. Musically, also, he deliberately adopted a Celtic idiom to free himself from the influence of Wagner and Strauss, and in the tone-poem *In the Faëry Hills*, first given at a promenade concert in 1910, he employed what he described as 'figures and melodies of a definitely Celtic curve'. A visit to Russia in the same year also contributed to Bax's formulative musical experiences, providing material for, amongst other works, the First Piano Sonata.

The orchestral tone-poems were the first of Bax's works to attract attention and *The Garden of Fand* (1916) is perhaps the most immediately appealing of them. No less important, however, are the later *Tintagel* and *November Woods* (both 1917) and *The Tale the Pine Trees Knew* (1931). None of these later works is based on Celtic subjects, and indeed this influence almost completely disappeared from his music in the twenties. Colin Scott-Sutherland has listed the following among the inspirational origins of Bax's music—Wagner, Strauss, Yeats, Swinburne, Shelley, Grieg, the Icelandic sagas, the pre-Raphaelites, Finland, the seascapes of the North. The turning-point from the Celtic to the Nordic was possibly the Symphonic Variations for Piano and Orchestra (1917) written for Harriet Cohen, and it is significant that *Winter Legends*, composed for the same pianist thirteen years later, should have a Nordic and not a Celtic setting.

The music critic Edwin Evans, writing about Bax's music in 1919, described it as containing two complementary and compensatory qualities—robustness and wistfulness. The first he regarded as responsible for the elements of structure and inventiveness, while the second provided the music with its chromatic character: 'to be wistful and at the same time robust is a combination of qualities that falls to few'. Although none of the symphonies had then been produced, Evans had already observed in Bax's music the emergence of a more abstract, austere art; 'the harmony has become more incidental to the polyphonic interest'. As if to prove the rightness of Evans's judgement, Bax composed the unaccompanied motet *Mater ora Filium* (1921), an exercise in pure polyphony which undoubtedly prepared him for the seven symphonies (1922–39) upon which his ultimate reputation rests.

The symphonies may be divided into two groups, the first three and the last three, with the Fourth Symphony, written in both Donegal and Inverness-shire, forming an extrovert interlude between these largely introspective works. Together with the symphonies must be considered the two important works for piano and orchestra already mentioned, the Cello Concerto (1932), which Bax considered one of his finest works, and the Violin Concerto (1937–8) distinguished both for its geniality and for its inventive musical structure.

Bax's orchestral virtuosity was equalled in the chamber music field, and his output of some thirty works includes several unusual instrumental combinations, such as the Nonet for string quartet, double-bass, flute, clarinet, oboe, and harp. The harp, indeed, is an instrument much exploited by Bax, as is the viola. The piano music, which includes four solo sonatas, is important, and there is much fine choral music and also many songs of character. Bax also composed ballet and film music, his principal works in these fields being the ballet *The Truth about the Russian Dancers* (1920), written in collaboration with Karsavina and Sir J. M. Barrie, and the film *Malta, G.C.* (1943). Like his contemporary John Ireland, he never showed any interest in opera.

Bax described himself as a 'brazen Romantic'. His life was conditioned both by literature and by nature: he was remarkably well read, and was never happier than when contemplating the ever-changing panorama of nature. Naturally such a man avoided public occasions whenever possible, and though he could mix easily with country people he had an almost claustrophobic distaste for urban society. The only time he could be seen in a crowd was at Lord's, for he was an enthusiastic lover of cricket.

In 1911 he married Elsita Luisa, a concert pianist, daughter of Carlos Sobrino, the Spanish pianist; they had one son and one daughter. Bax's increasing reputation as a composer brought him many honours, including a knighthood in 1937. He received honorary doctorates of music from Oxford (1934), Durham (1935), and the National University of Ireland (1947). In the last year of his life he was appointed K.C.V.O.

Possessing private means, Bax never needed to seek a musical appointment, which indeed would not have suited his temperament; when in 1942 he accepted the post of Master of the King's Musick, he did not overburden royal ears with occasional compositions. He probably found it embarrassing to 'shuffle around in knee-breeches', as he once put it, but he was a man who realized both the responsibility of the artist and the dignity of the composer.

He died in Cork 3 October 1953, on the day after he had taken part in the university's autumn music examinations. A memorial room dedicated to his memory has been created in Cork University which includes a death mask, his compositions, including some manuscripts, and the books he wrote as Dermot O'Byrne. A portrait, by Vera Bax, is on permanent loan to the Royal Academy of Music, and a drawing by Powys Evans is in the National Portrait Gallery.

[Sir Arnold Bax, *Farewell, my Youth*, 1943; R. H. Hull, *A Handbook on Arnold Bax's Symphonies*, 1932; Edwin Evans in *Musical Times*, March and April 1919; *Grove's Dictionary of Music and Musicians*; private information; personal knowledge.]

JULIAN HERBAGE

published 1971

DYSON George

(1883–1964)

Sir

Musician, was born at Halifax, Yorkshire, 28 May 1883, the eldest of the three children of John William Dyson, blacksmith, and his wife, Alice Greenwood, a weaver. In spite of poverty his parents had a cottage piano and George began to play at the age of five and to compose music when he was seven. He earned his first fee, as an organist, at the age of thirteen. He left Halifax in 1900 to take up an open scholarship at the Royal College of Music (organ and composition). At the RCM he studied composition with (Sir) C. V. Stanford. He played percussion in the orchestra and after a run-through of a new work by Stanford, Dyson played the piece from memory on the piano—early evidence of his phenomenal musicianship. In 1904 he was awarded the Mendelssohn travelling scholarship to Italy, Austria, and Germany. His first major composition, *Siena*, was played at Queen's Hall in 1907. In the same year he began his teaching career, first at the Royal Naval College, Osborne (1908–11), later at Marlborough (1911–14), and Rugby (1914).

On the outbreak of war he enlisted in the Royal Fusiliers and in 1915 became brigade grenadier officer, 99th Infantry brigade. His extraordinary versatility was manifest, for his *Grenade Warfare* (1915) became an army textbook. He was invalided home from France in 1916 suffering from shell-shock. During convalescence he worked for Edmund Speyer in a barrister's office. In 1917 he took the Oxford D.Mus. and in 1919 was commissioned major in the Royal Air Force to organize military bands. With (Sir) H. Walford Davies he composed *The Royal Air Force March*. He was appointed music master at Wellington in 1921, and in 1924 master of music at Winchester. He became director of the Royal College of Music in 1937, the first alumnus to do so, and retired in 1952 to Winchester, where he and his wife settled down among their old friends.

Dyson was a fastidious craftsman. His zest was shown in a stream of literary and musical works. He wrote three books—*The New Music* (1923), *The Progress of Music* (1932), *Fiddling While Rome Burns* (autobiography, 1954)—all of which showed great acuity of mind. His published musical output included twenty-eight instrumental compositions and ninety-two for voices. His best-known work is *The Canterbury Pilgrims*, portraying Chaucer's characters in music of great sympathy, wit, and grace. His three church services are in the repertoire of the cathedrals and college chapels. He wrote much for the 'Three Choirs' Festival. His most important compositions were: *In Honour of the City* (1928), *The Canterbury Pilgrims* (1931), *St. Paul's Voyage to Melita* (1933), *Nebuchadnezzar* (1935), *Quo Vadis* (1939), *Music for Coronation* (1953), and *Sweet Thames Run Softly* (1954). Everything he wrote was well made, but lacked a strong personal idiom which might have brought greater success. Both as a musical thinker and composer Dyson was a liberal conservative.

In *Fiddling While Rome Burns* he wrote, 'I am really what the eighteenth century called a Kapellmeister', and he often said that he could have succeeded in almost any career and it was chance which made it a musical one. Dyson's brilliant all-round qualities were particularly evident in his teaching appointments. At Marlborough, Beverley Nichols said of his first lesson with Dyson, 'This was, I think, one of the few "supreme moments" of my long life' (Beverley Nichols, *Father Figure*, 1972). At Wellington his arrival was described as 'positively elemental' for he had the rare gift of communicating and maintaining enthusiasm and his dry humour would round off a performance of a complex contemporary piece with 'Anyway, it's a lovely piano, isn't it'. At Winchester he exercised benevolent despotism not only in the college but the county round about. He kept the clever boy at full stretch and could coax a choir or orchestra to rehearse a two-hour programme in an hour and a half and give a performance better than was thought possible; even if he did remind them, 'You are supposed to be a symphony orchestra not an elastic band'.

Dyson changed the friendly and humanistic trend of the Royal College of Music to a small, tough, high-quality school for the training of professional musicians. He had an astringent style and brought the College to high professional and international repute. His administration covered the war period and the early post-war years of reconstruction. His decision in 1939 to keep the College open in London showed courage and foresight. He cut his own salary by half and slept in the College throughout the bombing. His ability for administration and financial acumen were outstanding and his innovations in government grants, buildings, syllabuses, and pensions, proved of lasting benefit. His love and pride for the Royal College of Music included ordinary people as well as talented musicians, as was exhibited in his generous tribute to a deceased College servant (*RCM Magazine*, vol. li, no. 2).

Outside the College his main work and interest was centred in the Carnegie United Kingdom Trust, of which he became a trustee in 1942 and chairman (1955–9). He considered the support of musical and artistic productions, by means of guarantee against loss, to be one of his major contributions to society.

Dyson was knighted in 1941 by King George VI, whom he had taught at Osborne, and was created KCVO in 1953. Many academic honours were conferred upon him, including FRCM (1929), Hon. RAM (1937), FICS (1950), FRSCM (1963), Hon. LLD Aberdeen (1942), and Leeds (1956). He was granted the Freedom of the Worshipful Company of Musicians (1944) and in 1963 the mayor and corporation of Winchester made him a freeman of the city, which symbolized what Dyson himself felt to be true—that Winchester was his spiritual home.

His most striking physical characteristics were his piercing blue eyes and his ready laugh. He had a vivid personality and a great capacity for enjoyment. He loved hill-walking and was an accomplished carpenter. His main driving force was dedication to home-made music, shown so well in his work and interest in the Winchester Music Club and Festival, and, later, when he became the first president of the National Federation of Music Societies (1935). He had great respect for first-rate professional musicians but little for the 'artistic temperament', pretentious talk about music, and 'academic' musicians. He had an agreeable and most attractive element of mischief in his nature—playing 'Pop Goes the Weasel' with one hand and 'God Save the Queen' with the other—and an endless fund of stories.

In 1917 Dyson married Mildred Lucy (died 1975), daughter of Frederick Walter Atkey, a London solicitor. Their daughter Alice (born 1920), became a medical social worker. Their son Freeman (born 1923), FRS (1952), became professor of natural sciences at the Institute for Advanced Study, Princeton, New Jersey. Dyson died in Winchester 28 September 1964.

A portrait of Dyson painted by Anthony Devas (1952) is in the possession of the Royal College of Music.

[George Dyson, *Fiddling While Rome Burns*, 1954; *The Wykehamist*, November 1964; *Royal College of Music Magazine*, vol. lxi, no. 1; *Yorkshire Post*, *The Times*, and *Daily Telegraph*, 30 September 1964; *Sunday Telegraph*, 4 October 1964; *Hampshire Chronicle*, 3 October 1964; *Music Trades Review*, June 1954; private information; personal knowledge.]

Keith Falkner

published 1981

BUTTERWORTH George Sainton Kaye

(1885–1916)

Composer, was born 12 July 1885 at 16 Westbourne Square, London. He was the only child of (Sir) Alexander Kaye Butterworth, solicitor and subsequently general manager of the North Eastern Railway Company, by his wife, Julia Marguerite, daughter of George Wigan, M.D., of Portishead, Somerset. John Kaye, bishop of Lincoln, was his great-grandfather, and John and Joseph Butterworth were ancestors in the direct male line. His first school was at Aysgarth, Yorkshire, whence he entered Eton as a king's scholar in 1899. He took part with credit in the intellectual, social, and athletic life of the school: music he studied with T. F. Dunhill, as well as with Christian G. Padel in York. From 1904 to 1908 he was in residence at Trinity College, Oxford; he took a third class in the honour school of *literae humaniores*, and was a prominent figure in musical circles, holding the presidency of the University Musical Club during the period October 1906 to March 1907.

After leaving Oxford, having abandoned his original intention of adopting the bar as a profession, Butterworth acted for a short time as one of the musical critics of *The Times*; and in 1909 accepted a teaching post at Radley College. In 1910 he returned to London, and worked for a few months at the Royal College of Music, studying the organ with Sir Walter Parratt, the piano with Herbert Sharpe, and theory with Charles Wood. The greatest influence on his musical ideals was derived from an intimate friendship with Ralph Vaughan Williams, whom he had first met in his Oxford days. He enlisted on the outbreak of war in August 1914, and was subsequently given a commission in the Durham Light Infantry. He was killed in action at Pozières, in the first battle of the Somme, 5 August 1916. He had won the military cross in the previous month and was again recommended for it shortly before his death.

Butterworth was greatly attracted by English folk-music, and gave much time to research in this field; he was also a prominent worker for the English Folk-Dance Society, of which he was one of the founders. He collected and arranged an album of Sussex folk-songs; and, in conjunction with Cecil J. Sharp, published several books of country and morris dances. His original compositions, few in number but of very distinctive quality, include about twenty songs (more than half to words from A. E. Housman's *A Shropshire Lad*), a suite for strings, and four orchestral pieces, three of which are idylls partially based on folk-song material, and the fourth a rhapsody thematically connected with some of the *Shropshire Lad* songs. This rhapsody (first produced under Arthur Nikisch at the Leeds festival of 1913) is his masterpiece, combining singularly individual imaginativeness with great command of orchestral technique; moods at once simple and intense made special appeal to him, and he expressed them with a sensitive intimacy that gives his work a notable place in contemporary English music.

[*Memoir*, privately printed, 1918; private information; personal knowledge.]

ERNEST WALKER

published 1927

WELLESZ Egon Joseph

(1885–1974)

Composer, music scholar, and teacher, was born in Vienna 21 October 1885, the only child of (Solomon) Josef Wellesz, textile manufacturer, and his wife, Ilona Lövenyi. He was educated at Vienna Hegel-gymnasium and studied musicology at the Vienna University under Guido Adler. He started composing at the age of thirteen and six years later became a private composition-pupil of Arnold Schönberg.

The greatest musical influence in his early life was that of Gustav Mahler, whose musical personality and methods he was able to study by frequently attending his rehearsals at the Opera. This double interest in the remoter past of music, as research student, and in the modern development of the art, as composer, was to mark the whole of his long life and to impart a quite unusual breadth of interest and vision to his work not only as composer but also as teacher.

Wellesz's first researches were into the music, and particularly the opera, of the baroque period in Venice and in Vienna itself. But the subject that was to be his life-work was the history of Byzantine ecclesiastical chant and its relationship to the Gregorian chant of the western church. His earliest publications on the subject date from 1914, and his successful deciphering of Middle Byzantine musical notation (1918) gave him a unique authority, of which the non-specialist musician can appreciate something in his *A History of Byzantine Music and Hymnography* (1949, 2nd edn. 1961). On the other hand his earliest published book (1921) was a study of Schönberg's music, which had a marked though by no means exclusive influence on the five operas and four ballets that Wellesz wrote between

1918 and 1930. If Richard Strauss was a strong influence in these works, their subject-matter and character owed even more to Strauss's librettist, Hugo von Hofmannsthal, a close friend who provided Wellesz himself with librettos for the ballet *Achilles auf Skyros* (1926) and the opera *Alkestis* (1924).

Ballet particularly interested Wellesz at this time, both as an avenue of escape from the Wagnerian conception of opera and also as a form related to the Bzyantine liturgy, conceived as a terrestrial reflection of the court of the Divine Pantokrator. This establishment of widely drawn parallels was an essential characteristic of Wellesz's mentality and explains his instinctive sense of the essential similarity between the new movements in all the arts of the day. His song-texts included poems by Stefan George and Francis Jammes and his friends included the writer Jacob Wassermann and the painter Oskar Kokoschka, whose portrait of Wellesz dates from 1911. The ballets and operas of these years were successful on German stages but, despite Wellesz's deep sense of belonging to a native Viennese tradition—both baroque and classical—he assiduously cultivated links with both France and England (which he visited for the first time in 1906, attending lectures at Cambridge) and he was active in the foundation and administration of both the International Society of Contemporary Music (1922) and the International Musicological Society. In 1932 he was the first Austrian composer since Haydn to receive an honorary doctorate of music from Oxford University. During these years he was professor of music history at Vienna University (1929–38).

It was therefore not wholly unexpected that when, in 1938, Hitler annexed Austria, it should have been England that offered Wellesz a new home. In that year Bruno Walter had conducted a major orchestral work based by Wellesz on *The Tempest* (*Prosperos Beschwörungen*) but the sudden and violent interruption of his career, and exile from the centre of new musical developments to the still musically insular atmosphere of England, caused a break of years in his development as a composer. During the 1930s he had taken an active interest in a movement aimed at the renewal, enlargement, and *aggiornamento* of the Catholic tradition in Austria; and this, with his Jewish origins and known hostility to National Socialism, would have made him an inevitable victim of persecution had he remained in Vienna. Through Henry Colles, the chief music critic of *The Times*, and other friends he was able to settle with his family in Oxford, where in 1939 he was made a fellow of Lincoln College and later university lecturer in the history of music (1944) and university reader in Byzantine music (1948). He was naturalized in 1946. It was now that his career as teacher assumed a primary importance, and it seemed for a time as though this and his Byzantine studies might well occupy the rest of his life. In 1957 appeared volume i, which he edited, of *The New Oxford History of Music*, of which he was one of the four editors.

Instead of this, however, Wellesz entered a new and extremely prolific period of creative activity. This began in 1944 with a chamber work based on Gerard Manley Hopkins's *The Leaden Echo and the Golden Echo*; and during the next thirty years he was to write a large quantity of music of all kinds, bringing the number of his string quartets (the first of which is dated 1911–12) to nine and including, most importantly, nine symphonies, written between 1945 and 1971. In all these works Wellesz, whose attitude to Schönberg's serialism had never been that of a doctrinaire, was clearly concerned to continue and expand the Viennese symphonic tradition, as represented particularly by Schubert, Bruckner, and, above all, Mahler. These works interested and were championed by a number of English musicians and, taken with Wellesz's activities as teacher, lecturer, and writer, played an important part in what may be called the 'de-insulation' of English music. On the Continent, however, and particularly in his native Vienna, enthusiasm for the music of first Schönberg and then Anton von Webern was inextricably associated with hostility to the ideas of defeated National Socialism: so that Wellesz's more traditionally based and basically eclectic 'Austro-European' music found at first little favour. Although he was made a fellow of the Royal Danish Academy of Science and Letters in 1946, became a fellow of the British Academy in 1953, and was appointed CBE in 1957, it was not until 1961 that he received the Austrian Great State prize. In the same year he was also made a Knight of the Order of Saint Gregory the Great.

He spent the rest of his long life in Oxford, though returning regularly to Austria during the summer months. He remained active until two years before his death, when he had a severe stroke. He died in Oxford 9 November 1974. In 1908 Wellesz married Emmy Franzisca, daughter of Ludwig Stross. There were two daughters of this marriage. If the specialist nature of his Byzantine studies (of which his greatest work was editing the *Monumenta Musicae Byzantinae*) has made it hard for the general musical world to appreciate fully his quality as a scholar, his activities as teacher, writer, and inspirer of a generation of musicians in Britain and his part in bringing British music 'into Europe' will always be remembered; and the profusion, variety, and craftsmanship of his music remain to reflect the warmth and generosity of his personality and the scope of his artistic interests.

[Robert Schollum, *Egon Wellesz*, 1963; Egon and Emmy Wellesz (ed. Franz Endler), *Egon Wellesz—Leben und Werk*, 1981; C. C. Benser, *Egon Wellesz*, 1985; Robert Layton, 'Egon Wellesz' in *The New Grove Dictionary of Music and Musicians*, ed.

Stanley Sadie, vol. xx, 1980; Walter Oakeshott in *Proceedings* of the British Academy, vol. lix, 1975; personal knowledge.]

MARTIN COOPER

published 1986

COATES Eric
(1886–1957)

Composer, was born 27 August 1886 in Hucknall, Nottinghamshire, the younger son and youngest of the five children of William Harrison Coates, a skilled surgeon and a notable personality greatly loved by the mainly mining community. From him Eric inherited his lifelong interest in photography and his aesthetic appreciation. His mother, Mary Jane Gwyn Blower, herself an artistic amateur singer and pianist, contributed the Welsh strain responsible largely for the musicality which showed itself at an early age. He demanded his first violin when only six; by the age of thirteen his attainments warranted lessons from Georg Ellenberger in Nottingham. Later, to complete an amateur ensemble, he took up the viola.

Coates had been intended for a commercial career but in 1906 his parents reluctantly allowed him to enter the Royal Academy of Music where Sir Alexander Mackenzie, on hearing his settings of poems by Robert Burns, assigned him to Frederick Corder for composition as his first study and to Lionel Tertis for viola. Many evenings became occupied in playing in various London theatres where he gained experience of practical orchestration and skilful arranging which later stood him in good stead as a composer. This led to engagements to play under (Sir) Thomas Beecham; and from 1910 for nine years he was successively sub-principal, then principal, viola in the Queen's Hall Orchestra under Sir Henry Wood. While still a student he had toured South Africa as viola in the Hambourg String Quartet which added much chamber music to his repertoire while releasing him from the drudgery of the theatre pit which aggravated the neuritis increasingly troubling his left arm.

Coates's first real song hit, 'Stone-cracker John', appeared in 1909 and the orchestral *Miniature Suite* was launched by Wood at the promenade concerts in 1911. In 1919, having established himself as a successful composer of songs and of excellent light music in the line of Sir Arthur Sullivan and (Sir) Edward German, he gave up playing; but he often conducted his works in Scarborough, Hastings, and other resorts which then boasted orchestras of considerable size, as well as in London and Bournemouth. Attractive and popular though his music was proving, it was the selection by the British Broadcasting Corporation of 'Knightsbridge March' from the *London Suite* to usher in 'In Town Tonight' in 1933 which suddenly made people conscious of Coates as a composer of exhilarating marches. His wartime 'Calling all Workers' had a similar and lasting success. The romantic serenade 'By the Sleepy Lagoon' written in 1930 achieved widespread popularity in the United States in the late thirties and subsequently in Britain and all over the world.

Although a lover of the peace and quiet of the country, Eric Coates found London with its ceaseless bustle of activity a more congenial place in which to compose. He was a first-class craftsman. Characteristic of his music are its freshness, melodiousness, gaiety, charm, and infectious rhythm. While it has an English flavour its language is so universal that it is popular in every country where western music is heard. He introduced the syncopation of modern jazz into many works which are thus very effective when played by large dance-type orchestras. His personal charm and humour were known to a vast public before whom, in concerts or on radio or television, he conducted his music in many countries in Europe and the Americas. That he received no official recognition would not have worried him for he was too busy encouraging and helping younger talent. He was a founder-member and director of the Performing Right Society of which in post-war years he proved to be an able and diplomatic delegate at international conferences as well as a conscientious member of its board.

In his autobiography, *Suite in Four Movements* (1953), Coates tells his personal love story: in 1911 he met a young fellow student, Phyllis, daughter of Francis Black, R.B.A., who was later to become a successful actress; it was a case of love at first sight. Two years later, parental objections overcome, they married and so began a partnership which lasted until he died in London 21 December 1957. Their only child, Austin, for whom the 'Three Bears' fantasy was written, became a successful writer.

[Private information; personal knowledge.]

KENNETH WRIGHT

published 1971

FACHIRI Adila Adrienne Adalbertina Maria (1886–1962)

Violinist, and her sister, Jelly D'Aranyi (1893–1966), also violinist, were both born in Budapest 26 February 1886 and 30 May 1893, the first and third of the three daughters of Taksony Aranyi de Hunyadvar, chief of police in Budapest, and his wife, Adrienne Nievarovicz de Ligenza, the fourteenth child of a Pole of good family from the Cracow district. Adrienne was the niece of Josef Joachim, the celebrated violinist and friend of Brahms. The entire family was musical and both girls began their musical training as children at the piano; Béla Bartók, as a student of twenty-two, was among their teachers and became a lifelong friend. It was as violinists, however, that the two entered the Budapest Academy of Music as children; they became pupils of the great violinist Jenó Hubay.

Adila began to play in public when she was fourteen, winning the approval of Budapest critics and the affection of audiences not only for her playing but also for the charm of her personality. In 1906, the year of her début in Vienna, she won the artists' diploma of the Budapest Academy and, although an impresario at once offered her a favourable contract, she went to Berlin to become the only private pupil of her celebrated great-uncle.

Although Joachim died in 1907, Adila's work with him had lasted long enough to imbue her with the principles which made him one of the most admired of musicians, a virtuoso whose gifts and personality were entirely dedicated to music rather than to display. It also brought her into contact with Joachim's circle, musicians as important as Grieg, Humperdinck, Casals, Ysaÿe, and the distinguished English musicologist, (Sir) Donald Tovey. Her work under Joachim included not only the standard concertos and the violin and piano works of the nineteenth-century masters but also the music of eighteenth-century composers, including the accompanied and unaccompanied violin music of Bach. At the same time, she never disdained effective show pieces by composers like Saint-Saëns, Sarasate, and Wieniawski.

At the time of Joachim's death, Adila was already winning a reputation as an unusually gifted violinist much influenced by Joachim but also capable of enjoying well-written display works. Joachim had planned to conduct her début in Berlin, with the Philharmonic Orchestra there, in November 1907, and the concert was given in spite of his death; the impression Adila made opened the doors of many other important concerts for her, and she travelled widely, introducing Jelly as a supporting artist and as her partner in Bach's D minor Concerto for Two Violins. Jelly's formal training thus ended by the time she was fourteen.

Joachim had planned Adila's English début, and she found in 1909 that her great-uncle's English friends and disciples—people of eminence in English music and social life—were eager to demonstrate their enthusiasm for her playing. Apart from their relationship with the much-lionized Joachim, the d'Aranyis were related through the violinist's banker brother, Henry Joachim, to the Russells, so that they began to move among the friends of Bertrand (later Earl) Russell in the intelligentsia. Their liveliness, personality, and quite un-English attractiveness made them welcome in England, and they kept the friends whom they made on their first visit throughout their lives. Fanny Davies, the pianist pupil of Clara Schumann, and Sir Henry Wood became, like Donald Tovey, friends and colleagues.

Thus, when war broke out in 1914 during their second English tour, and kept them in this country, they settled down to become a regular part of English musical life, assisted by such friends as the ex-prime minister Asquith and Balfour over any difficulties arising from their nationality. When, after 1919, their international careers could be resumed, England remained their base. Wartime music-making, much of it at private concerts in great houses, turned Adila's attention to chamber music (slow movements rehearsed, it is said, with tears and an intensity of emotion) rather than to concerto playing. The cellist Guilhermina Suggia was happy to play chamber music with the two sisters: other equally eminent friends gathered round to deal with a remarkably catholic selection of works, many of them unfamiliar, for chamber ensemble.

In November 1915, Adila married Alexander P. Fachiri, an American lawyer of Greek descent, and adopted her husband's name for professional purposes. In 1919 Alexander Fachiri took British citizenship and practised in international law. They had one daughter. Fachiri was, too, an accomplished cellist who had sometimes thought of making music his career, but a retiring disposition had made him unhappy at the thought of public performance. Nevertheless, he became effectively involved in his wife's chamber-music performances. Throughout this period Adila accepted frequent engagements to appear with Jelly in such works as the concertos for two violins by Bach and Gustav Holst, the latter work having been written for and dedicated to the two sisters.

The death of Adila's husband, 27 March 1939, restored her to the concert platform. Her broad, powerful style, responsive and high-spirited but essentially classical, remained unimpaired, and her readiness to tackle new music was as great as it had ever been. She was in demand as a teacher, and although after the war of 1939–45 she settled near Florence, in Italy, she returned from time to time to play in London, where she was last heard in 1957, playing in Bach's Double Concerto with her sister. She died in Florence after a short illness 15 December 1962.

It was customary, during the lifetime of the two sisters, to contrast the classical style of Adila Fachiri with the more impulsively romantic playing of Jelly d'Aranyi. The two were, however, such frequently and perfectly matched partners in many works of a variety of styles and periods that to hear them together was to realize that, essentially, they were in complete musical sympathy. Although Joachim died before he could become a direct influence on the younger of his two great-nieces, it seems that Adila passed on his tradition to her sister.

Jelly d'Aranyi's career began at the age of fourteen when she became the pupil of Hubay at the Budapest Academy of Music. During the 1920s and 1930s, when Adila Fachiri was heard less frequently in public as a soloist, Jelly d'Aranyi combined recitals with concerto performances with major European orchestras and established a reputation in the United States of America. As well as Bach's unaccompanied violin works, she played the concertos of Szymanowski, Respighi, and Vaughan Williams, whose *Concerto Accademico* was dedicated to her; she also played his *The Lark Ascending* very frequently. Her recital repertory included Ravel's *Tzigane*, perhaps the most important of all the works dedicated to either of the sisters; she played it both in its original version, with piano accompaniment, and in its later form as a work for violin and orchestra. She played the violin and piano sonatas of Bartók, written for her and her sister, and the sonatas of John Ireland, (Sir) Eugene Goossens, and Richard Strauss.

Jelly was partly responsible for the rediscovery of Schumann's Violin Concerto, and she first played it to the public in 1938. This concerto, dismissed as an inferior work by Clara Schumann, the composer's widow, had been allowed to become forgotten. What Jelly apparently called a 'game' with a wineglass on an improvised ouija board put her on to the track of a work she did not even know existed (the Violin Concerto was not at that time listed in catalogues of Schumann's compositions). It was found in the composer's manuscripts in the Prussian State Library.

Apart from her many appearances with her sister Adila, Jelly formed a close friendship and effective musical partnership with the pianist Myra Hess. The two played violin and piano music both in Britain and the United States. In 1933 Jelly suggested and began to carry out a series of charity recitals in English cathedrals. Her 'Pilgrimage of Compassion', as the series began to be called, happily extended itself far beyond her original plan. She was appointed CBE in 1946.

When Adila Fachiri retired and settled in Italy, Jelly d'Aranyi followed her after a short time. She died in Florence 30 March 1966.

The d'Aranyi sisters were both fine violinists of technical accomplishment and widely sympathetic musicianship. The teaching of Hubay and the strict artistic discipline of Joachim, which controlled their natural impulsiveness, made their appearance together memorable in music as diverse as that of Bach and their contemporary composers. In spite of their apparent differences of style, they brought the same tradition and same outlook to whatever music they played together.

Between the world wars the musical parties at their studio in Chelsea were much appreciated by their friends, for distinguished artists found it a pleasure to play or sing for such sympathetic and understanding hostesses.

Their popularity among eminent men and women came from a readiness of response to events, personalities, and surroundings, and was the result of charm which, on the platform, was inclined to be spectacular. Virtually self-educated, they read widely and were always ready to speak their minds, sometimes with a startling disregard for conventional notions of tact. Not only through the musical tradition they served, but also through richness of personality, they impressed themselves on the world as women of unusual gifts, both personal and musical.

There is a portrait of Adila Fachiri by the German artist Nelson (*c.* 1907). Portraits of Jelly d'Aranyi have been painted by Neville Lytton (1919), de Laszlo (1928), and Charles-Louis-Geoffrey-Dechaume. (Sir) William Rothenstein sketched her in 1920.

[*The Times*, 1 April and 17 December 1962; Joseph MacLeod, *The Sisters d'Aranyi*, 1969; personal knowledge.]

IVOR NEWTON

published 1981

BOOSEY Leslie Arthur

(1887–1979)

Music publisher, was born in Bromley, Kent, 26 July 1887, the eldest of five children (three sons and two daughters) of Arthur Boosey, music publisher, and his wife, Lucy Ashton. After some years at Malvern College he chose, instead of going to a university, to work for a time in the music publishing house of Durand in Paris, before joining the family business, a conservative and rather old-fashioned one largely associated at that time with the Boosey Ballad Concerts in the Albert Hall.

Long before 1914 Boosey had been a keen territorial officer, and throughout the war he served in France with the 22nd London Regiment. Captured, as a major, in the March offensive of 1918, he was put up against a wall to be shot for refusing to give information to the enemy: at the last moment, however, the German officer changed his mind: 'All right', he said, 'you can go back; you're a gentleman.' Boosey was recommended for appointment to the DSO, but the recommendation miscarried—the first but not the last occasion on which deserved recognition, sponsored by responsible people, was not forthcoming.

When he got back to the publishing business in 1920 Boosey had to adapt himself to conditions very different from those of 1914. Recording and radio transmission had created new problems and possibilities, and Boosey met the challenge by establishing firm friendships with many leading composers. A merger with the firm of Hawkes, completed in 1930, led to important developments in the manufacture of musical instruments and increased publishing activity, especially in the American market. The culmination of this vigorous expansion came with the acquisition in 1947 of the Koussevitsky catalogue, which added the names of Prokofiev, Rachmaninov, and Stravinsky to a list that already included those of Strauss, Bartok, Copland, and Britten. By this time the firm of Boosey & Hawkes, in its own field, was one of the most influential in the world.

Leslie Boosey was an adventurous and shrewd publisher, but he was also a very scrupulous one. His weakness, if weakness it was, lay in his readiness to trust everybody and to believe that people would not do to him the things he would never do to them: he lived to learn that this was over-optimistic. In the later years of his publishing career he began to find himself involved in circumstances that were distasteful; and in 1963, after some years of increasing discomfort, he severed his connection with the firm whose prosperity he had done so much to create and sustain.

Boosey retained until the end of his life a great influence in the Performing Right Society, which he had joined in 1926, and whose chairman he became in 1929. This office he held with distinction until 1954, when he gave up the post to Sir Arthur Bliss. During his period of office he attended all the great international conferences, where he was respected by publishers, authors, and composers alike. In 1976 he was awarded the International Society's gold medal: he was also a chevalier of the Legion of Honour and was honoured by the Royal Philharmonic Society of London, with which he was closely associated during most of his life.

Boosey should be remembered, if for nothing else, for the fact that in 1944, by his personal initiative, he saved the Royal Opera House from becoming a Mecca dance-hall. He had learnt that a lease was about to be signed which would produce that very result, and he acted quickly. With his partner Ralph Hawkes, having been to Washington to gain the support of Lord Keynes, he secured the lease for the firm of Boosey & Hawkes and the Covent Garden Opera Company. It was an achievement of great importance at the time and for the future.

A casual observer, meeting Leslie Boosey, might have taken him for a typically urbane and conventional business man: it would have been a mistake, for beneath the polished surface there lay a different reality. Experience in the trenches, which included the death of a loved brother and many friends, had led him to examine and reject most of the comfortable beliefs learnt at home and at school, and to search for more dependable convictions. His mind was naturally sceptical and critical: he read widely in philosophy, theology, history, and science, and wrote a great deal, though not for publication: he was always ready to submit his views to criticism and discussion. And these studies, continued until the onset of his last illness, were undertaken not as an intellectual pastime, but in order to discover a way of life. That he was successful in this endeavour is suggested by the fact that he was able to accept without bitterness the realization that a long and helpful career had passed without public recognition—a source of surprise and regret to those who knew his work. His gaiety, his lively mind, and his amused observation of the world and its ways, made him a sought-after companion in the Savile Club and elsewhere. To those fortunate enough to know him better he was a great deal more than that.

In 1921 he married Ethel Torfrida, daughter of Frank Marchant, paper maker; they had three sons and a daughter. He died at his home in Hampshire 5 September 1979.

[Personal knowledge.]

THOMAS ARMSTRONG

published 1986

EBERT (Anton) Charles

(1887–1980)

Actor and opera director, was born 20 February 1887 in Berlin, the eldest child of Count Potulicky, a Prussian government official in Berlin, who was Polish, and his wife, Mary Collins, who was Irish. He was legally adopted by Wilhelm and Maria Ebert of Berlin. Customarily known as

'Carl', Ebert was educated at Friedrich Werder'sche Oberrealschule, Berlin, and then at Max Reinhardt's School of Dramatic Art, Berlin. After a short spell as a clerk in a private bank to help to support his foster-parents he embarked on an acting career. He was accepted, even as a student, by Max Reinhardt for a number of important roles in productions at the Deutsches Theater, Berlin, which was under Reinhardt's direction. He then joined the Frankfurt-am-Main Drama Theatre and in the seven years up to 1922 played most of the major roles in that theatre. He joined the Berlin State Drama Theatre in 1922 and continued his career as one of Germany's leading actors until 1927.

In 1919 he had founded the Frankfurt Drama College and in 1925 he became director of the Berlin Academy of Music and Drama with the title of professor. In 1927 he became the first actor to be appointed Generalintendant of the Hessische Landestheater in Darmstadt where until 1931 he had the opportunity of practising his ideas on modernizing attitudes and methods in opera production. In 1931 he was appointed to the post of Intendant of the Staedtische Oper, Berlin.

When the Nazis took power in Germany Ebert decided, despite the offer of an enhanced position in the Berlin theatre, to build a new career abroad. He settled with his family in Switzerland. His first major assignment was as director of the opening production of the first 'Maggio Musicale' in Florence (1933). Subsequently he directed in the major opera houses of the world, including La Scala, Metropolitan Opera, Vienna State Opera, Teatro Colon Buenos Aires, and at the Salzburg Festival, among others.

In 1934 he was invited by John Christie and his wife Audrey to join with them and Fritz Busch to help to launch the Glyndebourne Opera. He accepted the appointment as Glyndebourne's artistic director, a position he held until 1959. During this period he directed almost every production mounted by Glyndebourne both in the festivals there and in the first Edinburgh Festivals of 1947 to 1955. His productions initially concentrated on the operas of Mozart, but soon embraced a wide variety of repertory extending from the British premier of Verdi's *Macbeth* and of Stravinsky's *The Rake's Progress* (the world première of which he had in 1952 directed in Venice) through the works of Strauss, Rossini, Debussy, Gluck, and Donizetti. His collaboration with Busch immediately gave Glyndebourne the hallmark of artistic excellence which established its reputation as a Festival of international importance. His subsequent work with a variety of conductors, in particular Vittorio Gui in the 1950s, maintained Glyndebourne's position at the forefront of operatic enterprise. Perhaps his greatest contribution to British opera was to establish it as a Gesamtkunst—an artistic synthesis—of music and theatre, giving dramatic credibility in the production of opera in a way that had been previously absent. Glyndebourne's artistic foundations and its policy of operation were to a major extent established by Ebert and Busch and the weight of their contribution has played a vital part in Glyndebourne's early years and as a heritage for its continued success since Ebert's final production there in 1962.

During World War II Ebert 'fathered' Turkish opera and drama, having from 1936 advised Kemal Ataturk on the establishment of the Turkish national opera and theatre companies and helped to establish music and drama academies there.

In 1948 he created the opera department of the University of Southern California, Los Angeles, the success of which resulted in the establishment of a new professional company, the Guild Opera Company of Los Angeles. At this time he obtained American citizenship. In 1954 he accepted an invitation to resume his pre-war position at the Staedtische Oper (later renamed the Deutsche Oper), Berlin. In 1961 he supervised the rebuilding and directed the opening production of the new opera house in Berlin.

Among Ebert's honours were: honorary doctorate of music, Edinburgh University (1954); honorary doctorate of fine arts, University of Southern California (1955); the Ernst Reuter plaque of the City of Berlin (1957); a knighthood of the Dannebrog Order of Denmark (1959); Grosses Verdienstkreuz mit Stern, Germany (1959); Grosse Ehrenzeichen for services to Mozart, Austria (1959); honorary CBE (1960); and grande medaille d'argent de la ville de Paris (1961).

He was a man of majestic appearance, powerfully built with in later years a mane of white hair. He was a man of considerable resolve, displaying on occasions a fiery temperament, but more often than not exercising a considerable amount of persuasive charm.

In 1912 Ebert married Lucie Karoline Friederike, daughter of Oskar Splisgarth, electrical engineer. They had one daughter, who became a prominent German actress and died in 1946, and one son, Peter, theatre producer and administrator, who was awarded an honorary D.Mus. of St. Andrews in 1979. This marriage was dissolved in 1923 and in 1924 he married Gertrude Eck (died 1979). Of the second marriage there were two daughters and one son. Ebert died in Santa Monica, California, 14 May 1980.

[*The Times*, 16, 22, and 28 May 1980; personal knowledge.]

George Christie

published 1986

BLOM Eric Walter

(1888–1959)

Music critic and lexicographer, was born 20 August 1888 in Berne, the only son and elder child of Frederick Walter Blom, bookseller and amateur singer of Danish origin, and his wife Anna Elise Rosalie Wenger. He was educated privately, and was always very reticent about his early years: he seems to have been largely self-taught in music. Blom settled in England shortly before the war of 1914–18, and after working for two music publishers—Breitkopf & Härtel in Berne and J. & W. Chester in London—began to make his name in 1919 as a writer of programme notes for the Promenade Concerts. His flair and knowledge led to his becoming London music critic of the *Manchester Guardian* in 1923; an appointment to the *Birmingham Post* followed in 1931; and from 1949 onwards he worked as music critic of the *Observer*. In all three tenures, Blom showed a wide range of musical sympathies and balanced judgements, and wrote with fine style and sensitivity. Of his dozen books, *Mozart* (1935) was by far the most successful. Written with insight and affection for the Master Musicians series (of which he was editor), it remained in print for over fifty years.

Blom's fluent command of languages was invaluable in his work as a lexicographer. His Everyman's *Dictionary of Music* (1946) revealed his gift for the systematic organization of a large quantity of material. Its success led at once to his appointment as editor of the fifth edition of *Grove's Dictionary of Music and Musicians*, a task which occupied him until 1954.

The fourth edition of *Grove* appeared in 1940, comprising a revision of the five volumes of the third edition of 1927, with a sixth, supplementary, volume. But clearly, by the late 1940s, an entirely new approach was required, and Blom was given a free hand to bring everything as up to date as possible. Of the eight million or more words to which the nine-volume fifth edition ultimately amounted, over half were entirely new articles or replacements of old ones, and nearly all else was revised. Though some of the original contributions by Sir George Grove were still retained, Blom was able to take account of the huge expansion of musical scholarship and history that had occurred during the preceding quarter of a century. In addition to planning and editing, he read the entire *Dictionary* in proof, a prodigious task for one man. The result was the crown of his life's work and his lasting monument. In 1950, because of pressure of work on *Grove*, Blom gave up the important editorship of *Music & Letters*, which he had held since 1937. He resumed it in 1954 and continued as editor until his death. In this capacity, his wisdom and tolerance gave much encouragement to young writers.

Blom was a man of sterling character—modest, kindly, humorous, hospitable, and friendly: he hated pretentiousness in any form. In 1955 he was appointed CBE and was awarded a D.Litt. by the University of Birmingham. He married in 1923 Marjory Spencer (died 1952), the daughter of a London photographer. There were a son and daughter of the marriage: the daughter married the humorous writer Paul Jennings. Blom died in London 11 April 1959.

[Stanley Sadie (ed.), *The New Grove Dictionary of Music and Musicians*, 1980; information from Celia Jennings (daughter); personal knowledge.]

ALEC HYATT KING

published 1993

TEYTE Margaret (Maggie)

(1888–1976)

Dame

Soprano, was born 17 April 1888 at Wolverhampton, the seventh of eight children (five boys and three girls) of Jacob James Tate, and his second wife, Maria Doughty. There were also two sons of a previous marriage. Jacob Tate was a prosperous wine merchant and a keen amateur musician who had once journeyed to Leipzig in order to take piano lessons with Theodor Leschetizky. Maria Tate was also musical, and sang. When the family moved to London in 1898, Maggie began to have some music lessons, at first in piano and theory at the Royal College of Music. She was invited to sing, as an amateur, at a church charity concert in 1903, and aroused the interest of her accompanist, a young man of social as well as musical background named Walter Rubens, the brother of Paul Rubens who composed musical comedies. She was in effect adopted by the Rubens family, who divined her promise and introduced her to Lady Ripon, the musical hostess and friend of Jean de Reszke.

In 1904 she was sent by her English patrons to study with de Reszke in Paris for two years, and at once impressed him with what seems to have been from the first a pure timbre and easy emission of tone. She quickly absorbed both the vocal training of de Reszke and the general artistic atmosphere of Paris. In 1906, when not yet eighteen, she made her first public appearances in a Mozart festival organized by Reynaldo Hahn and Lilli Lehmann, at which she sang in scenes from *Le Nozze di Figaro* (as Cherubino) and *Don Giovanni* (as Zerlina), still using the original spelling of her surname, which she was soon to change in order to preserve its correct pronunciation in France. On 7 February 1907 she made her stage début at Monte Carlo as Tyrcis in Offenbach's *Myriame et Daphné* (a new version of the first act of *Les Bergers*), as Zerlina, and as Rosa in Saint-Saëns's *Le Timbre d'argent*. On her twentieth birthday she made her first appearance at the Paris Opéra-Comique, as Glycère in *Circé* by the brothers Hillemacher, appearing there also in other roles, including that of Mignon.

Her chance came when she was chosen to succeed Mary Garden in the role of Mélisande in Debussy's *Pelléas et Mélisande*, and coached for the part by the composer himself (her first performance was on 13 June 1908). Debussy also accompanied her, both at the piano and as conductor, in performances of his own songs; and from that time French song in general, and the music of Debussy in particular, became the centre of her artistic career, at least in its more serious aspect. On her return to England in 1910 she sang Mélisande and her Mozart roles (adding to them Blonde in *Die Entführung aus dem Serail*), besides such leading parts as Madam Butterfly, Gounod's Marguerite (in *Faust*), and Offenbach's Antonia (in *The Tales of Hoffmann*), with the Beecham Opera Company and later with its successor, the British National Opera Company (BNOC), both at Covent Garden and on provincial tours.

For three consecutive seasons (1911–14) Maggie Teyte sang with the Chicago Opera Company, both in Chicago itself and on tour in Philadelphia and New York; among her parts with this company was the title-role in Massenet's *Cendrillon*, which was the sole occasion that she sang in the same production as Mary Garden, the Prince Charming. At Boston, where she was a member of the Opera Company from 1914 to 1917, her Mimi and Nedda were specially admired; but America was not to see her Mélisande until as late as 1948. In England, after World War I, she continued her appearances as Mimi, Butterfly, Hansel, and the Princess in the BNOC's first performances of *The Perfect Fool*, a satirical opera by Gustav Holst; but for a while she also made frequent sallies into operetta and musical comedy (*Monsieur Beaucaire, A Little Dutch Girl, Tantivy Towers*), and was at one time in some danger of being regarded as a lightweight artist.

It was therefore fortunate that in the mid-thirties her career should have received a fresh impetus from an unexpected source. Joe Brogan, a great admirer of her art who was the founder of the Gramophone Shop in New

York, had been campaigning for some authentic Debussy recordings from her, and in 1936 succeeded in persuading HMV to make an album. Maggie Teyte, accompanied by Alfred Cortot, made a recording that became famous. Thenceforward, her status as an interpreter of French song was indisputable; and during the next decade she made many further records of Fauré, Hahn, and other French composers with Gerald Moore as accompanist, as well as a few orchestrally accompanied songs by Berlioz, Duparc, and Ravel. Her London and New York recitals became notable events; and in 1948 her Mélisande was at last seen, at the New York City Center, some forty years after her first appearance in the part. In 1951 she sang Belinda in *Dido and Aeneas* by Purcell, to the Dido of Kirsten Flagstad, at the Mermaid Theatre (then located in Acacia Road, St. John's Wood); and on 17 April 1955 (her sixty-seventh birthday) she gave what proved to be her farewell concert at the Royal Festival Hall, still in remarkably good voice.

Maggie Teyte was small and slight, with a personality that was often charming, always downright, and sometimes abrasive. Throughout her long career, the quality of voice remained inimitable and unmistakable: it was a very pure sound, always under perfect control, with softly floated head-notes devoid of shrillness, and with an uncommonly free and fearless use of the chest register which gave strong character and humour to such renowned performances of hers as that of 'Tu n'es pas beau' from Offenbach's *La Périchole*. She could still sound fresh and youthful even in Ravel's taxing 'Shéhérazade' at the age of sixty. Although her French accent was not flawless (containing certain exotic intonations that were said to have charmed Debussy), she showed an acute sensibility to the colour and meaning of the phrase, and in such songs as Debussy's 'Chansons de Bilitis' she has hardly been surpassed. A slightly excessive use of the downward portamento occasionally introduced a sentimental touch into otherwise immaculate interpretations; but her combination of natural gifts, spontaneity, and musical taste secured for her a unique position in her chosen field which was eventually, if belatedly, recognized in official circles. In 1943, at a dinner given in her honour in London, she received the Croix de Lorraine accompanied by a letter from General de Gaulle; she was made a chevalier of the Legion of Honour in 1957, and appointed DBE in 1958.

In 1909 Maggie Teyte married Eugène de Plumon, a French lawyer. They were divorced in 1915 and in 1921 she married Walter Sherwin Cottingham, son of Walter Horace Cottingham, a Canadian-American millionaire; they were divorced in 1931. There were no children of either marriage. Maggie Teyte died in a London nursing home, after a long illness, 26 May 1976.

[Maggie Teyte, *Star on the Door*, 1958; Garry O'Connor, *The Pursuit of Perfection: A Life of Maggie Teyte*, 1979; personal knowledge.]

DESMOND SHAWE-TAYLOR

published 1986

CARDUS (John Frederick) Neville (1889–1975)

Sir

Writer and critic, was born possibly 2 April 1889 at 2 Summer Place, Rusholme, Manchester, the home of his maternal grandparents. His maternal grandfather was a retired policeman. His unmarried mother, Ada Cardus, died in 1954, and on his marriage certificate he gave the name of his father (whom he never knew) as the late Frederick Cardus, Civil Service clerk. In his *Autobiography* (1947) Cardus disclosed that his real father was 'one of the first violins in an orchestra' who vanished from his mother's life almost as soon as he casually entered it. His mother and his aunt he described as having joined 'the oldest of professions'. Even Cardus's year of birth is uncertain. Although he gave it in *Who's Who* as 2 April 1889, on his marriage certificate of 17 June 1921 he gave his age then as thirty-one. Cardus was equally evasive about his childhood and education at a board school, but Summer Place in Rusholme was not the slum that his book implies. He educated himself by reading and had various menial jobs. His first connection with journalism was in a printer's works, where he had to boil the type in a pan to clean it after it was removed from the page-formes. Later he sold chocolates in the Manchester theatre where the repertory company of Annie Horniman later performed. There his lifelong relish of the music hall began. In 1901 he first entered Lancashire's county cricket ground at Old Trafford, where he saw A. C. MacLaren hit a boundary before rain stopped play. But it was enough to start another passion; thereafter he went there often and watched the cricketers of the 'Golden Age'.

In 1904 Cardus was a clerk in a marine insurance agency, where his employers were indulgent towards his frequent absences in the reference library or at Old Trafford. He began to read the music criticism of Ernest Newman and the dramatic criticism, in the *Manchester Guardian*, of C. E. Montague, James Agate, and Allan Monkhouse, and he also began to write in imitation of them. This was Manchester's cultural heyday, when Hans

Richter and Adolf Brodsky guided its musical life. Cardus went to the Free Trade Hall on the night of 3 December 1908 when the First Symphony of Sir Edward Elgar had its first performance, and he educated himself in opera during the regular visits of the touring companies.

In 1912 he became assistant cricket coach at Shrewsbury School, where the headmaster was Cyril Alington. Cardus acted as his secretary from 1914. He volunteered for the army but was rejected because of his short sight. Returning to Manchester in 1916, Cardus was for three months Manchester music critic of the Socialist newspaper *Daily Citizen.* Unemployed and unfit for the army, he wrote to C. P. Scott, editor of the *Manchester Guardian*, seeking any kind of work on the paper. Scott took him on as a secretary, then decided he did not need one. But three months later, in 1917, he appointed Cardus to the reporting staff at 30 shillings (£1.50) a week. Soon the initials 'N.C.' appeared at the end of music-hall notices, but he made his real mark on the paper in the summer of 1919, after an illness, when the kindly news editor sent him to recuperate by reporting the opening of Lancashire's first post-war cricket season. Soon he was writing about cricket not merely as a reporter, but as an essayist, an observer of character. His prose was allusive, studded with poetical quotations and musical analogies. A game had not been written about in this way before. He adopted the pseudonym 'Cricketer', and before long was one of the *Guardian*'s chief attractions to readers. Other writers on cricket have displayed more strategic knowledge of the game; none has captured its spirit and atmosphere as perceptively and humorously. He created a Dickensian gallery of characters, as he admitted, and the characters themselves played up to him. In 1922 Grant Richards published Cardus's *A Cricketer's Book*. There followed *Days in the Sun* (1924), *The Summer Game* (1929), *Good Days* (1934), and *Australian Summer* (1937).

In spite of cricket, Cardus still hankered after the arts. His interest in music being known to Scott, in 1920 he became assistant to the paper's chief critic, Samuel Langford, succeeding him in 1927. Unlike some critics, Cardus did not isolate himself from the artists upon whom he passed judgement, for he enjoyed their company as much as their performances. Thus he became the friend of Sir Thomas Beecham, Kathleen Ferrier, Sir John Barbirolli, Artur Schnabel, and Claudio Arrau. In his writings on music, as on cricket, Cardus was more interested in aesthetics than technicalities, in emotional rather than intellectual response. Newman described him as a 'sensitized plate', and he did not demur. Cardus inherited Langford's championship of the music of Gustav Mahler. His essay on Mahler in *Ten Composers* (1945, revised as *A Composers' Eleven*, 1958), made as many converts to the music as Bruno Walter's 1936 recording of

Das Lied von der Erde. It is Cardus at his best, whereas his analytical study of the first five symphonies (*Gustav Mahler: his Mind and his Music*, 1965) was not a success and was significantly not followed by a planned second volume.

In January 1940 Cardus arrived in Australia where he wrote on music for the *Sydney Morning Herald* and gave many broadcasts. He returned to Britain in June 1947, writing on cricket for the *Sunday Times* while expecting to succeed the long-lived Newman as music critic. In 1951 he returned to the *Manchester Guardian* as its chief London music critic and occasional cricket contributor. He continued in this role to the end of his life although he felt increasingly out of sympathy with the paper after it loosened its Manchester ties. Even if he now visited his native city ever more rarely, his spiritual home remained Scott's *Guardian* in Cross Street. He was happiest in his late years holding court behind the Warner Stand at Lord's—he was a wonderful raconteur—or in the Garrick Club. He returned to Australia for brief visits in 1948, 1949, and 1954. After he had reached his mid-seventies, many honours came to him—the CBE in 1964, a knighthood in 1967, Austria's decoration of honour (1st class) for science and art in 1970, and honorary membership of the Royal Manchester College of Music (1968)—his sole Manchester honour—and of the Royal Academy of Music in 1972. But he valued highest the presidency of Lancashire County Cricket Club in 1970–1, seventy years after he had seen MacLaren's drive for four. His last book of essays, *Full Score*, was published in 1970.

In 1921 Cardus married Edith Honorine Watton (died 1968), a schoolmistress, daughter of John Thomas Sissons King, schoolmaster; there were no children. Edith was active with one of Manchester's most enterprising amateur stage companies, the Unnamed Society. Cardus died in London 28 February 1975.

[Neville Cardus, *Autobiography*, 1947, and *Second Innings*, 1950; Robin Daniels, *Conversations with Cardus*, 1976; Christopher Brookes, *His Own Man* (biography), 1985; *Daily Telegraph, Guardian*, and *The Times*, 1 March 1975; private information; personal knowledge.]

MICHAEL KENNEDY

published 1986

BOULT Adrian Cedric

(1889–1983)

Sir

Orchestra conductor, was born 8 April 1889 in Chester, the only son and younger child of Cedric Randal Boult, JP, oil merchant, and his wife, Katherine Florence Barman. The family were Unitarians. He was educated at Westminster School, and at Christ Church (of which he was made an honorary Student in 1940), Oxford, where he was president of the University Musical Club in 1910, and took a pass degree in 1912. After studying under the distinguished German conductor Arthur Nikisch at the Leipzig Conservatorium in 1912–13, he sat his B.Mus. examination at Oxford in 1913, receiving his degree in 1914. He achieved his Oxford D.Mus. in 1921.

Boult's talent for music had revealed itself at a remarkably early age. At sixteen months he was able to pick out tunes on the piano, and by his seventh birthday he had begun to compose. There was, therefore, never any doubt about his choice of profession. At the beginning of 1914 he joined the music staff of the Royal Opera House, Covent Garden, where he participated in the first British performances of Richard Wagner's *Parsifal* in February and March, playing the off-stage bells. As a young man he suffered from a heart condition which rendered him unfit for active service during World War I. He helped to drill recruits in Cheshire for two years, worked in the war office in 1916–18, and found time to organize concerts in Liverpool with a small orchestra drawn from the ranks of the Liverpool Philharmonic Society. This led to his being invited to conduct the full orchestra at a concert in Liverpool in January 1916. The programme of this, his professional début as a conductor, included works by Bach, Haydn, Liszt, and the contemporary composers Sir C. Hubert H. Parry and Arthur de Greef.

In 1918, at the invitation of its composer, Boult conducted the first performance of *The Planets* by Gustav Holst at a concert in the Queen's Hall, London. In the following year he joined the teaching staff of the Royal College of Music, where he remained until 1930, continuing to accept engagements as a conductor in London. His first experience as a conductor of opera was gained with the British National Opera Company, and in 1926 he rejoined the Covent Garden company as a staff conductor. He was also at this time the musical director of the City of Birmingham Symphony Orchestra (1924–30) and, from 1928 to 1931, conductor of the Bach Choir, London.

The most important phase of Boult's career began when he was invited to succeed Percy Pitt as director of music of the BBC at the beginning of 1930. In addition to his other administrative duties, this involved him in recruiting players for and becoming chief conductor of the newly formed BBC Symphony Orchestra which during the following years he developed into a first-class ensemble. From the beginning the orchestra gave public concerts as well as broadcasting from the BBC studios, and Boult took it on tour in Europe with great success in 1935 and 1936, giving concerts in Brussels, Paris, Zurich, Vienna, and Budapest.

Boult had by this time become well known abroad, having been invited to conduct the Vienna Philharmonic Orchestra in Vienna for the first time in 1933, and having later conducted in Salzburg, New York, and Boston. Nor did he lose contact with the world of opera, his performances of *Die Walküre* at Covent Garden in 1931 and *Fidelio* at Sadler's Wells Theatre in 1930 being considered outstanding. He also introduced much new music in his concerts with the BBC Symphony Orchestra, giving the first performances in England of Alban Berg's *Wozzeck* in 1934, and Busoni's *Doktor Faust* in 1937, perhaps his most notable and memorable operatic achievements.

Relinquishing the position of music director of the BBC in 1942, Boult became associate conductor of the Promenade concerts, and continued as conductor of the BBC Symphony Orchestra until 1950 when, having reached the age of sixty, he was retired by the BBC (the wife of whose new director of music Boult had married) and immediately became musical director of the London Philharmonic Orchestra with which he toured West Germany in 1951 and the Soviet Union in 1956. Although, in the following year, he announced his retirement from the London Philharmonic, he continued to make a number of guest appearances with orchestras at home and abroad, in Europe and the United States, and was able to devote a large part of his time to recording many of the works in his vast repertory, especially the music of Sir Edward Elgar and Ralph Vaughan Williams. He conducted the music at the coronations of George VI and Elizabeth II.

In 1959, the year of his seventieth birthday, Boult was offered and accepted the presidency of the Royal Scottish Academy of Music, in succession to Vaughan Williams. In the same year he became musical director of the City of Birmingham Symphony Orchestra for the second time (until 1960), and he returned to the Royal College of Music to teach from 1962 to 1966. Among the many honours he received were his knighthood in 1937, the gold medal of the Royal Philharmonic Society in 1944, and the Harvard medal in 1956. He was made a Companion of Honour in 1969. He had honorary degrees from six universities, including Cambridge (Mus.D., 1953) and Oxford (D.Litt., 1979).

One of the leading British musicians of his time, Boult was the least demonstrative of conductors on the concert platform, obtaining his effects by meticulous rehearsal, impeccable musicianship, and a natural authority. A tall man of erect, almost military bearing, Boult was taciturn by nature. However, his courteous manner could occasionally, at rehearsals, give way to storms of violent temper. He was always concerned to present the music as the composer conceived it, and was reluctant to impose his own personality upon a work in the name of interpretation. He excelled in the nineteenth-century classics as well as in the music of his British contemporaries, and was the author of two excellent books on conducting, *The Point of the Stick* (1920) and *Thoughts on Conducting* (1963), as well as a fascinating volume of memoirs, *My Own Trumpet* (1973).

In 1933 he married Ann Mary Grace, daughter of Captain Francis Alan Richard Bowles, RN, JP, of Dully House, Sittingbourne, Kent, and mother of four children from a previous marriage to Sir (James) Steuart Wilson. There were no children of this marriage. Boult died in a London nursing home on 22 February 1983.

[Adrian Cedric Boult, *My Own Trumpet*, 1973; Michael Kennedy, *Adrian Boult*, 1987; Ronald Crichton in *The New Grove Dictionary of Music and Musicians*, 1980 (ed. Stanley Sadie); personal knowledge.]

Charles Osborne

published 1990

GURNEY Ivor Bertie

(1890–1937)

Composer and poet, was born at 3 Queen Street, Gloucester, 28 August 1890, the elder son and second in the family of two boys and two girls of David Gurney, proprietor of a small tailoring business, and his wife Florence, daughter of William Lugg, house decorator. He was educated at the King's School as a chorister of Gloucester Cathedral, then as an articled pupil of the cathedral organist, (Sir) A. Herbert Brewer, and finally, on winning a composition scholarship (1911), at the Royal College of Music under Sir Charles Stanford.

Though rejected by the army in 1914 on grounds of defective eyesight, Gurney enlisted on 9 February 1915 while still a student and from 25 May 1916 served in France as a private with the 2nd/5th Gloucesters. He sustained a minor bullet wound on Good Friday 1917 and more serious gas injuries on or about 10 September 1917 during the third battle of Ypres

(Passchendaele). Invalided back to England, he spent time in various war hospitals and, after exhibiting signs of mental instability (including a suicide attempt on 19 June 1918), he was finally discharged in October 1918.

He resumed his studies at the Royal College but was unable to concentrate. He returned to Gloucester and, failing to find permanent employment, was obliged to live on a small disability pension and the charity of friends and family. Music and poetry now poured from him, but his behaviour (eccentric before the war) grew increasingly erratic. Further threats of suicide followed and in September 1922 he was diagnosed as suffering from paranoid schizophrenia and committed to Barnwood House Asylum, Gloucester. On 21 December 1922 he was transferred to the City of London Mental Hospital, Dartford, Kent, where he remained until his death.

As a composer Gurney found his voice in 1913/14 with the composition of *Five Elizabethan Songs*. Although he wrote chamber and orchestral music, songs were his true vocation. Manuscripts of more than 300 are to be found in the Gurney archive at the Gloucester city public library. Poetry was a secondary interest that grew only when conditions in the trenches made composition almost impossible. After the war he pursued both arts with equal fervour. Gurney's songs began to reach publication from 1920, but it was not until the Oxford University Press issued two volumes of twenty songs in 1938 that his true stature could be appreciated. Further collections followed in 1952, 1959, and 1979. These were made possible by the faith and industry of Gurney's friend, the musicologist Marion Scott, who had preserved his manuscripts, and the editorial expertise of the composers Gerald Finzi and Howard Ferguson. His manuscripts pose formidable ethical and aesthetic problems because so much of his work is uneven, unpolished, and sometimes incoherent.

Similar considerations afflict his poetry, of which over 1,700 items exist in the Gloucester archive. Two volumes were published during his lifetime: *Severn and Somme* (1917) and *War's Embers* (1919); and minor selections appeared in 1954 and 1973, edited by Edmund Blunden and Leonard Clark respectively. In 1982 the Oxford University Press issued a major selection of some 300 poems, edited by P. J. Kavanagh, and it is on the basis of this volume that his importance as a poet came to be recognized. Gurney's poems celebrate his love of the Gloucestershire countryside with the same unsentimental vigour as they report on the realities of trench warfare and chart his gradual descent into madness. His songs are equally forceful and direct, covering a wide range of emotional expression and empathizing with poets of every period, particularly his contemporaries, the Georgians. In both fields he was an individualist, and in both his successes mark him out as an artist of power and originality.

Gurney died from tuberculosis 26 December 1937 at the City of London Mental Hospital, Dartford, Kent. He was unmarried.

[Michael Hurd, *The Ordeal of Ivor Gurney*, 1978; R. K. R. Thornton, *Ivor Gurney: Collected Letters*, 1991.]

MICHAEL HURD

published 1993

HESS (Julia) Myra

(1890–1965)

Dame

Pianist, was born in London 25 February 1890, the daughter of Frederick Solomon Hess, a textile merchant, and his wife, Lizzie, daughter of John Jacobs, shopkeeper and moneylender of London. She was the youngest of four children of whom the eldest was her only sister. She grew up in a typical Jewish home in north London.

Myra Hess's general education, to her lasting regret, was of the superficial kind then deemed adequate for a young girl. But thanks to her obvious musical talent she was given piano and cello lessons from the age of five. The cello was abandoned when she began more serious study at the Guildhall School of Music, where her teachers were Orlando Morgan (piano) and Julian Pascal (theory). By far the most formative musical influence in her life, however, was that of Professor Tobias Matthay, with whom she studied piano for five years after winning the Ada Lewis scholarship at the Royal Academy of Music in 1903. She always maintained that he was her 'only teacher', and he regarded her as his 'prophetess'.

Myra's official début took place on 14 November 1907, when she gave an orchestral concert at the Queen's Hall in London, conducted by young (Sir) Thomas Beecham. She played concertos by Saint-Saëns and Beethoven (the G major, with which she was later so often associated), together with an obligatory group of solos. Newspaper reports of the concert, and of her first solo recital given at the Aeolian Hall two months later, were mainly enthusiastic. Yet engagements came in slowly and were rarely well paid, so for some years her livelihood depended to a large extent on teaching.

Her first great success came in Holland in 1912, when she took the place of an indisposed colleague to play the Schumann Concerto in A minor with the Concertgebouw Orchestra under Willem Mengelberg. This had a welcome effect on her career in England, where engagements with music clubs and orchestras steadily increased. Visits abroad became impracticable during the war of 1914–18; but on 17 January 1922 Myra made a highly successful American début with a recital at the Aeolian Hall, New York. Thereafter, up to 1939, she divided each year between a North American tour in the winter, concerts in England and Holland in the spring and autumn, and a working holiday, often in the country, during two summer months.

In the early part of her career Myra played a considerable amount of contemporary music, although even then she tended to favour the classical and romantic repertoire. This, and her abiding lack of interest in virtuosity, might suggest a rather forbidding character. But her strength of character was tempered by graciousness and an enchanting sense of humour, which bubbled out irresistibly not only in everyday life, but also whenever she played a light-hearted Scarlatti sonata or Mozart finale. Moreover, in spite of agonies of nerves before every concert, as soon as she stepped on a platform (a shortish but comfortable-looking woman, invariably dressed in black) her deceptive air of serenity made audiences feel that they were her friends, and that the only thing which mattered was the music they were about to enjoy together.

Myra delighted in taking part in chamber music. In the 1920s she regularly joined the London String Quartet for a week's music-making at the Bradford Chamber Music Festival; in the 1930s she had a sonata partnership with the Hungarian violinist Jelly d'Aranyi; and she appeared at the Casals summer festivals in Perpignan and Prades in 1951 and 1952. More important, and wholly characteristic, was her decision on the outbreak of war in 1939 to cancel an American tour in order to remain in England and organize, and take part in, the remarkable series of daily chamber-music concerts which she instituted at the National Gallery in London, with the assistance of Sir Kenneth (later Lord) Clark, the director. They ran uninterruptedly for six and a half years (apart from a short break at the end of the war), were attended by over three-quarters of a million people, and only ceased (to her bitter disappointment) when repairs to the war-damaged Gallery became inevitable.

The finish of the concerts allowed Myra to resume her regular tours in Holland and the United States where she was greeted as a beloved, long-absent friend, and as one who had served music and her country so selflessly. Audiences sensed, too, that her powers of interpretation had acquired a new simplicity, directness, and depth. Whereas formerly her quest for sheer beauty of sound had sometimes interfered with her sense of musical line, she had now achieved such complete technical control that she could concentrate entirely on the shape and meaning of a work, knowing that her fingers would reproduce exactly what her inner ear dictated. Furthermore, her instinctive understanding of whatever music awakened her love and interest had become unerring.

From the late 1950s Myra became increasingly troubled by arthritis of the hands and severe circulatory problems. Her last concert appearance was on 31 October 1961 at the Royal Festival Hall, London, when she played the Mozart Concerto in A major, K. 488, under Sir Adrian Boult. Although she still managed to give occasional lessons to a few gifted pupils, she lacked the physical and mental strength to reorientate her life in a way which might have made retirement tolerable. It was a sad end to a great career. She died at her home in St. John's Wood, London, 25 November 1965. She had never married.

The gramophone recordings made between 1928 and 1959 (a list is in both the books about Myra Hess cited below, but that in Marian McKenna's book is more complete) give little idea of the quality of her playing. She hated recording and, as Professor Arthur Mendel wrote, 'performance for her was *essentially* communication to an audience'. The recording which comes closest to capturing her beauty of tone, human warmth, and deep musical understanding, is probably the Beethoven Sonata in E major, Op. 109, issued in 1954. Of her few publications, immense popularity was achieved by her piano transcription (1926) of the chorale-setting from Bach's Cantata No. 147, familiarly known as 'Jesu, Joy of Man's Desiring'. Few artists have been so closely associated with one piece of music.

For her services to music Myra Hess was appointed CBE (1936), DBE (1941), and commander of the Order of Orange-Nassau (1943). She received the gold medal of the Royal Philharmonic Society (1942) and honorary degrees from the universities of Manchester (1945), Durham, London, St. Andrews (all 1946), Reading (1947), Cambridge (1949), and Leeds (1951).

A charcoal drawing of her (1920) by John Singer Sargent is on loan to the Museum of Fine Arts, Boston, and a bronze bust (1945) by (Sir) Jacob Epstein belongs to the Royal Academy of Music, London.

[The Myra Hess papers and the National Gallery Concerts papers in the British Library; *Grove's Dictionary of Music and Musicians*; Denise Lassimonne and Howard Ferguson (eds.), *Myra Hess by her Friends*, 1966; Marian C. McKenna, *Myra Hess, a Portrait*, 1976; personal knowledge.]

HOWARD FERGUSON

published 1981

TAUBER Richard

(1891–1948)

Austrian tenor, who was naturalized British in 1940, was born 16 May 1891 in Linz, Austria. He was illegitimate, and was christened Richard Denemy after his mother's maiden name. His father, (Anton) Richard Tauber, was an actor, and his mother, Elisabeth Denemy (later Seiffert), played musical-comedy roles. He studied at the conservatoire in Frankfurt 1909–11, and with Carl Beines in Freiburg, and made a youthful début in 1913 as Tamino in *The Magic Flute* at the Neues Stadt-Theater in Chemnitz, of which his father was director, with instant success. He was soon engaged on a five-year contract with the Dresden Opera, where he sang all the leading lyrical tenor parts. In 1915 he made his first appearance at the German Opera House, Berlin. From 1922 his career centred on Vienna, where he sang the classical repertory at the Staatsoper and operetta at the Theater an der Wien.

During the Mozart festivals in both Munich and Salzburg he became enormously popular as Tamino, Belmonte, and Don Ottavio. The famous Swedish Don Giovanni, John Forsell, declared that the young Tauber was the greatest Ottavio he had ever heard, and he was noted for the intense conviction with which he declaimed to his Donna Anna (in the German text then still generally in use, even at festivals) the solemn oath, 'Ich schwöre'. Among his non-Mozartian roles, those of Max in Weber's *Der Freischütz* and of Hans in the German version of Smetana's *The Bartered Bride* were especially successful.

His name and achievements became better known to the general public, however, in the sphere of lighter music: in operetta rather than in opera, and above all in the stage works of Franz Lehár, in which he charmed thousands by his sympathetic tenor quality and by the grace and variety of his vocal inflections. The song 'You are my Heart's Delight' from Lehár's operetta *The Land of Smiles* (1929) was one of his most famous, and it was in this work that he first came to England in 1931. He also showed marked ability as a conductor with the London Philharmonic Orchestra and as a composer. His operetta *The Singing Dream* (1934) was a great success in Vienna, and his other works included the operetta *Old Chelsea* (1943) and an orchestral *Sunshine Suite*. Except for a film version of Leoncavallo's *Pagliacci*, his film career was mainly an extension of his operetta activities.

It would not be quite true to claim that his wide experience of light music, and the strain of singing long parts, with numerous encores, throughout the week left no mark on either his style or his vocal chords; but he can be justly likened to two other similarly popular tenors, John

McCormack and Tito Schipa, in his ability to return successfully to serious music until the end of his career. In 1938 and 1939 he appeared under Sir Thomas Beecham at Covent Garden in his three greatest Mozartian roles and in a German-language *Bartered Bride*; and after the war he insisted on taking part there with his old colleagues, the visiting Vienna State Opera, as Don Ottavio in a *Don Giovanni* at Covent Garden which was to be his final stage appearance, in September 1947.

In appearance, Tauber was not handsome, but genial. His first marriage, in 1927, to the operetta singer, Carlotta Vanconti, was unsuccessful and led to protracted divorce proceedings, which were not finalized until 1936; in that year he married his second wife, the English stage and film actress, Diana Napier, and settled in England. After his death Diana Napier wrote (or collaborated in) three volumes of biography or memoirs. There were no children of either marriage. Tauber died from lung cancer 8 January 1948 in London.

[Diana Napier Tauber, *Richard Tauber*, 1949, and *My Heart and I*, 1959; Charles Castle and Diana Napier Tauber, *This was Richard Tauber*, 1971; Willi Korb, *Richard Tauber*, 1966 (in German).]

DESMOND SHAWE-TAYLOR

published 1993

HOWES Frank Stewart

(1891–1974)

Music critic of *The Times* and author, was born at Oxford 2 April 1891, the elder child and only son of George Howes, a grocer and confectioner of Oxford, and his wife, Grace Phipps. He was educated in his home town, at the Oxford High School, then at St. John's College (1910–14) where he obtained third classes in both classical honour moderations and *literae humaniores*, rowed for his college, and sang in the chorus for the performances of *Fidelio* and *Der Freischütz* conducted by (Sir) Hugh Allen. He became a schoolmaster, served a brief prison sentence as a conscientious objector, then went to the Royal College of Music (1920–2) as a member of the criticism class run by H. C. Colles. In 1925 he joined Colles on *The Times*, succeeding to the principal post on Colles's sudden death in 1943.

His first book, *The Borderland of Music and Psychology* (1926) and his editing of what became the *Journal of the English Folk Dance and Song Society*

(1927–45) soon indicated the cast of his mind, in which speculation was rooted in the soil of his native country. His *A Key to Opera* (with P. Hope-Wallace, 1939) revealed another enthusiasm, and in his *Full Orchestra* (1942) his experience as a lecturer together with his lively, lucid prose, produced a popular success.

He lectured at the RCM from 1938 to 1970, during the war coming up from his family retreat, a mill near Standlake, where the river Windrush flows into the Thames. When he took over *The Times* in 1943, readers were jaded, and both newsprint and music were in short supply. With vigour and assurance he directed the post-war expansion. He approved the anonymity then in force—though his own views and style were recognizable enough—as an aid to objective, responsible criticism without personal display. He insisted on a wide coverage, so that the paper reported débuts and amateur events as well as major national occasions. He refused to look at scores in advance and liked writing on the night, believing that the pressure made for immediacy, and also allowed no opportunity for outside influence. He retained the weekly music article, valuing the chance it gave him to expand on a remote or a topical point, and was once delighted to be complimented simply on the range of his subjects.

He threw his considerable weight behind such causes as opera in English (he himself had no modern languages), the building of the Festival Hall, and the founding of *Musica Britannica* while he was president of the Royal Musical Association (1948–58). His authority and urbane common sense made him much in demand on committees: he was chairman of the Musicians' Benevolent Fund (1938–56), and of the English Folk Dance and Song Society (1932–46), and also served the Arts Council, the British Council, the BBC, the British Institute of Recorded Sound, and Music in Hospitals. He gave the Cramb lectures at Glasgow University in 1947, and the first Crees lectures (1950) for the RCM. He was created CBE in 1954; he was an honorary fellow of the RCM, an honorary RAM, and an honorary freeman of the Worshipful Company of Musicians.

In spite of his many commitments, his early *William Byrd* (1928) was followed by valuable and substantial studies of *The Music of Ralph Vaughan Williams* (1954) and *The Music of William Walton* (2 vols., 1942, 1943, revised 1965). Though his approach was on the whole analytical, he was always concerned to uncover the thoughts behind the sounds, to relate music and ethics, to consider symbolism and aesthetics. These ideas he set out in *Man, Mind and Music* (1948). His wide sympathies extended notably to Lord Britten, but less to Stravinsky and hardly at all to Schönberg and his school; but his strong intellect and professional curiosity enabled him to write stimulatingly about music he disliked, and only occasionally could he be provoked to bluntness. His probity and good humour were respected even by those who might disagree with his taste.

He retired from *The Times* in 1960, and out of his study with its continuous murmur of the millrace came an account of *The Cheltenham Festival* (1965) while he was its chairman, and a jubilee record of *Oxford Concerts* (1969). But the major works, summarizing his life's interest, were *The English Musical Renaissance* (1966), a synthesis of a period he had largely lived through, and *Folk Music of Britain—and Beyond* (1969).

Howes was a deeply emotional but self-reliant man, to whom music was one of the humanities. He was a trenchant speaker who enjoyed great occasions; but was as happy among his family and close friends on his river bank. There in the end he suffered cancer, and he died in hospital at Oxford 28 September 1974.

Howes married Barbara Mildred, daughter of John Tidd Pratt, a solicitor, in 1929, and had one son and three daughters.

[Private information; personal knowledge.]

DIANA MCVEAGH

published 1986

BLISS Arthur Edward Drummond

(1891–1975)

Sir

Composer and Master of the Queen's Music, was born in Barnes, London, 2 August 1891, the eldest of the three sons (there were no daughters) of Francis Edward Bliss, an American business man resident in England, and his second wife, Agnes Kennard, daughter of James Davis, a minister of religion, of Great Yarmouth. There was also a son of a previous marriage. Arthur Bliss, whose mother died when he was four, was educated at Rugby and went in 1910, with a classical exhibition, to Pembroke College, Cambridge. There his mentors in music were the strict disciplinarian Charles Wood and the internationally minded Edward Dent. He took his BA and Mus.Bac. in 1913 and was then at the Royal College of Music for some months where he received constructive advice from Ralph Vaughan Williams and Gustav Holst. Shortly after the declaration of war on 4 August 1914 he enlisted and was on active service with the Royal Fusiliers and, later, with the Grenadier Guards; he was twice wounded, gassed, and mentioned in dispatches.

On his release from the army in 1919 he embarked upon a period of experimentation in unusual instrumental ensembles with, generally, a vocal line as an integral part, as in *Madam Noy, Rhapsody*, and *Rout* of 1918–20. Bliss began a lasting association with the world of the theatre by writing, in 1921, imaginative incidental music for Viola Tree's production of *The Tempest* at the Aldwych. He possessed an abiding interest in painting, particularly that of his contemporaries, and one of his earliest large orchestral pieces, the balletic *Mêlée Fantasque* (1921), written in memory of the stage designer, Claud Lovat Fraser, evokes something of his fascination with colour, movement, and changing patterns. The scrupulous attention which Bliss paid to the scoring of the heraldic *A Colour Symphony* (1922) had a lasting effect upon the orchestration of subsequent works. So, too, did the setting of a sequence of texts, by way of the *Pastoral* and the *Serenade* (1928 and 1929), upon one of his most powerful and individual compositions, *Morning Heroes* (1930). This symphony, which skilfully brings together a spoken part, chorus, and orchestra, was written in memory of his brother, Kennard, 'and all other comrades killed in battle' and through it he exorcized the lasting horror of his war experiences.

Bliss had paid his first visit to America, to Santa Barbara, California, in 1923, where he lived for two years. He and Gertrude ('Trudy') Hoffmann, a daughter of Ralph Hoffmann, an American, director of the Natural History Museum at Santa Barbara, were married there in 1925 and immediately took up residence in London. They had two daughters.

Between 1927 and 1933 Bliss wrote three important chamber music works, the Oboe Quintet, the Clarinet Quintet, and the Viola Sonata, for (Sir) Eugene Goossens, Frederick Thurston, and Lionel Tertis respectively. Again for particular soloists he wrote the Piano Sonata (1952) for Noel Mewton-Wood, the Violin Concerto (1955) for Alfredo Campoli, and the Cello Concerto (1970) for Rostropovich. It was with Solomon in mind as soloist that he wrote the Piano Concerto of 1939.

The composer, his wife, and their two young daughters were in America for the first performance of the Piano Concerto at the New York World Fair in 1939. He remained there as visiting professor (from 1940) at the University of California, Berkeley, and wrote two significant works, the *Seven American Poems* and the First String Quartet. Unhappy at not helping the war effort, he returned to England to join the BBC Overseas Music Service where, in 1941, he framed a far-reaching memorandum, his 'music policy statement', a motivating factor in the eventual creation of the Third Programme. He was BBC director of music from 1942 to 1944.

Bliss wrote music for six films commencing with that for *Things to Come* (released in 1936, produced by (Sir) Alexander Korda, with a script by H. G.

Wells), four ballets of which the first, *Checkmate* (1937), is the most widely known, and two operas, *The Olympians* (libretto by J. B. Priestley) produced at Covent Garden in 1949, and, for television, *Tobias and the Angel* (1960) to a libretto by Christopher Hassall. He delighted in working in new mediums and was adept in providing Fanfares, of which he wrote over thirty, each singularly apposite to the occasion celebrated.

In *Music for Strings* (1935) Bliss explored to the full the nuances obtainable from the string orchestra and achieved one of his tautest and most lyrical compositions. The Second String Quartet of 1950 he considered to be his best chamber-music work and he felt a particular affection towards his two large compositions of 1955, the Violin Concerto and the *Meditations on a Theme of John Blow*. There is a deep sense of awe underlying these orchestral variations and this same spirituality is found in the five cantatas written between 1961 and 1974. The first of these, *The Beatitudes*, was in fulfilment of an invitation to contribute a work for the opening in 1962 of the new Coventry Cathedral and the last, which he did not live to hear, was the *Shield of Faith*, written for the quincentenary in 1975 of St. George's chapel, Windsor. *The Golden Cantata*, written in 1963 to poems provided by Kathleen Raine, celebrated the giving of the first degree in music by Cambridge University in 1464, and is an essay in music of the act of musical composition. His last big orchestral score, *Metamorphic Variations* of 1972, embodies the dramatic, lyrical, and meditative qualities inherent in so much of Bliss's music.

Bliss wrote over a hundred and fifty compositions of which at least fifty are major works. Through his exceptional ability to turn from the needful isolation of the creative artist to the pressures imposed upon the committee man and administrator, to both of which roles he brought an appraising and incisive mind, he became one of the outstanding musical personalities of the twentieth century.

A dedicated Master of the Queen's Music (from 1953), he nevertheless accepted time-absorbing appointments in the service of music and of fellow musicians in this country and abroad; he was an early and active member of the International Society for Contemporary Music and was chairman of the music committee of the British Council from 1946 to 1950. In 1956 he led a group of British musicians to perform in Russia and, invited by Shostakovich, was in Moscow again in 1958 as a member of the jury for the Tchaikovsky competition for pianists. In 1964 he conducted at a number of centres in Australia, and in Japan. Throughout his life Bliss was a talented and sensitive conductor and gave authoritative interpretations of his own music in the concert hall and in the recording studio. He worked steadfastly for the Performing Right Society, as a director from 1947 and as president from 1954. In his memory an annual postgraduate scholarship in composition at the Royal College of Music was inaugurated in 1982 by this society.

Bliss's marriage was a happy one. He and his wife enjoyed many deeply shared interests and he entered closely into the pursuits, joys, and sorrows of his children and grandchildren. He never lost his enthusiasm for the game of chess; he was a brilliant conversationalist with a playful and pungent humour.

Bliss was knighted in 1950 and appointed KCVO in 1969 and CH in 1971. He received many further honours amongst which were honorary degrees from London, Cambridge, Edinburgh, Bristol, Glasgow, and Lancaster. He was honorary freeman of the Worshipful Company of Musicians (1954) and gold medallist of the Royal Philharmonic Society (1963). In 1953 he was made an honorary fellow of his Cambridge College, Pembroke.

Bliss died at his London home 27 March 1975.

[Arthur Bliss, *As I Remember* (autobiography to 1966), 1970; Bliss papers in Cambridge University Library and in the Imperial War Museum; George Dannatt, a critical appreciation of the life and works in *Arthur Bliss: Catalogue of the Complete Works*, ed. Lewis Foreman, 1979; private information; personal knowledge.]

GEORGE DANNATT

published 1986

HOWELLS Herbert Norman

(1892–1983)

Composer, teacher, and writer on music, was born at Lydney, Gloucestershire, 17 October 1892, the youngest in the family of six sons and two daughters of Oliver Howells, painter and decorator, and his wife, Elizabeth Burgham. Both parents were of Gloucestershire stock. While he was still at Lydney Grammar School his talent came to the notice of (Sir) A. Herbert Brewer, organist of Gloucester Cathedral, who taught him until in 1905 he was ready to be formally articled. Howells was therefore one of the last English musicians to be brought up in the old apprentice system under which the aspirant was bound to a master, generally the nearest cathedral organist, who accepted full responsibility for his training and entry into the profession.

Howells accordingly spent the next three years in the daily routine of cathedral music, playing and singing in the services, and open to the influences of the Anglican liturgy, the psalms, the Book of Common

Prayer, and the Authorized Version of the Bible, read by educated men in a noble building. He admitted, in later life, that this discipline had largely moulded him, and that the main lines of his development had already been laid down when in 1912 he won an open scholarship at the Royal College of Music and became a pupil of Sir Charles Stanford and Sir C. Hubert H. Parry, under whom, during the next five years, he wrote a great deal of music and acquired a formidable technique. Even more significant than Stanford's discipline and Parry's generous friendship were the social and literary influences that flooded over him in the new world that welcomed his romantic good looks, charm, and lively intelligence.

Recognition and a kind of maturity came early. 'Lady Audrey's Suite' (1916) and 'A Spotless Rose' (1918) were widely performed, but it was the Piano Quartet (1916) and the Phantasy String Quartet (1918) that gave fuller insight into the composer's powers. In 1916, whilst acting as assistant organist at Salisbury Cathedral, Howells suffered a complete breakdown of health, and it was not until late in 1918 that he was able to return to work and to London, where he lived for the rest of his life except for a sojourn in Cambridge during World War II.

At all times he had his living to earn, and after 1920 a family to support. He did this by teaching theory and composition at the Royal College of Music for over fifty years, and by lecturing and writing, for which he had a great gift. He was also much in demand as an adjudicator at music festivals. If he had not been a musician he could have excelled as a poet and essayist like his friend Walter de la Mare. From 1936 to 1962 he was director of music at St Paul's Girls' School, Brook Green. From 1955 to 1962 he was King Edward professor of music at London University. It was his powers of withdrawal and concentration that enabled Howells in a busy life to produce so much music, including, besides early orchestral works, three concertos, six quartets, five instrumental sonatas, a number of large choral works, among them the masterly 'Hymnus Paradisi' (1938), forty songs, and much church and organ music. He had an unfailing insight into what is possible with a small choir and organ. Howells also wrote many short choral pieces for school and festival use, some of which are among his most distinguished works, imaginative, beautifully composed, and fastidious in choice and treatment of poetry. In this and other respects he may be compared with his Tudor predecessors, John Dowland and Thomas Campion, with whom he clearly felt an affinity. It is significant that he chose to write for the clavichord, most intimate of instruments, for his music often conveys a sense of privacy, of direct address to one friend, or of solitary meditation.

Yet he was in no sense a miniaturist. Although he did not choose, in maturity, to work in the major symphonic forms, there are movements in the chamber music and the choral works that are designed on a massive scale; and he had, moreover, the power to create a sense of space even in short pieces. The Nunc Dimittis of the St Paul's service, for instance, in the building for which it was composed, sounds as vast as the cathedral itself. Howells's harmonic idiom was based on the tonal tradition, derived through Parry, Stanford, and Sir Edward Elgar, but extended by bold use of chords superimposed or used as appoggiaturas. No composer of his generation could remain aloof from the recent revivals of Tudor music, folk-music, and modal harmony, and Howells took from these sources all that he needed: but he was never dominated by them, or by the powerful proximity of Ralph Vaughan Williams, as were some of his contemporaries. There is, in his melodic style, as much of S. S. Wesley and Parry as of folk-song.

One finds in Howells's music depth of feeling, tenderness, humour, and a love of the English landscape, but seldom great exuberance. Especially after the death of his son in 1935, there is often a persistent note of nostalgia and regret that has led critics to compare him with Frederick Delius. But in Howells's music there are gleams of visionary hope that are not to be found in Delius and it is noticeable that in the last years of his life he wrote little or nothing except church music, as if, for the finale, he was returning home to Gloucester. Although as a young man he had not expected to live very long, he remained active, in spite of increasing deafness, until his death in Putney at the age of ninety, 23 February 1983.

In 1920 he married Dorothy (died 1975), daughter of William Goozee. There were two children, Michael, who died of poliomyelitis in 1935, and Ursula, the distinguished actress.

He received many honours. He was appointed CBE in 1953 and CH in 1972. Honorary degrees were conferred on him by Cambridge (1961) and the RAM. He was a D.Mus. of Oxford. He was elected an honorary fellow of St John's College, Cambridge, in 1962 and of The Queen's College, Oxford, in 1977. He served as master of the Worshipful Company of Musicians in 1959. In 1952 he was president of the Incorporated Society of Musicians, and in 1958–9 of the Royal College of Organists. After his death a memorial tablet was unveiled in Westminster Abbey, where his music is so often to be heard. There are portraits by Sir William Rothenstein and Brenda Moore in the RCM, and a fine photograph of Howells as a young man by Herbert Lambert of Bath.

[Christopher Palmer, *Herbert Howells*, 1978; Hugh Ottaway in *The New Grove Dictionary of Music and Musicians*, 1980 (ed. Stanley Sadie); private information; personal knowledge.]

Thomas Armstrong

published 1990

SORABJI Kaikhosru Shapurji

(1892–1988)

Composer, pianist, and critic, was born 14 August 1892 in Buxton Road, Chingford, Essex, as Leon Dudley Sorabji, the only child of a Parsee father, Shapurji Sorabji, mining engineer and iron merchant, and his wife, Madeline Matilda Korthy, a Spanish-Sicilian opera singer. He adopted the baptismal Parsee name by which he was universally known early in life, though near the beginning of his career he signed himself with various forms combined with Leon and Dudley. Latterly, he rejected enquiries into his nomenclature, as into the date of his birth, with the jealousy of his privacy that characterized his life. This refusal to countenance journalistic curiosity, coupled with the challenging letters with which he would bombard those who displeased him, was in contrast to the good humour, humanity, and generosity which he would show to those who came into personal contact with him.

Sorabji had a number of teachers, both as pianist and as composer, but no formal education. His keyboard technique was admired as 'fabulous' in the early part of his career, when he played in London, Paris, Vienna, Glasgow, and Bombay; but he came to dislike the circumstances of public music-making, and withdrew from the concert platform in December 1936. In part, this was a product of his distaste for playing to listeners of whom he knew nothing, and a preference for addressing himself to a circle of like-minded friends. Modest private means enabled him to pursue a life free from the commercial considerations he despised, though he continued to compose (up to 1982) and won himself a reputation as a trenchant and forceful critic. He wrote especially for the *New English Weekly* and for A. R. Orage's *New Age*. Some of these articles were later reprinted in two collections, *Around Music* (1932) and *Mi Contra Fa* (1947).

The allusion in the latter title is to the medieval theorists' description of two harmonically opposed notes: 'mi contra fa, diabolus in musica'. However, Sorabji's criticism was generally on the side of the angels. Composers he championed included those who later won international recognition, such as Karol Szymanowski, Nicolai Medtner, Ferruccio Busoni, and Charles-Henri Alkan (all influences on him), and some who have remained neglected even in their homeland, such as Francis George Scott and Bernard van Dieren. Though he had strong opinions, his attacks were mostly reserved for individuals and organizations whose attitudes he saw as betraying the loftiest standards. He expressed himself forcefully, even vituperatively, but always with an expressive bravura in his widely ranging sentences that made his prose an entertainment to read. A characteristic sally is contained in the dedication of what is probably his masterpiece, the 'Opus Clavicembalisticum', to his friend Hugh MacDiarmid, 'likewise to the everlasting glory of those few men blessed and sanctified in the curses and execration of those many whose praise is eternal damnation'.

The elaborate richness of Sorabji's own music reflects not so much the oriental luxuriance often attributed to it (nothing enraged him more than being described as Indian) as the profusion of his mind. His earliest music, such as 'In the Hothouse' (1918), is sensuously chromatic in a manner that might have appealed to Frederick Delius (who admired his 'Le Jardin Parfumé' of 1923). His First Piano Sonata (1919) makes some use of thematic cells, but the Second (1920) lacks any clear controlling form; his Fourth (1929) was accompanied by a rare analytical account (probably written as a concert introduction) and gave the music more traditional forms, such as passacaglia. He claimed to have found his direction with the First Organ Symphony (1924), a work lasting two hours (the later organ symphonies are longer). In this, an opening passacaglia provides an admirable tether for his far-ranging fantasy, a fugue develops some ideas strictly, and in the complex finale all the ideas are woven into a complex tapestry. Other works drew, with great technical virtuosity, on established forms as providing the basis for elaborate fantasizing. The 'Opus Clavicembalisticum' (1930) for solo piano combines into its time-span of four and a half hours a wide range of disciplines, of which the principal is fugue.

Sorabji gave the first performance himself in Glasgow in December 1930. It caused a sensation, but then an inadequate London performance of the first part by an inferior pianist contributed to Sorabji withdrawing his music from being performed without his express permission. This 'ban' was relaxed when, in the 1970s, there began to emerge virtuosi with the technique to master the music's difficulties and the intellectual curiosity to explore its substance. Sorabji was happy with performances by John Ogdon, Yonty Solomon, Michael Habermann, Geoffrey Douglas Madge, and the organist Kevin Bowyer.

He had by now long since withdrawn to what he called his 'granite tower', a small house on the outskirts of Corfe castle in Dorset, from which he repelled casual vistors with fierce notices, but welcomed friends with warmth and wit. Short of stature and bespectacled, with a shock of wild black hair that in later life became a heavy white mane, he was a delightful conversationalist whose independence of mind remained intact. Though he denied any formal doctrinal persuasion, he had a religious temperament that inclined towards Roman Catholicism while not excluding an interest in Parsee mysticism. He never married, and died in Winfrith Newburgh 15 October 1988.

[Sorabji archive, organized by Alistair Hinton, Easton Dene, Bailbrook Lane, Bath, BA1 7AA; personal knowledge.]

John Warrack

published 1996

TURNER Eva

(1892–1990)

Dame

Soprano, was born 10 March 1892 in Oldham, Lancashire, the elder child and only daughter of Charles Turner, chief engineer of a cotton mill, and his wife, Elizabeth Park. She was educated at Werneth Council School until she was ten, when her father moved to Bristol to take up an appointment as manager of another mill in the south-west of England. There she heard her first opera, performed by the Royal Carl Rosa Opera Company, and so struck was she by this that she was determined to become a singer herself. Her parents were musical and gave her every encouragement, sending her for lessons to Daniel Rootham, who taught (Dame) Clara Butt. Her studies were continued at the Royal Academy of Music in London from 1911 to 1915, during which time she was briefly betrothed. In 1915 she joined the chorus of the Royal Carl Rosa Opera Company and entered her new life with enthusiasm and with the serious determination and commitment that were to characterize her life. When not singing in the chorus, she never lost an opportunity to observe other performers from the wings, studying the action and learning the soprano repertory. Anxious for progress, she badgered the management to find her roles and she soon made her solo début as the page in *Tannhäuser*.

But she was still not satisfied and on the advice of the company's principal tenor she began to work with an Australian singer, Richard Broad, who had recently joined the management of the Carl Rosa. He had sung as a bass under Hans Richter at Covent Garden but it was as an authority on voice production that he was better known. This proved to be a most successful relationship and Broad continued as her coach, adviser, and friend until his death some twenty-five years later.

The small parts became larger and by 1920 she was assuming dramatic roles as her voice increased in power and weight. In that year the company gave a four-week season at Covent Garden, in which Eva Turner sang Santuzza (*Cavalleria Rusticana*), Musetta (*La Bohème*), Leonora (*Il Trovatore*), Butterfly (*Madame Butterfly*), Antonia (*The Tales of Hoffmann*), and Venus (*Tannhäuser*). *The Times* critic described her Leonora as promising. Another Covent Garden season followed a provincial tour in 1921. *Tosca* and *Lohengrin* were two operas added to her repertory that year. In 1922 she appeared as Eva in *The Mastersingers* with the Carl Rosa at Covent Garden and won a favourable review from *The Times*.

In 1924 the Carl Rosa was at the Scala Theatre, London, for a four weeks' season, which was to be a turning-point in her career. Amongst other roles she sang Butterfly on 3 June, a performance with which *The Times* did not find entire favour but which so impressed Ettore Panizza, Arturo Toscanini's assistant at La Scala, Milan, that he asked her to sing to the maestro. She auditioned successfully and was offered Freia and Sieglinde in the 1924–5 Scala season. Her characteristic loyalty persuaded her to tell the Scala that she was not free to accept because of her Carl Rosa contract. However, she was released from that and she spent the intervening period learning Italian and her roles in that language in preparation for her début, as Freia in *Das Rheingold*, conducted by Vittorio Gui.

Thus began the most important part of her career and a love affair with Italy, one of the outcomes of which was the Italianate colouring, with strongly enunciated consonants, that she applied to her speaking voice. She was then to sing in many Italian cities, including Brescia, where she first sang Turandot with conspicuous success. This became the role with which she was most identified, although from all accounts her portrayal of Aida was equally outstanding. She built and settled in a villa on Lake Lugano.

By now Eva Turner's international career was developing rapidly, with appearances in Europe and in North and South America. She returned to Covent Garden in 1928 in a season managed by the Covent Garden Syndicate and scored a major triumph with the press and public with Turandot. Nobody was prepared for such a magnificent performance. Nothing could then hold her back and with her glorious voice she took a leading place in the seasons at Covent Garden and abroad until the outbreak of war in 1939. Small of stature, Eva Turner had a vocal command which was astonishing, with a voice of extraordinary sumptuousness and steadiness that could project through the loudest orchestral sound without any loss of quality. She surmounted all the technical challenges of the German and Italian repertoire and left her audiences spellbound. Turner's colossal success did much to encourage British opera singers, who at that time were probably more noted for dependability than brilliance and rarely given chances to prove anything else. An English name was a handicap and Eva Turner was urged to change hers. Proud of her Lancastrian roots, she refused.

Undoubtedly the war deprived her of the final climax to her career, including the conquering of audiences at the Metropolitan in New York. After a performance of Turandot in Brescia in 1940 she returned to England, where she spent the war singing in concerts for the armed forces and the radio, and in the Proms. A staunch patriot, this was what she believed she needed to do and she declined invitations to work in America.

In the 1947 and the 1948–9 seasons at Covent Garden she joined the newly formed company for Turandot, in which once again she astonished and thrilled the public and press. Then, in 1949, she accepted an invitation to teach at the University of Oklahoma for one year and stayed for ten. After that she returned to London to teach at the Royal Academy of Music. Teaching occupied her for several more years and she passed on to many singers, established and young alike, her wealth of experience, with her inimitable generosity but also with a ferocious expectation of hard work and high standards in return. For her it was serious work which produced the results, however talented the individual. President of the Wagner Society from 1971 to 1985, she was appointed DBE in 1962. She was FRAM (1928), FRCM (1974), an honorary citizen of the state of Oklahoma (1982), and a first freeman of Oldham (1982). She was awarded an honorary D.Mus. from Manchester (1979) and Oxford (1984) and became an honorary fellow of St Hilda's College, Oxford (1984).

Well into her nineties and still immaculately groomed and handsome, she maintained her enthusiasm and capacity for work, serving on committees and lecturing endlessly to music clubs and societies. She was constantly to be seen at opera performances and concerts, travelling and coaching with an eagerness and display of energy that left many breathless. She never married, probably because she believed she could not find the time for the kind of relationship that marriage demanded. She led an intensely busy life, ably assisted by Ann Ridyard, her companion and secretary for thirty-five years, whose descent into senile dementia caused Eva Turner's last years to be burdensome. Eva Turner died 16 June 1990 in the Devonshire Hospital, Marylebone, London.

[*Record Collector*, vol. 11, no. 2, Feb./March 1957; John Steane, *The Grand Tradition*, 1974; Royal Opera House programme note by Harold Rosenthal for concert celebrating Eva Turner's ninetieth birthday, 14 March 1982; private information; personal knowledge.]

JOHN TOOLEY

published 1996

GOOSSENS Eugene

(1893–1962)

Sir

Conductor and composer of music, was born in London 26 May 1893. He came from a musical family of Belgian origin: his grandfather and father, both named Eugene, were both conductors of the Carl Rosa Opera Company, and his mother Annie was the daughter of the operatic bass singer Aynsley Cook. Eugene was the eldest son of the family; his younger brothers were Adolphe, a horn player who was killed in World War I at the age of eighteen, and Leon, the well-known oboist. His sisters Marie and Sidonie are equally well known as harpists.

Goossens was educated at the Muziek-Conservatorium in Bruges and the Liverpool College of Music: from the latter he won a Liverpool scholarship to the Royal College of Music in London in 1907. Here he studied the violin with Achille Rivarde, piano with J. St. Oswald Dykes, harmony with Charles Wood, and counterpoint with Sir Frederick Bridge. He was later admitted into Sir Charles Stanford's composition class. He began his professional career in 1912 as a violinist in the Queen's Hall Orchestra under Sir Henry J. Wood. He was rejected for military service in World War I on medical grounds, and began his conducting career with various opera companies, including the Beecham Opera Company in 1916 and the British National Opera Company: he was also a guest conductor with the London Symphony Orchestra, the Philharmonic Orchestra, and various provincial orchestras, the Royal Choral Society, and the Handel Society. He conducted for the Diaghilev Ballet during their London seasons: this involved performing a number of unusual works, especially modern ones, as Diaghilev had a very forward-looking taste in music and liked to present as many new works as possible.

Goossens was by now becoming known as a composer as well as a conductor: his choral work *Silence* was performed at the Gloucester Three Choirs' Festival of 1922 together with the *Colour Symphony* by Goossens's near contemporary (Sir) Arthur Bliss: both works were put into the programme at the request of Sir Edward W. Elgar. Goossens continued to compose in all forms for the rest of his life, and in the 1920s he was regarded as a member of the avant-garde of British music.

In 1923 Goossens was appointed conductor of the Rochester Philharmonic Orchestra in New York State. This orchestra had been founded by George Eastman, head of the Eastman Kodak Company, who believed in the civilizing influence of music without pretending to have any technical knowledge of it himself. In the eight years which Goossens spent at Rochester he established the orchestra's reputation, and it became one of the leading orchestras in the United States. Goossens conducted at Rochester during the winter season, returning to London in the summers. In 1923 he conducted Delius's incidental music to James Elroy Flecker's play *Hassan* in Basil Dean's famous production: in 1926 he composed and conducted incidental music for Margaret Kennedy's play *The Constant Nymph*, again directed by Basil Dean. His first opera, *Judith*, with a libretto by E. Arnold Bennett was produced at Covent Garden on 25 June 1929 under the composer's direction.

In 1931 Goossens was appointed conductor of the Cincinnati Symphony Orchestra, a position which he held till 1947: he was the musical director of the Cincinnati May Festival eight times, and made a number of guest appearances as conductor in New York, Boston, Philadelphia, San Francisco, Detroit, and other American cities, as well as conducting opera. On 24 June 1937 he conducted the first performance of his opera *Don Juan de Mañara* at Covent Garden as part of an unusually large repertory of operas performed in honour of the coronation of King George VI. Goossens conducted a number of other operas during this season.

In 1947 Goossens went to Sydney as conductor of the Sydney Symphony Orchestra and director of the New South Wales Conservatorium. He remained there till 1956, when he resigned after a law case, and considerably improved the standards of both institutions. After this he returned to England and made a number of guest appearances with orchestras in many countries. He was knighted in 1955. In 1934 he had been made chevalier of the Legion of Honour.

Apart from his two operas Goossens wrote a choral work, *The Apocalypse*, generally considered one of his finest compositions, two symphonies, a sinfonietta, a concertino for double string orchestra, and an oboe concerto for his brother Leon, as well as chamber music (including a work for his brother and two sisters), songs, and piano music. Though his music was frequently played in the 1920s and 1930s, performances of it have become rarer in recent years. This is probably due to changes in musical fashion, as Goossens always wrote expertly for whatever combination of voices or instruments he was using. Of his two operas *Judith*, in one act, develops and sustains the dramatic action successfully: in *Don Juan* he had to face competition with Mozart, and in addition had to set a libretto by Arnold Bennett, who was more at home writing novels than in dramatic works and was consequently unable to produce striking stage effects. Also the company assembled for the first performance was very much an *ad hoc* one, and not all the singers were really experienced. Goossens's style is chromatic, but does not approach the 'total chromaticism' of Schoenberg: there is always a tonal feeling in it. And Goossens had a very lively and varied feeling for colour. As a person he was charming, witty, and cultured, as may be seen from his autobiography, and he was always willing to help younger musicians. He was very much an all-round musician, of a kind which are not often found nowadays, and his conducting was invariably musical and alive.

Goossens was married three times: first, in 1919, to Dorothy Millar, daughter of Frederick C. Smith Dodsworth, and they had three daughters; secondly, in 1930, to an American, Janet Lewis, who bore him two daughters; thirdly, in 1947, to Marjorie Fetter Faulkrod, who survived him. In 1951 he published an autobiography, *Overture and Beginners*, describing the events of his life up to 1931 and also giving a good deal of information about the lives of his grandfather and father. A projected second volume was never completed. While returning from a visit to Switzerland he was taken ill on the aeroplane and died in Hillingdon Hospital 13 June 1962. There is a bronze bust of Goossens by Frank Dobson (1927).

[Grove's *Dictionary of Music*; Eugene Goossens, *Overture and Beginners*, 1951; private information; personal knowledge.]

HUMPHREY SEARLE

published 1981

HESELTINE Philip Arnold

(1894–1930)

Writer on music, and musical composer under the pseudonym Peter Warlock, was born in London 30 October 1894, the only child of Arnold Heseltine, solicitor, of London, by his wife, Edith Covernton. His father died when the boy was two years of age. He was sent to a private school at Broadstairs when he was about nine, and thence to Eton (1908–1911). In 1910 he made the acquaintance of Frederick Delius, with whom there followed a remarkable interchange of letters, and whose music became the chief formative influence on Heseltine's own compositions. The two years after Eton found Heseltine in Germany, where he spent some months at Cologne, and at his mother's home, Cefn Bryntalch, Abermule, Montgomeryshire. He went up to Christ Church, Oxford, in the autumn of 1913, but left at the end of the summer term of 1914. Thereafter, for a few years, he lived principally in London. He had liked neither Eton nor Oxford, and liked still less the patriotic attitude to the European War. His letters to Delius about this time reveal him a brooding, melancholy, yet passionate soul, an 'apparent misfit in any surroundings'. In November 1915 Heseltine met David Herbert Lawrence, whose personality and philosophy affected his music, and he stayed with Lawrence in Cornwall in the spring of 1916. About this time he also met Bernard van Dieren, the influence of whose music upon him was second only to that of Delius and ultimately became greater. In December 1916 he married Minnie Lucy, daughter of Robert Stuart Channing, a mechanical engineer. They had one son. From August 1917 to August 1918 he was in Dublin, and after that in London again. He first used the pseudonym 'Peter Warlock' as the signature to certain songs published in 1919. He founded *The Sackbut* (incorporating *The Organist*), a musical journal, in May 1920, and edited it until June 1921. During these two years he was abroad for long periods in France and North Africa. He settled at Cefn Bryntalch in the autumn of 1921, but, having separated from his wife in or about the year 1923, he left Wales in 1924 and after a few months in London went to live, early in 1925, at Eynsford, Kent. There he stayed until October 1928. After returning to Wales for a short time, he went again to London and lived there till his death, which took place at Chelsea, 17 December 1930, as the result of gas poisoning. At the inquest the jury were unable to determine whether he had committed suicide.

Heseltine left about a hundred songs with pianoforte accompaniment; *The Curlew*, a song cycle for tenor voice, flute, cor anglais, and string quartet (1920–1922); *Serenade* for string orchestra, in homage to Delius (1923); and other instrumental compositions, besides numerous choral works and part songs. He edited a large body of Elizabethan and Jacobean music, Purcell's *Thirteen Fantasies for strings*, and transcriptions of many works by Delius. He was the author, among other books, of *Frederick Delius* (written under his own name, 1923), *The English Ayre* (1926), and, in collaboration with Cecil Gray, *Carlo Gesualdo, Musician and Murderer* (1926).

Heseltine's music is that of a belated Elizabethan. His best songs—described by a writer in *The Times* as 'some of the most exquisite and original songs of our day'—have unusual purity of tone, a delicate clarity of utterance, and a learned simplicity. His books are scholarly contributions to their subjects.

[Cecil Gray, *Peter Warlock: A Memoir of Philip Heseltine* (containing a complete list of his works musical and literary), 1934; private information.]

E. O'Brien

published 1937

MOERAN Ernest John

(1894–1950)

Composer, was born at Osterley, Middlesex, 31 December 1894, the second son of the Rev. Joseph William Wright Moeran, vicar of St. Mary's church, Spring Grove, Heston, and his wife, Ada Esther Smeed Whall, of King's Lynn. His father was of partly Irish descent and his paternal grandfather was vicar of Bacton, Norfolk. He was educated at Uppingham and the Royal College of Music; after active service in the army, he studied composition privately for a time with Dr. John Ireland. He was a sufficient pianist to play publicly in his own chamber works and also studied the violin, but his life was devoted to composition. His father's induction as vicar of Salhouse, Norfolk, had a deep effect, for Moeran early became acquainted with the Norfolk peasants and their folk-music, in which he took much interest, becoming a field-collector and arranger.

Moeran's first phase was prolific; his string Quartet (1923) survives in performances, and there were also a Trio for piano, violin, and 'cello (1920), two orchestral rhapsodies (1922 and 1924), and a symphonic impression 'In the Mountain Country' (1921). The piano pieces, like 'Stalham River' (1921), somewhat influenced by Dr. John Ireland, are attractive, and there are a number of excellent songs, especially ''Tis time, I think, by Wenlock town' and the *Shropshire Lad* cycle, 'Ludlow Town' (1920). Already Moeran was showing how strongly affected he was not only by folk-song but by the countryside around him. Settings of actual folk-songs were less arrangements for voice and piano than re-creations of the originals' mood.

After a creative lull Moeran returned, around 1930, to chamber music of a more austere kind with his Sonata for two violins alone and his string Trio. He also turned to choral music, writing a suite of six part-songs in the English style to Elizabethan poems, entitled 'Songs of Springtime' (1933); between 1933 and 1939 he wrote six more, published as 'Phyllida and Corydon' (1939), where the style was nearer that of the madrigal, and the influence of Bernard van Dieren was evident. Southern Ireland had long attracted Moeran, and from 1934 he made his home for many months of the year at Kenmare, county Kerry. His last publication was a collection of Irish folk-songs, taken down aurally.

In 1926 Sir Hamilton Harty suggested that Moeran should write a symphony; after abandoning first attempts, he embarked on new ideas and, closely consulting Harty all the time, completed his G minor Symphony in 1937. It is a work redolent of the Atlantic coast of Eire. A later

'Sinfonietta' (1945), however, derives its inspiration from the Radnorshire hills, his family by then having moved to Kington, Herefordshire. The broader, more jovial side of his character is seen in his 'Overture for a Masque', written in the war of 1939–45 for the Entertainments National Service Association. The violin Concerto of 1942 is the most important of Moeran's later works—perhaps of them all. Sensitive, lyrical, it reflects the Southern Irish coast in full summer, with a scherzo representing a Kerry fair. In 1945 Moeran married Kathleen Peers Coetmore, 'cellist, daughter of Stanley Coetmore Jones, estate agent, of Lincolnshire. For her he wrote a 'cello Concerto (1945) which showed a new dramatic power, and a 'cello Sonata (1947) of even greater intensity and sense of struggle.

Physically Moeran was largely built and rubicund, his pale dreaming eyes contrasting with his peasant-like exterior. Lonely by nature, he had nevertheless a great gift for friendship and was happiest when among country folk in a village inn. There his shy talent for mimicry could develop, and also his broad laughter. Moeran's compositions are essentially musical in quality, expressive more of song than of dance, and despite certain roughnesses often touchingly emotional. He died at Kenmare 1 December 1950. There were no children.

[Private information; personal knowledge.]

HUBERT FOSS

published 1959

SARGENT (Henry) Malcolm (Watts)

(1895–1967)

Sir

Conductor, composer, pianist, and organist, was born in Ashford, Kent, 29 April 1895, the only son of Henry Edward Sargent of Stamford, Lincolnshire, and his wife, Agnes Marion Hall, daughter of a Hertfordshire landscape gardener. Henry Sargent, employed in a coal-merchant's business, was a keen amateur musician, an organist, and choirmaster, who carefully fostered his son's talent from the beginning: but the most important early influence was that of Frances Tinkler, an inspiring local teacher who greatly helped Sargent and, some years later, (Sir) Michael Tippett. At Stamford School Sargent was soon noted for irrepressible high spirits and quick intelligence. But his interests were never academic, and other possibilities were elbowed aside in the determined drive towards a career in music.

On leaving school in 1912 Sargent was articled to Haydn Keeton, organist of Peterborough Cathedral, and was one of the last to be trained in that traditional system, so soon to disappear. The discipline involved daily contact between master and pupil in a severe but balanced curriculum: and Keeton was an exacting tutor, old-fashioned perhaps, but highly professional. He taught the counterpoint of Fux, organ-playing in the style of Samuel Sebastian Wesley, and piano-playing in that of Mendelssohn and Sir W. Sterndale Bennett. Score-reading and continuo-realization were learnt not as academic subjects but in the daily practice of cathedral music, performed from the scores of William Boyce and Samuel Arnold. It was hard work, and Sargent loved it all. 'We had no money', he said in later years, 'and our future was quite uncertain: but it was music, music, music all the way.'

By the end of his articles Sargent was already recognized as a fine player, a composer of marked talent, and a well-equipped professional whose charm, vitality, and technical accomplishment were outstanding. But his ambitions, though ample, were not yet defined. Sometimes he thought of being a solo-pianist and, like a Rachmaninov, playing his own compositions all over the world. He could probably have done this. After a performance of *The Dream of Gerontius* in 1912, however, he told a group of friends about his intention to be 'a second Elgar'. For that destiny he was less well suited.

In 1914 Sargent was appointed organist of Melton Mowbray, and found himself among people able to appreciate his talent and to give him substantial help. It was made possible for him to have piano-lessons from Benno Moiseiwitch; a good orchestra was created for him to conduct in Leicester; opportunities were offered generously. In his Leicester concerts he appeared as pianist, composer, and conductor, and won the approval of Sir Henry J. Wood, who invited him to conduct, in the 1921 Promenade Concert season, his tone-poem 'Impressions of a windy day'. The performance was a triumph: but it was as conductor rather than composer that the young man was acclaimed, and on that evening the pattern of his career was settled. For a time he continued to work from his base in the Midlands, but in 1923, invited to join the staff at the Royal College of Music, he moved to London, where in the following year he married Eileen Laura Harding Horne, by whom he had two children, a son, Peter, and a daughter, Pamela. The marriage was terminated by divorce in 1946.

The ten years after 1923 were decisive in Sargent's career, and were a time of unremitting hard work and social activity. He was a restless man, for whom dancing till dawn after a concert seemed to be a necessary relaxation. With no private income and increasing responsibilities, as well as a natural inclination to spend freely, he was obliged to undertake whatever work was offered; and his schedule involved much travel, with varied programmes on limited rehearsal time. Only a musician of great talent and resilience could have done what he did. But he might have been wise to be more selective, even if the experience made him a general-purpose conductor of extreme efficiency, sometimes criticized for not being fastidious but also admired for being totally reliable.

Sargent's responsibilities at this time included the Robert Mayer concerts (1924), the Diaghilev Ballet (1927), the Royal Choral Society (1928) including the spectacular productions of *Hiawatha*, the Courtauld-Sargent concerts (1929–40), and the D'Oyly Carte Opera Company (1930). He conducted many performances of the British National Opera Company and numberless concerts in cities outside London. Among the works entrusted to him for first performance were *Hugh the Drover* by Ralph Vaughan Williams, (Sir) William Walton's *Belshazzar's Feast*, and Walton's opera *Troilus and Cressida*.

Success so brilliant and an enjoyment of its glamour so uninhibited were bound to provoke hostility and to 'excite the common artifice by which envy degrades excellence'. There began to be troubles with orchestras which Sargent tried to discipline. Methods that delighted his devoted choralists were less acceptable to experienced orchestral players: harsh things were said on both sides. Some critics described his performances as brash and superficial, and purists objected to adjustments that Sargent made in the scoring of well-known works, even though these were always effective, and generally less drastic than those made by other conductors. Sargent seemed to disregard these attacks: in fact he was deeply hurt, and they added to the strain under which he worked, a strain that was beginning by 1930 to affect the quality of his performances and his health.

In 1932 he suffered a complete breakdown, and there was doubt whether he would recover from the tubercular infection that involved serious abdominal operations. For two years he was out of action, but when he did reappear his performances had all the old zest and a new depth.

In 1944 a fresh blow fell when his much-loved daughter Pamela was smitten with polio and died. For months Sargent was almost a broken man, but music saved him, and he seemed in time to draw inspiration from the experience. There were, however, works that he never conducted again except as a kind of memorial to Pamela, and not a few of his many generous but strictly private benefactions to other sufferers were really an offering to her.

In 1950 Sargent was chosen to follow Sir Adrian Boult as conductor of the BBC Symphony Orchestra and entered the final, most influential, stage of his career. With that orchestra, the BBC Chorus, the Royal Choral Society, the Huddersfield Choir, the Promenade Concerts, and many appearances as guest conductor with other ensembles, he enjoyed unrivalled opportunities for music-making on a great scale. Old prejudices had largely evaporated, and his interpretations were now seen to be equal to those of any conductor in the world; as an accompanist, he was regarded by many exacting soloists as pre-eminent.

His influence in these years was extended by appearances on the Brains Trust, where he effectively represented the common sense and decency of the ordinary citizen, and proved himself more than a match for the plausible intellectuals who often appeared with him. In this as in other activities he used his gifts of personality and showmanship to spread the love of music and to insist upon its place in a good life.

Sargent was now accepted as a valuable ambassador for music, and especially British music, in many parts of the world; and it was on one of his numerous foreign tours that he was taken ill. There was a temporary recovery, and he returned to conducting, but again collapsed in Chicago in July 1967. On his return he was seen to be dying. During the months that remained he continued to present himself with courage and something of the old panache, and made an unforgettable farewell visit to his devoted audience on the last night of the Proms. He died a day or two later at his home in London 3 October 1967.

Sargent's death provoked a remarkable demonstration of public sorrow and admiration. During a career in which social success had played no small part he had won the affection and loyalty of countless ordinary music-lovers who recognized his sincerity and came to share his buoyant love of life and music. He once said in jest that his career had been based on the two Ms, Messiah and Mikado, and there was an element of truth in the comment, which was a characteristic example of his unguarded spontaneity. But he could have added that it also rested on a long record of fine performances, an unfailing devotion to music, and natural endowments of exceptional brilliance.

Sargent's character was a strange blend of simplicity and sophistication, of apparent self-confidence and a deep sense of insecurity. He was an extremely generous man, but could sometimes appear vain and arrogant, displaying a frank enjoyment of fame and success which more cautious persons would have concealed, not from modesty but from fear of ridicule.

The circumstances of his early life had permanently influenced him. If he had enjoyed the privilege of attachment to a great professional orchestra and its conductors he might have become a different musician but not necessarily a better one. As it was, in the tough campaign to make his own way, he won the equipment necessary for the work he had to do, a work that greatly forwarded the interests of British music. After Sir Henry Wood's death in 1944 there was nobody except Sargent who could carry on his particular task; and when Sargent himself passed from the scene his place was not filled.

Sargent was appointed honorary D.Mus. (Oxford) in 1942 and honorary LLD (Liverpool) in 1947, the year in which he was knighted. Among his many other honours were honorary RAM, honorary FRCO, FRCM, honorary FTCL, and FRSA.

There is a bronze bust by William Timyn in the Royal Albert Hall and a portrait in oils by Sir Gerald Kelly. Another portrait in oils by John Gilroy (1967) is in the Garrick Club.

[Charles Reid, *Malcolm Sargent*, 1968; private information; personal knowledge.]

THOMAS ARMSTRONG

published 1981

BAILLIE Isobel

(1895–1983)

Dame

Scottish soprano, was born 9 March 1895 at Hawick, Roxburghshire, the youngest in the family of one son and three daughters of Martin Baillie, master baker, of Hawick, and his wife Isabella, daughter of Robert Douglas, weaver, of Selkirk. She was christened Isabella Douglas and was educated at Princes Road board school and, with a scholarship, at Manchester High School. At a very early age it was noted that 'her voice is something different'. She studied first with Jean Sadler-Fogg and later with Guglielmo Somma. At the age of fifteen she made her first public appearance, for a fee of seven shillings and sixpence, and in the same year sang her first *Messiah* performance.

(Sir) H. Hamilton Harty took great interest in her career and gave her her first Hallé concert (1921). On his advice she studied with Somma in Milan (1925–6). Later Harty wrote to her, 'When you die I want someone to write on your grave, "She was a sweet singer who always respected Music".' He also advised her to change her professional name from Bella to Isobel. Her career developed rapidly in oratorio and in concert following her first London season in 1923 and she became the most sought after soprano in England for Handel, Haydn, Brahms, and Elgar oratorios. She was the first British artist to sing in the Hollywood Bowl in California (1933). In 1937 she sang in Gluck's *Orphée* at Covent Garden and in 1940 she gave many performances of Gounod's *Faust* in New Zealand, but she did not consider opera her true *métier*. She sang in every corner of Britain and appeared 51 times with the Royal Choral Society (which included 33 performances of *Messiah*). She sang for twenty-six consecutive years with the Hallé orchestra, and for fifteen consecutive years at the Three Choirs Festival. Between 1924 and 1974 she recorded 166 songs and arias covering 100 sessions, starting in the acoustic (horn) era and concluding in the stereo age.

At the height of her career Richard Capell, music critic, wrote: 'The character of Isobel Baillie's singing and her fine technique will be indicated if it is said that her performance in Brahms's *Requiem* has hardly been matched in her time. The trying tessitura of "Ye now are sorrowful" becomes apparently negligible and the term "angelic" has sometimes been applied to suggest the effect, not so much personal as brightly and serenely spiritual made here by her soaring and equable tones.' In Handel's *Messiah* her declamation of the Christmas music, the clarity and vitality of 'Rejoice Greatly', the serenity of 'I Know That My Redeemer Liveth' were acclaimed by all who heard her. *The Times* obituary referred to 'her gift for silken legato and silvery tone' and the *Telegraph* to 'that clear beautifully enunciated, entirely individual voice, capable of surprising richness'. Toscanini described her singing 'Right in the middle of the note and none of this', waving his hands in and out as if playing a concertina, indicating excessive vibrato.

Her red-gold hair and lovely complexion were outstanding physical traits. These together with complete dedication to her 'job', as she called it, captivated the audience. She delighted them by the care she gave to her own appearance for she felt that if people came to hear her she should look her best and *Never Sing Louder than Lovely*, the title of her autobiography (1982).

Sir George Dyson, impressed with her performance as the Wife of Bath in his 'The Canterbury Pilgrims', persuaded her to teach at the Royal College of Music (1955–7 and 1961–4). She was a visiting professor at Cornell University (1960–1) and later for many years at the Manchester College of Music. She was described as a teacher 'of rare genius and contagious enthusiasm'. After her retirement from the concert scene she travelled the world giving lecture-recitals. At the age of eighty-five she returned to lecture at Cornell University 'with very impressive vocal examples'. She sang her way through life and at the end quoted Hilaire Belloc: 'It is the best of all trades to make songs, and the second best to sing them.'

She was appointed CBE in 1951 and DBE in 1978. She became honorary RCM (1962) and honorary RAM (1971), and also had honorary degrees from Manchester (MA, 1950) and Salford (D.Lit., 1977).

In 1917 she married Henry Leonard Wrigley, who worked in the cloth trade, when he was on leave from the trenches in Flanders. They had met as fellow artists in concerts in Manchester before World War I. They had one daughter. She lived in Selborne, Hampshire, until her husband died in 1957, and later in St John's Wood, London. Finally she returned to Manchester to be among old friends. She died there 24 September 1983. There is a water-colour portrait of her (artist unknown) as Marguerite in *Faust*, in the possession of her daughter.

[*The Times*, 26 September 1983; *Daily Telegraph*, 21 November 1983; Richard Capell in *Grove's Dictionary of Music and Musicians*, 5th edn., 1954 (ed. Eric Blom); private information; personal knowledge.]

KEITH FALKNER

published 1990

COHEN Harriet

(1896–1967)

Pianist, was born 2 December 1896, the eldest of the three daughters and one son of Joseph Verney Cohen, a composer and business man, of London and Aldershot, and his wife, Florence, daughter of Benjamin White, a dental surgeon, of Ludgate Hill, London. Harriet Cohen's paternal grandfather had emigrated from Lithuania; her father was an amateur cellist and an amateur military historian who combined his two hobbies by writing music for military bands.

The young Harriet Cohen, known to family and friends as 'Tania', was educated at the Royal Academy of Music, which she entered in 1909 as the youngest student ever to hold the Ada Lewis scholarship; she was booked in the register as Harriette Pearl Alice Cohen. Her scholarship, originally awarded for three years, was extended to keep her at the Royal Academy until 1915, and as a student she won the Sterndale Bennett prize, the Edward Nicholls prize, the Hine prize, the RAM prize, the medal of the

Worshipful Company of Musicians, and the Chappell pianoforte prize. Having worked as a piano pupil of Felix Swinstead and a harmony pupil of Frederick Corder, she left the Royal Academy of Music for further study under Tobias Matthay, becoming the third of a trio of outstanding pianists—its other members were (Dame) Myra Hess and Irene Scharrer—who much enhanced the reputation of Tobias Matthay and the Matthay method of piano teaching. Already occupied as a pupil teacher, in 1922 Harriet Cohen joined the staff of the Matthay School as a professor. Her combination of beauty and elegance with real musicianship quickly established her on the concert platform, and the unusual programmes she offered made her recitals lively musical events. She was devoted to the music of J. S. Bach, whose works she played in a style perhaps more overtly expressive than would be approved by some modern critics; she did all she could to popularize the works of the Tudor composers represented in the *Fitzwilliam Virginal Book*, and she took many an opportunity of playing new music; her performances of the standard classics were no less popular. Manuel de Falla's *Nights in the Gardens of Spain*, Prokofiev's concertos and sonatas, and the piano music of Shostakovich, were music she did all she could to popularize, and she became the first pianist outside the Soviet Union to learn the *Twenty-Four Preludes* which Shostakovich composed in 1932 and 1933. Modern British music, in particular, won her allegiance, and (Sir) Arnold E. T. Bax, Ralph Vaughan Williams, John Ireland, and Constant Lambert all wrote works for her as, in a later generation, did Peter Racine Fricker. Her devotion to the music of Bach led a group of grateful composers (it included Sir G. R. Bantock and Bax among her seniors, and (Sir) William T. Walton among her contemporaries) to compile *A Bach Book for Harriet Cohen* (1932), which consisted of piano transcriptions of choral preludes and cantata movements. When, in 1936, she published *Music's Handmaid*, a book principally concerned with her ideas about interpretation, she wrote particularly of Bach, Mozart, Chopin, Brahms, de Falla, Debussy, Bartok, Vaughan Williams, and Arnold Bax. Bax, a close friend of Harriet Cohen since their student days, owed a great deal to the unswerving loyalty with which she played his music wherever she was heard in Europe and across the Atlantic.

Despite the inexhaustible energy which took her from end to end of the British Isles, across Europe, and over the Atlantic on frequent concert tours, Harriet Cohen's health was never strong. In 1925 a course of treatment enabled her to keep tuberculosis at bay, although it forced a lengthy interruption in her career. In 1948, at the Cheltenham Festival, an accident robbed her of the use of her right hand, but two years later she gave the first performance of the *Concertino for Left Hand* which Sir Arnold Bax had written for her. Despite failing sight and two major eye operations, she continued to act as vice-chairman of the Harriet Cohen International Music Awards, which she instituted under the presidency of Jean Sibelius and of which Bax was chairman. In 1938 she was created CBE for services to British music. Among many foreign honours bestowed upon her, she was commander of the Order of the Crown of Belgium (1947), and a member (first class) of the Order of the White Lion of Czechoslovakia; in 1950 she became an officer de l'Académie Française and in 1954 a cavalière of the Order of the Southern Cross of Brazil. She was also a freeman of the City of London (1954) and received an honorary doctorate from the National University of Ireland (1960).

She was energetic, widely read, and gifted with endless enthusiasm for literature as well as for music, and her continuous musical activities did not prevent her from leading a vigorous social life. She remained unmarried. Her friends, an impressive and international body of celebrities, included Sir Edward W. Elgar and those most prominent in the world of music; such literary eminences as G. Bernard Shaw, H. G. Wells, and E. Arnold Bennett; J. Ramsay Macdonald, the first Labour prime minister; and a glittering array of European and American intellectuals, Albert Einstein among them. They were great figures not only in music but in many branches of politics, learning, and the arts. Her autobiography, *A Bundle of Time*, (published posthumously in 1969 after her sudden death at University College Hospital, London, 13 November 1967) quotes extensively from the letters of the many celebrities who regularly corresponded with her. If her autobiography shows that she delighted in the eminence of her friends, the letters they wrote to her show that her beauty, intelligence, and vivacity delighted her friends as surely as their achievements delighted her.

There is a pen, ink, and wash drawing by Dame Laura Knight, and a drawing by Edmond X. Kapp (1921), entitled 'Harriet Cohen and Debussy'. There are also three portraits of her at the Royal Academy of Music by Stochell, Somorov, and an unknown painter.

[*A Bundle of Time: The Memoirs of Harriet Cohen*, 1969; Harriet Cohen, *Music's Handmaid*, 1936; *The Times*, 14 November 1967; personal knowledge.]

Ivor Newton

published 1981

GOOSSENS Léon Jean

(1897–1988)

Oboist, was born 12 June 1897 in Liverpool, the third of three sons and the fourth of five children of the conductor Eugene Goossens (1867–1958), himself the son of Eugene Goossens (1845–1906), conductor of the Carl Rosa Opera Company. His mother was Annie, daughter of the operatic bass singer Aynsley Cook. Of Belgian origin, the family had settled in England in the 1870s and 1880s; Léon's siblings were the conductor (Sir) Eugene Goossens, the horn player Adolphe (who was killed in World War I), and the harpists Marie and Sidonie. He was educated at the Christian Brothers Catholic Institute in Liverpool and Liverpool College of Music. After some study of the piano, he began learning the oboe with Charles Reynolds at the age of eight, and by the time he was ten had played professionally. After further study with William Malsch at the Royal College of Music (1911–14), he was appointed principal oboe of the Queen's Hall Orchestra at the age of seventeen. Throughout his career (apart from a brief period when it was stolen) he played the same oboe, made for him by Lorée of Paris.

During World War I Goossens volunteered in the Middlesex Yeomanry and subsequently served in the 8th Royal Fusiliers before being commissioned into the Sherwood Foresters. On leaving for France in 1915 he was given a silver cigarette case as a keepsake by his brother Eugene, who had been given it by (Dame) Ethel Smyth after a performance of one of her operas; it deflected a high-velocity bullet from the region of his heart, still wounding him sufficiently for him to be invalided home. He decided to accept an offer to join a friend on an Argentinian ranch; but, needing capital of £100, he began earning it by freelance oboe playing, which quickly brought so many engagements that the Argentinian plan was cancelled.

He rejoined the Queen's Hall Orchestra in 1918, moving to Covent Garden in 1924. In the same year he became professor of oboe at the Royal Academy of Music (until 1935) and at the Royal College of Music (until 1939). He also played in the Royal Philharmonic Society's orchestra and, on its foundation by Sir Thomas Beecham in 1932, the London Philharmonic Orchestra. His playing with Beecham lent added distinction to a fine orchestra, as can be heard on records and was heard with admiration in an early broadcast of his music by the aged Frederick Delius. Fritz Kreisler declared that among his greatest musical pleasures was listening to Goossens playing the solo in the Adagio of Brahms's Violin Concerto before his own entry. This, too, can be heard on records. Goossens was, in his own right, one of the most popular and prolific recording artists in the 1920s and 1930s. Recording companies were inexplicably slow to take him up again with the advent of the long-playing record, but he was making a comeback with a recording of J. S. Bach's Violin and Oboe Concerto, with Yehudi (later Baron) Menuhin, when an accident interrupted his career.

Goossens had by now acquired a world reputation (he frequently toured abroad) second to that of no other oboist. More, he had given the oboe standing as a solo instrument. He refined the sound from the conventional German breadth and reediness, while enriching the French slenderness but elegance of tone, to a warmth and sweetness hitherto unknown. By this, and by the highly personal elegance of his phrasing, he drew attention to lyrical possibilities that quickly excited the attention of composers, while his brilliant finger technique opened up a new range of virtuosity. Almost every English composer of note was drawn to write music for him: works which he inspired and first performed included concertos by Ralph Vaughan Williams and Rutland Boughton, chamber pieces by Sir Arnold Bax, Sir Arthur Bliss, and Benjamin Britten and an uncompleted suite by Sir Edward Elgar. He was appointed CBE in 1950 and FRCM (1962). He also became honorary RAM (1932).

In 1962, still at the height of his powers, Goossens suffered a car accident that severely damaged his teeth and lips, rendering him incapable of playing. After many operations, borne with great physical courage, and the no less courageous confrontation of the apparent end of his career, he began practising again with a newly learned lip technique. He then played in film and recording orchestras away from the public view, always with the affectionate support of his colleagues. He was able to resume his professional life, though he privately insisted that the standard of his playing was not what it had been. He continued playing into his eighties, sometimes with small ensembles and modest orchestras to whom he felt an old loyalty.

In his prime, Goossens had earned himself a reputation as something of a prima donna among orchestral players. He would demand his own microphone in recording sessions, on the grounds that the oboe's tone needed special consideration. Colleagues in the wind section would feel obliged to fit in with phrasing that was always personal and at times became mannered and unstylish. But with this awareness of his own worth, seen in his gracious platform manner in concertos, went an essential musical humility and a high degree of personal kindness. Self-disciplined in his personal life, in the interests of a musical professionalism inherited from his strict father, he enjoyed physical activities, which included yachting and farming. He was always generous with his time to younger oboists, while sometimes resisting those who represented a newer stylistic wave. His charm and humour, among friends, were unaffected and engaging. He was a tall, well-built man, with a deep chest that would have helped his phenomenal breath control. Like his conductor brother Eugene, he went bald early and had the family's characteristic slightly hooded eyes and charming smile.

In 1926 he married Frances Alice, daughter of Harry Oswald Yeatman, a port shipper who worked in London for Taylor, Fladgate & Yeatman. They had one daughter. This marriage was dissolved in 1932 and in 1933 he married the dancer Leslie Burrowes (died 1985), daughter of Brigadier-General Arnold Robinson Burrowes, of the Royal Irish Fusiliers. There were two daughters of this marriage. Goossens died 13 February 1988 in Tunbridge Wells.

[Barry Wynne, *Music in the Wind: the Story of Léon Goossens*, 1967.]

JOHN WARRACK

published 1996

HALL Henry Robert

(1898–1989)

Dance orchestra conductor, impresario, and BBC chat show host, was born 2 May 1898 at 23 Bonar Road, Peckham, London, the eldest son in the family of three sons and three daughters of Henry Robert Hall, blacksmith, and his wife, Kate Ellen Smith. Part of his childhood in a poor but happy Salvation Army family in Peckham was spent learning the trumpet. Whilst still at the London county council school in Waller Road, Peckham, he won a scholarship to Trinity College of Music, London, for trumpet, piano, and musical theory lessons on Saturday mornings. He left school at fourteen, but his musical education fortunately continued when he was employed at the age of sixteen as a music copyist at the Salvation Army head office in Judd Street, King's Cross. His employer, Richard Slater, worked him hard but helped to develop his talents as player and composer. His 'Sunshine March' was later the basis for his BBC signature tune, 'Here's to the Next Time'.

In December 1916 he enlisted in the Royal Field Artillery. His musical prowess was quickly recognized and he spent much time playing at troop concerts. After the war he undertook desultory engagements in the seedier music halls and played a cinema piano to finance advanced piano lessons at the Guildhall School of Music. In 1922 he accepted a Christmas job as relief pianist at the Midland Hotel, Manchester. A Chopin study played at a minute's notice in the hotel cabaret stopped the show and Arthur Towle, general manager of Midland Hotels, signed up Hall as resident pianist. Within a year he was musical director of the hotel band, within ten he was in charge of the bands in all thirty-two hotels in the LMS railway group, and when the Gleneagles Hotel opened in 1924, Hall persuaded the BBC to broadcast his band on the opening night. This was the start of a broadcasting career which lasted forty years. In 1932 he succeeded Jack Payne as musical director of the BBC Dance Orchestra, a move which involved a large cut in salary, but promised enhanced prospects.

Hall's purist style of music left some listeners lukewarm; but the impeccably played musical arrangements, often made by Hall himself, and his modest way of announcing the items were appealing. The repertoire of straight dance tunes interspersed with novelty items like 'The Teddy Bears' Picnic' soon made the band, broadcasting at teatime and in the evening, enormously popular. In 1934 he had the idea of inviting show-business stars to join him and his band in a programme called 'Henry Hall's Guest Night'. This was an instant success and ran for 972 performances over twenty-three years. The first chat show on British radio, it featured stars like (Sir) Noël Coward, Stan Laurel and Oliver Hardy, Danny Kaye, and (Dame) Gracie Fields, with whom he always established an immediate rapport. The programme made him a major figure in the golden age of radio.

A royal command performance, a film *Music Hath Charms* (1935), and an engagement to conduct the ship's band on the maiden voyage of the *Queen Mary* showed a widening recognition of his star status. By 1937, when many other dance bands were broadcasting, he asked permission to leave the BBC and take his band with him. Sir John (later first Baron) Reith granted it and agreed that they would not be replaced. It was said that forty million people listened to their final broadcast.

Hall now faced a freelance career touring the major variety theatres with his band topping the bill. Fears that the public would not support a wireless star in the theatre were groundless. 'Sold Out' boards were everywhere and Hall was frequently mobbed by the fans. The tours continued during the years of World War II, during which Hall also gave troop concerts and 'Guest Nights'. These strenuous and demanding years culminated in a second royal command performance (1948). After the war Hall began presenting stage shows, notably *Irma la Douce* (1958). Yet he continued to appear regularly on radio and television until

1964, finally announcing his retirement in 1970, when he was appointed CBE.

A tall dignified man, immaculately dressed, his dark hair brushed down, with a quizzical face and horn-rimmed glasses, Hall had flair and an engagingly hesitant style, which did not conceal a quiet authority inseparable from a lifetime of demanding high standards from himself and those around him. In return he received universal respect and affection. He was a showman completely in tune with the age in which he flourished. In 1924 he married Margery (died 1976), daughter of Robert Brook Harker, commercial traveller. It was a perfect partnership, and they had a son and a daughter. Hall died in Eastbourne after a long retirement, 28 October 1989.

[Henry Hall, *Here's to the Next Time*, 1955; BBC press books; private information; personal knowledge.]

Ian Wallace

published 1996

FOSS Hubert James

(1899–1953)

Musician and writer, was born at Croydon, Surrey, 2 May 1899, the thirteenth and youngest child of Frederick Foss, solicitor, mayor of Croydon (1892–3), and his wife, Anne Penny Bartrum. His grandfather was Edward Foss. An uncle, H. J. Foss, was bishop of Osaka, Japan; a first cousin was Brigadier C. C. Foss, V.C. (1885–1953). As a child Hubert Foss learnt to read exceptionally quickly and had a great feeling for words. Music attracted him intensely and obviously he possessed unusual talent. Soon he was put under Stanley Roper, sometime organist at the Chapel Royal, St. James's, who, impressed by his natural aptitudes and already marked talent for composition, undertook his musical education. This influence ripened into a friendship which lasted until his death.

His father having died when the boy was nine, his mother sent him to St. Anselm's School, Croydon. From there he won a senior classical foundation scholarship to Bradfield College, where he remained until 1917, leaving with a Stevens senior classical scholarship. At Bradfield, F. H. Shera and B. Luard Selby exercised a beneficent and widening influence on Foss, who contributed much to the musical life of the school.

He then served in the 5th Middlesex Regiment as a second lieutenant and was discharged early in 1919. Later that year he took a post in a preparatory school, leaving to become assistant editor of *Land and Water*, whilst also contributing music and art criticism to many prominent journals.

In 1921 he joined the Oxford University Press as senior assistant to the educational manager in London. There his intense interest in music soon made itself evident. With youthful drive and vision Foss envisaged a new music department organized on music trade lines, as distinct from the book trade. This project was favourably received by (Sir) Humphrey Milford, who appointed Foss its head and musical editor. Thus, at the age of twenty-five Foss began what was probably the most notable achievement of a brilliant but short life. Within a few years the Oxford University Press music department reached a world status second to none.

To the task of building up an international catalogue of music and books on music he brought an almost infallible instinct for what was vital and genuine in the work of young composers and writers. He published the first important works of (Sir) William Walton, from the famous *Façade* (1922) and *Belshazzar's Feast* (1931) to the later works. He also launched Constant Lambert whose vivid *The Rio Grande* achieved immediate success. Amongst other young composers Peter Warlock, E. J. Moeran, van Dieren, Rubbra, Rawsthorne, Britten, and John Gardner mostly owed their real start to Foss. The more established composers: Holst, Ethel Smyth, Ireland, Dyson, were glad to appear in the Oxford list. Above all Ralph Vaughan Williams became identified with the new department, and from 1925 onward many important works of his were issued under Foss's editorship.

A flow of important books on music was a natural development—amongst them the *Oxford Companion to Music* (1938) of Percy Scholes. And it was owing solely to Foss's patience and pertinacity that there appeared in permanent form as *Essays in Musical Analysis* (6 vols., 1935–9), the fruits of the encyclopedic learning of Sir Donald Tovey.

Towards the end of 1941, for personal reasons Foss felt impelled to resign his work, and when it was announced Vaughan Williams wrote: 'I did not know how much I counted on you. I know that I owe any success I have had more to you (except H. P. Allen) than to anyone else.' From 1942 a new phase began as freelance musician, author, and broadcaster. During the war he lectured for C.E.M.A. and for a period was music adviser to Eastern Command E.N.S.A. He was also an excellent and sympathetic broadcaster, and spoke on a wide variety of subjects on both the Home and Overseas services. In addition he wrote many excellent programme notes for the promenade concerts and others. As author and critic by *Music In My Time*

(1933) he made his mark, and later came *Ralph Vaughan Williams—A Study* (1950). In 1947 he edited *The Music Lover* and in 1952 reissued Warlock's book of 1923 on Delius with additional valuable chapters from his own pen.

His early 'Seven Poems by Thomas Hardy' (1925) for baritone solo and male voice choir had revealed him as a sensitive composer, and much important music followed. And his acknowledged expertise as typographer and printer led to the founding of the Double Crown Club in conjunction with Oliver Simon. Thus he contributed notably to almost every form of musical and literary activity, and achieved in his fifty-four years more than many enjoying a far longer life.

Early in 1952 he underwent a major operation but continued his work for another year. Then his appointment as editor of the *Musical Times* was announced. But he did not live to take up this post for he died unexpectedly in London 27 May 1953.

Foss talked well, had a rare sense of humour, and could be an entertaining mimic. Certainly he had a genius for friendship, his friends coming from every walk of life, and he was loyal, generous, and considerate to them all. His humility in face of criticism and his ready acceptance of it ended by making his critics admire the totality of the man.

In 1920 Foss married Kate Frances, daughter of Charles Carter Page, seed merchant; there were two daughters. The marriage was dissolved. His second marriage in 1927 was to a gifted singer Dora Maria, daughter of Alfred Stevens, managing director; they had a son and a daughter.

[Private information; personal knowledge.]

Norman Peterkin

published 1971

PAYNE John Wesley Vivian (Jack)

(1899–1969)

Bandleader, was born in Leamington 22 August 1899, the only son of John Edwin Payne, music warehouse manager, and his wife, Sarah Vivian Clare Gunn, of 10 Church Street, Leamington. Jack Payne first became interested in dance music during his service with the Royal Flying Corps in 1918, playing the piano in various amateur bands in the Service. After demobilization he took up dance music as a profession and formed a small band which secured a position in the Hotel Cecil in London in the summer of

1925. With this he made his first records (Zonophone, Aco). When the BBC began relaying dance music from the hotel, four extra musicians were added, increasing the number to ten. In February 1928 Jack Payne was appointed director of dance music to the BBC, a position he held from 2 March 1928 until 14 March 1932. In that period, he and the BBC Dance Orchestra recorded exclusively for Columbia, and made daily broadcasts of about an hour from Station 2LO, later known as the National Programme. He was the first bandleader to introduce and close each broadcast with a signature tune, in this case Irving Berlin's 'Say It With Music', and was one of the first to announce his music and sing the vocal refrains himself. In April 1930 Jack Payne and the BBC Dance Orchestra appeared at the London Palladium, returning there in August 1931. The full strength of the band was then sixteen, and it remained so for many years.

On leaving the BBC, Jack Payne took his band on nationwide tours, recording for Imperial Records; the labels showed his portrait in place of the gold crown trade-mark, and a gold facsimile of his signature. He is the only dance bandleader in this country to have been accorded this honour. Late in 1932 he and the band appeared as the central figures in a film called *Say It With Music*, for which his arranger, Ray Noble, wrote the score. Towards the end of 1933 the band was reorganized, and continued to record on Rex Records, which had replaced Imperial as the principal product of the Crystalate Gramophone Record Manufacturing Company. At the end of 1935 Jack Payne and his band made another film, *Sunshine Ahead*, on completion of which they visited South Africa very successfully during the summer of 1936.

In May 1937 Jack Payne gave the members of his band two weeks' notice, and retired to his Buckinghamshire farm to concentrate on stock-breeding; but he returned to the popular-music business in January 1938, resumed recording (for Decca), and touring. During the war of 1939–45 he and the band entertained the Services extensively, but within a year of the end of the war Jack Payne again withdrew from the scene and became a very popular 'disc-jockey', host on his own television show, artists' manager, and, finally, manager of a hotel in Tonbridge. The last venture was not a success, and failing health and financial difficulties contributed to his death at the age of seventy.

Jack Payne was also a composer. In 1930 he had published two waltz ballads which were very successful—'Blue Pacific Moonlight' and 'Underneath The Spanish Stars'—and, in 1931, another waltz 'Pagan Serenade', among other numbers. His band was very versatile, and in the course of a single show would play all kinds of popular tunes of the day, mostly romantic but freely intermixed with rousing chorus songs in 6/8 time, *paso-dobles*, Afro-American rhythms, comedy songs involving cameo-sketches in which Jack Payne himself would play cockney, north country, American, and 'Oxford-English' character-parts, and sometimes concert arrangements of standard classics, one of the most popular being Ravel's 'Bolero'. One of his most spectacular pieces of showmanship was to simulate a huge engine, appearing to be running out of the stage backdrop into the stalls of the London Palladium, with the members of the band seated on various parts of the engine, as they played a popular instrumental number of the time (1931) called 'Choo Choo'. As a man, Jack Payne was a perfectionist, a disciplinarian, an obvious leader, frank and sincere to a fault. These characteristics did not always find favour with his associates, but he has left an indelible mark on the pages of the history of British dance music.

Payne was twice married: firstly, in 1923, to Doris Aileen (died 1939), the daughter of Colonel H. H. Pengree, Royal Field Artillery, and secondly, in 1942, to Peggy, daughter of Thomas Andrew Cochrane, LLB (Edinburgh). A daughter was adopted in the second marriage. Payne died at his home in Tonbridge, Kent, 4 December 1969.

There is a cartoon sketch of Payne by Kapp reproduced as the frontispiece to Payne's autobiography, *Signature Tune* (1947), and another by Bond in the *Radio Times*, 17 March 1933, p. 656. A cartoon was also used by the Crystalate Gramophone Record Company for their publicity material in 1932 and for a year or so thereafter.

[Jack Payne, *This is Jack Payne*, 1932, and *Signature Tune*, 1947; Peggy Cochrane, *We Said it with Music*, 1979.]

BRIAN RUST

published 1981

BARBIROLLI John (Giovanni Battista) (1899–1970)

Sir

Conductor and cellist, was born in London 2 December 1899, the elder son and second of the three children of an *émigré* Italian violinist, Lorenzo Barbirolli, and his French wife, Louise Marie Ribeyrol, of Paris. He began to play the violin when he was four, but a year later changed to the cello. He was educated at St. Clement Dane's school and, at the same time, from 1910, was a scholar at the Trinity College of Music. He made his public début in a cello concerto in the Queen's Hall in 1911. In 1912 he won a scholarship to the Royal Academy of Music, which he attended from 1912 to 1916. He was elected an associate of the Academy at the age of thirteen. From 1916 to 1918 he was a freelance cellist in London, playing in the Queen's Hall Orchestra, in opera under Sir Thomas Beecham, and in theatre and cinema orchestras.

He served in the Suffolk Regiment 1918–19 and, on demobilization, resumed his orchestral career, although he was gifted enough to be soloist in Sir Edward Elgar's Cello Concerto at Bournemouth in 1921. In 1924 he became the cellist in both the Music Society and Samuel Kutcher string quartets. However, his ambition since childhood had been to conduct and later that year he formed his own string orchestra. He gradually attracted attention and in 1925 was invited to conduct for the British National Opera Company, making his début in C. F. Gounod's *Romeo and Juliet* in Newcastle upon Tyne in 1926.

When the BNOC foundered financially in 1929, Barbirolli was appointed conductor of the Covent Garden Opera touring company and also became a regular conductor at the Royal Opera House, Covent Garden, in the Grand Opera season. In 1931 the company staged thirteen operas, including the revival of Dame Ethel Smyth's *The Wreckers*. In 1933 he became conductor of the Scottish Orchestra, rejuvenating the playing and the programmes and winning most favourable opinions. Even so, no one was prepared for the sensation in 1936 when the Philharmonic-Symphony Society of New York, having been forced by public protests to withdraw their invitation to Wilhelm Furtwängler to succeed Arturo Toscanini as conductor, asked Barbirolli for the first ten weeks of the 1936–7 season. He conducted in Carnegie Hall for the first time 5 November 1936 and a month later was offered a three-year contract.

The years in New York were both rewarding and scarring for Barbirolli. Working with a great orchestra, with whom he was always on excellent terms, and with the most talented of the world's soloists, matured him musically; but the handicap imposed upon him by having succeeded Toscanini, who was idolized in New York and for whom a rival orchestra was created, was almost insurmountable. The critics, whose power and influence in New York at that time were notorious, were savage in their attacks on Barbirolli's interpretations. Nevertheless, in 1940 his contract was renewed for a further two years. When in April 1943 he was invited to become permanent conductor of the Hallé Orchestra at a time of crisis in its history, he accepted without hesitation, not wishing to avoid Britain's wartime privations.

Barbirolli arrived in Manchester to find that he had a month in which to recruit forty players to add to the thirty-five under contract. He scoured the country for talent, no easy task in 1943, and launched a virtually new orchestra which was soon acclaimed as the best in the country. This period, when he recreated the orchestra, bound him emotionally and indissolubly to the Hallé, so that despite lucrative offers from elsewhere and despite his own exasperation with its post-war financial problems, he could not be lured away. He was knighted in 1949 and was awarded the Royal Philharmonic Society's gold medal in 1950. In 1959 he accepted engagements in America and returned to a rapturous welcome from public and critics in New York. From 1961 he was a regular and much-admired guest conductor of the Berlin Philharmonic, and from 1961 to 1967 was conductor-in-chief of the Houston Symphony Orchestra. But the Hallé was still his principal concern and, after twenty-five years with it, in 1968 he was appointed conductor laureate for life. He was made a Companion of Honour in 1969. For some years he had suffered from heart disease and he died in London 29 July 1970 after a day of rehearsal in preparation for concerts with the New Philharmonic Orchestra in Japan.

Barbirolli was a complete musician. His magnetism as a conductor was exemplified by his ability to obtain quickly the special quality of sound which he liked from an orchestra. His aim was to lead players and listeners into the composer's world: this power of commitment was his strength, as his recordings testify. If concentration on broad lines and expressive phrasing meant some loss of rhythmical impulse, that was a weakness which was usually outweighed. In the music of Mahler, Elgar, Sibelius, Brahms, and Vaughan Williams he was at his greatest, combining power and poetry, but his excellent Haydn was underrated and it was most unfortunate that after 1936 he conducted comparatively little opera. No one who saw him—dynamic, with a touch of arrogance in his demeanour on the rostrum, small of stature but big in every other way—would have guessed that after a concert he would often lapse into deep depression. He was prey to an insecurity which partly stemmed from experiences during his rise to fame, was partly the result of his years in New York, and was also due to his own genuine humility in the face of great music. But with his sardonic humour, his courage, and his gift for friendship, he concealed these human failings from all but his intimates. His capacity for work was prodigious and he demanded most from himself.

In 1932 Barbirolli married Marjorie Parry, a soprano. The marriage was not a success and they were divorced in 1939, when he married a celebrated oboist, Evelyn, daughter of R. H. Rothwell, a tea-dealer, of Wallingford, Berkshire. There were no children of either marriage. Barbirolli was a fellow of the Royal Academy of Music (1928), and an honorary freeman of Manchester, King's Lynn, and Houston, Texas. Honorary degrees were conferred on him by the universities of Manchester (1950), Dublin (1952),

Sheffield (1957), London (1961), Leicester (1964), and Keele (1969). He received the Bruckner (1959) and Mahler (1965) medals and was decorated by the governments of Italy, Finland, and France. There are drawings of him by Augustus John and Harold Riley, and a triptych sculpture by Byron Howard is in Manchester Town Hall.

[Michael Kennedy, *Barbirolli, Conductor Laureate*, 1971; Charles Reid, *John Barbirolli*, 1971; Charles Rigby, *John Barbirolli*, 1948; personal knowledge.]

MICHAEL KENNEDY

published 1981

MOORE Gerald

(1899–1987)

Pianist and accompanist, was born 30 July 1899 in Watford, Hertfordshire, the eldest in the family of three sons and a daughter, who died in childhood, of David Frank Moore, who owned a men's outfitting establishment, and his Welsh-born wife, Chestina Jones. He was educated at Watford Grammar School. Musical, with perfect pitch, he learned the piano locally with Wallis Bandey. When, owing to a financial crisis, the family decided to emigrate to Toronto, Canada, the thirteen-year-old Gerald had to start again with his piano studies. His mother arranged an audition with Michael Hambourg, founder of a school of music in Toronto. This resulted in a scholarship and much expert coaching. Hambourg's cellist son, Boris, later took Moore as his accompanist on a tour of forty engagements in western Canada. When Moore finally was shipped back to London, in 1919, it was another Hambourg son—Mark Hambourg, the well-known pianist—who offered to take over his training.

But Moore was not cut out for a career as a soloist and on the advice of (Sir) Landon Ronald, then principal of the Guildhall School of Music, he concentrated on accompanying. He went on tour with baritone Peter Dawson and was engaged on an exclusive basis by the tenor John Coates. Coates taught him to work and awakened his realization of the importance of the piano part in the basic structure of the song: Moore said he owed everything to him.

In 1921 Moore made his first record (for HMV), with Renée Chemet, the French violinist. The studio had a large horn contraption into which the violinist played. In spite of the piece being a gentle lullaby Moore had to play fortissimo throughout in order to be heard at all on the record.

A vital step forward for Moore was the arrival on the recording scene of the microphone. At last his playing would be faithfully reproduced on records. At first he was greatly shocked by hearing himself. But by listening carefully he was able to improve, technically and musically, and raise his playing to a new standard, which took him to the top. Apart from many instrumentalists, his famous vocal partners included Elena Gerhardt, Elisabeth Schumann, (Dame) Maggie Teyte, John McCormack, Hans Hotter, Kathleen Ferrier, (Dame) Elisabeth Schwarzkopf, Victoria de los Angeles, Dietrich Fischer-Dieskau, and (Dame) Janet Baker.

When (Dame) Myra Hess started her series of lunchtime concerts in the National Gallery, during World War II, she asked Moore to give a talk at the piano on his experiences as an accompanist. He revealed a sense of verbal timing of which any professional comic would be proud. His unique blend of wit and wisdom not only pleased the cognoscenti but also won over ordinary people who had no idea that classical music could be fun. This kind of treatment has its dangers, but not with Moore, who always put the music first and used the jokes to sugar the pill. The talk became immensely popular.

Moore played throughout the world as an accompanist and included many tours of America as a lecture-recitalist. His favourite festivals included Edinburgh, Salzburg, and King's Lynn (where he played piano duets with Ruth, Lady Fermoy).

Moore retired from the concert platform in 1967, at the comparatively early age of sixty-seven, when he was at the top of his form. A farewell concert, which was recorded, was given in his honour at the Royal Festival Hall on 20 February 1967. After Moore gave up public playing his great affection for Schubert became an obsession: he embarked on the huge task of recording over 500 Schubert songs. Three sets of these—'Schöne Müllerin', 'Winterreise', and 'Schwanengesang', all with Fischer-Dieskau—were issued on compact disc and form a lasting tribute to his work. His playing was remarkable for flawless technique and a rare ability to make the piano 'sing'.

Moore was a talented writer. His best-known book was the autobiography *Am I Too Loud?* (1962). He became CBE (1954), honorary RAM (1962), FRCM (1980), honorary D.Litt., Sussex (1968), and honorary Mus.D., Cambridge (1973).

Moore was a stocky, thickset figure not readily associable with the ravishingly delicate effects he could obtain from the piano. His zest for living, his enormous vitality, and his sense of humour were strong preservatives in a very hard-working life. Away from music Moore enjoyed in early life tennis and golf and, later, bridge, gardening, and watching cricket. He had an ideal partner in his wife, Enid Kathleen (died 1994), daughter of Montague Richard, ironmonger, of Beckenham, whom he called 'the most perfect of all accompanists'. They had no children. Moore had had a previous marriage, in Canada in 1929, which lasted only three or four years and which ended in divorce. Moore died in his sleep at home in Penn, Buckinghamshire, 13 March 1987.

[Gerald Moore, *Am I Too Loud?*, 1962, *Furthermoore*, 1983, and *Collected Memoirs*, 1986; family information; personal knowledge.]

JOSEPH COOPER

published 1996

SILVESTER Victor Marlborough

(1900–1978)

Dance instructor and bandleader, was born 25 February 1900 at the vicarage of St. John's church, Wembley, the younger son and second of the six children of the Revd John William Potts Silvester and his wife, Katherine Hudson. Victor was so named because a victory in the Boer war was reported on the day he was born; his second name was in honour of the bishop of Marlborough. His father was a stern disciplinarian but his mother was more understanding and approachable.

He ran away from each of the schools he was sent to: Ardingly College in Sussex; St. John's, Leatherhead, Surrey; and John Lyons' School at Harrow in Middlesex. In November 1914 he joined the army by lying about his age. He spent six months in France, in the front line near Arras, until he was discovered to be under age, when he joined the 1st British Ambulance Unit in Italy, where he was wounded in 1917 by shrapnel in the leg and won the Italian bronze medal for military valour. Returning to England in December 1917, he was given a commission but demobbed immediately the war ended.

He applied to go to Sandhurst but meanwhile he was noticed at a tea dance by Belle Harding, who employed him to partner dancers at her headquarters in Kensington. He soon became one of her team of instructors and, although he went to Sandhurst in September 1919, he left there after three weeks and returned to London to work as a dancing partner and teacher.

On 17 December 1922 he married Dorothy Frances (died 1981), daughter of Frank Newton, a schoolmaster. Five days later he won the world ballroom dancing championship at Queen's Hall in London, partnered by Phyllis Clarke. When Phyllis Clarke married, his wife became his dancing partner. In 1923 the Silvesters opened a dancing school at Rector's Club in London. Their only child, a son—Victor Newton—was born in 1924. In that year the Imperial Society of Teachers of Dancing invited Silvester on to the committee of their newly formed ballroom branch, which codified the standard steps of ballroom dancing. He became chairman of the society in 1945; during the 1960s he was made its first life president.

The dancing school moved to 19 Maddox Street, off Regent Street, and then—in 1927—to 20 New Bond Street. In 1927 Silvester published *Modern Ballroom Dancing* of which more than a million copies were sold, the book reaching its fifty-seventh edition in 1974. His later books included *Theory and Technique of Ballroom Dancing* (1932), *Sequence Dancing* (1950), and *Dancing for the Millions* (1952).

In August 1935, dissatisfied with the lack of strict-tempo recordings for dancers, Silvester formed his Ballroom Orchestra. His first recording—'You're Dancing on my Heart'—sold 17,000 copies and became his signature tune. Eventually over 75 million copies of his records were sold: more than any other dance orchestra in the world. His orchestra produced a unique sound, keeping closely to the melody but decorating it with the twinkling sound of two pianos. It began broadcasting for the BBC in April 1937. By 1939 it was more successful than the dancing school, which Silvester closed on the outbreak of war to concentrate on broadcasting. In 1941 he started 'BBC Dancing Club', in which he became famous for his spoken instructions for dances ('Slow, slow, quick, quick, slow'). In 1949 he started 'Television Dancing Club' on BBC television, which continued until 1964. In 1953, 1954, 1956, and (posthumously) 1978, he won the Carl-Alan award for services to ballroom dancing.

In 1957 he opened the first of twenty-three 'Victor Silvester Dancing Studios' in collaboration with the Rank Organization. His orchestra appeared at the royal command performance in 1958, the year he published his autobiography, *Dancing is My Life*. In 1961 he was appointed OBE for his services to ballroom dancing. Although his son took over the running of the orchestra in September 1971, he continued to take an active interest in it. In 1972 he was president of the Lord's Taverners. For twenty-eight years up to 1975, he had a weekly request programme on the BBC's World Service. In 1977 he was presented with a golden microphone by the BBC for forty years of broadcasting.

He died 14 August 1978 of a heart attack after going for a swim on holiday at Aiguebelle, near Le Lavandou in the South of France. A tall, athletic man, he was an enthusiast for physical culture and trained regularly in a gymnasium. More than anybody else, he popularized ballroom dancing in Britain and symbolized that popularity.

[Victor Silvester, *Dancing is My Life*, 1958; *The Times*, 15 August 1978; *Guardian*, 15 August 1978; information from Victor Silvester (son).]

TONY AUGARDE

published 1986

FINZI Gerald Raphael

(1901–1956)

Composer, was born in London 14 July 1901, the son of John Abraham Finzi, ship broker, and his wife, Eliza Emma Leverson. His general education was undertaken privately but from 1918 to 1922 he studied music under (Sir) Edward Bairstow, organist of York Minster. Later, in 1925, he became a private pupil of R. O. Morris, a leading British authority on the aesthetics and technique of sixteenth-century polyphony, but this formal tuition lasted only a few months. For three years (1930–33) Finzi was a professor of composition at the Royal Academy of Music, but London was uncongenial to him and he held no other post save during the war of 1939–45 when he was employed in the Ministry of War Transport.

Finzi's art is rooted in English music, in English letters, and in the English countryside. As to music, composers so diverse as Parry, Elgar, and Vaughan Williams all had a traceable influence on his thought. Finzi was, however, a wide reader and a real scholar. No composer so inveterately polyphonic as he could remain unaffected by the textures, and occasionally the forms, of J. S. Bach. Thus Finzi's counterpoint is often a concealed source of vitality and clarity in passages which, in clumsier hands, would have sounded thick and muddy. Its unobtrusiveness may be compared with those beautiful details of medieval architecture which do not show unless specially looked for.

He was devoted to English poetry for its own sake and his knowledge of the English masters was profound. It is in his settings of such intractable verses as those of Thomas Hardy that Finzi shows his special spark of genius. His ear for the music of words, alike as to sound and sense, was so acute that he was able, at his best, to create, within the orbit of pure melody and true musical inflexion, an integrated result akin to stylized or even idealized reading aloud; for him Voice and Verse were, in a special way, harmonious sisters. His love of the Wessex countryside and its history, his interest in rural pursuits such as apple-growing (at which he was expert), and not least his happy countrified family life all contributed to the personality which lay behind his music. He was musician first and foremost but his music was evoked and nourished by the wealth and warmth of his other enthusiasms.

Sir Donald Tovey said of Schubert that all his works were early works. In a sense this was true of Finzi who died in 1956 just when opportunity, largely through the West Country Festivals, was bringing him experience and confidence in the handling of big designs. He responded, notably in matters of dynamic energy, to the scale and scope of work on a broader canvas, but his style did not undergo a radical change. It is not that his imagination or his technique were unequal to the handling of large resources but rather that his very genius in lyric forms precluded mastery in those matters of sustained development which are of the essence of extended movements. His large choral works amply justify themselves on their own merits and they are highly individual. His *Intimations of Immortality* (Wordsworth), Op. 29 (1950), could not have been written by anybody else and his short Christmas Scene *In Terra Pax*, Op. 39 (1954), was surely a presage of things to come. In this, which in the event proved to be his last choral work, he had returned to Robert Bridges, a poet with whom he was specially in sympathy and from whose verses he had already made 'Seven part-songs', Op. 17, in the thirties. Nevertheless it is doubtful whether Finzi's delicate art could ever have produced, in large forms, works more significant than the best of his songs with piano or his 'Dies Natalis' (Traherne), Op. 8 (1939), for solo voice and string orchestra. Indeed the short 'Intrada' to this work is among his most beautiful instrumental pieces.

Thus it is essentially as a composer of vocal music that Finzi has left his mark, and his finest writing is undoubtedly to be found in his songs for solo voice. There are three books of Hardy settings: Op. 14 (1933), Op. 15 (1936), and Op. 16 (1949). The collection of five Shakespeare songs Op. 18 (1942) called 'Let us garlands bring' is not a cycle but, in Finzi's words, 'put together as the only thing I can offer at present' (owing to his war work) as a greeting for Vaughan Williams on his seventieth birthday. It includes a specially sensitive setting of the Dirge from *Cymbeline* ('Fear no more') and in this song, for all its originality, he pays a subtle tribute to an earlier setting by Vaughan Williams himself.

Finzi's instrumental works are, however, by no means insignificant. Yet they derive from a vocal standpoint and from invention which is naturally melodic and declamatory. His orchestral output is comprised in five works including a Clarinet Concerto, Op. 31 (1949), and a Violoncello Concerto,

Op. 40 (1956), with an especially beautiful slow movement. There are two chamber works, Op. 21 (1936), Op. 24 (1942), and a set of 'Bagatelles for Clarinet and Pianoforte', Op. 23 (1945).

The works which Finzi acknowledged are embodied in some thirty compositions or collections. His method of writing makes chronological reference a baffling business. He generally had several works 'on the stocks' at the same time and he allocated the opus numbers at the time of their inception. His meticulous criticism often meant that he withheld a work, already numbered, until after later ones had been completed and published. (Thus his Op. 5 and 21 are both of 1936, whereas Op. 9 is dated 1945.) It sometimes took years of intermittent sketching and patching before a piece reached what Finzi regarded as its definitive form. He did, in fact, withdraw altogether the early work ('A Severn Rhapsody', 1924) which had been published by the Carnegie Trust and which had first brought him to the notice of musicians. During the war his original work was in abeyance, but he founded a string orchestra at Newbury for which he edited works of eighteenth-century composers, notably of John Stanley. Those which have been published show his practical musicianship as well as his careful scholarship.

Finzi made no bid for personal recognition, much less for popular appeal, but he was vigorous in bringing good music to the people around him. He kept his orchestra going after the war and took it about the countryside playing in churches and village halls. The pains he took over finding, preparing, and rehearsing this music is typical of his deep interest in all things old and odd. It also indicates the warmth of his feeling for friends and neighbours and not less his constant willingness to place his musical gifts at the service of the community. It is primarily owing to Finzi's sympathy, initiative, and persistence that the songs of Ivor Gurney have been preserved.

Finzi's music is of a restrained and contemplative order; sometimes withdrawn in its very eloquence, and often foreboding. Paradoxically, his most buoyant and least foreboding works were produced during his last few years when he knew his days were numbered; such is the nature of courage, and courage was of the essence of Finzi. He died in Oxford 27 September 1956.

In 1933 he had married Joyce Black; there were two sons.

[Private information; personal knowledge.]

HENRY HAVERGAL

published 1971

RUBBRA (Charles) Edmund (Duncan) (1901–1986)

Composer, pianist, and symphonist, was born 23 May 1901 at 57 Cambridge Street, Northampton, the elder son (there were no daughters) of Edmund James Rubbra, journeyman, shoe-last maker, clock and watch repairer, and, later, jeweller, and his wife, Mary Jane Bailey. The name Duncan was not on his birth certificate; it was the surname of his first wife and he used it after his first marriage. According to family tradition, the Rubbras originated from Bologna in Italy. He left school at fourteen and worked briefly as an errand boy and then a railway clerk. In his home there was a deep love of music and as a youngster he was much drawn to the music of Cyril Scott and Claude Debussy. Eventually he took lessons with Scott, and then went on to study composition at Reading University, where Gustav Holst taught, and counterpoint at the Royal College of Music with one of the great theorists of the day, R. O. Morris.

After leaving the RCM in 1925, he pursued a freelance career as a pianist, taking whatever teaching, performing, and journalistic work came to hand. His repertoire included both Arnold Schoenberg and Alexander Scriabin, and he was a perceptive exponent of J. S. Bach. During the 1930s he attracted increasing attention with such works as the *Sinfonia Concertante* for piano and orchestra (1934) and his First Symphony (1937).

During World War II he served in the army, as an anti-aircraft gunner in the Royal Artillery and then in the army music unit, and made an appearance in battledress at London's Henry Wood Promenade Concerts to conduct the first performance of his Fourth Symphony (1942). Rubbra spent much of his army service entertaining the troops with the trio he had formed with Erich Gruenberg and William Pleeth (and was very fond of telling how the three were once introduced as being 'at the top of the tree in their various string combinations'). The Rubbra–Gruenberg–Pleeth trio continued for some years after the war until the combined pressures of Rubbra's creative work and teaching led to its demise. In 1947 he was appointed lecturer in music at Oxford University, becoming a fellow of Worcester College in 1963. He remained at Oxford until 1968. In 1961 he also joined the staff of the Guildhall School of Music, where he taught composition until 1974.

Rubbra belonged to the same generation as Sir William Walton, Sir Lennox Berkeley, and Sir Michael Tippett but had little in common with them and even less with such European contemporaries as Karl Amadeus Hartmann, Luigi Dallapiccola, and Dmitri Shostakovich. It has been said that his music was not of his time, yet could have been composed at no other. It is rooted in place—England—and, more specifically, England's musical heritage lies at its heart. There is little of the pastoral school in it, though Rubbra revered Ralph Vaughan Williams and also possessed a keen sense of nature's power, which is clearly evident in the Fourth (1941–2) and Seventh symphonies (1957). Rubbra's outlook was far from insular: he set to music poetry ranging from the time of the Chinese T'ang dynasty and of Icelandic ballads to medieval Latin and French verse, and his interest in eastern culture, which arose in childhood, remained lifelong. In his book, *Counterpoint* (1960), Rubbra argued that western music had grown out of melody and in particular the interaction of independent melodic lines; this was certainly a dominant principle in his own music. Such was the eloquence and quality of his vocal music that some critics spoke of his symphonies as 'motets for orchestra'. His choral music was finely fashioned and elevated in feeling, and his symphonies likewise were touched by a preoccupation with linear growth. Matter, not manner, was his central concern.

His early symphonies are difficult, though not in the way that some contemporary music is, for the musical language itself is quite straightforward. There is nothing abstruse about the symphonies' tonality and harmony, which is basically diatonic, but they are difficult because the continuity of their melodic and polyphonic growth is logical and unremitting. The first two symphonies were composed in quick succession (both were finished in 1937) and it was obvious that, whatever their failings, Rubbra was a symphonist to be reckoned with. The Third, which he finished in 1939, was a positive reaction to the experience of the Second, and is outwardly the most genial and relaxed of the early symphonies. The orchestration is much cleaner and the first movement much closer to sonata form. The opening of the Fourth Symphony is beautiful and free from any kind of artifice, having serenity and quietude. This symphony, like the Third, is not so dense contrapuntally as the first two, and though practically every idea evolves in some way or another out of the opening figure, its first movement is a sonata design. Nothing could be further removed from the grim years of World War II than this symphony. In 1948 came the Fifth and most often played of the Rubbra symphonies; it enjoyed something of a vogue in the 1950s. Sir Adrian Boult premièred it, Sir John Barbirolli recorded it, and Leopold Stokowski briefly included it in his repertoire.

After the Seventh Symphony (1957), Rubbra's music fell on hard times and enjoyed relatively little exposure. His Eighth Symphony (1968) had to wait three years for a performance and the Ninth (*Sinfonia Sacra*, 1971–2), for soloists, chorus, and orchestra, possibly his masterpiece, also suffered relative neglect. It tells the story of the resurrection, and with its soloists and chorus would closely resemble a passion were it not for its symphonic cohesion. Like most of Rubbra's finest music, it unfolds with a seeming inevitability and naturalness, and a powerful sense of purpose that justify its inclusion in the symphonic canon. His scoring has been criticized, but conductors such as Arturo Toscanini, Eugene Ormandy, and Neeme Järvi recorded his orchestration of Brahms's *Variations and Fugue on a Theme of Handel*.

Rubbra was of medium height and was for most of his adult life bearded. He possessed a beatific smile and exercised great personal charm. Always courteous, a supportive and illuminating teacher, he radiated warmth and spirituality. His deeply religious nature shines through much of his music: the Canto movement of the Sixth Symphony (1954), for example, and the Eighth, subtitled *Hommage à Teilhard de Chardin*. (Although he was much influenced by Buddhist teachings, Rubbra was received into the Catholic faith in 1947.) He never lost this feeling for organic growth essential to the symphony: his Tenth (1974) and Eleventh (1979) are highly concentrated one-movement affairs of much substance.

His output was extensive and ran to over 160 works. Apart from the symphonies, his most important works included a Viola Concerto in A Major, op. 75 (1952); a Piano Concerto in G Major, op. 85 (1956); a Violin Concerto, op. 103 (1959); an Improvisation for Violin and Orchestra, op. 89; four string quartets: F Minor, op. 35 (1933, revised 1946), E flat, op. 55 (1952), op. 112 (1962–3), and op. 150 (1976–7); two piano trios: op. 68 (1950) and op. 138 (1973); two violin sonatas: op. 31 (1931) and op. 133 (1967); and a Cello Sonata in G Minor, op. 60 (1946). Eight of his symphonies have been commercially recorded, and there is an extensive discography which includes his two masses. His last work was the Sinfonietta for large string orchestra, op. 163, which he completed in 1980, in his late seventies, shortly before suffering a stroke, from which he eventually died.

Rubbra was appointed CBE in 1960. He became MRAM (1970) and FGSM (1968). He had honorary degrees from Leicester (LL.D., 1959), Durham (D.Mus., 1949), and Reading (D.Litt., 1978). His music does not possess the dramatic power which characterizes that of Vaughan Williams and Walton but has a sense of organic continuity that is both highly developed and immediately evident to the listener. Perhaps the most distinctive and individual quality that shines through his most inspired music, such as the opening of the Seventh Symphony or the *Missa in Honorem Sancti Dominici* (op. 66, 1948), is breadth and serenity.

Rubbra's first marriage, which lasted only a few months, was to Lilian Annie Duncan. There were no children. In 1933 he married the violinist Antoinette Chaplin, from France, daughter of William Chaplin, engineer;

they had two sons. He separated from his second wife during the 1950s and in 1975, following her death, he married Colette Muriel Marian Yardley, daughter of Harold Evans, a Sunbeam Motors salesman. They had one son. Rubbra died 14 February 1986 in Gerrards Cross.

[(Ronald) Lewis Foreman (ed.), *Edmund Rubbra: Composer*, 1977; Ralph Scott Grover, *The Music of Edmund Rubbra*, 1993; personal knowledge.]

ROBERT LAYTON

published 1996

GOODALL Reginald

(1901–1990)

Sir

Musician and conductor, was born in Lincoln 13 July 1901, the elder son of Albert Edward Goodall, solicitor's clerk, and his wife, Adelaide Jones. There was also a half-sister from Albert Goodall's previous marriage. Reginald went to Lincoln Cathedral Choir School from 1910 to 1914, after which his education continued at Springfields, Massachusetts, USA, and in Burlington, Ontario, Canada, following the breakdown of his parents' marriage and their decision to emigrate, his mother to the United States and his father to Canada. He left school at fifteen and undertook a variety of work, as a messenger for the railways, a clerk in an engineering works, and in a bank in Burlington. His earnings enabled him to study at the Hamilton Conservatoire of Music, which led to his appointment as organist of St Alban the Martyr Cathedral, Toronto, and as a music master at Upper Canada College. As the result of meeting Sir Hugh Allen in Canada, he became a student at the Royal College of Music, London, in 1925.

It was not until 1935 that Goodall conducted his first opera, *Carmen*, with a semi-professional company in London. In the mean time he had established himself as organist and choirmaster of St Alban's church, Holborn, and he gave the first performances in England of Bruckner's F Minor Mass and other works. Each year he travelled on the Continent as piano accompanist for the teacher and lieder singer Reinhold von Warlich. He was thus able to hear some of the world's great conductors, such as Wilhelm Furtwängler and Hans Knappertsbusch. In 1936 Goodall was engaged by Covent Garden to train the chorus for *Boris Godunov*, conducted by Albert Coates. He did this so well that he was asked to remain for the winter season. An invitation for the 1937 summer season followed, but he declined this in favour of other artistically less rewarding but financially more secure work. The 1930s were difficult for Goodall and the prospect of war filled him with gloom, as he envisaged the collapse of the German culture which he had come to know and love. Politically naïve, but at heart a serious pacifist, he supported Sir Oswald Mosley and his demand for negotiations with Hitler.

Apart from a brief spell of military service, in the Royal Army Ordnance Corps from April to September 1943, Goodall spent the war conducting, first the Wessex Philharmonic Orchestra and then the Sadler's Wells Opera. The latter introduced him to a repertoire with which he was not familiar and much of which he did not admire. However, he conducted the première of *Peter Grimes* by Benjamin (later Baron) Britten, at the reopening of the Sadler's Wells theatre on 7 June 1945. So impressed was the composer that he invited Goodall to conduct the première of *The Rape of Lucretia* at Glyndebourne's first postwar season the following year, although he shared the conducting with Ernest Ansermet. In 1947 Goodall became second conductor with the newly formed opera company at Covent Garden. This was a low period for him, with much of his time devoted to conducting Verdi, a composer he despised. In 1951 his contract as conductor was terminated and he continued as a coach. He was an invaluable teacher to the many singers who passed through his hands. There were occasional excursions into conducting for Covent Garden.

In 1968 Goodall conducted *The Mastersingers* at Sadler's Wells and again revealed his understanding of Richard Wagner. Following this huge success, Sadler's Wells invited him to conduct the four *Ring* operas at the Coliseum. These were nothing short of triumphant. He then went on to conduct *Tristan and Isolde* with the Welsh National Opera in 1979, and *Parsifal* with the English National Opera. Critical and public response was ecstatic, and both these performances were recorded.

A small, dishevelled, and sometimes cantankerous man, Goodall gave at first sight little indication of the strong inspirational force that he undoubtedly was as a conductor and coach. His conducting technique in a conventional sense was sketchy, but given time for preparation and rehearsal with singers and orchestra, which not every opera company could provide, the resulting performances were astonishing and profoundly moving in their revelations. He had a rare understanding of the architecture of Wagner's music. The long, slowly unfolding spans were wonderfully shaped and realized with unforced sonority. Goodall allowed the music to flow naturally and at the same time gave singers the greatest support without drowning them. He was appointed CBE in 1975 and knighted in 1985. He had honorary degrees from Leeds (1974), Newcastle (1974), and Oxford (1986).

In 1932 Goodall married Eleanor Katherine Edith (died 1979), schoolteacher, daughter of Montagu Gipps, of independent means. They had no children. Goodall died 5 May 1990 in a nursing home at Bridge, near Canterbury.

[John Lucas, *Reggie: the Life of Reginald Goodall*, 1993; personal knowledge.]

JOHN TOOLEY

published 1996

WALTON William Turner

(1902–1983)

Sir

Composer, was born in Oldham, Lancashire, 29 March 1902, the second son in the family of three sons and one daughter of Charles Alexander Walton, the son of an Inland Revenue official, and his wife, Louisa Maria Turner, the daughter of an upholsterer. Both his parents were singing teachers, who instructed pupils at their home. Charles Walton, one of the first enrolments at the Royal Manchester College of Music, had sung oratorio and operatic roles there. As the organist and choirmaster of St John's, Werneth, he had an excellent choir, which included both William and his brother Noel.

In 1912, at the age of nine, Walton took a voice test for a probationer chorister at Christ Church Cathedral Choir School, Oxford, and, on being accepted, became a boarder at the school, remaining there for six years. Then, after being squeezed into Oxford University (Christ Church) at the age of sixteen, without much secondary education, he studied under (Sir) Hugh Allen, the professor of music, and on 11 June 1918 passed the first part of the Bachelor of Music examination, but failed responsions at three attempts. He passed the second part of the examination on 8 and 9 June 1920.

While an Oxford undergraduate, Walton completed the writing of a string quartet and a piano quartet. After being revised in the early 1920s, the first of these was performed at the festival of the International Society of Contemporary Music at Salzburg on 4 August 1923; the latter gained a publication award from the Carnegie Trust Fund in 1924. Among his boyhood compositions were three notable works: *Tell Me Where is Fancy Bred* (1916), a Choral Prelude on *Wheatley* for organ, and *A Litany*, a setting of a poem by Phineas Fletcher. Despite early influences acquired from the study of other composers, Walton's own characteristics soon showed in his music.

During this period he made enduring friendships with the poets Siegfried Sassoon and I. Roy Campbell, and the novelist Ronald Firbank. He also met (Sir) Sacheverell Sitwell, who, designating him a musical genius, brought his brother (Sir) Osbert Sitwell to Oxford in February 1919 to meet him and to hear him play his Piano Quartet. Osbert Sitwell was greatly impressed by the music, and as a result the young composer, after leaving Oxford, went to live with the Sitwells at Swan Walk, Chelsea, and at Osbert's house, 2 Carlyle Square, London, in effect becoming another member of the family.

His 'adoption' by the Sitwells, already achieving some literary fame, opened up exciting vistas of opportunity. Combining with Dr Thomas Strong, the dean of Christ Church, and with Lord Berners and Sassoon, in guaranteeing him an income of £250 a year, they enabled him to spend his life composing. By introducing him to famous writers, musicians, and painters, they helped to broaden his cultural and social outlook. In the spring of 1920 and on subsequent occasions, he visited Italy with his benefactors; an experience which undoubtedly influenced his music. If he was short of money, his generous friend Sassoon provided it. He even found some for the impoverished Baroness Imma Doernberg, with whom Walton had a romantic association. Born the Princess Imma of Erbach-Schönberg on 11 March 1901, she was the daughter of Alexander, Prince of Erbach-Schönberg. Fortune smiled on the composer in 1932 when Elizabeth Courtauld, wife of Samuel Courtauld the industrialist, died, bequeathing him a life annuity of £500.

Walton had gone to live with the Sitwells in 1919 and he remained with them until 1934, when, having started a romance with Alice, Viscountess Wimborne, he moved into her house. The younger daughter of the second Baron Ebury and a cousin of the Duke of Westminster, she married Ivor Guest, first Viscount Wimborne, heir to the Guest Steel fortune, in 1902. Walton's affair with Imma Doernberg seems, at some time in 1933, to have gone adrift. While staying with the Sitwells, he had composed several works, including *Façade, Portsmouth Point*, the *Sinfonia Concertante*, the Viola Concerto, the First Symphony, and *Belshazzar's Feast*.

Drawn to the world of film music by Dallas Bower, he was commissioned by the British and Dominion Film Corporation in 1934 to write a score for *Escape Me Never*, in which the young (Dame) Margot Fonteyn appeared. The fees for this and other commissions helped him to purchase his own house in Eaton Place, London. In 1935 he collaborated with (Sir) C. B. Cochran by writing a short ballet, *The First Shoot*, which formed part of *Follow the Sun* (1935), a spectacular review. After King George V died, Walton was commissioned by the BBC to provide a Symphonic March for the coronation of King George VI in Westminster Abbey on 12 May 1937, and he wrote *Crown Imperial*, which was played for the entry of Queen Mary just before the ceremony began.

He was in America in the spring of 1939, completing the Violin Concerto commissioned by Jascha Heifetz, who gave him some useful technical advice. In the same year Paul Czinner's film *A Stolen Life*, for which Walton had composed music, had its première at the Plaza Theatre, London.

On 28 December 1940, during World War II, he finished work on his comedy-overture *Scapino*, and, about the same time, was attached to the films division of the Ministry of Information as a composer. Walton wrote several film scores for the MOI and these included *The Next of Kin* (1942), *The Foreman Went to France* (1941), *The First of the Few* (1942), and *Went the Day Well?* (1942). Released by the MOI in 1945, he completed his Second String Quartet; then, towards the end of the year, he accepted an invitation from six Scandinavian orchestras to tour Scandinavia, conducting his own music. Imma Doernberg died on 14 March 1947 and Lady Wimborne on 17 April 1948, the latter leaving him £10,000, Lowndes Cottage in Westminster, and various effects. Shortly after settling in a new home on the island of Ischia, off the coast of Italy, in 1949, Walton started work on his opera *Troilus and Cressida*, completing it in 1954. Following the death of King George VI in 1952, he composed a coronation march, *Orb and Sceptre*, and a *Te Deum*: these were performed at the Coronation of Queen Elizabeth II in Westminster Abbey on 2 June 1953.

In the years that followed, Walton wrote many fine works. They included such orchestral pieces as the film music for Laurence (later Lord) Olivier's *Richard III* (1956), the *Johannesburg Festival Overture*, the Cello Concerto, the *Partita* for Orchestra, and the Second Symphony. He composed a one-act opera, or extravaganza, *The Bear*, and among the choral and vocal pieces were *Anon in Love* (1960), *A Song for the Lord Mayor's Table* (1962), a Missa Brevis, and a Magnificat and Nunc Dimittis (1975).

Walton toured the United States in 1955 and appeared there for the first time as a conductor, leading a performance of his *Crown Imperial* at the United Nations. In 1963 he made a return visit, conducting an all-Walton concert at the Lewisohn Stadium, New York.

In January 1957, while travelling along a road near Rome, he was involved in a car crash, sustaining a cracked pelvis and other injuries. He made his first visit to Canada in February 1962 and shared a Canadian Broadcasting Corporation programme with the American composer Aaron Copland and Louis Applebaum from Canada; then in June the same year he was in Los Angeles for the American première of his *Gloria*. He went to Israel in 1963 and conducted three concerts of his own music there, one taking place in July, when the first performance of *Belshazzar's Feast* in Hebrew was given by the Tel Aviv Choir and the Israeli Philharmonic Orchestra in Tel Aviv, Haifa, and Jerusalem. In the first half of 1964 he toured New Zealand and Australia, again acting as an ambassador for, and conductor of, his own compositions. Commissioned by United Artists Ltd. to write music for a new film, *Battle of Britain*, he showed bitter anger when, after he completed the score in February 1969, it was rejected because there was not enough music to fill a long-playing record.

Walton visited Russia for the first time in 1971, accompanying André Previn and the London Symphony Orchestra, whose performance of his First Symphony before a Moscow audience was described by the *Financial Times* as 'a phenomenal success'. His seventieth birthday was celebrated in Britain by special concerts and tributes from press, radio, and television. Edward Heath, then prime minister, gave a concert for him at 10 Downing Street on 29 May 1972, with the Queen Mother heading the distinguished guests.

Walton's manifestations of ill health surfaced alarmingly in November 1976, when, after attending all the performances of *Troilus and Cressida* at the Royal Opera House, he returned to Ischia, showing definite signs of a stroke, and became a very sick man, unable to work. He made only a partial recovery, but, with characteristic gallantry, visited Britain in March 1977 and 1982, for the London concerts given to celebrate his seventy-fifth and eightieth birthdays. Back on Ischia, a semi-invalid in a wheelchair, with a restricted range of movement and energy, Walton continued to compose in a small way, but the end was near.

To look back over his life is to realize the lofty scale of his achievements. Like Sir Edward Elgar, he was largely self-taught as a composer, but, like Elgar, he became a supreme professional. For many people, *Façade*, skittish, catchy, and beautiful by turns, marked him as the brilliant English counterpart of the Parisian playboys of the 1920s, and although this work, which uses strange, capricious poems by (Dame) Edith Sitwell, was booed and hissed at its première, it was soon recognized as a concept of rarest originality. The public waited for Walton to repeat the phenomenon. He never did. Between the first performance of *Façade* in 1923 and that of the *Sinfonia Concertante* in 1928 he averaged only one small piece a year, the most impressive of which was *Portsmouth Point* (1926).

The poet in Walton came into his own with the Viola Concerto (1929), when he could with complete conviction write what the critics and music lovers of the day seemed to want. This composition, closely modelled on Elgar's Cello Concerto, has maintained its pre-eminence, like the Violin Concerto (1939), a miracle of delicate, haunting lyricism and elegiac feeling. Between Walton's two concertos came *Belshazzar's Feast* (1931), whose high-flying drama and savage ferocity, offset by passages of songful serenity, broke the bonds of conventional oratorio.

Most of the great masters of the previous generation had avoided the symphony, arguing that it had no relevance to the musical situation of the day, but there was in the early 1930s a definite movement backwards towards this large-scale form. Walton felt sure that he could speak eloquently through the symphony, but his confidence had been shaken by the rather cool response to *Belshazzar's Feast* shown at the 1933 ISCM Festival. Despite doubts and difficulties, his First Symphony proved to be a masterpiece. He was, for a time, unable to find a satisfactory solution to the problem of writing the final movement, and on 3 December 1934 he allowed the symphony to have a première in its unfinished state. Almost a year elapsed before he completed the last movement, and not until 6 November 1935, in London, did the public hear the full score. The tragic nature of the work, with a scherzo marked 'Presto con malizia', reveals the influence of Sibelius.

Walton wrote music for fourteen films, of which *Dreaming Lips* (1937) is not usually included in his list of credits. The score for *Henry V* (1944) is magnificent. He drew a fine line between true 'background' music and those elements of musical pastiche that were needed to evoke the atmosphere of a particular historical period. The most thrilling facet is the Agincourt battle sequence, where the sound effects of horses' hooves, rattling harness, and clinking armour, make the charge of the French knights fearsomely real. Outstanding among the film scores which he wrote for the Ministry of Information during World War II is *The First of the Few* (1942), from which the 'Spitfire Prelude and Fugue' was later published as a separate concert piece.

The comedy-overture *Scapino* (1941), a brittle portrayal of a rascally character of the *commedia dell'arte*, contains the best of all the exhilarating tunes he ever wrote. Both this work and *Portsmouth Point* are superior to the *Johannesburg Festival Overture* (1956). One of his most glorious achievements at this time was the massive and picturesque score which he created for the BBC's radio drama *Christopher Columbus*, used in a transatlantic broadcast on 12 October 1942, the 450th anniversary of the great explorer's first voyage to America.

Walton's String Quartet in A minor (1947) has an air of easy composure, despite the rhythmic vitality of the scherzo and the finale, while the slow movement has a gentle inwardness that emphasizes the Ravelian aspect of much of his art. Like the First Symphony, it was not ready for the publicized première. It seems that, at different stages of his life, unease and doubt over the direction he was taking interrupted his flow of inventiveness.

Uncertainty and discontent haunted him also while he was composing *Troilus and Cressida* (1954), and sometimes irascibility surfaced between him and his librettist, Christopher Hassall. He knew that there was a feeling of disillusionment about English opera, *Gloriana* by Benjamin (later Lord) Britten and *The Midsummer Marriage* by (Sir) Michael Tippett having been poorly received. *Troilus and Cressida*, a love story in the grand manner, with a Chaucerian text, struck some critics as being old-fashioned, but Walton's passionate score, full of gorgeous harmonies and luminous orchestration, inspired much praise after the initial reaction.

His second coronation march *Orb and Sceptre* (1953), enriched by music of coruscating brilliance, proved to be more complex than the previous one, *Crown Imperial* (1937), a work of simple, diatonic grandeur. The other new coronation piece he composed, the *Te Deum* (1953), covered a big expanse of sound and, in its noble utterance, outshone most of the remaining choral works that were sung on this great occasion. Walton's Cello Concerto (1957) also captivated the listener, revealing a warm, Italianate glow and a really fresh invention.

In complete contrast to its mighty predecessor, his Second Symphony (1960) showed him in a more subdued, reflective vein: gone were the truculence, the spiky rhythms, and the restless unease of former years. Because of this, some people complained that he had taken a wrong turning, that he had failed to 'advance' in his style. But after the Cleveland (Ohio) Orchestra, under George Szell, made their splendid recording of the symphony, it was recognized as a feat of orchestral virtuosity which few, if any, British composers could match. The music not only represented a natural development from the preceding period, but introduced entirely fresh ideas that were treated in a quite different way.

Walton's second opera, *The Bear* (1967), has a witty libretto with rhyming lyrics by Paul Dehn based on a short play of the same title by Chekhov, and is a comedy of manners, not of plot. His pungent, high-spirited score never holds up the pace of the merry making, and there is fun for the listener in identifying in the music certain droll parodies of contemporary composers.

He used a spare melodic style of scoring in *Improvisations on an Impromptu of Benjamin Britten* (1970), just one of a stream of finely crafted works too numerous to catalogue fully here. They include the dreamy, skittish miniature *Siesta* (1926), piano pieces *Duets for Children* (1940), a Spenserian ballet *The Quest* (1943), the exquisite setting of the poem by John Masefield *Where Does the Uttered Music Go?* (1946), the *Partita* for Orchestra (1958), the *Gloria* (1961), and the elegant, poetic *Variations on a Theme of Hindemith* (1963). Walton was always a slow, painstaking perfectionist, who revised a number of his scores after publication.

At a time when a reaction against nineteenth-century romantic music had set in, he had to work extremely hard to find a personal idiom and he did, in fact, create a tone and a rhythm that were unmistakably his own. His pre-1939 compositions were very popular in the concert halls of Europe and America: so that, in winning a reputation abroad, he also acted as an ambassador for his own country. Walton introduced no pioneering techniques into his music, but he demonstrated, most eloquently, that to scale lofty heights a man of genius looks, not necessarily for new forms, but simply for the best means to express his own ideas.

As he grew older, during the post-1945 phase of his career, the inventive quality in his music declined, but he became more prolific, with a greater variety of expression. One example is the *Capriccio Burlesco* (1968), with its sly musical gesticulations and saucy ideas. Walton could not possibly have written this in his so-called *enfant terrible* days.

In the matter of gramophone recordings, Walton conducting Walton became a revelatory, as well as definitive, experience. Sir Eugene Goossens, renowned for his brilliance in handling contemporary scores, taught the young composer a technique for mastering the swift nervous changes of rhythm in his own music. Most of Walton's recordings, especially those made for Columbia in the 1950s, are bright, unpretentious, and vibrant with life.

Despite occasional flashes of anger and hostility, there were many appealing facets to his character. He had an endearing habit of self-denigration and once described *Belshazzar's Feast* as 'a beastly noise'. There was no pomposity in his make-up. He loved to tease his friends. A very private person, he often retreated into a haven of brooding silence when questioned about his music or his views. Walton had a curious way of smoking his pipe, balancing it precariously on his lower lip in the centre of his mouth.

He was knighted in 1951, given the freedom of the borough of Oldham in 1961, and admitted to the Order of Merit in 1967. He held honorary doctorates from the universities of Durham (D.Mus. 1937), Oxford (Mus.D. 1942), Dublin (D.Mus. 1948), Manchester (D.Mus. 1952), Cambridge (D.Mus. 1955), London (D.Mus. 1955), and Sussex (D.Litt. 1968). He had a number of honorary fellowships, including those at the Royal

College of Music (1937), the Royal Academy of Music (1938), and the Royal Manchester College of Music (1972). Appointed an honorary member of the Royal Swedish Academy of Music (1945) and an Accademico Onorario di Santa Cecilia (Rome) (1962), he was awarded the Benjamin Franklin medal (1972), the gold medal of the Royal Philharmonic Society (1947), and the medal of the Worshipful Company of Musicians (1947).

In 1948 he married Susana Valeria Rose Gil Passo, daughter of Enrique Gil, a prosperous Buenos Aires lawyer. After their marriage the couple settled on the island of Ischia, where 'La Mortella', a beautiful villa with an exotic garden, was built specially for them. Walton died there 8 March 1983. He had no children.

[Neil Tierney, *William Walton: His Life and Music*, 1984; Susana Walton, *William Walton*, 1988; Michael Kennedy, *Portrait of Walton*, 1989; information from Lady Walton and Dr Stewart R. Craggs; private letters and documents.]

NEIL TIERNEY

published 1990

SOLOMON (1902–1988)

Pianist, was born 9 August 1902 at 39 Fournier Street, in the East End of London, the youngest in the family of four sons and three daughters of Harris Cutner (formerly Schneiderman), master tailor, the grandson of a Polish *émigré* from Cutnow, and his wife, Rose Piser. Showing exceptional musical talent from early childhood, at the age of seven he came to the attention of Mathilde Verne, a fashionable London piano teacher and former pupil of Clara Schumann. She persuaded Solomon's parents to sign a contract, relinquishing him into her care for five years, and within a year she had launched him successfully as a child prodigy, with a début at the Queen's Hall in June 1911, playing Mozart's Concerto in B♭ ('the little B♭'), the slow movement of Tchaikovsky's first Piano Concerto, and a Polacca by Alice Verne. The concert was conducted by Theodor Müller-Reuter, another of Clara Schumann's pupils. Billed from the outset as 'Solomon', sometimes wearing a sailor suit, sometimes in velvet knickerbockers and a lace collar, he captivated his audiences. He was invited to play at Buckingham Palace in 1912, and he made his Proms début in 1914 playing Beethoven's Second Piano Concerto.

After Solomon had spent five miserable years with Mathilde Verne, forced to practise for many hours a day in a locked room, his parents refused to sign another contract, and for a year he gave concerts throughout England chaperoned by one of his brothers. In 1916 he decided to give up all public performances, and, after a farewell recital at the Wigmore Hall shortly before his fourteenth birthday, he began studying with Dr Simon Rumschisky in London, while attending King Alfred School in the North End Road in the mornings. His studies were financed through a fund set up by an American, Mrs Colson. He spent three years with Rumschisky, a medical doctor who had studied the physiological aspects of playing the piano. Solomon later claimed that he was one of the greatest teachers in the world, and had taught him all his technique. In 1919, financed by Mrs Colson, Solomon went to Paris, where his teachers included Lazare Lévy, Marcel Dupré, and Alfred Cortot.

Still only nineteen, Solomon returned to the concert platform with a Wigmore Hall recital in 1921. The 1920s were difficult years for him, for English audiences then preferred foreign pianists such as Arthur Schnabel. Although he toured the USA in 1926, he remained relatively unknown outside England. Thanks to Sir Henry Wood he performed regularly at the Queen's Hall Promenade Concerts. (Sir) Arthur Bliss wrote his Viola Sonata (1933) for Solomon and Lionel Tertis, and when Solomon was asked by the British Council to represent Great Britain at the New York World Fair in 1939, he commissioned Bliss to write a piano concerto. During World War II Solomon joined the Entertainments National Service Association (ENSA) and gave many concerts, both for troops abroad and in army camps and hospitals at home, making many converts to classical music. Through his concerts on the wards at St Mary's Hospital, Paddington, he came into contact with Sir Alexander Fleming, and was successfully treated for a septic thumb through the inhalation of penicillin in the very early days of its development as an antibiotic.

After the war Solomon became an international celebrity, following an enthusiastic reception in the USA on his tour in 1949. He spent the next few years touring and recording, before a stroke ended his career in 1956. He was left with an active brain, but a speech impediment. Though he struggled to express himself his playing days were over. In the remaining years of his life he could take no interest in his career, achievements, or recordings.

Solomon was one of the three greatest English pianists of the twentieth century, with Dame Myra Hess and Sir Clifford Curzon, and possibly the greatest twentieth-century British interpreter of Schumann. During his early career he was best known for his performances of Chopin, but he later concentrated on Mozart, Beethoven, Schumann, and Brahms. Critics commented on the elegance and purity of his playing, its clarity and accuracy, and the controlled nature of his performances. Famous recordings from the early 1950s include those of the Brahms 'Variations and

Fugue on a Theme by Handel', Beethoven's 'Moonlight' Sonata, the two Brahms piano concertos, and Schumann's 'Carnaval'. He also played chamber music, recording the Beethoven cello sonatas with Gregor Piatigorsky, and he formed a trio with Zino Francescatti and Pierre Fournier for the 1955 Edinburgh festival.

Solomon was short and stocky, almost completely bald from an early age, with short, thick fingers. He displayed none of the temperamental behaviour usually associated with great artists, and despite his years of adulation as a child prodigy he developed into a charming and modest person, nicknamed 'Solo' by Walter Legge, manager for artists and repertory at the Gramophone Company. He had a passion for betting and gambling, possibly originating in his trips to the races with the elderly mother of his landlady while he was studying in Paris, and he loved to visit the casinos in Cannes and Monte Carlo. He enjoyed bridge and golf, and for years played tennis daily with his old friend Gerald Moore.

Solomon was appointed CBE in 1946 for his wartime work. He had honorary degrees from Cambridge (Mus.D., 1974) and St Andrews (LL.D., 1960). In 1970 he married, after a long friendship begun in 1927, a former pupil, Gwendoline Harriet, daughter of Patrick Byrne, an Irish doctor and surgeon. They had not married earlier because Solomon was an orthodox Jew and Gwendoline a gentile. They had no children. Solomon died 22 February 1988 in London.

[Mathilde Verne, *Chords of Remembrance*, 1936; Gerald Moore, *Am I Too Loud?*, 1962; David Dubal, *The Art of the Piano*, 1990; Reginald Pound, *Sir Henry Wood*, 1969; Brian Crimp, *Solo*, 1995; BBC Sound Recordings archive; private information.]

ANNE PIMLOTT BAKER

published 1996

WEBSTER David Lumsden

(1903–1971)

Sir

Theatre administrator, was born in Dundee 3 July 1903, the only child of Robert Lumsden Webster, advertising agent, and his wife, Mary Ann Alice, née Webster. In 1913 the family moved to Liverpool where he was educated at the Holt School. In 1921 he won a scholarship to Liverpool University where he read economics and became deeply involved in university life as secretary of the University Guild and chairman of the Dramatic Society. Such was his interest in the theatre that many believed that it was there that he would find a career.

Following postgraduate studies in education at Oxford and Liverpool, Webster joined the retail store organization run by F. J. Marquis (later Earl of Woolton). He quickly made his mark and in 1932 was appointed general manager of the Bon Marché in Liverpool. On the outbreak of World War II he became general manager of Lewis's. Meanwhile he maintained his interest in opera and in the theatre, becoming in 1940 chairman of the Liverpool Philharmonic Society. During his tenure of office (which lasted until 1945), he made the Liverpool Philharmonic Orchestra into a permanent body.

In 1942, on the recommendation of Lord Woolton, Webster was seconded from Lewis's to the Ministry of Supply with the brief to improve productivity and quality at ordnance factories. This mission was successfully completed and at its conclusion in 1944 Webster was offered and accepted a post with Metal Box.

Boosey & Hawkes, the music publishers, who had acquired a lease on the Royal Opera House, Covent Garden, intended (contrary to the practice of the inter-war years) to present opera and ballet throughout the year and began to search for a person to organize this inspired venture. Their choice fell upon David Webster, who was released from his Metal Box commitment and took up his Covent Garden post, as administrator of its preliminary committee, in August 1944. In 1946 he was appointed general administrator of the Royal Opera House. For many it was an unlikely choice and for years Webster was the subject of harsh criticism which he bore silently, but not painlessly. Few understood the formidable task of setting up permanent opera and ballet companies at Covent Garden and this hostility and lack of understanding drove Webster, a shy man, into an obsessive secretiveness and desire for procrastination, which was not always for his good, but which he could use to good effect on occasions.

For ballet, there was a relatively simple solution. The Sadler's Wells Ballet, founded by (Dame) Ninette de Valois in 1931, was again at its theatre in Rosebery Avenue and was beginning to look for bigger challenges. Covent Garden offered these and eventually the Sadler's Wells governors agreed to release the company to the Covent Garden Trust, which had been created in February 1946, under the chairmanship of Lord Keynes, to supervise the running of the opera house. It became known as the Royal Ballet.

For opera, there was no simple answer, for nothing of permanence had been created in the inter-war years. It was thus a matter of starting from scratch and after the appointment of Karl Rankl as music director, work on the formation of a company (known as the Royal Opera) began with the selection of soloists, choristers, and orchestral musicians.

A lesser man than Webster would not have survived these early and chequered years, but such was his faith in Covent Garden and in those who performed and worked there, and such were his patience and skill, that the enterprise prospered through many financial crises, through various changes of policy in relation to language and presentation of performances, and through changes of music director (Karl Rankl 1946–51, Rafael Kubelik 1955–8, and Sir George Solti 1961–71). In many ways the years of interregnum between music directors were the happiest for Webster. He enjoyed the freedom of choice of repertory and of artists just as he sometimes felt that he would like to run Covent Garden without a board of directors, although inwardly he knew the value of that and the depth of support which he could expect from it. Webster also had a flair for discovering singers and furthering their careers at home and abroad—for example, (Dame) Joan Sutherland, Jon Vickers, and (Sir) Geraint Evans.

Webster also developed his interests in other directions. From 1948 he was chairman of the Orchestral Employers' Association. He became governor and treasurer of the Royal Ballet School in 1955 and governor and general administrator of the Royal Ballet Company in 1957. In 1962 he became general administrator of the London Opera Centre. From 1957 he was a director of Southern Television Ltd. and from 1965 chairman of the London Concerts Board. He held visiting lectureships at the universities of Bristol (1955–6) and Liverpool (1958). He became president of the Wagner Society in 1957 and worked hard to raise the reputation of Wagner's work in Britain.

The strain of the vast tasks which Webster had undertaken since the mid-1940s and the burden of maintaining and improving standards of performance at Covent Garden in the face of general under-finance, and the early days of fierce criticism, eventually took their toll. The last few years at Covent Garden were not happy for him. He was unwell and he became prey to doubts and fears about himself and his ability to carry on. In July 1970 he retired and was appointed KCVO (he had been knighted in 1960). He also became honorary FRCM and RAM, was an officer of the French Legion of Honour, and had Swedish, Portuguese, and Italian honours.

Webster enjoyed food and wine and giving parties, which he frequently did with great style at his house in Weymouth Street. From 1931 his companion was James Cleveland Belle. Webster died at his London home 11 May 1971.

[Montague Haltrecht, *The Quiet Showman: Sir David Webster and the Royal Opera House*, 1975; *The Times*, 12 May 1971; personal knowledge.]

JOHN TOOLEY

published 1986

BERKELEY Lennox Randal Francis

(1903–1989)

Sir

Composer, was born 12 May 1903 at Melford Cottage, Boar's Hill, near Oxford, the younger child and only son of Captain Hastings George FitzHardinge Berkeley, of the Royal Navy (the eldest son of George Lennox Rawdon Berkeley, seventh Earl of Berkeley), and his wife Aline Carla, daughter of Sir James Charles Harris, KCVO, former British consul in Monaco. His father did not succeed as eighth Earl of Berkeley because Captain Berkeley's parents were unmarried until prior to the birth of their third son, who succeeded to the earldom. After early schooling in Oxford, he was educated at Gresham's School in Holt, St George's School in Harpenden, and Merton College, Oxford, where he coxed the college rowing VIII and took a fourth class in French (1926). He became an honorary fellow of Merton in 1974.

He had shown no outstanding musical abilities at school (though a contemporary remembers him playing the piano with much flourishing of hands), but while at Oxford he had several of his compositions performed and eventually made up his mind to be a composer. In this he was supported by the young British conductor Anthony Bernard, who was to conduct first performances of a number of Berkeley's early works.

On advice from Maurice Ravel, he went to Paris in the autumn of 1926 to study with Nadia Boulanger, and stayed with her for six years. For the first of these she allowed him to do nothing but counterpoint exercises, a discipline which often reduced him to tears at the time, but for which he was to remain grateful all his life. He had works performed in Paris and London and his 'Polka for Two Pianos' (1934) was a notable success, inaugurating his ties with the publishers J. & W. Chester. But the BBC broadcast of his oratorio *Jonah* (1935) in 1936 and the Leeds festival performance of it the following year led many critics to look at him askance as a purveyor of modernism. From 1932 to 1934 he lived on the Riviera with his invalid mother.

In 1936 he met Benjamin (later Baron) Britten and the two became close friends, sharing a house in Snape just before World War II. Although rather daunted by what he felt to be Britten's superior talent, Berkeley was able to find a distinctive voice in the 'Serenade for Strings' (1939), the First Symphony (1940), and the 'Divertimento' (1943). From 1942 to 1945 he worked for the BBC, first in Bedford and then in London, as an orchestral programme planner. The authorities noted with dismay that when Berkeley was labouring on a commission his BBC work suffered, and he was happy to accept an appointment as professor of composition at the Royal Academy of Music in 1946. He remained in the post until 1968 and numbered many of the country's best composers among his pupils, including David Bedford, Peter Dickinson, William Mathias, (J.) Nicholas Maw, and John Tavener.

Until he succumbed to Alzheimer's disease in the early 1980s, he produced a succession of works which made him many friends and admirers in the musical community, even if he never became famous outside it. He wrote for performers such as the pianist Colin Horsley, the oboist Janet Craxton, and the guitarist Julian Bream, and produced a considerable body of fine chamber music. He was particularly at home with the voice, and his vocal and choral works, such as the *Four Poems of St Teresa of Avila* (1947), the *Stabat Mater* (1947), and *The Hill of the Graces* (1975), show a love and understanding of words at least equal to Britten's. His four operas—*A Dinner Engagement* (1954), *Nelson* (1954), *Ruth* (1956), and *Castaway* (1967)—display at times an individual view of what constitutes opera, and one which critics and impresarios have not always shared; certainly he was not always fortunate with his librettists. But *Nelson* suffered from less than adequate London performances and deserves to be revived. From the late 1960s Berkeley, like many composers, experimented with serial techniques and, though they never took over his music, he admitted that thanks to them his musical language had expanded. The Third Symphony (1969) is perhaps his most impressive exercise in this new vein. The 1970s found Berkeley still true to his principles of writing with performance in mind and never *in vacuo*. At the time his last illness struck he was working on a fifth opera, 'Faldon Park'.

In 1959 he said, 'I know quite well I'm a minor composer, and I don't mind that.' It is true that he was not an Arnold Schoenberg or an Igor Stravinsky. His music made no revolutionary claims, partly because revolutionaries have to be destroyers and Berkeley was too respectful of tradition to set about it with a hatchet. If his studies with Boulanger taught him to be at ease with counterpoint, they also inculcated a love of 'la grande ligne', which Boulanger had inherited from Gabriel Fauré. Berkeley's music, like Fauré's, eschews surprises and, for the most part, grand gestures (though, again, *Nelson* showed what he could achieve in this more public, extrovert manner). His colleague Edmund Rubbra referred to his work as offering 'so much in sanity and honesty of purpose'. These attributes have in general been misprized in the twentieth century and Berkeley's refusal to jettison them meant that his reputation likewise matured without sudden surprises. He was notable for attending to the needs of the amateur: it is unusual, for example, to come across a flautist who has not at some time played his *Sonatina*. But his larger works, though always expertly written, demand patience and close attention to be fully appreciated. Even if his music always remains basically tonal, it can sometimes be fierce and gritty, very often as a result of his essentially linear thinking. Perhaps too much has been made of his music's Frenchness, and too often critics have used this as an excuse to deny his work profundity, but at the very least he managed to avoid the vapid pastoral meanderings of some of his English predecessors. The history of twentieth-century music may not have been greatly changed by his passing across it, but without him it would have been immeasurably the poorer. He was a man dedicated, as his pupil Peter Dickinson has said, to 'passing on the love of music as a spiritual imperative in a foreign, material age'.

He was appointed CBE in 1957 and knighted in 1974. Among many other honours were the papal knighthood of St Gregory (1973), honorary membership of the American Academy and Institute of Arts and Letters (1980), honorary doctorates of music from City University (1983) and Oxford (1970), and an honorary fellowship of the Royal Northern College of Music (1976). He also served as president of the Performing Right Society (1975–83), the Composers' Guild of Great Britain (from 1975), and the Cheltenham festival (1977–83).

Berkeley was, above all, graceful: he had been a good tennis player in his youth and remained all his life a tireless walker. As with his music, there was no hint of otiose flesh, rather of a strength which he was careful to hide beneath beautiful manners. As well as being a kind and approachable man, he was always quick to see the funny side of things. During his time with Boulanger, he and Igor Markevitch were members of a mildly disruptive 'back row', while in later life an eye would twinkle in response to persons on committees who treated 'criteria' as a singular noun or interposed with, 'Mr Chairman, I have a trepidation about that one.' Although determined to do what he saw as his civic duty, he never courted public notice unless forced by the strength of his own opinions. He had become a Roman Catholic in 1928 (when he took the name Francis), and, in the wake of the second Vatican council, wrote in the press urging the retention of the tridentine mass, since he believed the authorities were ignoring a legitimate desire expressed by a large body of Roman Catholic laymen. In private he wrote of those 'for whom the overthrow of the old tradition appears to be an end in itself', an end which, in religion as in music, he was unable to approve.

In 1946 he married Elizabeth Freda, daughter of Isaac Bernstein, a retired shopkeeper. They had three sons, of whom the eldest, Michael, became a composer. Berkeley died in St Charles's Hospital, Ladbroke Grove, London, 26 December 1989.

[Peter Dickinson, *The Music of Lennox Berkeley*, 1988; BBC archives; private information; personal knowledge.]

ROGER NICHOLS

published 1996

WALCAN-BRIGHT Gerald

(1904–1974)

Dance-band leader and musician who used the name Geraldo, was born in Islington, north London, 10 August 1904, the twin son (there were also three daughters) of Isaac Walcan-Bright, master tailor, and his wife, Frances Feldman. Like his brother, Sidney, he was musical from an early age. He started to learn the piano when he was five and he continued his training at the Royal Academy of Music, after attending the Hugh Middleton Central School at Islington. His first professional engagement was as a relief pianist accompanying silent films at a cinema in the Old Kent Road. His first band was formed in 1924 to play at the Metropole in Blackpool, but recognition came for him during the five years he spent as musical director at the Hotel Majestic, St. Anne's on Sea. His band broadcast from the hotel three times a week and became the most popular dance orchestra in the north of England.

In 1929 he disbanded the orchestra and went to South America, where he spent some time in Argentina and Brazil studying Latin-American rhythms. Returning to London, he formed his Gaucho Tango orchestra, which started playing at the Savoy Hotel in August 1930. He remained there for ten successful years. During this time, he changed his stage name from Gerald Bright to Geraldo. He made his first recordings in 1930 with the orchestra, which gave more than 2,000 broadcasts from the Savoy. In

1933 they appeared at the royal command performance. In September that year he formed a new orchestra for the Savoy, widening his repertoire to include dance music and changing his signature tune from 'Lady of Spain' to 'I Bring You Sweet Music' (it later became 'Hello Again'). This orchestra made brief appearances in the films *Lilies of the Field* and *Ten-Minute Alibi* and played the whole score for *Brewster's Millions.* At one time during the 1930s, Geraldo was leading four bands and employing more than 200 musicians.

At the outbreak of World War II, he was appointed supervisor of the bands division of ENSA (Entertainments National Service Association) and director of bands for the BBC. Broadcasting several times a week in such programmes as 'Tip-Top Tunes', 'Over to You', and 'Dancing Through', Geraldo's orchestra became the most popular in Britain. His wartime band was more oriented towards jazz and swing than his groups of the 1930s—it included such men as trombonist Ted Heath, trumpeter Leslie 'Jiver' Hutchinson, and clarinettist Nat Temple, who all led their own orchestras later. Geraldo took the orchestra to entertain the troops in the Middle East, North Africa, and Europe, covering nearly 20,000 miles and twice crash-landing (in Italy and Gibraltar).

After the war he ran several orchestras, the largest comprising seventy-five musicians, but he became more interested in the business side of music, supplying orchestras for liners (including the Cunard Line), dance halls, theatres, and restaurants. His own orchestra continued to broadcast, and he was the first bandleader to appear on British television when it reopened after the war. He was a founder-director of Harlech Television and, for a while, musical director of Scottish Television. In the early days of ITV, he appeared in a long-running television series called 'Gerry's Inn'.

Although his public appearances diminished, he returned for a series of nostalgic concerts at the Royal Festival Hall from 1969, which led to a television series recalling the era of swing music. He was still recording in the 1970s. His last public appearance was at a concert in Eastbourne a few weeks before his death.

Geraldo was of medium height, sturdily built, with dark brown hair and brown eyes. He was always immaculately dressed and his voice had a slight cockney accent. He loved classical music but firmly believed in the value of dance music. When (Sir) Malcolm Sargent criticized dance music in 1942, Geraldo said that he would conduct Sargent's orchestra in any piece of classical music if Sargent would conduct Geraldo's orchestra in a piece of swing music. Sargent refused the challenge.

He married Alice Plumb in 1948 and they were divorced in 1965, when he married Marya, daughter of Leopold Detsinyi, a Hungarian textile-manufacturer. He died 4 May 1974 of a heart attack while on holiday with his wife in Vevey, Switzerland.

[*The Times*, 6 and 20 May 1974; *Guardian*, 6 May 1974; Julien Vedey, *Band Leaders*, 1950; Albert McCarthy, *The Dance Band Era*, 1971; private information.]

TONY AUGARDE

published 1986

WESTRUP Jack Allan

(1904–1975)

Sir

Musician, author, and conductor, was born in Dulwich, London, 26 July 1904, the second of the three sons (there were no daughters) of George Westrup, insurance clerk, of Dulwich, and his wife, Harriet Sophia Allan.

He was educated at Alleyn's School, Dulwich, where he was a scholar, and then gained a Nettleship scholarship in music to Balliol College, Oxford. There was no honours degree in music at that time, so he first read classics in which he gained first class honours in moderations (1924) and second class honours in *literae humaniores* (1926) before proceeding to the B.Mus. degree in 1926. He took an active part in music in the university both as a keyboard and brass player. However, his most important contribution to Oxford music was his part in the foundation of the University Opera Club whilst still an undergraduate to which he returned later as conductor, when he was elected to the Heather professorship in 1947.

In spite of a research grant on going down from Oxford—when he worked on 'Noëls Provençaux' in Avignon—appointments for musical scholars were then so scarce that he went back to his old school and taught classics. Then in 1934 he returned to music as a critic on the *Daily Telegraph* until the war virtually put an end to concerts in London, whereupon he did another short stint as a schoolmaster. His chance to enter academic life came in 1941 when he was offered and accepted a lectureship at King's College, Newcastle upon Tyne, and this was followed by his election to the Peyton and Barber chair of music at Birmingham University in 1944. He flourished at Birmingham, making full use of the excellent facilities offered by the Barber Institute library, and the opportunities for conducting.

Oxford conferred upon him the degree of honorary D.Mus. in 1944, and in 1947 he returned to his old university as Heather professor of music. Much as this pleased him, it was not an easy time for him, as there were some Oxford musicians who did not welcome his election. However, in 1950 the university finally allowed music to become an honours course and Westrup was mainly instrumental in designing a new syllabus which demanded a wider knowledge of musical scholarship than the old B.Mus. This gave him satisfaction and confidence.

His energy was remarkable. Not only did he fulfil meticulously his duties as professor, but during his twenty-four years at Oxford he conducted seventeen operas for the University Opera Club—mostly unfamiliar and including one first performance and one British première—, edited *Music & Letters* from 1959 and was president of the Royal Musical Association (1958–63), the Incorporated Society of Musicians (1963), and the Royal College of Organists (1964–6).

As a man Westrup was a person with complete self-control and with a presence which alarmed those who did not know him well. He did not suffer fools gladly and had no patience with the yes-man. If one disagreed with him his face would light up and his interest immediately would be stimulated. In matters of detail he was most meticulous and expected others to be likewise. But to those who had the fortune to know him well he was a kind and humble man, never too busy to offer help and almost incapable of saying 'no' to the most mundane of requests.

Apart from his university degrees he was a fellow of the British Academy (1954), the Royal College of Organists (1942), Trinity College, London (1946), the Royal College of Music (1961), and the Royal School of Church Music (1963). He was also honorary RAM (1960). For his services to music he was knighted in 1961.

It was to the lasting regret of his friends and colleagues and a serious loss to music that while at Oxford his energies were not directed more towards the writing of books. It was hoped—nay, assumed—that he would follow up his outstanding books on *Purcell* (1937), *Handel* (1939), and *An Introduction to Musical History* (1955) with works of similar stature. Instead he indulged in much editing (in 1947 he became chairman of the editorial board of *The New Oxford History of Music*), writing articles, compiling lexicons, and lecturing abroad which, although of importance, were no substitute for what a man of his talent should have achieved.

His versatility—as a practical musician and as a musicologist—can best be summed up by two quotations from his 1945 Deneke lecture (published in 1946): 'Nothing can better aid our endeavours than performance—performance not merely by amateurs, to whose enthusiasm we so often owe a lively acquaintance with the past, but by expert musicians who unite with their skill an understanding of what they are trying to do.' And: 'Perhaps the virtue that we need most of all is humility—not the crawling acquiescence that accepts great reputations and can find no flaw, but the readiness to believe in lesser men until we can prove them to be charlatans.' The last paragraph of this lecture might well have been written of him rather than by him: 'The great historians of music are those who have carried musical souls about them, who to industry and scholarship have added vision and found the power to share it with their readers.'

In 1938 he married Solweig Maria (died 1984), daughter of Per Johan Gustaf Rösell, musical director of an infantry regiment in Linköping, Sweden; they had one daughter and three sons. Westrup died at his home in Headley, Hampshire, 21 April 1975.

[Gerald Abraham in *Proceedings* of the British Academy, vol. lxiii, 1977, P. Dennison in *The New Grove Dictionary of Music and Musicians* (ed. Stanley Sadie), vol. xx, 1980; J. A. Westrup, *The Meaning of Musical History* (Deneke lecture), 1946; private information; personal knowledge.]

BERNARD ROSE

published 1986

ABRAHAM Gerald Ernest Heal

(1904–1988)

Musical scholar and leading authority on Russian music, was born 9 March 1904 in Newport, Isle of Wight, the only child of Ernest Abraham, manufacturer, and his wife, Dorothy Mary Heal, a jeweller's daughter. In spite of his strong musical interests, he planned a naval career, attending a naval crammer in Portsmouth. Ill health forced him to abandon this, though he retained a lifelong interest in naval history, and after studying for a year in Cologne he published his first book on music, a study of Alexander Borodin (1927), an autodidact like himself. Apart from some early piano lessons, he was self-taught but, during the following years, he contributed widely to musical periodicals and also published monographs on Nietzsche (1933), Tolstoy (1935), and Dostoevsky (1936), as well as an introduction to contemporary music, *This Modern Stuff* (1933), renamed *This Modern Music* in later reprints. He taught himself Russian and published two collections of his primarily analytical essays, *Studies in Russian Music* (1935) and *On Russian Music* (1939). In collaboration with M. D.

Calvocoressi, he wrote *Masters of Russian Music* (1936). In 1935 he joined the BBC as assistant editor of the *Radio Times* and subsequently served as deputy editor of the *Listener* (1939–42), remaining its music editor until 1962.

During World War II, when interest in Russian music was at fever point, he published *Eight Soviet Composers* (1943) and made a valuable behind-the-scenes contribution to broadcasting as director of gramophone programmes (1942–7), helping to lay the foundations of the Third Programme in 1946. He returned to the BBC in 1962, as assistant controller of music, after having spent the intervening years (1947–62) as the first professor of music at Liverpool University. He spent a further year as chief music critic of the *Daily Telegraph* (1967–8), before becoming the Ernest Bloch professor of music at the University of California at Berkeley (1968–9). His lectures there were subsequently published under the title, *The Tradition of Western Music* (1974).

Although the public tended to associate him with Slavonic and Romantic music, his scholarship was of quite unusual breadth and depth. He edited symposia on Tchaikovsky (1945), Schubert (1946), Sibelius (1947), Grieg (1948), Schumann (1952), and Handel (1954). He set in motion The History of Music in Sound (gramophone records and handbooks) and the *New Oxford History of Music*. The latter occupied him for the best part of three decades; he edited three of its ten volumes personally—the third, *Ars Nova and the Renaissance, 1300–1450*, in collaboration with Dom Anselm Hughes (1960), the fourth, *The Age of Humanism, 1540–1630* (1968), and the eighth, *The Age of Beethoven, 1790–1830* (1982). He also brought out his magisterial, synoptic overview of western music, *The Concise Oxford History of Music* (1979). He was closely involved in *The New Grove Dictionary of Music and Musicians* (1980). His selfless work as an editor is nowhere better exemplified than in his completion of Calvocoressi's Master Musicians study of Mussorgsky (1946) and his work on seeing Calvocoressi's larger study through the press in 1955 (published in 1956).

Abraham was of medium height, with a genial and warm personality. His writings are exceptional in the field of musicology for not only their scholarship, which was always worn lightly, but also their freshness, originality, and readability. He had the rare ability to stimulate the interest and engage the sympathies of the less informed as well as the specialist reader, and commanded a ready wit with the gift for a felicitous and memorable phrase. Although Abraham wrote widely on Russian music and literature, he was also the author of a penetrating study of *Chopin's Musical Style* (1939), which was a model of lucidity, economy, and good style. Always a Wagnerian, Abraham long planned a book on Wagner's musical language. In the 1940s he even made a conjectural reconstruction of a quartet movement that was published by the OUP. He also made a conjectural completion of Schubert's 'Unfinished' Symphony in 1971.

He held honorary doctorates from Durham, Liverpool, Southampton, and Berkeley in California, was a fellow of the British Academy (1972), and president of the Royal Musical Association (1969–74). He was appointed CBE in 1974. From 1973 to 1980 he was chairman of the British Academy's Early English Church Music committee. Some of his finest and most absorbing writing is to be found in *Slavonic and Romantic Music: Essays and Studies* (1968). Whether as a lecturer or broadcaster, Abraham's erudition was always tempered by a keen sense of humour. The publication of *Slavonic and Western Music: Essays for Gerald Abraham*, edited by Malcolm Hamrick Brown and Roland John Wiley (1985), paid him fitting and timely tribute.

In 1936 he married (Isobel) Patsy, daughter of Stanley John Robinson, pharmacist; they had one daughter. Abraham had an abiding love of the English countryside and the music of Sir Edward Elgar, and from the early 1960s lived in a converted school in Ebernoe near Petworth, until his death at the King Edward VII Hospital, Midhurst, 18 March 1988.

[Malcolm H. Brown and Ronald J. Wiley, *Slavonic and Western Music: Essays for Gerald Abraham*, 1985; Sir Jack Westrup (ed.), 'A Birthday Greeting to Gerald Abraham', *Music and Letters*, vol. lv, 1974; personal knowledge.]

ROBERT LAYTON

published 1996

LAMBERT Constant

(1905–1951)

Musician, was born in London 23 August 1905, the younger son of the Australian painter George Washington Lambert, A.R.A., and his wife, Amelia Beatrice Absell. He was the brother of the sculptor Maurice Lambert. He was educated at Christ's Hospital and the Royal College of Music, where he studied with Ralph Vaughan Williams and R. O. Morris. He was introduced by Edmund Dulac to Diaghilev who commissioned him to write the ballet *Romeo and Juliet*. At this time Lambert was still a student and he was the first English composer to be commissioned by Diaghilev. The ballet which consists of thirteen short movements in classical forms was first performed in 1926 at Monte Carlo, with choreography by Nijinska.

Earlier Lambert had become acquainted with the Sitwells and he shared brilliantly with (Dame) Edith Sitwell the speaking part in the 1922 and 1923 performances of *Façade,* the entertainment with poems by Edith Sitwell and music by (Sir) William Walton. His second ballet, *Pomona,* was written at the Sitwell family home at Renishaw in Yorkshire in 1926; the story concerns the successful wooing of Pomona, the goddess of fruit, by the god Vertumnus. The ballet was first produced in Buenos Aires in 1927, again with choreography by Nijinska. Later in 1926 he set eight poems by the Chinese writer Li-Po for voice and piano, and afterwards made an arrangement of them for voice and a small combination of instruments. In 1927 came *Music for Orchestra,* a brilliant orchestral work which showed a masterly command of the medium. An 'Elegiac Blues' in memory of the negro singer Florence Mills showed Lambert's interest in jazz music, and this was shown even more strikingly in *The Rio Grande,* a setting of (Sir) Sacheverell Sitwell's poem for piano, chorus, and orchestra, which contains a number of jazz effects. This was first performed on 12 December 1929 in Manchester by the Hallé Orchestra conducted by the composer; the orchestra's regular conductor, Sir Hamilton Harty, played the difficult solo piano part. This performance was repeated on the following day at the Queen's Hall, London, and *The Rio Grande* remained Lambert's most popular work during his lifetime.

Between 1928 and 1931 Lambert wrote two works in classical forms, but also showing some influences of jazz: these are the Piano Sonata and the Concerto for piano and nine instruments (Lambert was an expert pianist himself). The Concerto was dedicated to the memory of Lambert's close friend Philip Heseltine (Peter Warlock) and ends with an elegiac slow movement.

In 1930 Lambert became conductor of the Camargo Society, and he conducted Vaughan Williams's ballet *Job* in his own version for theatre orchestra at the 1931 festival of the International Society for Contemporary Music in Oxford. From the Camargo Society grew the Vic–Wells Ballet (later the Sadler's Wells Ballet), of which Lambert became the first musical director, holding this post until 1947, after which he remained its artistic adviser. He was awarded the Collard fellowship of the Musicians' Company in 1934 and this enabled him to complete his largest work, the choral masque *Summer's Last Will and Testament*, to poems of Thomas Nashe. This was first performed in January 1936 at the Queen's Hall, with the composer conducting. Although Lambert here again makes use of classical forms, the work is not in the least archaistic, and shows a brilliant command of voices and instruments in combination.

Lambert's next ballet, *Horoscope*, was first performed at Sadler's Wells in 1938, with choreography by (Sir) Frederick Ashton; the story concerns the love of a man born with the sun in Leo and the moon in Gemini and a woman born with the sun in Virgo and the moon in Gemini. (Lambert's own birthday was on the cusp between Leo and Virgo.) The ballet begins with an extraordinary palindrome, unique in Lambert's work, which the composer believed to have been dictated to him by his friend and colleague Bernard van Dieren, who had died shortly before.

Later works of Lambert include a setting for male voices and strings of the Dirge from Shakespeare's *Cymbeline* (1940) which is one of his most moving works; it is dedicated to Patrick Hadley, Lambert's fellow student and later professor of music at Cambridge. In 1940 Lambert was with the Sadler's Wells Ballet in Holland and narrowly escaped capture at the time of the German invasion. This experience was reflected in the *Aubade Héroïque* for orchestra (1942) in which pastoral and warlike elements are strikingly combined; Lambert dedicated this work to his teacher Vaughan Williams on his seventieth birthday. His last ballet, *Tiresias*, was given at Covent Garden in 1951, shortly before his death, again with choreography by (Sir) Frederick Ashton and décor by his wife Isabel Lambert. The composer conducted the initial performances.

While director of the Sadler's Wells Ballet Lambert made many arrangements for them, including music of Meyerbeer (*Les Patineurs*), Purcell (*Comus*), Auber (*Les Rendezvous*), and Boyce (*The Prospect Before Us*). He also chose the late Liszt piano pieces used in *Apparitions* and orchestrated Liszt's Dante Sonata for the company. Other transcriptions include works by Boyce, Handel, and Thomas Roseingrave, an Irish pupil of Domenico Scarlatti. Lambert did a great deal of conducting, at the promenade concerts, where he was associate conductor (1945–6), on the B.B.C. Third Programme, where he was always willing to perform unusual but interesting works, and at Covent Garden, where among other works he gave memorable performances of Purcell's *Fairy Queen* and Puccini's *Manon Lescaut* and *Turandot*. His book on the music of the twenties, *Music Ho!* (1934), subtitled 'A Study of Music in Decline', was brilliantly written and showed a wide and erudite knowledge of the arts and of life in general, if some of its conclusions have subsequently been questioned. Lambert also wrote musical criticism for the *New Statesman, Figaro*, the *Sunday Referee*, and other papers, and he contributed a number of extremely witty articles on non-musical subjects to *Lilliput* and other magazines. Apart from his brilliance as a composer and conductor, he was a warm and generous personality, a brilliant conversationalist, and a man of enormous knowledge who made a unique contribution to English music during the last twenty-five years of his short life.

Lambert married in 1931 Florence Chuter and had one son; the marriage was dissolved and in 1947 he married Isabel Delmer. He died in London 21 August 1951.

A portrait by Michael Ayrton is in the Tate Gallery. Of two by Christopher Wood, one is at Covent Garden and the other in the National Portrait Gallery. The family owns a sculptured head by Maurice Lambert and a pencil drawing by his father. A portrait of him as a boy at Christ's Hospital by his father is at Christ's Hospital.

[*Grove's Dictionary of Music and Musicians*; personal knowledge.]

HUMPHREY SEARLE

published 1971

RAWSTHORNE Alan

(1905–1971)

Composer, was born in Haslingden, Lancashire, 2 May 1905, the younger child and only son of Hubert Rawsthorne, medical practitioner, of Haslingden and Southport, Lancashire, and his wife, Janet Bridge. He was educated, after preparatory school, at Sandringham School, Southport, for two years, then continued his education with a private tutor, also in Southport. His parents were initially opposed to his following the profession of music and consequently he briefly and abortively studied dentistry and architecture. He did not begin serious musical training until, at the age of twenty, he entered the Royal Manchester College of Music. Here he studied piano under Frank Merrick and cello under Carl Fuchs, gaining diplomas in teaching and performance and becoming a gold medallist and later (1943) an honorary fellow of the college. He continued his piano studies abroad, notably under Egon Petri in Berlin. In 1932–4 he taught, played the piano, and was generally responsible for the music in the School of Dance Mime at Dartington Hall.

It was not until the mid-1930s that he settled in London, married in 1934 as his first wife the orchestral violinist, Jessie, daughter of Herbert Hinchcliffe, schoolmaster, and began to devote himself solely to composition.

In the few years before World War II he began to make his mark, notably with his Theme and Variations for Two Violins (1938) and Symphonic

Studies for Orchestra (1939). Both were performed in the annual festivals of the International Society for Contemporary Music (London, 1938, and Warsaw, 1939, respectively). With the dislocation of war—Rawsthorne served in the army from 1941 onwards—his career was hampered but not at a standstill. Both his First Piano Concerto (1942) and the *Street Corner Overture* (1944) were successes. After the war, he was to have a working life of only twenty-five years. They were productive but not prolific. Major post-war works included three symphonies, a Second Piano Concerto written for the 1951 Festival of Britain; Concertos for Violin, Cello, Oboe, and Orchestra; a Concerto for String Orchestra; chamber music including three String Quartets and an outstanding Sonata for Violin and Piano; works for piano solo, few in number unfortunately, since he wrote beautifully for the instrument; and some extended cycles or cantatas both for solo voice and for chorus, with orchestra: these did not perhaps display his gifts as fully as his purely orchestral and instrumental work did.

Much of this output was written after he left London and moved to a fairly remote village in Essex in the 1950s. He was divorced in 1954 and in the following year married the painter Isabel Delmer Lambert, daughter of Philip Owen Nicholas, master mariner. She was the former wife of D. Sefton Delmer and the widow of Constant Lambert, who died in 1951 and who was one of Rawsthorne's closest friends and musical associates. There were no children by either marriage. Isabel Lambert was responsible for the décor of Rawsthorne's ballet, *Madame Chrysanthème* (Covent Garden, 1955). This was his only stage work, though he was planning at the end of his life to write a full-length opera, and earlier in his career he had composed music for numerous films.

'A musicians' composer' is a phrase commonly applied to Alan Rawsthorne and with some justice. Certainly the meticulously clean writing, the polish and refinement which inform his work appeal to professional musicians and to the more knowledgeable listeners, rather than to a wider public. Yet there is much to enjoy in his best work: the clarity of thought and expression, at times witty, more often introspective, with a gentle melancholy yet not without occasional bursts of power and intensity. His style was remarkably consistent throughout his career though it lost some of its precise texture in his last years. It was a style that was as remote from the traditional twentieth-century English school as it was from the European avant-garde. In the crucial period of Rawsthorne's post-war development, fashion and taste in England tended to follow one or other of these two opposed movements and thus his music, not conforming to either, probably suffered in public esteem. But in any historical assessment of mid-twentieth-century English music, his place is assured. Influences on his writing are to be found, in composers such as Hindemith, Roussel, and Prokofiev. But Rawsthorne was always very recognizably himself, certain of his 'trade marks' (such as his liking for rapidly shifting tonalities) sometimes becoming near to mannerisms.

As a man he displayed several of the characteristics to be found in his music. Quiet, unhurried, and courteous in manner, his conversation nevertheless had a sharp cutting edge: he chose his words with the same precision as he did his black-and-white notes. At heart an intensely serious man, there was yet an urbanity about him and a stylish elegance which is reflected in the immaculate manuscript of his scores. He was well versed in literature and the pictorial arts, and, though not generally gregarious, he had many friends among painters, sculptors, actors, and poets. By his fellow musicians he was held in unusually warm regard.

Rawsthorne was appointed CBE in 1961 and received three honorary doctorates (University of Belfast, 1969; Liverpool, 1969; Essex, 1971). He became an honorary fellow of Downing College, Cambridge, in 1969. He died in Cambridge 24 July 1971.

[*The Times*, 26 July 1971; Peter Evans, 'Alan Rawsthorne', *The New Grove Dictionary of Music and Musicians*, ed. Stanley Sadie, vol. xv, 1980; private information; personal knowledge.]

ALAN FRANK

published 1986

DYKES BOWER John

(1905–1981)

Sir

Cathedral organist, was born at Gloucester 13 August 1905, the third of four sons (there were no daughters) of Ernest Dykes Bower MD, surgeon, and his wife, Margaret Dora Constance Sheringham. Two brothers (Michael and Wilfrid) became well-known doctors; Stephen, architect, designed the baldaquin at St Paul's. All four sons inherited from their parents a powerful interest in music, and as children were daily set to practise the piano during the hour before breakfast. The family worshipped regularly at Gloucester Cathedral.

Dykes Bower was educated at Cheltenham College and at the same time was a pupil of (Sir) A. Herbert Brewer, organist of Gloucester

Cathedral. From Cheltenham he went in 1922 to Corpus Christi College, Cambridge, having won the John Stewart of Rannoch scholarship in music. He was again awarded a Rannoch scholarship, together with his brother Wilfrid, in 1925. At Corpus he was organ scholar in succession to Boris Ord; his brother Wilfrid succeeded him. Ord and Dykes Bower were lifelong friends, both dedicated to the pursuit of perfection in the performance of church music and very austere in the demands they made on choirs. Both hated any element of 'show-biz' about the conductor's role.

From Cambridge Dykes Bower went to be organist at Truro (1926–9), where Bishop Walter Frere as musician and liturgist made his stay congenial. At Truro he succeeded in expelling from his choir a tone-deaf lay clerk who was mayor and a potentate in the city. This difficult achievement commended him to H. A. L. Fisher, warden of New College, Oxford, and Sir Hugh Allen, when New College needed an organist in 1929. In 1933 he was invited to be cathedral organist at Durham, with a university lectureship. His Cambridge college simultaneously elected him a (non-resident) fellow, 1934–7. The incomparable acropolis of Durham was congenial to him, but there were also difficulties to contend with (he did not get on well with those who wanted no changes and resented his perfectionism); and in 1936, aged only thirty-one, he was appointed by W. R. Matthews, the dean, to St Paul's to succeed (Sir) Stanley Marchant. Matthews and Dykes Bower became instinctively drawn together in friendship as well as by their common responsibility for cathedral services. They perfectly understood their respective spheres. Moreover, Dykes Bower was a punctilious administrator and letter-writer. He enjoyed to the full the great occasions that come to St Paul's, like the thanksgiving service after World War II or Sir Winston Churchill's state funeral in 1965, when the huge congregation singing the 'Battle Hymn of the Republic' was totally controlled by masterly rhythmic playing on the part of Dykes Bower.

St Paul's had resources making it possible for him to include music of a complexity that other cathedrals could hardly attempt. Characteristically, unless an anthem were unaccompanied, he would always direct from the organ loft; his intense sense of pulse and rhythm was conveyed with the minimum of external sign. He disliked anything flamboyant or histrionic. In part this reflected the quiet reticence of his personality. But it was more an expression of his deep feeling that the sublimity of church music is diminished or even destroyed if the performance and the performers are perceived to be somehow distinct from the act of worship to which they help to give expression.

During World War II the cathedral was under frequent threat from the air. In the destruction of the city of London by fire-bombs in December

1940 Dykes Bower lost everything, including his exquisite grand piano to which he was devoted; he was at least as fine a performer on the piano as on the organ. In 1940 he joined the RAFVR and, with the rank of squadron leader, worked in the Air Ministry with a group which included the viola player Bernard Shore, with whom he used to give occasional wartime recitals when life made such relaxation possible. After the war he combined his continued work at St Paul's with the post of associate director of the Royal School of Church Music (1945–52). He held the professorship of organ at the Royal College of Music (1936–69), and sent out a series of distinguished pupils to many of the major cathedral posts in England. Only Boris Ord at King's College, Cambridge, had a comparable influence on the standard of musicianship in English cathedrals.

In 1967, aged sixty-two, his eyesight was threatened by cataract and once, playing some difficult Bach at the end of a service, he suddenly found himself unable to see the printed page. Immediately he decided to retire from the great position he had held so long. He also had such an attachment to W. R. Matthews, with whom he had collaborated for thirty-one years, that he did not want to continue after Matthews's retirement from the deanery. He took a flat near Westminster Abbey which he attended regularly. Weak sight robbed him of the earlier pleasure of reading Victorian novels, and railway timetables, on which he was remarkably expert. (He loved to plan imaginary cross-country journeys with *Bradshaw*.) But he continued to do much for the Royal College of Organists, of which he was president (1960–2).

He was appointed CVO in 1953 and knighted in 1968. Oxford made him an honorary D.Mus. (1944) and Corpus Christi, Cambridge, made him an honorary fellow (1980). He was master of the Worshipful Company of Musicians (1967–8). He did much for the council of *Hymns Ancient & Modern*, of which he was chairman. The hymn writer J. B. Dykes (1823–76) was his forebear.

His fastidiousness and relentless quest for flawless performance made him hard to please, and could combine with his quiet reticence to make him silent where a word of encouragement could have been beneficial. A very private man with a horror of the limelight, he asked only to be allowed to offer perfection through music in the worship of the Church of England. He inspired awe but also deep affection in everyone who worked alongside him. He was unmarried. He died 29 May 1981 in hospital at Orpington, Kent.

[Personal knowledge.]

Henry Chadwick

published 1990

NEEL (Louis) Boyd

(1905–1981)

Conductor, teacher, and administrator, was born 19 July 1905 at 30 Ulundi Road, Blackheath, the only child of Louis Anthoine Neel, a paint manufacturer, and his wife Ruby Le Coureur—her family came from Jersey. He was educated at the Royal Naval College of Osborne and Dartmouth, which he left to study medicine at Gonville and Caius College, Cambridge (BA, 1926). He then went to St George's Hospital, London, and became MRCS Eng. and LRCP Lond. (1930). Meanwhile he grasped every chance to conduct amateurs, took lessons at the Guildhall School of Music, and listened to Sir Thomas Beecham, Wilhelm Furtwängler, and Bruno Walter. While still in medical practice, he founded the Boyd Neel Orchestra, which made its début at the Aeolian Hall, London, on 22 June 1933; Neel delivered a baby later that night.

For reasons of economy and repertory the group was small and at first consisted mostly of students. At the time little romantic, let alone baroque, string music was played, and then only by symphony orchestras; Neel saw a gap waiting to be filled. He brought forward works by Dvořák, Sir Edward Elgar, Grieg, Gustav Holst, and Tchaikovsky. The *Tallis Fantasia* of Ralph Vaughan Williams, Bloch's *Concerto Grosso*, and Stravinsky's *Apollon Musagète* were in the orchestra's twentieth-century repertory; and *Variations on a Theme by Frank Bridge*, composed by E. B. (later Lord) Britten for them to play at the 1937 Salzburg Festival, established the composer's international reputation and their own. Based on eighteen strings who worked together regularly, the BNO developed a true and distinctive chamber style, finely suited to the concertos of Mozart (often with Kathleen Long or Frederick Grinke) and to revivals of composers such as Torelli, Vivaldi, and Geminiani. A debonair and restrained figure on the podium, Neel had an instinctive gift for just tempos and lucid textures in Bach and Handel. Among the orchestra's many fine recordings, those of Handel's Concerti Grossi Op. 6, pioneering when they were made, held their own when they were reissued in the more critically informed 1970s.

During World War II Neel returned to medicine but also performed at the National Gallery concerts in London. He then branched out into opera, conducting briefly for Sadler's Wells and D'Oyly Carte, and also took the Sir Robert Mayer Children's Concerts. Even during the war, the Boyd Neel Orchestra managed to celebrate its tenth anniversary, for which Britten composed his Prelude and Fugue. Then came their widespread tours, in Britain and elsewhere in Europe, in Australia and New Zealand in

1947, in Scandinavia in 1950, in Canada and the USA in 1952. In 1950 Neel published *The Story of an Orchestra*; he also contributed the chapter on string music to *Britten: A Commentary* (ed. Donald Mitchell and Hans Keller, 1952).

The success of the 1952 Canadian tour led to his move to Toronto in 1953, as dean of the Royal Conservatory of Music and head of the university faculty of music. Without academic musical training, Neel might have seemed a figurehead; but, finding the premises inadequate, he immediately turned his energy to the planning of the Edward Johnson Building, named after the great Canadian tenor. Opened in 1962, this provided the reorganized faculty with an opera theatre, a concert hall, rehearsal, lecture, and practice rooms, a library, and many other facilities, all air-conditioned and sound-proofed. Neel's good humour and skill in communication stood him well in his relationship with both the university and the community (where he was highly regarded), and found another outlet in his work as a popular lecturer and broadcaster.

In 1955 he founded the Hart House Orchestra, a chamber group similar to his London one (which, directed by R. Thurston Dart, who had played continuo for Neel, became the Philomusica). Neel had quickly realized that Canada trained more performers than it could then employ, and that a professional orchestra based on the university would stimulate the community; and he himself needed active music-making. The Hart House Orchestra toured widely over North America, and visited the Brussels World Fair in 1958 and Aldeburgh, at Britten's invitation, in 1966. Neel was also in demand as a guest conductor, particularly after he retired in 1971 from his academic post, where his work had substantially raised the prestige of music in the university. A relaxed, buoyant figure, and a convivial homosexual, he became one of the best-known, most influential musicians in his adopted country. He was appointed CBE (1953) and a member of the Order of Canada (1973). He was honorary RAM. He died in Toronto 30 September 1981. He was unmarried.

[L. Boyd Neel, *My Orchestras*; private information.]

DIANA MCVEAGH

published 1990

KENTNER Louis Philip

(1905–1987)

Pianist, was born 19 July 1905 in Karwzn, Silesia, Hungary, the only son and elder child of Julius Kentner, stationmaster, and his wife, Gisela Buchsbaum. He was educated at the Gymnasium in Budapest and the Royal Franz Liszt Academy of Music, also in Budapest. This was a remarkable beginning: he was only six years old, and simultaneously a school pupil and an academician. He studied the piano with Arnold Szekely and composition with Hans Koessler, Leo Weiner, and Zoltan Kodály. Both Weiner and Kodály were lifetime influences. He gained a diploma in musical composition.

Composition was his first ambition. Three sonatinas were published (by Oxford University Press) in the 1930s, and there were later performances of a string quartet and a divertimento for chamber orchestra. But it was the piano that was to become the centre of his musical life. His concert career began with a recital in Budapest when he was thirteen. From the 1920s he undertook a ceaseless round of concerts around the world, his fame spreading rapidly. He went back to Hungary, but with the political situation worsening emigration beckoned, and he decided to move to England in 1935, becoming one of the mid-Europeans who transformed Britain's musical life. He became a British citizen in 1946, and London remained his home until his death.

In an early review (in the *Sunday Referee* of 11 October 1936), headed 'A new—and great—pianist comes to England', Constant Lambert wrote: 'What gives Kentner's playing its exceptional quality, however, is not so much his technical ability, which he shares with several virtuosos, but the remarkable intelligence and musical instinct which direct this ability . . . I have never heard a pianist of such power who at the same time has such delicacy and subtlety of tone gradation . . . a pianist with a brilliant future.' Lambert immediately discerned Kentner's exceptional musicianship, as did (Sir) William Walton and the Sitwells, who were warm supporters and friends. He became an admired performer in solo recitals and concertos—an early Mozart concerto with Sir Thomas Beecham was a landmark—as also in chamber music, a lifelong passion. For some years there was a trio with Yehudi (later Baron) Menuhin and the cellist Gaspar Cassado. Music-making with Menuhin, who married Kentner's second wife's sister, was an important activity over the years.

His repertory was enormous and ranged from Bach to Bartók. He was especially noted for his Chopin and Liszt, the latter being most remarkable. Liszt's music had been regarded as superficial and it was 'not done' to perform it. It was largely due to Kentner's championship and deeply felt performances that Liszt came to be treated as a composer of serious beauty. In 1951 he was one of the founders of the Liszt Society, and from 1965 to his death its president.

He gave the first performances of Bartok's Second Piano Concerto (conducted by Otto Klemperer, 1933) and—in Europe—his Third Concerto (conducted by Sir Adrian Boult, 1946), the First Piano Concerto of Alan Rawsthorne in 1942, the Piano Concerto of (Sir) Michael Tippett (1956), and, with Menuhin, of Walton's Sonata for Violin and Piano. He was gifted with a formidable technique and a faultless memory. But what governed his playing was a constant quest for musical truth and his faithfulness to the composer's intention, with which he wished to identify. So his performances moved one both through their effortlessness—though he never tried to dazzle—and his sensitivity, accuracy, and, above all, musical humility. He seemed to be communing with the composer, and this musicianship transmitted itself to the listener. He was one of the last great romantic pianists and his eightieth birthday concert in the Queen Elizabeth Hall, London, caused a spontaneous standing ovation. Fortunately, a number of splendid recordings were made.

The same qualities inspired his teaching, whether in master classes at the Yehudi Menuhin School of Music or with individual pupils in his studio. His standards were high and criticisms tough, though spiced with good Hungarian sarcasm ('Why play the wrong note when the right one is next door?'). There was no didactic method, just a search for musical truth. Technique was taught *through* the music, and Kentner could translate brilliantly musical points into words. He wrote: 'no teacher can put anything into a pupil which is not already there. He can only awake what is already lying dormant, and guide it towards possible short cuts, tending and nurturing it as it grows.' And so his pupils were inspired. He also liked writing, and his little book, *Piano* (1976), is necessary reading for any aspiring pianist. He became an honorary member of the Royal Academy of Music in 1970 and was appointed CBE in 1978.

Physically, he was small in build, and he looked even smaller on his very low (collapsible) piano stool. He had a beautiful head, and an ever-hovering smile. A gentle warmth emanated from him, coupled with a special sense of humour, sometimes wicked, always witty. He was a brilliant raconteur, equalled only by his wife Griselda. His wide reading made him into a typically cultured mid-European.

In 1931 he married a pianist, Ilona, daughter of Ede Kabos, journalist and writer. They were divorced in 1945 and in 1946 he married Griselda Katharine, sister of Diana, who married Yehudi Menuhin the following year, and daughter of Gerard Louis Eugene Gould, of the special branch in the Foreign Office, who died in 1916, and his wife, the pianist Evelyn Suart. There were no children of either marriage. Kentner and Griselda shared the remainder of his life, and he spoke often of how central to his playing and life Griselda was: he wrote of her as 'beautiful, talented, angelic, highly musical withal'. Kentner died at their home at 1 Mallord Street, Chelsea, 22 September 1987.

[Harold Taylor (ed.), *Kentner: a Symposium*, 1987; personal knowledge.]

CLAUS MOSER

published 1996

LUTYENS (Agnes) Elisabeth

(1906–1983)

Composer, was born at 29 Bloomsbury Square, London, 9 July 1906, the fourth of five children and third of four daughters of (Sir) Edwin Landseer Lutyens, architect, and his wife, Lady Emily, daughter of Edward Robert Bulwer Lytton, the first Earl of Lytton, statesman. She was educated at Worcester Park School, Westgate-on-Sea. She turned to music at an early age, not because of any conspicuous talent for it, but 'as another form of my need for privacy'. The family's reaction to her musical aims was at first more of apathy than outright opposition, and after a period of private piano and violin lessons, in January 1922 she was permitted, at the age of sixteen, to go to France to study at the École Normale in Paris. In 1926 she entered the Royal College of Music, London, becoming a pupil of Harold Darke for composition and Ernest Tomlinson for viola. She had cause to be grateful to Darke, who managed to arrange for almost everything she composed at this time to be performed. This was most unusual for the RCM, where 'Brahms was the god of *new* music.' Lutyens was emphatically not sympathetic to Brahmsian ideals, yet working in this style for exercises enabled her to develop a powerful compositional technique. Among her friends from this time were Anne Macnaghton, the violinist, and Iris Lemare, and together they founded the Macnaghton-Lemare concerts which began in 1931 at the Mercury Theatre, Notting Hill Gate. The main aim of the concerts was, and still is, to 'discover and encourage composers of British nationality by having their works performed'.

On 11 February 1933 Elisabeth Lutyens married Ian Herbert Campbell Glennie, who had also been an RCM student. He was the son of William

Bourne Glennie, a minor canon of Hereford. They had a son and twin daughters. They were divorced in 1940, and in 1942 Elisabeth Lutyens married Edward Clark (died 1962), a tireless champion of new music, who had previously worked for the BBC in Newcastle and London. He was the son of James Bowness Clark, coal exporter, of Newcastle. They had one son.

For much of her life Elisabeth Lutyens endured relative poverty (with occasional help from her family over such things as housing and children's education), a considerable amount of ill health, physical and mental, and widespread lack of recognition of her originality and achievement. None the less, she never ceased to compose, her opus numbers extending at least to 135, in addition to which there are a hundred film scores from 1944 to 1969 and about the same number of musical commissions for radio. She admitted that the continual steady drinking involved during discussions of the radio projects turned her into an alcoholic. Most of her life, apart from moves to Northumberland and other areas during World War II, was spent in and around London.

She was a prolific and versatile composer, one for whom neglect may have been discouraging but made no essential difference to her development and productiveness. From the outset she veered away from what Constant Lambert termed 'the cowpat school of English music' and described integrity as 'not a virtue [but] a necessity for an artist'. She was the outstanding pioneer of serial music in England, and while she would have liked more performances of her works, her fulfilment was in the composition of them. Her first work to become known through performance was a setting for a ballet *The Birthday of the Infanta* (1932) after Oscar Wilde. This was given at an RCM Patrons' Fund concert while she was still a student (the score has since been withdrawn). The main work of the pre-war years was the Chamber Concerto op. 8 no. 1 for nine instruments (1939) which antedated by several years any knowledge of Webern's concerto for a similar ensemble. The first work to be performed abroad was the String Quartet no. 2 op. 5 no. 5 given at the International Society for Contemporary Music festival at Cracow in 1939. Possibly her best-known work is *O Saisons, O Châteaux!* op. 13 (1946) for soprano and strings, to a poem by Rimbaud. A very high proportion of her later works make use of words, some written by herself, and others by an enormous range of writers, among them Stevie Smith and Dylan Thomas, with whom she was personally acquainted. At a relatively late stage she turned to dramatic music, and her opera 'Charade' *Time off? Not a Ghost of a Chance!* op. 68, 1967–8, to her own libretto, was staged at Sadler's Wells theatre in 1972.

She relished company and good talk, and could be provocative and outrageous, as when ringing up a Jewish pupil at 1 a.m., saying 'the PLO's all right'. Her sitting-room was very welcoming to a new pupil, with a large pot of steaming tea on the table, a standard lamp created from a French horn bell, and the work-desk with its stop-watches and slanting architect's board—the sense of excitement and joy in the act of composing this generated in a young composer can be imagined. She had various rather unsatisfactory arrangements with publishing firms, and eventually formed her own, the Olivan Press, which in the 1960s and 1970s published many more works than all the other publishers had managed over her entire career. In 1969 she was appointed CBE and awarded the City of London Midsummer prize. York University awarded her an honorary D.Mus. (1977). She died in Hampstead, London, 14 April 1983.

[Elisabeth Lutyens, *A Goldfish Bowl*, 1972 (autobiography); M. S. Harries, *A Pilgrim Soul: The Life and Work of Elisabeth Lutyens*, 1989; information from Robert Saxton.]

James Dalton

published 1990

CURZON Clifford Michael

(1907–1982)

Sir

Pianist, was born 18 May 1907 in London, the younger son and second of three children of Michael Curzon, antiques dealer, and his wife, Constance Mary Young, an accomplished amateur singer. His uncle, the composer Albert Ketèlbey, tried out his latest compositions on the family piano and gave the boy his first abiding musical memories. Curzon's first studies were on the violin. At the unusually early age of fourteen he was admitted to the senior school of the Royal Academy of Music where his professor was Charles Reddie through whose own teacher, Bernhard Stavenhagen, Curzon could claim to be a great-grand-pupil of Liszt. Curzon's pianistic ability to learn new repertory at speed impressed Sir Henry J. Wood, then conductor of the RAM first orchestra. Wood gave Curzon his first promenade concert appearance in 1922 as one of the soloists in a Bach triple-keyboard concerto and took him as his concerto pianist on concert tours of Britain. Curzon left the RAM with the McFarren gold medal and other prizes. At this time his repertory centred on Romantic and post-Romantic virtuoso piano works which better-known pianists did not play—for example, pieces by D'Indy and Frederick Delius. He also gave the first performance of Germaine Tailleferre's *Ballade*. Although later Curzon regretted his 'neglect of music of the first quality' this was a suitable repertory for an ambitious pianist whose seniors might well have found him too immature for great classic masterpieces. Nevertheless the young Curzon was specially praised for his account of Schubert's *Wanderer* Fantasia in Liszt's then more popular transcription for piano and orchestra.

It was through his familiarity with Delius's Piano Concerto that Curzon gained his entrée to the repertory which was to become his speciality. The pianist Katharine Goodson wished to rehearse this work with another pianist taking the orchestral part; Reddie recommended her to Curzon who subsequently accompanied her at home in numerous of the great piano concertos which he had hitherto neglected, an experience of value when he came to learn the solo parts himself. In 1926 his father had to abandon his business through illness: the son took a sub-professorship at the RAM to support his family by teaching the piano, while still undertaking concert engagements. An unexpected legacy enabled him to spend two years in Berlin as a pupil of Artur Schnabel. It was from him that Curzon inherited the intellectual seriousness and perfectionism of technique and style which subsequently established his international reputation as an interpreter par excellence of the Viennese classics and German romantics. Among these were Liszt, whose B Minor Sonata Curzon included in the Berlin recital which he gave before leaving Schnabel's tutelage, together with Beethoven's 'Les Adieux' Sonata, Schubert's 'Moments Musicaux', and a recent work by Ernst Lothar von Knorr, a Berlin pedagogue—Curzon always preferred his recitals to include a contemporary work.

Curzon then went to Paris where he studied the harpsichord with Wanda Landowska and attended the classes of Nadia Boulanger. These two great musicians undoubtedly supplemented Schnabel's Teutonic practical and intellectual tuition. In Paris he also met and married in 1931 the American harpsichordist Lucille Wallace (died 1977), daughter of Edward Wallace, a Chicago businessman. Her acute sense of style in performance came to match his own. They adopted the two sons of the soprano Maria Cebotari after her and her husband's untimely death in 1949.

Curzon returned to England in 1932 to build a new international career in the classic repertory, though his programmes still included more recent music. He was the best exponent of the Piano Concerto of John Ireland and was a witty and poetic first soloist in the Second Piano Concerto of Alan Rawsthorne during the Festival of Britain in 1951. In 1946 he introduced (Sir) Lennox Berkeley's Piano Sonata which is dedicated to him. A wartime friendship with Benjamin (later Lord) Britten found them giving concerts as a two-piano team for which Britten composed the *Scottish Ballad*, premièred by them at the Proms in 1944. Later, at Britten's Aldeburgh Festival, Curzon was often a visiting soloist.

In America, which he visited for the first time in 1938, Curzon continued regularly to play a large repertory. His concert schedule was calculated to allow for lengthy preparation with frequent intervals for sabbatical study. In Britain in 1945 he concentrated increasingly on that 'music of the first quality' which he had ignored in his youth—Mozart, Beethoven, Schubert, Brahms. It had been Schnabel's repertory; Curzon played, not in Schnabel's way, which was sometimes uncommunicative, but frankly, generously, yet with the utmost attention to every note and its relative weight in context. The virtues which he applied to Mozart's piano concertos—he regarded them as the most perfect music ever composed—included line-drawing that colours itself and a control of structure through harmony and feeling for ensemble, which was overwhelming when the conductor was sympathetic. He achieved them with Britten often, and also with Daniel Barenboim and Sir Colin Davis. In chamber music he gave unforgettable readings of Schubert's Trout Quintet, Dvorak's and Elgar's Piano Quintets, and the Mozart and Schumann concerted works with piano. Curzon seldom played chamber music at public concerts, but it was evident that chamber music was a necessary element of his art. He was an ideal host, a lively raconteur, a keen connoisseur of painting and literature, and appreciative of other countries and their cultures, food, drink, and language. On the concert platform he appeared nervous in his middle years (he always played from score) but latterly had learned to calculate every note for perfect effect and when he was clearly no longer physically powerful, his mastery of the piano seemed even more magical and potent.

Curzon was awarded many honours, notably honorary doctorates in music at Leeds (1970) and Sussex (1973) and the gold medal of the Royal Philharmonic Society in 1980. He was appointed CBE in 1958 and knighted (a rare honour for a pianist) in 1977. He died in London 1 September 1982.

[*The Times*, 3 September 1982; Max Loppert in *The New Grove Dictionary of Music and Musicians*, 1980 (ed. Stanley Sadie); A. Blyth, 'Clifford Curzon', *Gramophone*, vol. xlviii, 1971, p. 1794; information from Kenneth Loveland.]

William Mann

published 1990

HOLST Imogen Clare

(1907–1984)

Musician, was born in Richmond, Surrey, 12 April 1907, the only child of the composer Gustav Theodore Holst and his wife, Isobel, daughter of an artist, Augustus Ralph Harrison. From the first music was her environment and her nourishment. She was formally educated at St Paul's Girls' School where the curriculum was wide, interesting, and lively. There she developed her lifelong habit of disciplined study and took part in much music-making. Her father was the school's director of music and a major influence on her life and that of many of his other pupils.

In 1926 she entered the Royal College of Music to study piano with Kathleen Long, composition with (Sir) George Dyson and Gordon Jacob, and paperwork with her father's great friend Ralph Vaughan Williams. She also studied dancing and took part in many college stage performances. In 1927 she won an open scholarship for composition. In 1930 a scholarship for study abroad allowed her to travel widely in Europe. Although she lived frugally she was able to enjoy concerts and picture galleries and to experience the civilization of Europe between the wars.

When phlebitis in her left arm prevented her from becoming a concert pianist she turned to teaching and to arranging music for plays, for the English Folk Dance and Song Society as well as for amateur choirs and orchestras which she conducted and for whom she also composed original works. After her father's death in 1934 she wrote his biography (*Gustav Holst*) which was published in 1938.

In April 1939 she went to Switzerland to study the music of fifteenth- and sixteenth-century composers. Returning before the outbreak of war she served on the Bloomsbury House refugee committee concerned with musicians from Germany and Austria. In January 1940 she became one of the six organizers appointed by the Pilgrim Trust (taken over by the Council for the Encouragement of Music and the Arts, the forerunner of the Arts Council) to organize amateur music in wartime Britain. She had responsibility for seven counties in the west. With little help, means of transport, or money she managed to create choirs and instrumental groups among local residents, evacuees, land girls, and service men and women whom the chances of war had temporarily brought together. To them she offered days of music-making which enriched their leisure. In 1942 ill health forced her to resign, and after a recuperative year at Dartington Hall in Devon she became director of music at the arts department there. She trained her students to become music teachers and organizers, teaching them as her father had taught at St Paul's and at Morley College, always drawing in others to share the pleasures of making and of listening to music. She found time to study medieval European music and wrote a severely critical book about her father's works (*The Music of Gustav Holst*, 1951). In 1951 she spent two months at Santiniketan, the university of Sir Rabindranath Tagore in West Bengal, learning about the folk music of India. That summer she left Dartington to travel and study in Europe.

In 1952 she moved to Suffolk where Benjamin (later Lord) Britten had invited her to be his amanuensis. She also helped with the Aldeburgh Festival, of which she was an artistic director (1956–7). In 1953 she founded the Purcell Singers, a group she conducted until 1967. She wrote books for children on Henry Purcell, William Byrd, Bach, and Britten.

In 1964 she ceased to work for Britten in order to concentrate on Holst's work, editing scores for performance and publication and conducting and supervising recordings. In 1974 she produced an informative, definitive *Thematic Catalogue of Gustav Holst's Music* and just before her death a reconsidered edition of her 1951 book.

Though an intensely private person she enjoyed good company and friendship. She had a charming speaking voice which added to her success as a lecturer. Her books are written with the same clarity and persuasive talent that marked her work as teacher and as lecturer. Her own compositions she described as 'useful'. Though written to serve individual needs or special occasions they bear her stamp of professionalism and originality.

Imogen Holst was appointed CBE in 1975. She became a fellow of the Royal College of Music in 1966, and an honorary member of the Royal Academy of Music in 1970. She received honorary degrees from the universities of Essex (1968), Exeter (1969), and Leeds (1983). She died 9 March 1984 at Aldeburgh, where she is buried. She was unmarried.

[Personal knowledge.]

URSULA VAUGHAN WILLIAMS

published 1990

SEMPRINI (Fernando Riccardo) Alberto (1908–1990)

Pianist and conductor, was born 27 March 1908 in Bath, the second of three sons (there were no daughters) of Arturo Riccardo Fernando Semprini, musician, from Rimini, Italy, and his wife, Elizabeth Tilley, opera singer, from Dudley, Worcestershire. The family settled in Bath until Alberto was nine, when his father, a horn player, was appointed librarian to the Scala Opera House, Milan. The boy was intensely musical and won a state scholarship to the Conservatorio Verdi to study piano, composition, and conducting. When he was only sixteen Arturo Toscanini, chief conductor of the Scala, auditioned him for the fiendishly difficult orchestral piano part in Igor Stravinsky's ballet *Petroushka* and gave him the job.

On his vacations he played the piano on transatlantic liners, and while in New York was enthralled by jazz groups and the popular concert orchestra of André Kostelanetz. He discovered he could play this sort of repertoire far better than most classically trained pianists, and this seems to have proved a decisive influence in shaping his career. Another consideration was his marriage in Italy in 1931 to Brunilde Regarbagnati and the arrival of three sons to clothe, feed, and educate.

Semprini left the Conservatorio in 1929 with a doctorate of music and though he occasionally conducted at the Scala and elsewhere, the piano was his first love. In the 1930s he and another Italian pianist Bormioli toured Europe as a popular piano duo, and later he formed his own rhythm orchestra in Italy, with which he made records, broadcast, and played in a number of musical films. The outbreak of war in 1939 halted his career. He had angered the Fascist authorities by playing western music against their orders, and though he had dual Italian and British citizenship, both passports were confiscated, obliging the family to keep a low profile. When eventually the Allies advanced into southern Italy he managed to get to Rome, where he volunteered for ENSA, the Services entertainments organization, and gave many front-line concerts, his piano on the back of an army truck.

Among his troop audiences was the actor Michael Brennan, who offered to be his manager if he ever came to England. But immediately after the war he went to work and study in Spain, where he fell in love with a young Spanish dancer, Maria de la Concepción Consuelo Garcia Cardoso, daughter of Generoso Jose Garcia Inglesias, house painter. Sadly his first marriage had not survived the stresses of a musician's peripatetic life. He took Consuelo to England in 1949 and after his divorce in 1952 married her the same year. There were two sons of this happy and enduring union.

When they arrived in England Brennan secured Semprini a BBC audition. He was immediately engaged to play in a series of fifteen-minute programmes in the style of the recently deceased Charlie Kunz, a popular pianist whose German name had caused public resentment. The style of Semprini quickly took over, pleased the listeners, and led to a short programme with orchestra, for which he chose, arranged, and orchestrated all the music. It was entitled *Semprini Serenade*, and was a subtle blend of classical pieces interspersed with selections from theatre and film music and the work of popular composers like George Gershwin, impeccably performed and introduced quietly and economically from the piano. Soon the programme stretched to an hour; it remained on the air for twenty-five years.

Semprini appeared rarely on television, but was a great favourite from 1952 in the surviving variety theatres, sharing the bill with rising stars like Peter Sellers and (Sir) Harry Secombe, and touring the country in a caravan pulled by an ancient ambulance that contained a piano and a long table for doing orchestrations. Later, driving his beloved Jaguar, he gave many concerts with a more classical content both in Britain and abroad. Whenever possible he drove home through the night to *L'Espérance*, a sailing ship converted into a houseboat at West Mersea, where the family lived happily for many years.

Some critics regretted that Semprini did not pursue a more serious musical career. Certainly he could have performed at the very top of his profession, but he was master of his genre and millions of radio listeners and concert-goers loved his music. In 1972 he was made an officer of the Order of St John and he was appointed OBE in 1983—both recognitions of his considerable efforts for charity. He was a tall, dark, dignified man with fine features, always immaculately dressed, but his gravity was often dispelled by a strong sense of humour and a charming smile. He looked Italian, but he was an Englishman at heart. He died in Brixham from Alzheimer's disease, 19 January 1990.

[Information from relatives, friends, and Kathleen Davey, his personal assistant and music librarian for many years; personal knowledge.]

Ian Wallace

published 1996

LOSS Joshua Alexander ('Joe')

(1909–1990)

Bandleader, was born 22 June 1909 in Spitalfields, east London, the youngest of the family of two sons and two daughters of Israel Loss, of Russian origin, a cabinet-maker who had an office furnishing business, and his wife, Ada Loss. His mother and father were first cousins. Israel Loss recognized his son's musical talents and started him with violin lessons at the age of seven. It was hoped that he might become a concert violinist, and, after education at the Jewish Free School, Spitalfields, he studied at the Trinity College of Music and the London College of Music.

His interests lay in lighter fields and, after playing in cinemas during silent films and in various bands, at the end of 1930 he formed his own first band to play at the Astoria Ballroom (then known as the Astoria Danse Salon) in Charing Cross Road, becoming, at the age of twenty, the youngest bandleader in the West End of London. Under the name of Joe Loss and his Harlem Band, his musicians first played as the no. 2 unit, Joe Loss leading on violin, with three saxophones, trumpet, piano, and drums. Later they added a special tango section, which featured two accordions and two violins. Occasionally they deputized for the Percival Mackey Band at the Kit-Kat Club, and when Mackey left to go into vaudeville at the beginning of 1932, Joe Loss took over to initiate a new 'popular price' policy, playing for daily tea, dinner, and supper dances, supported by and often combining with Fred Spedbury's Coney Islanders. He returned to the Astoria in 1934 to become the no. 1 band and remained there until the outbreak of war in 1939.

During this period he began to record for the Regal-Zonophone label and his first really big hit came with a recording made in July 1939 of 'Begin the Beguine', with Chick Henderson (who was killed by shrapnel in 1944) as vocalist. During the war years Joe Loss toured the country and after D-Day played to the forces at various venues in Europe. His was to become the most prestigious society dance orchestra in the country, its qualities based on his love of a strong rhythm. From 1939 it played a regular engagement at Buckingham Palace and later at the weddings of Princess Margaret, Princess Anne, and Princess Alexandra. After the war there were residencies at the Hammersmith Palais, the Villa Marina in the Isle of Man, and Green's Playhouse, Glasgow, and there were frequent trips on the liner *Queen Elizabeth II*. The band was now always at least eighteen strong, usually with three vocalists—his singers, at various times, including Monte Rey, Howard Jones, Ross McManus, and Rose Brennan. (Dame) Vera Lynn was amongst those given encouragement in the early stages of an illustrious career. In 1970, when Loss left Hammersmith, the band, in the face of economic demands, became smaller.

His recording career was a busy one. In 1940 he had a second big hit with 'In the Mood', which became his signature tune, and many others followed. Despite the emergence of pop, he continued to record his swinging strict-tempo music and in the 1970s had two albums which sold a million copies—'Joe Loss Plays Glenn Miller' and 'Joe Loss Plays the Big Band Greats'. He continued to record with EMI until the end of his career, and became a well-known name on radio and television, notably with the long-running *Come Dancing* series.

Loss was a great supporter of such charities as the Variety Artists' Federation Sunshine Coach Fund. He was appointed OBE in 1978 and LVO in 1984. He was awarded the Queen's Silver Jubilee medal in 1978 and became a freeman of the City of London in 1979. Posthumously, he was made a fellow of the City University when his wife, who continued to run the Joe Loss Agency, started in the 1930s, presented the library with his collection of big-band scores.

Loss's generosity, kindness, and courtesy, and his dislike of star treatment, made him one of the best-liked figures in the world of popular music. He was five feet eight inches in height, with a trim figure and sleek black hair, which tumbled over his face when he was conducting in his typically energetic way. He was always well dressed, in later years in a white silk suit, and usually had a broad, friendly smile. Away from the relentless hard work of sixty years as a bandleader, celebrated by a Variety Club luncheon in 1989, he was a devoted family man. In 1938 he married Mildred Blanch Rose, daughter of a Latvian from Riga, Barnet Rosenberg (who later changed his name to Rose), master tailor. They had a son and a daughter and were delighted to have grandchildren who followed in Loss's musical footsteps. Loss died in a London hospital 6 June 1990.

[Private information; personal knowledge.]

PETER GAMMOND

published 1996

PEARS Peter Neville Luard

(1910–1986)

Sir

Tenor, was born 22 June 1910 at Newark House, Searle Road, Farnham, Surrey, the youngest in the family of four daughters, one of whom died in infancy, and three sons of Arthur Grant Pears, civil engineer and later a director of Burma Railways, and his wife, Jessie Elizabeth de Visme Luard. Pears's parents were married in Bombay in 1893. Much of his father's working life was spent overseas, which meant that Peter had little contact with him until after 1923, when Arthur Pears retired, to live in England. Pears's mother too was often absent, though it is clear from his letters that his relationship with her was a fond one and sustained throughout his young manhood. His brothers followed naval careers, continuing a family tradition in which there was a strong service element: his mother's father had been a general. But there was also another and altogether different strand in Pears's ancestry, that of the Church and, more particularly, the influence of Pears's great-great-grandmother, Elizabeth *Fry, the Quaker reformer. A bonding with Quakerism was to continue throughout Pears's life and was reflected in his pacifism, his sense of values, and his virtues. There was indeed something of the patrician Quaker in his looks, manners, and deeds. His habitual charm and courtesy rarely deserted him.

Pears's childhood, even though it may have lacked the continuity of a settled home, seems to have been a happy one, as indeed were his school-days at Lancing College, Sussex, which he entered as a classical scholar in 1923. At Lancing he became aware of his homosexual nature, though it was to be some years before it found fulfilment. In this respect he was to live at ease with himself throughout his life. It was at school, too, that his musical and theatrical gifts and inclinations showed themselves. He was a capable pianist, took part in operatic and dramatic productions, and involved himself in the school's cultural life. He was an accomplished cricketer. As his school-days ended, his love of painting seems to have begun: his taste and judgement aided him in the acquisition across the years of a notable private collection which included many examples of the work of the best British artists of the period.

In 1928 he went to Keble College, Oxford, to study music, but again without a very clear musical goal in mind. For a while he had a post at Hertford College as temporary organist. But his Oxford career was short-lived. He failed his pass moderations, left Oxford, and never returned. He went back to his preparatory school, The Grange (Crowborough), in 1929, but this time as a teacher, and resumed his interest in cricket. At this point Pears's instinct for music finally located itself in his voice. This led to his undertaking, for the first time, professional vocal studies at the Royal College of Music in London, initially on a part-time basis and then, in 1934, as a full-time student (he was an operatic exhibitioner). Again, however, he never completed the course. He left after only two terms, during which he participated in college operatic productions, to begin his professional career as a singer, with the BBC Singers (1934–7) and, in 1936, the New English Singers, with whom he made his first visit to the USA. In finally making his commitment specifically to a singer's life, he was helped by Nell Burra. She was the twin sister of Peter Burra, a close friend of Pears at Lancing and Oxford, whose life Pears was briefly to share in 1936 and 1937. It was a friendship which was to have a momentous consequence for Pears and indeed for the history of British music.

Burra, a gifted writer on the arts, had met the young composer, Benjamin (later Baron) Britten, in Barcelona in 1936, and the two men became friends. This was before Pears and Britten themselves had met. It was Burra's untimely death in an air accident in 1937 that brought Pears and Britten together. Their remarkable partnership had its inception in April of that year when, as Burra's friends, they jointly sorted out his personal papers. Thus the end of one friendship was the beginning of another; and thereafter the careers of Pears and Britten were inextricably interlinked, as were their lives (they began to share a flat in 1938), though it was not in fact until 1939 in Canada that the love each had for the other finally declared itself. It was to be sustained over thirty-six years. Pears had left England for North America with Britten in the same year and they were not to return until 1942, when both men, convinced pacifists of long standing, sought and were granted exemption from military service, provided they continued their wartime work as performing musicians.

Pears, already in 1938, had had professional experience of opera as a member of the chorus at Glyndebourne, when he was described by a fellow artist as 'tall, fair-haired, reserved and poetic-looking', most of which characteristics were to remain unchanged. Britten's phenomenal development as a composer for the opera house, which had begun in the USA, inevitably brought with it a comparable development in Pears, for whom Britten wrote an extraordinary number and variety of leading roles in almost all of his principal operas, from *Peter Grimes* (1945) to *Death in Venice* (1973). It was in that last opera, dedicated to Pears, that Pears was to make his début at the Metropolitan Opera, New York, in 1974, at the age of sixty-four. But while it is true that Britten's operas shaped Pears's destiny as an opera singer, it must be remembered that Pears, on his return to England from America, had established himself independently as a notable member of the Sadler's Wells company, appearing in such roles as Alfredo in *La Traviata*, Ferrando in *Così fan tutte*, the Duke in *Rigoletto*, Almaviva in *The Barber of Seville*, and Vašek in *The Bartered Bride*. His performances attracted critical attention for their exceptional musicality and intelligence and admiration from Britten, who was often in the theatre as a member of the audience. It was his growing confidence in Pears's theatrical and vocal skills that enabled Britten to write the title role of *Peter Grimes* with Pears's voice in mind (he had at one time thought of Grimes as a baritone). The famous world première of the opera on 7 June 1945 placed the composer in the front rank of musical dramatists of his time and Pears as his principal interpreter.

It was not only as a singer that Pears and his unique voice had an influential role to play in Britten's operas. In one of them, *A Midsummer Night's Dream* (1960), he collaborated with the composer in converting Shakespeare's text into a libretto. He was also the inspiration of the long series of song sets and song cycles that Britten composed between 1940 (the *Seven Sonnets of Michelangelo*) and 1975 (*A Birthday Hansel*), a legacy of song perhaps without equal in the twentieth century. This rich fund of songs reflected the prowess of Pears and Britten as performers. They were to establish themselves as one of the most celebrated and accomplished voice and piano duos of the postwar period, with an extensive repertory that included much of the work of Henry Purcell (when his songs were by no means the staple diet of recital programmes) and the great nineteenth-century classic song cycles—for example, Schubert's *Winterreise* and Schumann's *Dichterliebe*—in interpretations which themselves achieved classic status, and have been preserved on gramophone records. His partnership with the lute virtuoso Julian Bream was to become almost as celebrated, perhaps especially for performances of the Elizabethan master, John Dowland, of incomparable sensitivity and skill from both singer and accompanist. Of equal note was Pears's Evangelist in the Passions of Heinrich Schütz and J. S. Bach, roles to which he brought not only a predictable sensitivity but also an overwhelming sense of immediacy, as if he were a participant in the drama that was being unfolded. This was musical 'theatre' of an unusually exalted order.

The pattern of Pears's life, inextricably woven with the pattern of Britten's (until he suffered a slight stroke in 1973 as a result of his heart operation Britten was virtually the only pianist to accompany Pears), took the shape of strenuous recital tours, at home and abroad, recording and broadcasting; and planning the policy of the English Opera Group (of which he was a co-founder, in 1947) and the programmes of the annual Aldeburgh Festival (of which too he was a co-founder, in 1948). He played a leading role in both organizations as a performer and a stimulating, highly individual impresario.

It was Britten's name, as opera and song composer and pianist, that was inevitably most closely associated with Pears's. But his distinctive interpretations of roles other than Britten roles will not be forgotten: his Tamino in *The Magic Flute*, Idomeneo (in Mozart's opera), David in *The Mastersingers*, and Pandarus in *Troilus and Cressida* by (Sir) William Walton, were all marked by the exceptional musicality and intelligence that characterized him as a singer and, above all, by his exceptional response to, and articulation of, words. He was as sensitive to the sounds of words as he was to pitches. It was a gift that enabled him to bring even a 'dead' classical language to life, as in his masterly performance as Oedipus in Igor Stravinsky's opera-oratorio, in which he collaborated with the composer. He was an enquiring and adventurous singer too, as the long list of first performances by living composers other than Britten amply demonstrates, among them commissions which he himself generously funded. His commitment to the singer's life and art, which had begun so tentatively in the 1930s, found further reflection in his later years when he was an active teacher in the Britten–Pears School for Advanced Musical Studies. This he had co-founded with Benjamin Britten in 1972, and, after the incapacitating stroke he suffered in 1980 which brought his career as a performer virtually to an end, he devoted more and more of his time to it. It was entirely appropriate that he should die at home at Aldeburgh, the focus of his personal and musical life for so many years, having completed, the day before, a full day's teaching at the School—a course, as it happened, on Bach's Passions—passing on to future generations his own unique experience of music, of creative partnership, of the spectrum of the arts, of life itself. It was the totality of all of these that coloured and informed Pears's voice and made it the unique instrument that it was. There were some who found it difficult to come to terms with its peculiar timbre. But his admirers, who were worldwide, rightly regarded it as a vehicle of civilization and sensibility without equal among English singers of his time.

He was appointed CBE in 1957 and knighted in 1978. He received honorary degrees from the universities of York (1969), Sussex (1971), Cambridge (1972), Edinburgh (1976), East Anglia (1980), Essex (1981), and Oxford (1981). Keble College made him an honorary fellow in 1978. From 1957 he and Britten lived together in the Red House in Aldeburgh, Suffolk. After Britten's death in 1976 Pears continued to live in the house until his own death there 3 April 1986. He was buried beside Britten in the churchyard of the parish church of St Peter and St Paul, Aldeburgh.

[Christopher Headington, *Peter Pears: a Biography*, 1992; Marion Thorpe (ed.), *Peter Pears: a Tribute on his 75th Birthday*, 1985; Donald Mitchell and Philip Reed, *Letters from a Life: the Selected Letters and Diaries of Benjamin Britten 1913–1976*, 2 vols., 1991; personal knowledge.]

DONALD MITCHELL

published 1996

MOORE (Charles) Garrett (Ponsonby) (1910–1989)

Eleventh Earl of Drogheda

Chairman of the *Financial Times* and the Royal Opera House, Covent Garden, was born at 40 Wilton Crescent, London, 23 April 1910, the elder child and only son of Henry Charles Ponsonby Moore, tenth Earl of Drogheda, diplomat, and his wife Kathleen, daughter of Charles Maitland Pelham Burn, of Grange Park, Edinburgh. He was educated at Eton and Trinity College, Cambridge, which he left early, without a degree. After two years' bookkeeping at the Mining Trust, the first turning-point of his career came in 1932 when, at Brooks's Club in London, he met Brendan (later Viscount) Bracken, and went to work for him at the *Financial News*, selling advertising space. He worked hard at mastering the detail of the newspaper business, made a considerable impression on Bracken, and developed a long, close relationship with him. In World War II he served briefly in France, as a captain with the 53rd battalion of the Heavy Anti-Aircraft Regiment, Royal Artillery, and was then appointed to the staff of the war cabinet secretariat (1941) and later the Ministry of Production (1942–5). By the end of the war he was back at the *Financial News*, as managing director.

In 1945, at Bracken's instruction, he went out and bought the *Financial Times*. The two newspapers merged under the one title. For twenty-five years, as managing director of the *Financial Times* (1945–70), Drogheda (who succeeded his father in 1957) devoted himself to its commercial expansion and editorial improvement, taking particular pleasure in stimulating its coverage of the arts, the other great passion and interest of his life. He allowed the editor, Sir L. Gordon Newton, to edit, but pursued him daily with a string of memoranda, demanding answers to pertinent questions. If none was received Drogheda persisted.

He used the same tactic at Covent Garden, where, after serving as secretary to the board from 1951, he was its chairman from 1958 to 1974. He bombarded the general administrators, Sir David Webster and later Sir John Tooley, with the same missives, which were known as Droghedagrams. At Covent Garden Drogheda attempted to insist that the board was entitled to approve executive artistic decisions, such as the choice of designer for a particular opera. Webster resisted and (Sir) Georg Solti, engaged by Drogheda as musical director from 1961, never tolerated such interference. Solti's appointment, the decision to give opera in the original language rather than in English, and the high standards that resulted were the principal achievements of Drogheda's chairmanship, which also saw the birth and growth of the Friends of Covent Garden. The Droghedagrams were addressed also to those critics on the *Financial Times*'s pages and elsewhere whose views did not, in the author's opinion, do the opera house justice. These would arrive by messenger on a motor cycle early in the morning the review appeared. It was not unknown for them to be brought round, should the victim live close enough to his house in Lord North Street, by Drogheda himself, in slippers, pyjamas, and dressing-gown.

Drogheda's handsome looks and languid appearance concealed an iron determination to secure his ends. Charming, but obdurate; a dandy, but determined; debonair, but persistent, he would stop at nothing on the newspaper's or the opera house's commercial behalf, pursuing advertisers or possible benefactors without compunction. He struck up friendships with employees of every rank, and treated very many with great personal kindness. He had an acute mind, which expressed itself fluently and clearly on paper, but was guided, he himself thought, always by instinct.

Drogheda was chairman of Financial Times Ltd. (1971–5) and of the Newspaper Publishers' Association (1968–70). He chaired the London celebrations committee for the queen's silver jubilee in 1977. From 1941 he served as a director of the *Economist*, to which he was much attached. He was a commander of the Legion of Honour of France (1960) and of the Order of Merit of Italy (1968) and was grand officer of the Order of Leopold II of Belgium (1974). He was appointed OBE in 1946, KBE in 1964, and knight of the Garter in 1972.

He married in 1935 Joan Eleanor, daughter of William Henry Carr, who left her mother when she was born. She was an excellent pianist, whose immaculate musical taste served him often in good stead. They had one child, a son. Drogheda died 24 December 1989, at Englefield Green, Surrey, eight days after his wife. He was succeeded in the earldom by his son, Henry Dermot Ponsonby Moore (born 1937).

[David Kynaston, *The Financial Times: a Centenary History*, 1988; Frances Donaldson, *The Royal Opera House in the Twentieth Century*, 1988; Garrett Drogheda, *Double Harness, Memoirs*, 1978; private information; personal knowledge.]

JEREMY ISAACS

published 1996

FERRIER Kathleen Mary

(1912–1953)

Singer, was born 22 April 1912 at Higher Walton, near Preston, Lancashire, the third surviving child of William Ferrier and his wife, Alice, daughter of James Murray. Her parents endowed her with a mixture of English, Welsh, Scottish, and Irish blood. Appointed headmaster of St. Paul's School, Blackburn, William Ferrier sent Kathleen to the high school which she left at fourteen to become a Post Office telephonist. Born into a musical family, she showed signs of ability on the piano at an early age and became a pupil of Miss Frances Walker when she was nine. At eighteen she had passed her A.R.C.M. and L.R.A.M. examinations for piano, had developed into a useful accompanist, and was winning prizes in local festivals. A move to Silloth near Carlisle after her marriage in 1935 brought a life of teaching the piano and many musical evenings with friends. As yet singing was for her own amusement. For a shilling wager she entered the Carlisle musical festival in 1937 for singing as well as pianoforte and won the Rose Bowl. Maurice Jacobson, the adjudicator, encouraged her to take singing lessons. From the autumn of 1939 until 1942 she studied with Dr. Hutchinson of Newcastle and gradually gained a solid local reputation which was extended when she was offered concerts with the Council for the Encouragement of Music and the Arts (C.E.M.A.) which became the Arts Council.

Valuable introductions followed. (Sir) Malcolm Sargent heard her sing and introduced her to John and Emmie Tillett, the London concert agents, who advised her to move to London. A flat was found in Hampstead into which she and her sister Winifred moved on Christmas Eve 1942, joined later by their widowed father. From February 1943 Kathleen Ferrier put herself in the hands of Roy Henderson with whom she had recently sung in *Elijah*. He became her 'Prof', an association which lasted for the rest of her life. Intensive training followed for the next three or four years, during which time she built up a national reputation, chiefly with choral societies.

Joint recitals with her professor gave her experience in *Lieder* and art songs. Broadcasts and recording, chiefly for Decca, followed.

Benjamin Britten wrote the name part of his opera *The Rape of Lucretia* for her which she performed in 1946 at Glyndebourne where in the following year she made a profound impression in Gluck's *Orpheo*. The Glyndebourne manager, Rudolf Bing, asked Bruno Walter to hear her; the result was world fame. Here was the ideal Mahler singer Walter was seeking. Concert tours, the operas *Lucretia* and *Orpheo*, and choral works followed in many European countries; Salzburg, Edinburgh, and the English festivals, as well as tours in the United States and Canada. Bruno Walter accompanied her at a few recitals, a rare mark of respect; but her favourite accompanist, who helped her throughout her career, was Gerald Moore who, in his turn, recorded that without her his life would have been 'immeasurably poorer' (*Am I too Loud?*, 1962).

Early in 1951 Kathleen Ferrier had a serious operation. Despite regular visits to hospital for deep X-ray treatment, she was singing as well as ever within three months. But the disease could not be arrested. Her last triumph was in 1953 at Covent Garden in *Orpheo* conducted by her great friend Sir John Barbirolli. Although she was in great pain her glorious voice was in no way impaired. It was a superb end to a meteoric career. She died in London 8 October 1953, having been appointed C.B.E. and awarded the Royal Philharmonic Society's gold medal earlier in the year. The impact of her death on the musical world and her vast public was immense. Many were unable to obtain admission to the memorial service at a crowded Southwark Cathedral. Friends raised money for cancer research at University College Hospital where she had been a patient. The proceeds of a *Memoir* and choral societies provided money for Kathleen Ferrier scholarships for young singers.

The noble quality of Kathleen Ferrier's splendid voice, the great warmth of her heart, her gaiety, sense of humour, and the radiance of her personality, her fine musicianship, and above all her deep sincerity, all contributed to her success.

Her many hobbies included golf, photography, and, in later years, painting. It was, however, in her many friends that she found her greatest pleasure. To audiences and those who knew her best she was the most beloved singer of her time.

Her marriage in 1935 to Albert Wilson, bank clerk, was annulled in 1947. There were no children.

There are busts by Julian Allan at the Free Trade Hall, Manchester, and the Usher Hall, Edinburgh. Another, by A. J. Fleischmann, is in the Blackburn Art Gallery. A portrait by Maurice Codner is owned by Miss Winifred Ferrier.

[*Kathleen Ferrier, a Memoir*, ed. Neville Cardus, 1954; Winifred Ferrier, *The Life of Kathleen Ferrier*, 1955; personal knowledge.]

ROY HENDERSON

published 1971

BRITTEN (Edward) Benjamin

(1913–1976)

Baron Britten

Composer, was born in Lowestoft 22 November 1913, the youngest of four children (two sons and two daughters) of Robert Victor Britten (1878–1934), dental surgeon, and his wife, Edith Rhoda, daughter of Henry William Hockey (1874–1937), King's messenger at the Home Office, London. Hockey was also an active amateur singer and pianist and the secretary of the Lowestoft Choral Society. Benjamin Britten much admired his father but his mother was the dominant influence on his early years. His musical gifts declared themselves astonishingly early, his first attempts at composition dating from *c.* 1919. His mother gave him his first music lessons and a local piano teacher, Ethel Astle, succeeded her in 1921. His family were his first patrons and performers, many of his juvenilia being written for their use.

In 1923 Britten entered South Lodge Preparatory School, Lowestoft, and began viola lessons with Audrey Alston. His prodigious talent for music—he passed Grade VIII of the Associated Board piano examination at the age of twelve—did not affect his conventional school success: he was academically bright, was an excellent and enthusiastic sportsman, and became head boy in 1927. Although these years were largely happy, his leaving prep. school was shadowed by the fuss caused by an essay in which he argued against hunting, thus revealing his budding pacifist and humanist convictions. The choice of Gresham's School, Holt—at the height of its reputation as a 'progressive' public school—reflected his parents' desire to find an environment that would accommodate his views and neither stifle nor disparage his musical gifts. Whatever its merits, Gresham's was not altogether a happy experience: the music teaching and activities—his diaries make frequent caustic references to performances by his teachers—fell far below his expectations and standards.

Two juvenile works, *Quatre Chansons Françaises* for voice and orchestra (1928) and *Quartettino* (1930), disclose a creative precocity which will stand comparison with Mendelssohn's or Mozart's. That Britten's gift was so technically advanced by this time was due largely to the teaching of the composer Frank Bridge whom he had first met in 1927. From Bridge he acquired the integrity of his technique, his professionalism, and his awareness of the 'new' music in Europe. Bridge was a viola player and a pacifist—reasons for an immediate sympathy between master and pupil—and Britten regarded him as his 'musical conscience' throughout his creative life. In 1930 Britten won an open scholarship to the Royal College of Music, London. At Bridge's insistence he studied with another composer, John Ireland, while continuing at the college his piano lessons with Arthur Benjamin (1893–1960), having previously studied the piano, for about a year, with Harold Samuel (1879–1937). Britten was an industrious, conscientious, and ambitious student, twice winning the Ernest Farrar composition prize (1931 and 1933) and funds (though not the award) from the Mendelssohn scholarship, but it was his life outside the college—London's music, cinemas, and theatres—that gave him the enlarged horizons that influenced his development.

John Grierson, the innovative head of the GPO Film Unit, employed Britten—on the recommendation of the college—to write some film music and he soon became in effect the unit's resident composer and music editor. He found himself in sympathy with the leftish social and political preoccupations of the unit and significantly assisted in the development of the documentary film, incidentally developing his own gifts as a dramatic composer. In 1935 he began his collaboration with W. H. Auden, then working for the unit as script-writer and occasional director, on two of the most memorable of British documentary films, *Coal Face* (1935) and *Night Mail* (1936). Auden's influence was profound: the apostle incarnate of bohemianism blew away any vestiges of provinciality still clinging to Britten and it was probably about this time that he began to acknowledge and accept his homosexual nature. His work in films led to his writing music for the theatre (principally for Rupert Doone's Group Theatre) and radio. He had achieved his ambition to enter on full-time employment as a composer without any transitional period whatever. Key works from this period include *A Boy was Born* (chorus, 1933); *Phantasy* (oboe and string trio, 1933); and *Variations on a Theme of Frank Bridge* (string orchestra, 1937). *Our Hunting Fathers* (voice and orchestra, 1936), with a text devised by Auden, is notable for its technical virtuosity and for its reflection of the poet's and composer's impassioned reaction to the threat of European Fascism. Exhilarating optimism was equally of Britten's nature and the 'Bridge' variations brought him further international recognition at the

Salzburg Festival of 1937 (earlier successes had been at International Society for Contemporary Music festivals in 1934 (Florence) and 1936 (Barcelona).

Despite the signs of a career of high promise and achievement, Britten, with the singer (Sir) Peter Pears (born 1910), left England for the USA in May 1939. Various factors influenced this decision: the worsening political situation; the persuasive examples of Auden and Christopher Isherwood (born 1904), who had already emigrated; loosening family ties (his father had died in 1934, his mother in 1937); discouraging reviews of his music in the English press; and the growth of his friendship with Pears. The two men made their life together from 1937 onwards, an exemplary personal relationship that developed into one of the most distinguished and celebrated voice and piano duos of the twentieth century. They travelled first to Canada and then to New York. For two and three-quarter years they lived in the USA, mainly on Long Island, at Amityville, where they shared the family home and life of Dr and Mrs William Mayer, moving briefly (in 1940) to the Brooklyn house of which Auden was proxy landlord and spending the summer of 1941 at Escondido, California. When World War II began they were advised officially not to attempt to return to England, and it was not until March 1942 that they made the Atlantic crossing from Halifax, Nova Scotia, to Liverpool. Their return was the result of anxiety at wartime separation from friends and relatives and a profound sense, on Britten's part, of deracination. What finally fired his resolve to quit the USA was the chance reading of an article by E. M. Forster on the Suffolk poet, George Crabbe, which sowed the seed of the opera *Peter Grimes*. While in the USA Britten composed or completed a number of works in the larger instrumental forms, among them the Violin Concerto (1939), *Sinfonia da Requiem* (1940), and String Quartet No. 1 (1941), the first cycle of songs, the *Seven Sonnets of Michelangelo* (1940), composed especially for Pears, and the operetta *Paul Bunyan* (libretto by Auden), his first full-length stage work—a failure on its first performance in New York in 1941 and withdrawn by the composer until 1976.

On their return to England Britten and Pears registered as conscientious objectors. Britten was granted exemption from military service on the condition that he and Pears gave concerts for CEMA (Council for the Encouragement of Music and the Arts). The principal work to emerge from the wartime years was *Peter Grimes*, which affirmed the composer's Suffolk roots and his preoccupation with the English language, already revealed in the *Hymn to St. Cecilia* for chorus (1942, words by Auden), *A Ceremony of Carols* for treble voices and harp (1942), and *Serenade* for tenor, horn, and strings (1943). One may note the oddity of the première, at Sadler's Wells Theatre on 7 June 1945, of so bleak and pessimistic a work coinciding with the Allies' triumph in Europe, an irony compounded by the opera's unprecedented public success. *Grimes* was a watershed in Britten's life. Its success established his international reputation and was the brilliant first step in the creation of a national tradition of opera. He composed no fewer than nine further operas—among them *Billy Budd* (1951), *Gloriana* (for the coronation of Queen Elizabeth II in 1953), *The Turn of the Screw* (1954), *A Midsummer Night's Dream* (1960), and *Death in Venice* (1973)—three church parables, and three theatrical works for children.

From 1947 Britten lived in the small coastal town of Aldeburgh, Suffolk, and established a special relationship with the community of which he saw himself to be part. His prowess as a pianist of exceptional gifts was almost exclusively devoted to accompanying Pears in song recitals. As a conductor he was known as a 'musicians' conductor', orchestral players admiring his insight and unfussy technique. His opera conducting was the result of an invitation from John Christie to reopen the post-war Glyndebourne season with a new opera. In 1946 Ernest Ansermet conducted Britten's *The Rape of Lucretia* at Glyndebourne, but in 1947 Britten conducted his *Albert Herring* there himself. Earlier that year he and a group of colleagues had formed the English Opera Group, dedicated to the commissioning of chamber operas from Britten's contemporaries, the first performances of which invariably took place at the annual Aldeburgh Festival; and from 1947, with only occasional exceptions, all Britten's musico-theatrical works were written for and first performed by the Group. The Aldeburgh Festival, which he, Peter Pears, and Eric Crozier founded in 1948, was in its twenty-ninth year when Britten died. Such was his prestige that many of the best performing artists of his time were drawn to Aldeburgh each June. Composing; directing and inspiring the English Opera Group and Aldeburgh Festival; partnering Pears; recording and occasionally conducting: this was the agenda that kept Britten preternaturally busy for most of his life. There were frequent trips overseas, of which two require special mention: a concert tour of the German concentration camps with Yehudi Menuhin in August 1945; and the round-the-world journey with Pears in the winter of 1955–6. His encounter with oriental music, in Japan and Bali, had profound consequences for his technical development from *Curlew River* (1964) onwards. The pattern of his life was determined by his composing; the only interruptions were due to occasional bouts of ill health and the building (1967) and rebuilding (after the 1969 fire) of the Maltings Concert Hall at Snape.

Britten composed prodigiously in almost every genre: songs and song cycles (of which he was an acknowledged master); chamber music (e.g. four string quartets); orchestral music (e.g. the Sinfonietta (chamber orchestra, 1932), at the beginning of his professional career, and the Symphony for Cello and Orchestra (1963), written at the height of his mature powers, both showing the scale, conviction, and vigour of his instrumental thinking); and diverse works for chorus and orchestra. One of the largest of these was *War Requiem* (1961), which gave fullest expression to his long-standing pacifist and antimilitarist beliefs and caught the imagination of a whole generation. *Owen Wingrave* (opera for television, 1970) used a mass medium to put across the same message. For his music for children and young people he developed quite specific musical techniques—different in kind from a mere simplification of his established musical usage—and his masterpiece in this area was undoubtedly *Noye's Fludde* (1957). Britten regarded himself as a communicator, a role which, at least in part, was responsible for his unshakeable attachment to the principle of tonality, although that principle underwent continual scrutiny, modification, and revision. He was open always to almost every aesthetic and technical influence and incorporated what he found useful or stimulating into his own eclectic but highly individual musical language.

Despite the assurance of public acclaim of a scale and global spread that had been enjoyed by no other British composer, Britten remained inwardly uncertain of his achievements. This insecurity was undoubtedly responsible for the unquestioning support he exacted of his friends and collaborators, and led in later years to an intellectual climate which did not much favour debate or dissonance, in contrast with the challenges and engagements of the pre-war period. He was a truly modest, gentle, courteous, and generous man; but he could be ruthless when it came to professional standards or the achieving of a creative ambition, when he would absolutely not be thwarted. He was ready to sacrifice himself and others if the musical task demanded it.

In 1973, while completing his last opera, *Death in Venice*, he was dogged by increasing ill health; and in May he underwent open heart surgery for the replacement of a defective valve. The operation was not wholly successful and he suffered a slight stroke during it. He showed great courage and fortitude during his last years and continued to compose, often at a very high level of inspiration. He was unsentimental about death, a convinced humanist rather than a man of religious belief, and on 4 December 1976 he died calmly at Aldeburgh, with his lifelong companion, Peter Pears, by him.

He was created CH in 1953; was admitted to the Order of Merit in 1965; and in 1976 was created Baron Britten, of Aldeburgh in the county of Suffolk, the first time a life peerage had been bestowed on a British composer. He received honorary doctorates from Cambridge (1959), Oxford (1963), and nine other British universities, and was an honorary fellow or member of many colleges and institutions. Among his many prizes and awards were the Coolidge medal (1941), the Hanseatic Goethe prize (1961), the first Aspen award (1964), the Wihuri-Sibelius prize (1965), the Ravel prize (1974), and the Mozart medal (1976). His executors were approached with a request for his burial in Westminster Abbey but he had declared a preference for the graveyard of Aldeburgh parish church, where he was laid to rest on 7 December 1976. A thanksgiving service took place at Westminster Abbey on 10 March 1977. The abbey was packed, fitting tribute to the foremost British composer of his time.

[D. Mitchell and J. Evans (eds.), *Benjamin Britten (1913–1976): Pictures from a Life*, a pictorial biography, 1978; D. Mitchell, *Britten and Auden in the Thirties: The Year 1936* (T. S. Eliot memorial lectures for 1979), 1981; B. Britten, *On Receiving the First Aspen Award*, 1964; Peter A. Evans, *The Music of Benjamin Britten*, 1979; Michael Kennedy, *Britten*, 1981; private information; personal knowledge.]

DONALD MITCHELL

published 1986

SEARLE Humphrey

(1915–1982)

Composer and writer on music, was born 26 August 1915 at Oxford, the eldest of the three sons (there were no daughters) of Humphrey Frederic Searle, of Oxford, a commissioner in the Indian Civil Service, and his wife, Charlotte Mathilde Mary ('May'), daughter of Sir William Schlich, the pioneer of forestry studies at Oxford. He was educated at Winchester College (1928–33) and New College, Oxford, where he obtained a second class in classical honour moderations (1935) and a third in *literae humaniores* (1937). In 1937 he became Octavia scholar at the Royal College of Music (his teachers were John Ireland, Gordon Jacob, and R. O. Morris), and at the Vienna Conservatorium (1937–8). In Vienna he took private lessons from Anton Webern.

In 1938 Searle joined the BBC music staff. From 1940 to 1946 he served with the Gloucestershire Regiment, Intelligence Corps, and General List, and after the war, when still in Germany, assisted Hugh Trevor-Roper (later Lord Dacre of Glanton) in research for *The Last Days of Hitler* (1947). He resumed producing at the BBC, leaving in 1948 to work free lance. An enthusiast for promoting new music, he was general secretary of the

International Society for Contemporary Music (1947–9). In 1951–7 he served as music adviser to Sadler's Wells Ballet.

A distinguished Liszt scholar, he was generous in imparting knowledge to colleagues. He compiled a new catalogue of Liszt's works (*Grove's Dictionary of Music and Musicians*, 1954 edn.; updated in *The New Grove*, 1980), and wrote a seminal book *The Music of Liszt* (1954). He founded the Liszt Society along with his friends Constant Lambert, (Sir) William Walton, (Sir) Sacheverell Sitwell, and others, and was its first honorary secretary (1950–62). Other books included *Twentieth Century Counterpoint* (1954), *Ballet Music* (1958), and *20th Century Composers: Britain, Scandinavia and the Netherlands* (1972). He also edited Schoenberg's *Structural Functions of Harmony* (1977), and translated Josef Rufer's textbook on twelve-note composition (1954) and a selection of Berlioz's letters (1966).

His compositions show the influence of Liszt, Webern, and Schoenberg. This radical continental outlook encouraged a style not then fashionable in Britain, and Searle remained an unfashionable though vigorous, independent, and prolific composer. The neglect of his large output of colourful, powerfully emotional works, written in strongly personal idiom and with a predilection for unusual forms, never seemed to daunt him. *Night Music* (for Webern's sixtieth birthday, 1943) closely approached twelve-note technique. His first truly serial work, *Intermezzo for 11 Instruments* (1946), was written in memory of Webern. Almost all his subsequent compositions use the 12-note method. His finesse in instrumental detail and subtle nuance is the legacy of Webern; his natural romanticism has affinities with the romantic Schoenberg; his fascination with Liszt is seen in the metamorphosis of themes in his Piano Sonata (1951).

A powerful trilogy for speakers, chorus, and orchestra (1949–51) set texts by (Dame) Edith Sitwell and, as centre-piece, *The Riverrun* by James Joyce. Between 1953 and 1964 he produced five symphonies, the Piano Concerto no. 2, three ballets, and two operas: *The Diary of a Madman* (after Gogol; premièred at the Berlin Festival of 1958 and awarded the Unesco Radio Critics prize), and *The Photo of the Colonel* (1964, after Ionesco). He also wrote much other chamber, orchestral, vocal, and incidental music. A BBC production, *The Foundling*, for which he wrote the music, won the Italia prize. His final opera was *Hamlet* (Hamburg 1968, Covent Garden 1969). Many of these works richly deserve revival.

A shy man, Searle's integrity and cosmopolitan outlook won respect among his students. He was composer-in-residence at Stanford University, California (1964–5); professor of composition at the Royal College of Music from 1965; guest composer at the Aspen Music Festival, Colorado (1967); and guest professor at the Staatliche Hochschule für Musik,

Karlsruhe (1968–72) and at the University of Southern California, Los Angeles (1976–7).

His deep interest in the spiritual nature of humankind is reflected in his later choral-orchestral works: *Jerusalem, Kubla Khan, Dr Faustus*, and *Oresteia*. Colour and his love of adventure permeate orchestral works like *Labyrinth* (1971) and *Tamesis* (1979). His humour is seen in splendid settings of Edward Lear's *The Owl and the Pussy Cat* and T. S. Eliot's *Skimbleshanks the Railway Cat*. For all his reserve and professional detachment he loved conviviality, and the memoirs (as yet unpublished) of this fine writer and friend of Cecil Gray, Dylan Thomas, Constant Lambert, and the Sitwells are a fascinating record of his times.

He was appointed CBE in 1968; honorary FRCM (1969); and an honorary professorial fellow, University College of Wales, Aberystwyth (1977).

In 1949 Searle married Margaret Gillen ('Lesley'), daughter of John Gray, a cartage contractor. In 1960, three years after her death, he married an actress Fiona Elizabeth Anne, daughter of John Wilfred Nicholson, a forest officer in the service of the Indian government. There were no children of either marriage. Searle died 12 May 1982 in London.

[*The New Grove Dictionary of Music and Musicians*, 1980 (ed. Stanley Sadie); *The Times*, 13 May 1982; private information; personal knowledge.]

DEREK WATSON

published 1990

LEWIS Anthony Carey

(1915–1983)

Sir

Musician and founder of *Musica Britannica*, was born 2 March 1915 in Bermuda, the youngest of the three sons (there were no daughters) of Major (later Colonel) Leonard Carey Lewis, of the Lincolnshire Regiment and Royal Army Ordnance Corps, then chief ordnance officer in Bermuda, afterwards of Hampton, Middlesex, and his wife, Katherine Barbara, only daughter of Colonel Henry George Sutton, Indian Army, of Hartington, Derbyshire. At an early age Lewis revealed exceptional musical gifts. He went to Salisbury Cathedral choir school, and when he was eight was admitted a chorister at St George's chapel, Windsor, where he sang under Sir Walter Parratt, Edmund Fellowes, and Sir H. Walford Davies.

In 1928, after several months at the Royal Academy of Music, where his composition professor was William Alwyn, Lewis entered Wellington College as the first music scholar. He became proficient at the oboe, achieved concerto standard as a pianist, and in 1932 won the Bernard Hale organ scholarship at Peterhouse, Cambridge. He now studied composition and research with Professor Edward J. Dent, whose teaching and example influenced him profoundly. He won the John Stewart of Rannoch scholarship in sacred music in 1933, and the award of the Leith studentship enabled him to study composition in Paris with Nadia Boulanger during the summer of 1934. A year later he graduated BA and Mus.B., winning the Barclay Squire prize for musical palaeography.

In September 1935 Lewis joined the music staff of the British Broadcasting Corporation, under (Sir) Adrian Boult. Inspired by Dent's view that the standard classics should not be allowed to obscure other music of importance, Lewis brought before the public many revivals of unfamiliar pre-nineteenth century works. He produced the long-running series 'Foundations of Music' and other similar programmes, and later became responsible for all broadcast chamber music. His composition *A Choral Overture*, in which an eight-part unaccompanied choir vocalizes to varying syllables, received its première in the 1938 season of Queen's Hall Promenade concerts.

On the outbreak of war in 1939 Lewis joined the Royal Army Ordnance Corps. He was posted as a major to the Middle East in 1942, became deputy assistant director of ordnance services in 1943, and for a short period in 1945 was assistant director, with the rank of lieutenant-colonel, displaying administrative abilities which were to benefit music and musicians greatly in the years ahead. Under the auspices of the British Council and ENSA he helped to organize the provision of music for the troops, himself conducting the Cairo Symphony and other orchestras.

He returned to the BBC in February 1946, undertaking the planning and supervision of all music for the new Third Programme. The introduction of the network on 29 September 1946, under (Sir) George Barnes, was soon recognized as the most important development for music since the beginning of broadcasting, and Lewis's contribution to laying its foundations was not the least of his achievements.

At the end of the year he left the BBC, and in 1947 succeeded (Sir) Jack Westrup as professor of music in the University of Birmingham. It was from the Peyton and Barber chair that his greatest achievement as a musicologist was undertaken, the foundation of *Musica Britannica* as a national collection of the classics of British music. His proposals were submitted to the council of the Royal Musical Association in 1948. An editorial committee was appointed, with Lewis as general editor (which function he fulfilled for the rest of his life) and R. Thurston Dart as secretary; and the first three volumes were published in 1951, as part of the Festival of Britain celebrations.

It was Lewis's constant aim to see that the fruits of scholarly research should be enjoyed through practical performance; and during his time at Birmingham, where his compositions included concertos for trumpet, horn, and harpsichord, he conducted many revivals of baroque music, notably Handel operas, together with premier recordings of works by composers such as Lully, Rameau, Handel, and especially Henry Purcell. He served as honorary secretary of the Purcell Society (1950–76) and artistic director of the Festival of Britain's Purcell series (1951), and was chairman of the Arts Council's music panel (1954–65), the Purcell-Handel Festival (1959), and the British Council's music committee (1967–73). He was also dean of the faculty of arts at Birmingham University (1961–4), and was president of the Royal Musical Association (1963–9).

In 1968 Lewis succeeded Sir Thomas Armstrong as principal of the Royal Academy of Music. The balance between scholarly and artistic work which characterized his life was now demonstrated by the fact that for the next fourteen years he presided over many important developments in an institution where the emphasis was on performance and composition. This phase saw the publication of his contributions to *The New Oxford History of Music*—'English Church Music' for volume v, *Opera and Church Music (1630–1750)* (1975), of which he was joint editor, and 'Church Music' for volume viii, *The Age of Beethoven (1790–1830)* (1982). During this period he was president of the Incorporated Society of Musicians (1968), a director of the English National Opera (1974–8), and chairman of the Purcell Society (1976–83).

Lewis was a musician of rare accomplishment, widely skilled in the science and practice of music. His knowledge as an editor, experience as a composer, insight as a conductor, and eloquence as a writer, were all combined in solving the manifold problems surrounding practical performance, particularly of the neglected treasures of the national heritage. His appearance was imposing, his manner reserved; yet behind this lay a vigour which was essentially creative. He liked to see things grow. His chief recreation was gardening, a pastime which gave him much pleasure. He was genial and kindly, and had a lively sense of humour. His sustained vision, patient advocacy, and practical wisdom enabled him to blaze fresh trails. The foundation of *Musica Britannica* was an act of high imagination and courage; and, with over fifty volumes completed by the time of his death, this growing collection had achieved the early aim of ranging from

Dunstable to Parry, and stood four-square as 'a living tribute to British musical achievement through the centuries'.

He was appointed CBE in 1967 and knighted in 1972. The honorary degree of D.Mus. was conferred on him by Birmingham University in 1970. He was an honorary member of the Royal Academy of Music (1960) and the Guildhall School of Music and Drama (1969), and was also honorary FTCL (1948), FRCM (1971), FRNCM (1974), and FRSAMD (1980). He was a governor of Wellington College (1953–83).

In 1959 Lewis married Lesley Lisle, daughter of Frank Lisle Smith, bank manager, of Northland, New Zealand. There were no children. He died at his home in Haslemere, Surrey, 5 June 1983. A portrait by Pamela Thalben-Ball (1976) is at the Royal Academy of Music.

[Anthony Lewis, 'Musica Britannica', *Musical Times*, May 1951; *Royal Academy of Music Magazine*, summer 1982 and autumn 1983; David Scott in *The New Grove Dictionary of Music and Musicians*, 1980 (ed. Stanley Sadie); John L. Holmes, *Conductors on Record*, 1982; family papers; personal knowledge.]

Michael Pope

published 1990

MATTHEWS Denis James

(1919–1988)

Pianist, composer, and teacher, was born 27 February 1919 in Coventry, the only child of Arthur Matthews, director of the Norman Engineering Company at Leamington Spa, and his wife, Elsie Culver, schoolteacher. His father committed suicide when Denis was twelve. He was educated at Warwick Grammar School, where his musical gifts brought him to the attention of visiting adjudicators including Herbert Howells, who encouraged him to consider a career in music. Another was the pianist Harold Craxton, who offered to teach him. Winning the Thalberg scholarship to the Royal Academy of Music in 1935, he studied composition with William Alwyn and the piano with Craxton, who welcomed him into a large and musical family circle, giving him a home as well as tuition and encouragement. His interests were initially in composition, and early works included songs and chamber music, which he later described as 'cosily derivative and romantic'. However, a piano trio, performed at a student concert, excited favourable press attention; and in 1937 he added a composition scholarship to that for piano. His performing and composing abilities were sometimes combined, as when Sir Henry Wood conducted his Symphonic Movement for piano and orchestra. The list of his compositions eventually included a Violin Sonata, Five Sketches for violin and piano, a string quartet, and a Partita for wind quintet for a fellow student, the horn player Dennis Brain.

Though some of his works were taken up by performers, and even published, Matthews found that his deepening interest in the classics—Bach, Mozart, and Beethoven, in particular—was directing him towards playing. His professional début came with a Promenade Concert in 1939, when he played Beethoven's Third Piano Concerto under Sir Henry Wood. Beethoven was to remain central to his interests, and was the subject of many lecture recitals, some records expounding the sketchbooks, and two BBC Music Guide booklets, *Beethoven Piano Sonatas* (1967) and *Brahms Piano Music* (1978). Matthews's writings also included a chapter on Beethoven, Schubert, and Brahms in a symposium he edited, *Keyboard Music* (1972), *Arturo Toscanini* (1982), and an autobiography, *In Pursuit of Music* (1966).

Having graduated from the Royal Academy of Music in 1940 with the LRAM (to which he added the Royal College of Music's ARCM, as well as the Worshipful Company of Musicians' medal, 1938, for the most distinguished student), Matthews earned a living accompanying for opera and ballet classes, playing for social occasions such as City dinners, and occasionally giving concerts either alone or with student friends. He remained all his life an excellent sonata pianist, though latterly he seldom accompanied singers in lieder.

In 1940 he was called up, entered the Royal Air Force, and, together with a number of other musicians who were to go on to make distinguished careers, joined the central band at Uxbridge. He toured Germany at the end of the war with the central band, playing piano solos at the Potsdam conference to Josef Stalin, (Sir) Winston Churchill, and Harry S. Truman. He also shared the keyboard with Truman.

Demobilized in 1946, Matthews was taken up by musicians including Dame Myra Hess, and solo engagements began to come in. He played concertos with (Sir) John Barbirolli, (Sir) Malcolm Sargent, Sir Thomas Beecham, Sir Adrian Boult, and other leading conductors, and toured widely; he had also begun making records in 1941, in a repertory centring on Mozart and Beethoven (and including a classic version of Beethoven's Horn Sonata with Dennis Brain), but also embracing modern British composers. He was closely associated with the London Mozart Players, founded in 1949 by another friend from the central band, Harry Blech. Concerts and recordings brought him wide popularity, and he embarked upon a career that took him all round the world. In 1955 he settled in

Henley, where he and his friends took part in festival music-making. However, divorce in 1960 brought him back to London.

With the emergence of a postwar generation of virtuosi, Matthews found his career prospering less well in the 1960s. To his friends, he was candid about his powers, believing that he had been fortunate to make a career at a time when competition was less fierce. He was never a great technician, but the musicality of his playing gave his performances at their best an illuminating quality, and a sense of the music's essential structure and meaning. His interest in conveying this found a new outlet when in 1971 he was invited to be the first professor of music at the University of Newcastle. He ran an enterprising and successful department, while continuing to maintain a performing career. He retired in 1984. He was appointed CBE in 1975, and had honorary degrees from St Andrews (1973), Hull (1978), and Warwick (1982).

Though prey to private melancholy, Matthews was an amusing and warm-hearted companion. He was slightly built, with sandy hair and an expressive face that remained impassive during performance but could take on a lively, animated expression in the discussions about music which were his greatest joy. He retained a somewhat boyish appearance and manner. He married three times. In 1941 he married Mira Howe, a cellist, and they had one son and three daughters. The marriage was dissolved in 1960 and in 1963 he married Brenda, who had been brought up by Dr Samuel McDermott, a general practitioner in Swindon, and taken his surname. They had one son and one daughter. The marriage was dissolved in 1985 and in 1986 he married Beryl, a piano teacher, daughter of Arthur Harold Jordan Perry, owner of a textile firm. Matthews died by his own hand in Birmingham, 24 December 1988, having suffered from bouts of severe depression, particularly after his marriage to Brenda McDermott broke up.

[Denis Matthews, *In Pursuit of Music* (autobiography), 1966; private information; personal knowledge.]

John Warrack

published 1996

BRAIN Dennis

(1921–1957)

Virtuoso horn-player, was born in London 17 May 1921. Educated at St. Paul's School and the Royal Academy of Music, he was the younger son of Aubrey Harold Brain (1893–1955), who was the principal horn of the B.B.C. Symphony Orchestra from its foundation until 1945. His mother, Marion Beeley, was at one time a Covent Garden singer.

Dennis Brain was the third generation of a distinguished family of horn-players, his grandfather and uncle (Alfred Brain) having also made notable careers, the latter in the United States. His brother Leonard became one of the most prominent oboe and cor anglais players in London of his day.

Dennis Brain's career began during the war which he spent as principal horn in the Royal Air Force Central Band and Orchestra, and he became widely known as a soloist immediately upon demobilization in 1946. A number of important works were composed especially for him, notably by Benjamin Britten and Paul Hindemith.

Brain's playing was characterized by a remarkably natural facility and unthinking assurance. It seemed as if the pitfalls of this notoriously unreliable instrument simply never occurred to him, and he executed perfectly passages of hair-raising difficulty in the manner born. He was, to use his own phrase, 'game for anything', while his infectious grin and abrupt bellowing laugh typified a character which never lost an endearing schoolboy ingenuousness and enthusiasm. He was entirely unspoilt by the success which came to him during his latter years and he was as much universally loved in the profession as admired by the musical world.

He was short, and somewhat stocky in appearance, but with great energy and agility. He became very fond of contract bridge, but his abiding interest was in motor-cars of which he had a considerable knowledge and experience. He was in the habit of driving to and from engagements in a single journey, no matter what distance, and it was this which cost him his life. He met with a fatal accident returning to London in the small hours from an Edinburgh Festival concert, 1 September 1957.

His death came at a time of gradually increasing restlessness. A musician of broad interests and culture (he was also an accomplished organist), his profound artistry needed a greater outlet than the limited repertoire of the horn could supply. He had begun a number of ambitious ventures to supplement his normal activities as soloist and orchestral musician, such as a wind ensemble and even a small chamber orchestra which he was beginning to conduct, although he had previously been doubtful of his potential in this direction.

He was an inveterate lover of the country and even entertained wistful dreams of an eventual retirement, perhaps as a chicken farmer. This basic simplicity of outlook may indeed hold the key to his entire character and to the charm and humility of his essentially natural personality.

He married in 1945 Yvonne, a pianist, whom he met at the Royal Academy of Music, daughter of Edward Ralph Coles, bank accountant, of Petersfield, Hampshire; they had a son and daughter.

[Private information; personal knowledge.]

NORMAN DEL MAR

published 1971

DART (Robert) Thurston

(1921–1971)

Musicologist and harpsichordist, was born at Surbiton, Surrey, 3 September 1921, the only child of Henry Thurston Dart, metal merchant's clerk, and his wife, Elizabeth Martha Orf. He was educated at Hampton Grammar School and was a chorister at the Chapel Royal, Hampton Court, subsequently studying at the Royal College of Music in 1938–9 and then at University College, Exeter, where he read mathematics and took the London external degree of BA in 1942. He became ARCM in the same year. He served in the RAF from 1942 to 1945, using his mathematics training within the field of operational research. He was mentioned in dispatches. A minor hand injury caused him some concern but fortunately did not affect his subsequent performing career. His ex-service gratuity enabled him to study in Brussels in 1945–6 with Charles van den Borren. Returning to England he established himself quickly as a harpsichordist, and as one knowledgeable in early music, English particularly, and in early musical instruments. In 1947 he was appointed assistant lecturer in the Cambridge music faculty and in 1952 university lecturer in music.

Dart had a prodigious capacity for work. From 1947 to 1955 he was editor of the *Galpin Society Journal*, the society having been founded the previous year by Dart and others to commemorate and continue the work of Canon Francis Galpin (1858–1945) on early musical instruments. From 1948 onwards he became a regular broadcaster for the BBC's new Third Programme, equally at home speaking or performing. He was secretary to the editorial board of the series Musica Britannica (1950–64) and remained a vigorous member of its committee until his death, seeing thirty-three volumes through the press, a number of which were edited by young scholars he himself had trained.

Dart was a fellow of Jesus College, Cambridge, from 1953 to 1964, visiting lecturer at Harvard University in 1954, and recipient of the Cobbett prize in 1957. His book *The Interpretation of Music* appeared in 1954, incorporating many of his discoveries and hypotheses relating to early music. It was from around 1950 that he began his long association with the firm of L'Oiseau-Lyre, Monaco, both as editor of music publications and as performer on L'Oiseau-Lyre recordings. He became a lifelong friend of the proprietor, Mrs Louise Hanson Dyer, and her husband; their patronage was undoubtedly influential in furthering his career.

From 1955 to 1959 Dart was artistic director of the newly-formed Philomusica of London (formerly the Boyd Neel Orchestra). With Granville Jones and then Neville Marriner as concert masters, he directed numerous performances and recordings from the harpsichord (and latterly as conductor). The recordings were based on editions he had prepared from autographs and other prime sources and in some cases tested certain hypotheses; they thus remain a valuable testament to Dart's scholarship and musicianship. He made about ninety recordings in all of solo, chamber, and orchestral music.

In addition Dart undertook the editing of a large amount of music and the re-editing of the monumental series on English madrigalists and the works of William Byrd (first prepared by E. H. Fellowes). Yet his work as university lecturer and teacher was by no means neglected. His lectures were memorable for their meticulous preparation, excellent delivery, and stimulating content; and his influence as a teacher was perhaps his most considerable contribution, a whole generation of students (for whom Dart and Cambridge were virtually synonymous) being affected by him, not a few becoming in turn influential in the field of English music.

In 1962 he became professor of music at Cambridge and, as ever, brought fresh thinking to bear upon old problems and conventions. He found it virtually impossible to change established customs however and resigned the chair in 1964 to take up the challenge of establishing a new faculty of music at King's College, London, which he did most successfully as King Edward professor of music, a post he held until his death.

Dart was a complete musician, an instinctive performer (he played harpsichord, clavichord, viols, recorder, other woodwinds, and sang) and one whose intellect and imagination were unusually matched. Indeed, despite his reputation as solo performer his most outstanding performances were probably those in which he played harpsichord or organ continuo (often directing the ensemble at the same time), for it was in such performances that his perfect sense of rhythm, his self-discipline, his scholarly approach, and at the same time his creative flair for musical improvisation, were most fully matched and realized.

As a scholar Dart was concerned chiefly with English music of the sixteenth to eighteenth centuries, but also with aspects of French music of the period and, especially, Handel and J. S. Bach. (He was engaged in recording a particularly controversial account of Bach's *Brandenburg Concertos* at the time of his final hospitalization resulting from the cancer of which he died.) He had a wide and practical knowledge of earlier musical notations, western and non-western, and wrote on the subject in the fifth edition of *Grove's Dictionary of Music and Musicians* (1954). He also had an unusual knowledge of music-printing past and present. However, he by no means confined himself to early music. He often played Chopin for private relaxation, he commissioned a harpsichord concerto from Roberto Gerhard, and his music syllabus at London paid due attention to the nineteenth and twentieth centuries, and to electronic and non-western music.

In person 'Bob' Dart was large and somewhat formidable. He did not suffer fools gladly, particularly as demands on his time increased. His hobby-horses were not always securely stabled. However, to those who had worked with him and knew him well he was brilliant and amusing (with a delightful sense of the absurd) and generous in spirit and deed. He had a large library of books and scores and possessed many early instruments, most of which he gave away. He collected paintings and enjoyed the good things of life.

Dart was unmarried. He died in London 6 March 1971.

[I. D. Bent, '(Robert) Thurston Dart', *The New Grove Dictionary of Music and Musicians*, ed. Stanley Sadie, vol. v, 1980; *The Times*, 8, 12, and 24 March 1971; S. Jeans, *Galpin Society Journal*, vol. xxiv, 1971; N. Marriner, *Gramophone*, vol. xlix, 1971; A. Percival, *Musical Times*, vol. cxxii, 1971, and in *Source Materials and the Interpretation of Music: a Memorial Volume to Thurston Dart*, ed. I. D. Bent, 1981; private information; personal knowledge.]

Gerald Hendrie

published 1986

PRITCHARD John Michael

(1921–1989)

Sir

Operatic and orchestral conductor, was born 5 February 1921 at 17 Cromwell Road, Walthamstow, London, the younger son (there were no daughters) of Albert Edward Pritchard, violinist, and his wife, Amy Edith Shaylor. He was educated at Sir George Monoux School in London, and he studied privately with his father and other music teachers. In his teenage years he visited Italy to listen to opera. When World War II broke out Pritchard registered as a conscientious objector, to his father's dismay. He therefore underwent an army medical examination, but, because of an earlier attack of pleurisy, was registered unfit to serve. In 1943 he took over the Derby String Orchestra and was its principal conductor till 1951. Meanwhile he joined the music staff of Glyndebourne Opera (1947) and was appointed chorus master there (1949). He succeeded Reginald Jacques as conductor of the Jacques Orchestra (1950–2). By 1951 he was sharing with Fritz Busch major Mozart productions at Glyndebourne and at the Edinburgh Festival.

Important opportunities came his way in 1952. At Edinburgh he appeared with the Royal Philharmonic Orchestra, replacing Ernest Ansermet, who was ill; and he made his débuts at the Royal Opera House in Covent Garden, and at the Vienna State Opera. He appeared regularly with the Vienna Symphony Orchestra (1953–5). He continued to work at Glyndebourne, conducting their productions of Mozart's *Idomeneo* and Richard Strauss's *Ariadne auf Naxos* at the Edinburgh festivals of 1953 and 1954. After the latter he conducted the Glyndebourne production of Rossini's *La Cenerentola* at the Berlin Festival. The performance was a triumph.

At home, he was appointed principal conductor of the (Royal) Liverpool Philharmonic Orchestra (1957–63) and within a year had launched the Musica Viva series at which contemporary music was introduced, illustrated, performed, and then discussed. During five seasons, unfamiliar music by many living composers was heard for the first time in Britain. Pritchard's success in Liverpool led to his appointment as musical director of the London Philharmonic Orchestra (1962–6). At Glyndebourne he became music counsellor (1963), principal conductor (1968), and musical director (1969–77). In 1969 he took the London Philharmonic to the Far East and made his American début, at the Chicago Lyric Opera. Appearances at the San Francisco Opera (1970) and the Metropolitan Opera

(1971) followed. In 1973 he conducted the London Philharmonic in China—the first visit by a western orchestra.

By 1980 Pritchard had conducted many of the world's greatest orchestras, including the Berlin Philharmonic, the Leipzig Gewandhaus, the Dresden Staatskapelle, and the Philadelphia Orchestra; he had appeared at the Salzburg festival, the Maggio Musicale in Florence, and the Munich State Opera. He was a regular guest at the Royal Opera House, Covent Garden, at the Proms, and with the BBC Symphony Orchestra, whose chief conductor he became in 1982. Overlapping posts included at that time the musical directorships of the Cologne Opera (1978), the Théâtre de la Monnaie, Brussels (1981), and the San Francisco Opera (1986).

Pritchard's innate musicality, his quick grasp, his range of sympathies, and his gift for getting the best out of the musicians (with whom he was very popular) combined to bring him a career of astonishing concentration and variety. No conductor can have had a fuller diary. Although this sometimes led to a perfunctoriness bordering upon indolence, he was, at his best, an interpreter of lasting distinction. His Mozart and Strauss were superbly idiomatic, but he also excelled in nineteenth-century Italian opera. And he could surprise his public with, for example, some tough Shostakovich. He was not, however, a great star; he did not make enough recordings to achieve that status. But he was appointed CBE in 1962 and was knighted in 1983. The coveted Shakespeare prize (Hamburg) was awarded him in 1975.

Pritchard's much imitated manner of speech—bland, almost epicene—was an outward sign of his unabashed homosexuality, but there was nothing effeminate about his music-making. He had friends in every walk and style of life and was loyal and generous to them. Witty and well-informed, he lived in some style (in a number of homes, including an elegant house near Glyndebourne and a villa in the Alpes-Maritimes above Nice). Indeed his enjoyment of good food and wine became a problem when he needed to lose weight for a hip replacement operation not long before his death. It was a problem he observed with rueful detachment. Though already ill, with a blood clot, he conducted the last night of the Proms on 16 September 1989 and made a touchingly prescient and self-deprecating speech. He died 5 December 1989 in San Francisco, where he was musical director of the San Francisco Opera. He left a large part of his estate to Terry MacInnes, his partner.

[Spike Hughes, *Glyndebourne*, 1965; Nicholas Kenyon, *The BBC Symphony Orchestra*, 1981; John Higgins (ed.), *Glyndebourne, a Celebration*, 1984; personal knowledge.]

ROBERT PONSONBY

published 1996

HOFFNUNG Gerard

(1925–1959)

Cartoonist and musical humorist, was born Gerhardt Hoffnung in Grünewald, Berlin, 22 March 1925, the only child of German-Jewish parents, Ludwig Hoffnung, a wealthy grain merchant, and his wife Hilde, a widow, whose first husband, Schnabel, was killed in World War I. His mother was a keen amateur musician and artist who encouraged his artistic talents. From his earliest years he was interested in the macabre—fairy tales, practical jokes, and the comic drawings of the famous German illustrators and caricaturists.

In the wake of the Nazi persecutions the Hoffnungs left Germany in 1938. Ludwig Hoffnung settled permanently in Israel. Gerard and his mother went to London, renting a house in Hampstead Garden Suburb which was to be Hoffnung's home for the rest of his life. In 1939 Hoffnung became a pupil at Highgate School, where he was remembered for his anarchic spirit. He studied at Hornsey College of Art but was expelled and became art master at Stamford School in 1945 and later at Harrow. He was already working as a freelance cartoonist and his work appeared in a number of magazines. He developed a distinctive style which owed something to the German illustrator Wilhelm Busch. His illustrations in colour for Colette's libretto for Ravel's opera, *L'Enfant et les sortilèges*, were outstanding. Much of Hoffnung's humour centred on the world of music, particularly the various instruments of the orchestra with which he was fascinated. He taught himself to play the tuba. In 1953 he published *The Maestro*, the first of a series of six little books of cartoons on musical themes which had a worldwide success. He broke new ground in musical humour when in 1956 he organized the first of a series of concerts of symphonic caricature at which new music, some of it by respected composers like Malcolm Arnold, was played on ludicrous instruments or to the accompaniment of vacuum cleaners or road rammers. These concerts, which became more and more elaborate, proved highly popular with the public.

In 1950 Hoffnung began a career as a broadcaster, during the course of which he made many appearances on the radio as both raconteur and panel member. He was a brilliant improviser with a dry wit and a masterly sense of timing. An Oxford Union speech in 1958 in which he told 'The Story of the Bricklayer' became a classic recording. The story, involving a bricklayer's misfortunes as he attempted to lower some bricks from the top of a building in a barrel, was not especially funny, but Hoffnung's manner and delivery reduced his audience to hysterics. In appearance Hoffnung was stocky, bald, and benign. Nicolas Bentley described him as looking like a 'Teutonic Pickwick'. His manner, voice, and looks were those of a much older man and his wife was sometimes mistaken for his daughter.

In 1952 he married Annetta, daughter of Percy Alfred Bennett, electrical contractor, of Folkestone. They had one son and one daughter. Hoffnung was only thirty-four when he died of a cerebral haemorrhage in Hampstead 28 September 1959.

[*The Times*, 29 September 1959; Annetta Hoffnung, *Gerard Hoffnung*, 1988.]

RICHARD INGRAMS

published 1993

ARNOLD Denis Midgley

(1926–1986)

Musicologist, was born 15 December 1926 in Sheffield, the only son and younger child of Charles Arnold, company director, and his wife, Bertha Ball. He was educated at High Storrs Grammar School in Sheffield, and Sheffield University. He graduated BA in 1947 and B.Mus. in 1948, and received an MA in 1950 for a dissertation on Thomas Weelkes, partly written during service in the Royal Air Force.

The orientation of his life's work as a musicologist was determined by the award in 1950 of an Italian government scholarship enabling him to go to Bologna to study Italian music of the years around 1600. In 1951 he was appointed lecturer (reader, 1960) in music in the department of adult education at the Queen's University, Belfast; he also worked for the music department. His experience in adult education confirmed another of Arnold's conspicuous qualities: his powers as an educator and communicator, addressing widely varying audiences in plain language and with engaging enthusiasm. This stance, moreover, informs all his writings, even the most specialized. It was during his Belfast years that he began publishing the stream of articles in learned journals that continued up to his death. Through them he quickly made a name as a major scholar on the music, mainly secular vocal, of late Renaissance and early baroque Italy, and as one of Britain's leading musicologists, a reputation reinforced by his many editions of the music itself.

In 1964 Arnold moved as senior lecturer in music to the University of Hull at about the time he published his first book, the 'Master Musicians' volume on *Monteverdi* (1963). He was joint editor of, and a contributor to, the *Monteverdi Companion* (1968; new edition as *The New Monteverdi Companion*, 1985) and, perhaps surprisingly, the *Beethoven Companion* (1971). It was natural that he should welcome the chance to communicate with a potentially larger readership through a series of short studies of composers with whom he was particularly identified: *Marenzio* (1965), *Monteverdi Madrigals* (1967), *Giovanni Gabrieli* (1974), *Monteverdi Church Music* (1982), and *Gesualdo* (1984), as well as *Bach* (1984).

In 1969 Arnold became professor of music at the University of Nottingham and from 1975 to his death was Heather professor of music at the University of Oxford. He had always been a keen conductor, and he threw himself into performance at both universities with renewed zeal. He increasingly became a public figure on a wider scale too. For many years he toiled as editor of, and contributor to, *The New Oxford Companion to Music* (1983); he was president of the Royal Musical Association (1978–83) and British representative on the directorium of the International Musicological Society (IMS) from 1978 to his death; and he served as chairman of the Oxford Playhouse and the music panel of Southern Arts. Amid this activity he wrote his largest study, *Giovanni Gabrieli and the Music of the Venetian High Renaissance* (1979) and, with his wife, *The Oratorio in Venice* (1986), the fruit of an increasing interest in his later years in Italian, especially Venetian, music of the century and a half after the period on which he concentrated for much of his career.

Arnold was short of stature but in every other respect a 'big' man: ebullient, generous, and gregarious, as well as informal and unpretentious; an industrious scholar who produced eminently approachable books and practical editions that helped transform the general view of music and its contexts in Italy in the age of Gabrieli and Monteverdi. All were based on solid research: a public figure in his element as lecturer, conductor, or conference-goer, he was perhaps never happier than when working in libraries and archives, especially in his beloved Venice.

Arnold was appointed CBE in 1983. In 1980 the honorary degree of D.Mus. was conferred on him by two universities, Sheffield and Queen's, Belfast. He was an honorary fellow of the Royal Academy of Music (1971) and Royal College of Music (1981). He became FBA and an honorary foreign member of the Accademia Nazionale dei Lincei, Rome (both 1976), and in 1977 was awarded the Premio Internazionale Galileo Galilei dei Rotary Italiani at Pisa University for services to the study of Italian music.

In 1951 Arnold married Elsie Millicent, a trained musicologist, daughter of John William Dawrant, schoolmaster, of Liverpool. They had two sons.

Arnold died suddenly, of a heart attack, 28 April 1986 in Budapest while representing Britain at a meeting of the directorium of the IMS.

[Nigel Fortune in *Proceedings of the British Academy*, vol. lxxiii, 1987; private information; personal knowledge.]

NIGEL FORTUNE

published 1996

MONRO Matt

(1930–1985)

Singer of popular music, was born Terence Parsons 1 December 1930 in Shoreditch, London, the youngest in the family of four sons and one daughter of Frederick Parsons, druggist packer, and his wife, Alice Mary Ann Reed. He began singing when he joined the army in 1947, at the age of seventeen. He became a tank instructor and divided his time between tanks and talent contests while serving in Hong Kong. It was there that he decided to become a professional singer. After demobilization in 1953 he became a long-distance lorry driver, electrician, coalman, bricklayer, stonemason, railway fireman, layer of kerbstones, milkman, baker, offal boy in a tobacco factory, plasterer's mate, builder's mate, and general factotum in a custard factory. Using the name Al Jordan, he took a semi-professional job with Harry Leader and his orchestra. It meant months of travelling from town to town. Eventually he decided to abandon the work and became a London bus driver instead. However, the desire to become a fully professional singer persisted and he recorded a demonstration disc of 'Polka Dots and Moonbeams' with a small rhythm section. One of its members was so impressed it was forwarded to the pianist Winifred Atwell who arranged a number of important meetings. At this point he decided on a change of name. Terence Parsons became Matt Monro—'Matt' from Matt White, the first journalist to write about him, and 'Monro' from the first name of Winifred Atwell's father.

For the newly named Matt Monro there followed a series on Radio Luxembourg in 1956, a regular singing spot with Cyril Stapleton's show band, and a recording contract with Decca. However, his career took off almost by accident. The record producer George Martin, of EMI/Parlophone, was at this time making a name for himself in the comedy record field, and was looking for someone to sound like Frank Sinatra for an LP for Peter Sellers, *Songs for Swingin' Sellers*. He chose Matt Monro with his rich, clean-cut baritone voice. Everyone connected with the recording was impressed, especially Martin who asked if he would like to record under his new professional name (on the LP he had used the name Fred Flange).

Monro's first single, 'These Things Happen', was followed by 'Love Walked In'. His third recording, 'Portrait of my Love', which he thought one of the most uncommercial songs he had ever heard, entered the list of British best-selling records in December 1960 and reached no. 3. This was followed by 'My Kind of Girl' which climbed to no. 5 in 1961, 'Why Not Now?/Can This Be Love?', 'Gonna Build a Mountain', 'Softly as I Leave You', 'When Love Comes Along', 'My Love and Devotion', 'From Russia with Love', 'Walk Away', 'For Mama', 'Without You', and 'Yesterday'. He was to achieve his final singles record success in Britain in 1973 with 'And You Smiled'. Oddly, 'Born Free' and 'We're Gonna Change the World', two of his most requested records on radio programmes, never achieved success in the British best-seller lists, although the former won an Academy Award for the best song in a motion picture in 1965. Amongst his best known albums were *Walk Away, I Have Dreamed, My Kind of Girl, The Late Late Show*, and *Softly*. Monro came second in the Eurovision Song Contest in 1964 and was voted best male singer in England in 1965.

Monro spent a considerable amount of time in the United States of America, where he turned increasingly to cabaret. His first visit was in 1960 on a special exchange agreement. He sang at the Pentagon in Washington, while Ella Fitzgerald appeared in Great Britain. In 1966 Monro signed with Capital Records and he resided in the United States during 1967. He was a constant traveller, appearing in cabaret and concerts in Australia, New Zealand, Japan, Hong Kong, the Philippines, Malaysia, Canada, South Africa, Scandinavia, and most European countries. He travelled approximately 150,000 miles a year.

Monro's hobbies were golf, the cinema, and watching television programmes, especially westerns. He once said 'the worst fate that can befall me is to be stranded in a town without a television set'. His favourite film was *The Magnificent Seven*. He was a man of great natural charm and was highly respected by his colleagues, including Frank Sinatra, Tony Bennett, and Bing Crosby, who all regarded him as 'a singer's singer'. According to his old friend, George Martin, he 'had the rare gift of getting to the heart of a lyric and delivering it in such a way that it became a personal message to his audience'. Monro is rightly considered one of the best singers of popular music Britain has ever produced.

In 1955 Monro married Iris, daughter of Frederick Jordan, factory wallpaper dyer. A son, Mitchell, was born the same year. The marriage was dissolved in 1959 and in the same year Monro married Mickie, daughter of Adolph ('Dolly') Schuller, dentist. They had a daughter Michele in 1959 and a son Matthew in 1964. Monro died in the Cromwell Hospital, Kensington, London, 7 February 1985.

[Private information; personal knowledge.]

DAVID JACOBS

published 1990

OGDON John Andrew Howard

(1937–1989)

Pianist and composer, was born 27 January 1937 in Mansfield Woodhouse, Nottinghamshire, the youngest in the family of three sons and two daughters of Howard Ogdon, teacher, who wrote about music, and his wife, Dorothy Mutton, a former secretary, who also encouraged her children's musicianship by ensuring that they learned the piano from an early age. John began piano lessons when he was four years old. His gifts were such that at the age of eight he went to the Royal Manchester (later the Royal Northern) College of Music as a pupil of Iso Elinson. After attending Manchester Grammar School, he returned in his mid-teens to the college, where he found a gifted group of contemporaries—Alexander Goehr, (Sir) Harrison Birtwistle, (Sir) Peter Maxwell Davies, and Elgar Howarth—who were later known as the 'Manchester School'. Ogdon took piano with Elinson, Claude Biggs, and Gordon Green, and composition with Richard Hall.

Ogdon's superlative sight-reading gifts and his phenomenal musical memory enabled him to tackle the most difficult scores virtually at sight, but his technical mastery was allied to a deep intellectual grasp, which soon marked him out as a recreative musician of extraordinary range and depth. When he was still a child, his father had suffered a schizophrenic breakdown; it may well have been that this experience chastened Ogdon's own development: musically, he was prodigiously gifted, and physically he was (so described by Alexander Goehr) 'a big, clumsy, untidy, roly-poly boy'. His character was shy and reserved, his speech quietly withdrawn; only at the piano, it seemed, did his personality publicly flower, when he was overwhelming.

As a student he entered the Belgian Queen Elisabeth Competition in 1956 but was unsuccessful. On graduating soon afterwards (with distinction in every subject), he gave Brahms's D Minor Concerto, conducted by Sir John Barbirolli, which prompted Ogdon's Hallé Orchestra début at the age of twenty. Postgraduate work with Denis Matthews in London and

Egon Petri (a pupil of Ferruccio Busoni) in Basle led, in 1958, to Ogdon's playing Busoni's vast Piano Concerto from memory, conducted by (Sir) John Pritchard in Liverpool. The Busoni performance was much praised and on 8 August 1959, at less than forty-eight hours' notice, Ogdon made his Promenade Concert début in Franz Liszt's E Flat Concerto, after coming second in the Liverpool International Piano Competition, and a month before his Wigmore Hall début in London.

Married in July 1960 to Brenda Lucas (Peter Maxwell Davies was best man), the newly-weds made a notable two-piano team. In December Ogdon began his record career with a Busoni–Liszt album for EMI. Although he later recorded for other labels, his main recorded legacy is with EMI. In January 1961 he took first prize in the Liszt Competition and achieved world fame as joint winner (with Vladimir Ashkenazy) of the first prize at the Tchaikovsky Competition in Moscow in 1962.

One of the most sought-after artists of his day, Ogdon travelled widely, notably to the USA and Russia, where he was adored. Unlike other virtuosos, he championed new and unusual music, including concertos written for him by Alun Hoddinott (with whom he founded the Cardiff music festival in 1967), Robert Simpson, and Gerard Schurmann, alongside standard repertoire. He also found time to compose, among other music, a piano concerto, a symphony, solo piano works, and two string quartets. His immense energy ensured a full engagement book, yet his chain-smoking and excessive drinking, his unkempt appearance, and a tendency to overwork meant that the strains thus placed upon him took their toll.

In 1973 Ogdon began to exhibit symptoms of an alarming personality change. This previously gentle man became prone to degenerative mental and physical violence, eventually attacking his wife with such ferocity that she was hospitalized: he attempted suicide on numerous occasions. His condition at first eluded diagnosis, his treatment ranging from drugs and electric shock to psychotherapy. Some of his earlier treatment was experimental; he seemed to suffer from paranoid schizophrenic psychosis. Ogdon spent eighteen months in London's Royal Maudsley Hospital; by 1977 he had improved enough to take his first teaching post, at Indiana University in Bloomington, where he stayed until 1980. Under care, he resumed concert-giving, which he had never really abandoned: an American doctor who had observed Ogdon for a year concluded that he was not schizophrenic but manic depressive and prescribed lithium, claiming Ogdon was an obsessive genius living a vital inner life against which the 'real' world can appear remote.

The treatment was a success and, although never 'cured', he was able gradually to resume his career. His history meant that his condition was watched constantly; his earlier instability led to his affairs being taken over by the Court of Protection. Symptomatic of a new confidence was his recital of the legendary three-and-a-half-hour solo piano work *Opus Clavicembalisticum* by Kaikhosru Sorabji in 1988, which he also recorded. Ogdon was a fellow of the Royal Manchester College of Music (1962) and the Royal Academy of Music (1974), and an honorary fellow of the Royal Northern College of Music (1986). He was also a recipient of the Harriet Cohen international award (1960). His publications included contributory chapters to *Franz Liszt: the Man and his Music* (ed. Alan Walker, 1976) and *Keyboard Music* (ed. Denis Mathews, 1972).

In 1960 Ogdon had married Brenda Mary, daughter of John Gregory Lucas, civil servant; they had a son and a daughter. In late July 1989 Ogdon complained of feeling unwell. He saw a new doctor, who asked if he had been diagnosed as diabetic, and who arranged for him to be examined by several specialists some days later. But his condition worsened, and his wife found him unconscious on the morning of 31 July, the day of his first specialist visit. Rushed to Charing Cross Hospital, he was found to be in a diabetic coma. He had, moreover, contracted bronchial pneumonia, from which he died in hospital early the following day, 1 August 1989.

[Brenda Lucas Ogdon and Michael Kerr, *Virtuoso*, 1981; *Independent*, 3 August 1989; private information; personal knowledge.]

ROBERT MATTHEW-WALKER

published 1996

LENNON John Winston

(1940–1980)

Musician and composer of popular music, was born in Liverpool 9 October 1940, the only child of Alfred Lennon, a ship's steward, and his wife, Julia Stanley. The father was away when his son was born; the mother's sister, Mary, was present and named him John. Aunt 'Mimi' and her husband George Smith raised the boy at their house. Lennon attended Dovedale Primary and Quarry Bank High School. His academic work deteriorated as he cultivated a fondness for practical jokes, and he failed all his O levels by one grade. In 1957 he entered the Liverpool College of Art, but he obtained no degree.

That year a mutual friend brought (James) Paul McCartney to see Lennon's skiffle group the Quarrymen. One week later Lennon invited McCartney to join. He accepted, and in a few months brought his younger friend George Harrison into the group. In the four years that followed the act changed its name and its membership. In 1960 they became the Beatles and in August 1962 Ringo Starr became their drummer. None of the four could either read or write music.

It was while appearing in clubs in Hamburg from 1960 to 1962 and in the Cavern, Liverpool, in 1961–2 that the Beatles received invaluable experience. They played for hours, mastering a rock and roll repertoire while Lennon and McCartney wrote new songs. Lennon's controlled hysteria on the Isley Brothers' 'Twist and Shout' was an exciting example of rock and roll singing.

On 6 June 1962, the Beatles successfully auditioned for George Martin, the Parlophone label manager, and on 5 October they released their first single, 'Love Me Do', which was produced by Martin. It slowly climbed to number seventeen in the charts.

In 1963 the phenomenon known as Beatlemania swept Britain. 'She Loves You' was the first single to exceed sales of one and a half million in the United Kingdom. Hysterical crowds greeted the group's every appearance. In 1964 the fever spread to the United States, where six of their records reached the top of the charts in the first year. In one week in April, the Beatles held the top five positions in the national hit parade, an achievement never equalled. Throughout the 1960s the Beatles were the leading recording act in the world.

It is difficult to distinguish between the contributions of the individual Beatles at the beginning of their popularity. Lennon and McCartney were writing their songs together, and as a performing unit it was as John, Paul, George, *and* Ringo that they captivated the world as the 'Fab Four'. The Beatles were the first major pop group to write, sing, and play their own material; subsequent rock stars would be expected to do the same. The unprecedented demand for their long-playing discs put rock music on albums, which were previously predominantly the territory of film soundtrack or stage cast recordings.

The considerable foreign exchange the Beatles brought to Britain was a factor in their investiture as MBEs on 26 October 1965. On 26 November 1969 Lennon, who was passionately involved in left-wing and utopian politics, returned his MBE to the Queen as a protest against Britain's role in Biafra, Britain's support for American involvement in Vietnam, and the slipping sales of his Plastic Ono Band single 'Cold Turkey'. The other Beatles happily kept their decorations. The rebel of Dovedale Primary School never became an establishment figure, unlike Paul McCartney, who seemed to thrive on success and mass acceptance. After 1966 Lennon embraced transcendental meditation, drugs, and mystical religion.

The Beatles translated their success to other forms with a series of popular films and Lennon's two best-selling collections of stories and drawings, *John Lennon in his own Write* (1964) and *A Spaniard in the Works* (1965). It was around the time the latter work was published that Lennon and McCartney began to write songs individually. 'Help', 'In My Life', and 'Strawberry Fields Forever' were particularly outstanding Lennon pieces. In 1965 the Beatles released *Sergeant Pepper's Lonely Hearts Club Band*, which was considered the finest rock music album.

Lennon's association with the Japanese avant-garde artist Yoko Ono led him to lose interest in the Beatles, and by the time the group split in 1970 (the partnership was finally wound up in the High Court in 1971) Lennon had already made several 'solo' recordings. These almost inevitably included contributions from or were partly inspired by Yoko Ono. In 1971 Lennon composed 'Imagine', which became his best-known song. During the 1970s Lennon's relationship with Yoko Ono went through a rocky period, partly due to his use of drugs. He had difficulties with the United States Immigration Service which wanted to deny him permission to live there because of a British conviction for drug offences, but in 1972 the permission was granted.

Lennon's post-Beatle work was uneven but punctuated by heights of artistic achievement. His 1970 set *Plastic Ono Band* contains gripping examples of how emotional suffering can be conveyed musically. The single 'Cold Turkey' accurately recalls the agony associated with heroin withdrawal. 'Woman', from *Double Fantasy*, his 1980 collaboration with Yoko Ono, generates the warmth the artist himself was enjoying in his domestic life. For five years he had kept house and cared for his young son while Yoko Ono managed the business side of the marriage, buying property.

In 1962 Lennon married Cynthia, daughter of Charles Edwin Powell, commercial traveller. They had one son, (John Charles) Julian. This marriage ended in divorce in 1968 and on 20 March 1969 Lennon married Yoko, daughter of Eisuke Ono, of the Yokohama specie bank, Tokyo. They had one son, Sean Ono. Lennon was shot dead outside his New York City apartment 9 December 1980. The gunman made him a martyr in fans' eyes, proving that the words of 'All You Need Is Love' and 'Give Peace a Chance', which in moments of cynicism seemed trite, had meaning. At the time of his death Lennon's fortune was estimated at £100 million.

[Philip Norman, *Shout! The True Story of the Beatles*, 1981; *Sunday Times, John Lennon The Life and the Legend*, 1980; personal knowledge.]

PAUL GAMBACCINI

published 1986

FURY Billy

(1941–1983)

Singer of popular music, was born Ronald Wycherley 17 April 1941 in Garston, Liverpool, the elder son (there were no daughters) of Albert Wycherley, shoe repairer, and his wife, Jean Homer. As a child he suffered rheumatic fever which left him with a damaged heart. He was educated at Wellington Road School, Liverpool. On leaving he worked as a tugboat hand on the River Mersey. His interest in music was stimulated as he listened to records brought back from New York by seamen, particularly the rock and roll records of Elvis Presley. He bought a guitar, dressed as a Teddy Boy, began to write songs, and started emulating Marty Wilde, then one of Britain's most popular performers.

In 1958 he auditioned for Larry Parnes who immediately engaged him for a series of package shows touring Britain. It was Parnes who conceived the name Billy Fury and negotiated a recording contract with Decca Records. His first single, his own composition, 'Maybe Tomorrow', was released in March 1959 and was an instant hit. It climbed to no. 18 and remained for a total of nine weeks on the British list of bestsellers.

Fury was hailed by the media as 'The Blond Presley' and 'The British Teen Dream' and was certainly Britain's first major rock singer. Within the first six months of his professional career, he appeared in a television play, *Strictly for Sparrows*, by Ted (later Lord) Willis. Fury had a large number of fans but he also had his critics. In October 1959 the curtain was dropped on his act at Dublin's Theatre Royal when part of his performance was considered too suggestive. With his hair combed slickly back at the sides, ruffled at the front, his shoulders hunched, eyes hooded, dressed in bomber jacket, open-necked plaid shirt, and cowboy boots, Fury conveyed a look which with his hip swivelling and hand movements impressed his female fans, but brought so much criticism that the act was 'cleaned up'. The jackets, plaid shirts, and boots were replaced by a golden suit, shiny silk shirts, and shoes. On stage Fury continued to include beat numbers in his act as part of his rock image, but more ballads were included to project a wider image.

In the two years following 'Maybe Tomorrow' Fury enjoyed moderate success with his next six records. Then, in May 1961 his recording of the rock ballad, 'Halfway to Paradise', reached no. 3, stayed for twenty-three weeks in the bestseller lists, and brought him his first silver disc. Fury followed this with 'Jealousy' which went to no. 2. However, in the years between 1959 and 1966 when all his twenty-six records appeared on the top forty, he never had a no. 1 hit in Britain. It was one of his greatest disappointments. On record he concentrated more on ballads. On stage he developed a 'little boy lost' look which also helped stimulate his female following. He also appeared frequently on television in such programmes as *Oh! Boy, Boy Meets Girls, Wham, Thank Your Lucky Stars*, and *Saturday Spectacular*. In 1962 Fury appeared in the first of three films, *Play it Cool*, directed by Michael Winner. It was essentially a low budget picture and did little for his career. Three years later Fury appeared in *I've Gotta Horse* which told of a singer who put his horse before his career. It was a biographical reflection of his love for animals and also featured his own racehorse, Anselmo, which finished fourth in the 1964 Derby. His only other movie appearance was as a rock singer in *That'll be the Day* in 1973.

With the coming of the Beatles, solo singers began to struggle and Fury was feeling the winds of change. He tried to enlarge his career by attracting a wider audience through Christmas pantomimes such as *Aladdin*, in which he played the title role, and the night club circuit.

In 1966 Billy Fury parted company with Decca Records and signed with Parlophone and later Red Bus. Neither company, however, brought him any new recording success.

Shortly after the release of the film *That'll be the Day* in 1973 Fury underwent open heart surgery and retired to his farm near Brecon, Wales. Only occasionally did he appear on stage, preferring to spend his time breeding horses and bird-watching. In 1978 Fury was declared bankrupt and compelled to pay a tax bill of £16,000.

He returned to the recording studio in July 1981 and recorded a new single, 'Be Mine Tonight', for Polydor but was unsuccessful. On 8 March 1982 Fury collapsed, suffering partial paralysis and temporary blindness and was rushed to hospital. He survived and was planning to return to the concert stage when he collapsed and died 28 January 1983, in St. John's Wood, London.

In 1969 Billy Fury married Judith Hall. They divorced in 1973. There were no children.

[Personal knowledge.]

David Jacobs

published 1990

MUNROW David John

(1942–1976)

Early woodwind instrumentalist, was born in Birmingham 12 August 1942, the only child of Albert David Munrow, director of physical education in Birmingham University, and his wife, Hilda Ivy Norman. He was educated at King Edward VI School, Birmingham, where he became proficient on the bassoon and recorder, and after a period of teaching and travelling in South America (which laid the foundations of his considerable collection of exotic and folk instruments) he read English at Pembroke College, Cambridge (1961–4), obtaining a second class in both parts of the tripos (1963 and 1964). His enthusiasm and organizational energy quickly brought him to the forefront of university musical life (he was elected president of the University Music Club in 1964), and a partiality for early music (especially Purcell and the English baroque) was encouraged by Thurston Dart and bore fruit in a recorder consort, several chamber ensembles, and many large-scale concerts, including the first modern performance of William Boyce's *Cambridge Ode*. His lecture–recitals demonstrating many species of woodwind instrument (given first with Christopher Hogwood and later with his wife Gillian Reid) marked the start of a career of evangelistic communication with all levels of music-lover.

In 1964 he enrolled at Birmingham University for an MA on a study of D'Urfey's *Pills to Purge Melancholy*, and from 1966 to 1968 he was a member of the wind band of the Royal Shakespeare Company, providing incidental music in Stratford and London, during which time he founded the ensemble with which he was associated for the remainder of his life, the Early Music Consort of London. This made its début in Louvain in 1967 and first appeared in London in 1968. With a variety of well constructed and strikingly presented programmes this ensemble (James Bowman, Oliver Brookes, Christopher Hogwood, and, later, James Tyler) conveyed his enthusiastic and colourful ideas on music ranging from early medieval to late baroque to a world-wide audience, with frequent international tours (the Middle East in 1973, Italy in 1973 and 1975, Australia in 1974, USA in 1974 and 1976), an annual series of London concerts, and regular recordings for Decca (Argo) and later EMI, which attracted major awards, such as the Grammy award in 1975 and the Edison award in 1976. He became honorary ARAM in 1970.

Between 1967 and 1974 he was a part-time lecturer in the music department of Leicester University, and in 1968 became professor of recorder at the Royal Academy of Music, London, a post he held until 1975. During this period he was in demand as a virtuoso exponent of the repertoire for the baroque recorder (he recorded Bach's Brandenburg Concertos several times under conductors including Sir Adrian Boult and Neville Marriner) and made several recordings which displayed and documented the full range of the recorder family (particularly *The Art of the Recorder*, EMI, 1975).

Munrow was constantly willing to experiment; in addition to the wide range of little known repertoire which he researched for the consort's programmes and recordings (Dufay, Mouton, Landini, Binchois, Josquin), he co-operated with folk musicians such as Dolly Collins and The Young Tradition in studio recordings, and arranged (occasionally composed) music for television and cinema where he felt it could increase the public awareness of early instruments and their repertoire (*The Six Wives of Henry VIII*, *Elizabeth R.*, *A Man for All Seasons*, *The Devils*—with Peter Maxwell-Davies—*Zardoz*, *La Course en Tête* etc.). First performances given by the consort and Munrow include *Translations* (1971) and *Recorder Music for Recorder Player and Tape* (1973) by Peter Dickenson, and Elisabeth Lutyens's *The Tears of Night* (1972). Almost all his published writings were associated with recordings, in particular *Instruments of the Middle Ages and Renaissance* (1976), a popular and well illustrated book that incorporated and assessed current thinking on organology, combining musicological tenacity with a player's insight. Such a venture he held to be meaningless without the accompaniment of a series of recordings to bring the instrumental sounds to life.

He devised and presented radio and television programmes with vitality and wit, the most influential being a BBC Radio 3 series, *Pied Piper*, which ran from 1971 to 1976 with four programmes a week, and attracted an audience far wider than the younger listeners for whom it was designed. The same impetuous enthusiasm, restrained by a very conscious self-discipline, informed all his music-making; he abhorred the idea of remoteness, and as a keen (though diminutive) athlete and sailor (once an Outward Bound instructor), a lover of literature and paintings, an informed historian, a good linguist, and an animated mimic and raconteur he was the antitheses of an academic specialist. While at the start of his public career showmanship sometimes got the better of discretion and a certain brashness was criticized in his performances, he later developed a strong feeling for the liturgical repertoire of the late medieval and Renaissance periods; shortly before he died he was planning a reformed consort to explore this territory. His last recordings (*Music of the Gothic Era*) reflect this maturity.

In 1966 he married Gillian Veronica, daughter of William Robert Reid, principal officer in the Ministry of Home Affairs in Northern Ireland.

There were no children. Munrow died by his own hand, at Chesham Bois, Buckinghamshire, 15 May 1976.

[David Scott, 'David (John) Munrow', *The New Grove Dictionary of Music and Musicians*, vol. xii, 1980; *Early Music*, vol. iv, 1976; *The Times*, 17 and 18 May 1976; *Musical Times*, vol. cxvii, 1976; personal knowledge.]

CHRISTOPHER HOGWOOD

published 1986

DU PRÉ Jacqueline Mary

(1945–1987)

Cellist, was born 26 January 1945 in Oxford, the younger daughter and second of three children of Derek du Pré, financial writer and editor, who became secretary to the Institute of Cost and Works Accountants, and his wife, Iris Greep, who taught piano at the Royal Academy of Music. The family name had twelfth-century origins in Jersey. In 1948 the family went to settle in Purley, a suburb south of London. At four years of age, Jacqueline heard a cello for the first time and wanted to have such an instrument; she was given one for her fifth birthday. Her mother soon recognized that her daughter showed unusual talent; even when singing, neither her intonation nor her rhythms could be faulted. She arranged lessons and jotted down little tunes for her. With such support, coupled with Jacqueline's own outstanding talent and enthusiasm, the girl's early music lessons could not but succeed. After one year the six-year-old Jacqueline began studying at the London Cello School, directed by Herbert Walenn; when seven, she gave her first public performance at a children's concert.

The well-known teacher William Pleeth entered her life when she was ten; she was to stay with him for the next seven years. It was from him, she said later, that she learned to love the big concertos she was to play with unmatched brio, as well as the chamber music for which she always had a particular affection. She had a private tutor for general schooling. When she was eleven Jacqueline du Pré won London's first Suggia gift, an international cello prize, a remarkable result in a competition which set its age limit at twenty-one. From then on her tuition was financially secure, enabling her to study in Paris with Paul Tortelier, who predicted a great future for her. After being awarded all possible prizes at the Guildhall School of Music, London, including the gold medal 'for the outstanding instrumental student of the year', Jacqueline du Pré gave her first recital in March 1961, at the Wigmore Hall in a sonata programme, accompanied by Ernest Lush. This recital brought her to the attention of the public and of professional musicians, and from then on her career was assured.

In her first appearance in a chamber music recital for the National Trust Concert Society, she was joined by Yehudi (later Baron) Menuhin and his sister Hephzibah at Osterley Park. In March 1962 she played with the BBC Symphony Orchestra, at London's South Bank, Sir Edward Elgar's Cello Concerto, which she was to repeat at two Promenade Concerts under Sir Malcolm Sargent and which was to become the work with which her audiences would associate her for years to come. She then launched into a career that was to take her to the Continent and the USA. In 1966 there followed an intense time of study with Mstislav Rostropovich at the Conservatoire of Moscow, from where she wrote to Yehudi Menuhin: 'Over the past two years I have felt extremely lost with my work and generally fatigued by it. Now, under Rostropovich's tuition, I am finding a new freshness in it, and the old desire to go ahead with what I love so deeply is returning.' From this honest declaration it would appear that her meteoric rise to fame had taken its toll. The following year saw her return to London for concerts with the BBC Symphony Orchestra. An extensive tour of the United States and Canada further established the fame which had followed her first visit in 1965. American critics wrote about 'waves of intensity and love', her 'awesome gifts', her 'dazzling technique'. Beyond her cultivated and deeply musical approach to her playing she almost compelled the music to yield its utmost intensity, passion, and emotional abandon and was at one with it.

A first casual meeting with the young Argentinian-born Israeli pianist Daniel Barenboim (only son of Enrique and Aida Barenboim, pianists) turned out to lead not only to a musical partnership which was to become legendary but to Jacqueline adopting his Jewish faith before their marriage on 15 June 1967 in Israel, a country then at war. The following day they were the soloists in a concert with the Israel Philharmonic in Tel Aviv. On the programme were Schumann's Cello Concerto, which Barenboim conducted, and a Mozart Piano Concerto which he played, the conductor being Zubin Mehta. From then on the young Barenboims were involved in three musical careers: his, hers, and theirs. Their knowledge of each other's interpretive ideas was almost uncanny; they thought as one and their performances radiated this complete understanding. Though visual opposites—Jacqueline tall, with long, flowing, blonde hair and lively light-blue eyes, Daniel slim and slightly shorter with dark curly hair and intense brown eyes—they were beautiful to behold as a pair; their exuberance and joy in music-making and their deep respect for composer and score, together with their love of performance, never failed to reach the audience. Their musical partnership, which began at great speed, was to last for just four years, but this short period was filled with recitals, concerts, and recordings, the latter embracing a large catalogue, mainly on the EMI label, with which Jacqueline du Pré had an exclusive agreement. She recorded virtually the entire cello concerto repertoire with the greatest orchestras and conductors of her time, as well as numerous sonatas and other cello pieces with eminent pianists, amongst them Gerald Moore.

When in the autumn of 1973 odd symptoms, which had begun to disturb her playing two years earlier, were diagnosed as signs of the beginning of the crippling illness multiple sclerosis, which allows only brief periods of remission, all happiness and hope for the future were taken away and the musical world was stunned. Jacqueline du Pré took this fatal blow without complaint. With typical spirit she taught, gave master classes, cooked, and, whenever possible, played chamber music with her husband and friends. Her generosity of character and unselfish nature made her an ideal chamber music player. She became a familiar and beloved sight in her wheelchair at many London concerts, and she would ask people to come and play to her. Alexander Goehr wrote his *Romanze* for her (1968).

She was appointed OBE in 1976, was a fellow of the Guildhall School of Music (1975) and the Royal College of Music (1977), and was an honorary fellow of the Royal Academy of Music (1974) and of St Hilda's College, Oxford (1984). She won the gold medal of the Guildhall School of Music and the Queen's prize (both 1960), the City of London midsummer prize (1975), and the Incorporated Society of Musicians' musician of the year award (1980). She had honorary doctorates from Salford (1978), London (1979), the Open University (1979), Sheffield (1980), Leeds (1982), Durham (1983), and Oxford (1984). She had no children. In her final years she was saddened by her husband's relationship with Helena Bachkirev and the birth of their two children. At times she gave way to depression. She died 19 October 1987 in her flat at Chepstow Villas, and was buried at the Jewish cemetery in Golders Green.

[Carol Easton, *Jacqueline du Pré*, 1989; private information; personal knowledge.]

Yehudi Menuhin

published 1996

Alphabetical Index

Alphabetical Index